Silicosis

Silicosis
A World History

Edited by Paul-André Rosental

Johns Hopkins University Press | Baltimore

© 2017 Johns Hopkins University Press
All rights reserved. Published 2017
Printed in the United States of America on acid-free paper
9 8 7 6 5 4 3 2 1

Johns Hopkins University Press
2715 North Charles Street
Baltimore, Maryland 21218-4363
www.press.jhu.edu

Library of Congress Cataloging-in-Publication Data

Names: Rosental, Paul-André, editor.
Title: Silicosis : a world history / edited by Paul-André Rosental.
Description: Baltimore : Johns Hopkins University Press, 2017. |
    Includes bibliographical references and index.
Identifiers: LCCN 2016013185| ISBN 9781421421551 (hardcover :
    alk. paper) | ISBN 9781421421568 (electronic) | ISBN 1421421550
    (hardcover : alk. paper) | ISBN 1421421569 (electronic)
Subjects: | MESH: Silicosis—history | Occupational Exposure—
    history | History, 19th Century | History, 20th Century
Classification: LCC RC774 | NLM WF 11.1 | DDC 616.2/44—dc23
LC record available at http://lccn.loc.gov/2016013185

A catalog record for this book is available from the British Library.

*Special discounts are available for bulk purchases of this book. For more
information, please contact Special Sales at 410-516-6936 or specialsales@
press.jhu.edu.*

Johns Hopkins University Press uses environmentally friendly book
materials, including recycled text paper that is composed of at least
30 percent post-consumer waste, whenever possible.

Contents

Preface

The present volume is the outcome of an experiment in the collective writing of world history. It was begun in 2007, thanks to the support of the French Agence Nationale de la Recherche (ANR), and was accomplished with the aid of a European Research Council (ERC) Advanced Grant for study into the epidemiological implications of the historical construction of medical knowledge. Sciences Po and the Institut National d'Études Démographiques (INED) in Paris also supported the project.[1] It has brought together social, economic and public health historians, as well as two physicians, all of whom specialize in the history of 11 countries located on five continents (Australia, Belgium, France, socialist Czechoslovakia, Germany, Italy, Japan, South Africa, Switzerland, the United Kingdom, and the United States). Most of them had previously completed national studies of a particular country, but the underlying idea was to produce a book that would *not* be a collection of monographs. Rather, the project would be a collective attempt to achieve a truly integrated text that would be historically consistent and cover the main aspects of the world history of silicosis.

One of the well-known limits of world history's large syntheses is that, by definition, they often oblige their authors to rely mainly on secondary sources. Our project is unique in that it has united historians and physicians who, for the most part, have firsthand knowledge of the archival material. Moreover, from its inception, it has intentionally followed a collective research process, demanding a transcendence of national particularities and styles in writing history.

Primary research was undertaken when necessary. This was the case for the former Eastern European "popular democracies," for which special research was conducted on socialist Czechoslovakia.[2] Documenting the transnational history of silicosis also involved original research on the role of international organizations—the International Labour Organization/Office (ILO), the League of Nations (LN), the World Health Organization (WHO), and the European Coal and Steel Community (ECSC)—in defining and attempting to combat the disease.[3] Special issues of the *Journal of Modern European History* and the *Revue d'histoire moderne et contemporaine* allowed us to publish our early findings.[4]

The scientific coordination among the members of this international team was made possible by a series of meetings that took place in 2007 in Paris at the École des Hautes Études en Sciences Sociales (EHESS); in 2008 at the Wissenschaftszentrum Berlin für Sozialforschung, thanks to Dieter Gosewinkel; and in 2009 at the École Française de Rome, thanks to Luc Berlivet and Marilyn Nicoud. Other institutions also supported the organization of these meetings, such as the Bergbau-Berufsgenossenschaften in Bochum, Germany; the Charité Hospital and the Institut für Geschichte der Medizin at Humboldt University in Berlin, thanks to the help of Volker Hess; and Sciences Po and INED in Paris. Joint participation in international conferences, as well as research stays at the EHESS in Paris and support from the Centre d'Etudes Européennes and the Centre d'Histoire at Sciences Po in Paris, allowed us to go further in this process of collective writing. To complete the manuscript, in 2014–2015 I benefited from a one-year research stay in the IGK "Arbeit und Lebenslauf in Globalgeschichtlicher Perspektive" (re:work) at Humboldt University in Berlin, where I profited from the support of Andreas Eckert and Felicitas Hentschke. Among the numerous colleagues and friends who lent their support in preparing this volume, I would like to particularly thank Catherine Courtet from the ANR; Catherine Cavalin, Odile Macchi, Michel Vincent, Jean-François Bernaudin, Harriet McHugh Dillon, and Sophie Lagnier from the ERC Silicosis Project; Marie-Thébaud Sorger and Luc Berlivet from the Centre National de la Recherche Scientifique; Thomas Cayet from EHESS's Études Sociales et Politiques des Populations (ESOPP) research team; and Nathalie Jas from INRA for their help, advice, and inspiration. I am also grateful to Harriet McHugh Dillon and Penny O'Hara for an initial copyediting of the manuscript, and to all the Johns Hopkins University Press team and collaborators for their warm support and intellectual rigor, particularly Kelley Squazzo, Robin Coleman, and Kathleen Capels who did an extraordinarily careful second copyediting.

Silicosis: A World History is the end result. Part one covers the emergence of silicosis as a disease and a public health concern in the first decades of the twentieth century, a time in which economic considerations were at least as important as medical ones. In chapter 1, Gerald Markowitz and David Rosner detail why silicosis became a major issue in the world political economy during that period. In the following chapter, Alberto Baldasseroni and Francesco Carnevale trace the history of pulmonary occupational diseases in the nineteenth century. The gradual integration of these diseases under the heading of silicosis, a term and concept coined in 1871, would serve as the basis for the ILO's successful world crusade in the 1930s. In chapter 3, Jock McCulloch, Joseph Melling, and I examine how the ILO was helped in this process of transnational recognition by the South Africa gold-mining industry, which played a pioneering but quite ambiguous role, where health care went along with a desire to optimize use of the workforce on a racial basis.

Part two analyzes the history of silicosis after the progressive steps leading to its official recognition, beginning in the 1920s. In chapter 4, Martin Lengwiler and Julia Moses, together with Bernard Thomann and Joseph Melling, trace recognition of the disease in various industrialized countries, without these authors falling into the trap of a legalistic vision of history. They demonstrate that, while circumscribed by the often fierce opposition of employers, the significance of this recognition lies as much in what it conceals or makes conditional as in what it grants. In chapter 5, Bernard Thomann and I study employers' strategies for minimizing the costs to them arising from the disease and the difficulties workers' movements had in implementing an appropriate response. In chapter 6, Éric Geerkens describes the history of silicosis prevention policies, which exemplifies the ambiguities inherent in the fight against occupational diseases.

The concluding chapter evokes the new challenges raised by the growing number of medical discussions about a link between silica exposure and cancer—a debate that is all the more important in light of present concerns over occupational cancers—as well as the rapid increase in silicosis cases in emerging countries. It also studies the epidemiological move from silicosis to silica hazards, and from occupational lung diseases to systemic diseases. The long-term history brought together in this volume will help map new avenues in medical research through an unprecedented link between history and epidemiology.

NOTES

1. ANR SEST 2006 034 01 and ERC-2011-ADG-20110406—Project ID 295817. This research has also been supported by an Alliance Program Grant 2013 to Columbia University and Sciences Po; Sciences Po 2013 Scientific Advisory Board, "The Dusts of Givors"; and INED UR 11P-11-1-0.

2. Mackova and Rosental, "Les démocraties populaires."

3. Cayet et al., "How International Organisations Compete."

4. Rosental, "Health and Safety at Work"; Rosental and Omnès, "Les maladies professionnelles."

Silicosis

Silicosis and Global Public Health

Paul-André Rosental

It may seem odd to choose silicosis as a topic for research in 2017. This disease, induced by the inhalation of free crystalline silica dust in variable proportions over time, is usually associated in collective memory with a remote and outdated past: the coal-mining industry, a sector now relegated to a marginal position in most Western countries after having been economically and politically central throughout most of the nineteenth and twentieth centuries. The defeat of the coal miners' unions by Margaret Thatcher in the United Kingdom during the long 1984–1985 strike is perhaps one of the most powerful symbols of the decay of traditional industrial activities inherited from the Industrial Revolution in Europe and North America.

Silicosis, however, remains a crucial issue, not only for historians, but also for public health. This incurable chronic disease—which, in many cases, leads to an inescapable death that is preceded by disability and terrible suffering from an increasing inability to breathe—unfortunately promises to be a twenty-first-century scourge on a global scale. Silicosis, which is still present in various economic sectors in older industrial countries, is rapidly expanding in emerging countries, increasing at the same pace as their rate of industrialization. China, which is highly dependent on domestic coal production, is probably the country at highest risk, with at least hundreds of thousands of potential victims.

The coal industry is not the only sector in which silica dust is a killer. Silica is the main component of the earth's crust, and most industrial sectors—including the metallurgical, glassworking, foundry, stonecutting, construction, and tunneling industries—expose their workers to its lethal dust. Dental prosthodontists are also liable to come in significant contact with silica, as are those who produce pencils, which is the case in India. One of the most perilous activities is sandblasting. Exposure to concentrated sand squirt—whether in oil-tank cleaning, as in Texas; in shipbuilding, as in Brazil; or in the fading of bluejeans, as in Turkey—can cause silicosis in just a couple of years, whereas it sometimes takes decades in other sectors, depending on the intensity of the labor and the turnover of workers in the most dangerous jobs.

The World Health Organization and the International Labour Organization believe that millions of workers are at risk around the world. In 2000, they initiated a joint decennial eradication program that, at this point, is far from having achieved its aim. For historians, this goal tragically recalls preceding failures: as the concluding chapter shows, this is not the first time in history that international organizations have vainly striven to eliminate silicosis. A similar hope that a remedy would be found remained unrealized from the 1920s to the 1970s.[1]

Silicosis, then, looks set to remain a massive workplace killer in the near future. Moreover, it has probably been the most lethal occupational disease in history. By the end of the twentieth century, asbestos replaced silica as the symbol for health hazards in the workplace. Its effects are devastatingly fast growing today and are particularly visible, because asbestos-related diseases affect many white-collar employees who worked in office buildings constructed in the 1960s to 1980s or even later. But silicosis has been rife in many sectors since antiquity and has decimated workers in coal and metal-ore mines (chapter 2), and its damage spread significantly in the twentieth century with the mechanization of the mining industry, the digging of deeper and deeper wells, the generalized use of explosives, and a massive increase in the mining workforce.

Beyond this demographic importance, silicosis also matters as a historical precedent. In many ways, the issues it raises are comparable with those of asbestos, and silicosis has acted as a legal and medical template for the later response to asbestos. In many countries, both diseases have long been included within the same legal category. The very notion of a threshold of exposure—the idea that one can allow a worker to be in contact with a dangerous product, as long as this remains below a certain level, which has proven to be so detrimental in the case of asbestos—was, to a large extent, developed in response to silicosis.

Diagnosing silicosis is complex. Clinically, it takes years, or even decades, before it becomes apparent. X-rays, which can give an early diagnosis of its presence, only became available in the twentieth century. Even with this tool, delivering a clear diagnosis of silicosis is far from guaranteed: it requires well-trained specialists, good equipment, and reasonable-quality film—a set of conditions that has not always converged in the mining industry. Most of all, silicosis can easily be mistaken for similar diseases. Tuberculosis has been its main diagnostic competitor, not without a calculated bias on the part of the mining industry, which preferred its workers to be financially compensated by social security or private insurance for a "personal" ailment attributed to alcoholism or poor housing, rather than by the industry's own funds for an occupational disease.

Was silicosis an entity distinct from tuberculosis (TB)? Or, if acknowledged at all, was it just an outcome of TB? When not bluntly denying its existence, the mining industry did everything it could to minimize an understanding of the origins, range, and consequences of the disease. Throughout the world, only a handful of medical experts and trade unionists (and, in the United States, actuaries) managed to accumulate enough evidence to be able to argue for the dangerousness of silicosis. Yet this growing body of medical knowledge was never enough, in itself, to bring about recognition of the disease, for the history of silicosis is far from being a purely medical one. It is the story of a struggle among competing interests and their eventual negotiation of an intricate balance of power. To understand it, we must examine the way in which a complex set of factors converged: the economic interests of industry; the division of medical experts into two camps, "crusaders" for workers' health and "mercenaries" on the payroll of industry; the ability of workers to organize and exercise agency; and the involvement of private-insurance companies and social security systems. This power struggle also encompassed governments and transnational organizations.

Silicosis and World History

Understanding why silicosis is a global disease requires us to complement purely medical considerations with a political history of the disease. Although silicosis is an ancient disease that has always affected women and has primarily struck men at work, it remained barely visible over the centuries. In industry, it appeared only in certain sectors and, in spite of the efforts of some medical experts, only resulted in local recognition. Workers in some industries and regions knew that they were exposed to occupational hazards that were probably caused by dust, but this knowledge, although sometimes sophisticated (chapter 5, for Japan), remained limited to its geographical and occupational community. In mining, this invisibility was particularly pronounced, as that sector had long used forced labor, such as slaves or prisoners, and had often been located in remote rural areas. Thus mining was long considered a mysterious, almost magical activity. As late as 1700, when Bernardino Ramazzini published his famous book on craftsmen's diseases, he spoke of the mines as places haunted by devils, close to the classical representation of an inferno, or hell.[2]

Things only started to change at the turn of the twentieth century, largely due to technical innovations. In the expanding mining sector, dynamite and drills (sometimes nicknamed "the widow-makers" by the workers) dramatically raised the volume of dust and the mortality rates. This increased danger extended to several industrial sectors, such as the grinding industry, where steam power, introduced in the nineteenth century, drove the increased incidence of disease among workers and made this sector particularly visible from a health standpoint (chapter 2).

This impact coincided with a period of political turmoil. Both private insurance and social insurance were expanding, as were welfare states. Mechanization was disrupting traditional conceptions of individual responsibility: even a "cautious" and "well-behaved" worker could become the victim of a steam-machine explosion—a phenomenon that the introduction of Taylorism (or "scientific management," a theory that analyzed and integrated workflows) into the labor process would accentuate in the following decades.[3] During this same period, revolutionary pressures (anarchist and socialist before 1914, communist after 1917) affected the power struggles between industrialists and unions. Governments started to feel the need to include the previously "dangerous classes" in the management of the nation, a move that was accelerated by World War I and the Russian Revolution. In the interwar period, silicosis became "the king of occupational diseases," but for the opposite reasons in Europe than in America (chapter 1).

In Europe, an extension of the compensation system for workplace injuries to include occupational diseases, and the incorporation of silicosis into the emerging welfare system, stumbled over a financial hurdle: because of the frequency and seriousness of silicosis, its acknowledgment was considered a major economic, social, and political challenge. By contrast, in the United States, where unions were kept out of the new political and social compromises, silicosis played a role that was perhaps even more important: it probably was one of the main issues that made the introduction of some welfare regulations necessary.

In a period so strongly dominated by colonial and national imperialism, the process of recognizing and offering compensation for silicosis was triggered by a semicolonized country and by transnational dynamics. In the first three decades of the twentieth century, South Africa, then a British dominion, became the pioneering country for silicosis in medical, legislative, and institutional terms (chapter 3). It was the first country to officially recognize the disease, to issue compensation for it, to try to monitor it through a systematic (but racially hierarchized) medical examination system, and to produce a massive radiographic body of evidence. To some extent, South Africa, like the United States, belongs to the collection of countries where social legislation was partially built around silicosis.

But South Africa's historical prominence lies elsewhere. It is also the country that triggered the transnational process of recognition of the disease (chapter 3). Initially, this move was reactive, rather than proactive. Around 1900 and the Second Boer War, the Rand mining industry came under strong pressure from the British government, because of the terrible mortality rates experienced by the highly trained miners and foremen it imported from Cornwall. Coping with the pressure exerted by the British press and public opinion, and replacing British immigrant workers with Afrikaners, triggered South African medical and legal voluntarism. This, however, was based on a purely racial and colonial hierarchy: for the most part, prevention and monitoring targeted white, skilled miners, whereas black workers were discreetly left in the background.

From a transnational standpoint, this reaction occurred at a propitious moment. Both before and, mostly, after World War I, the reformist networks that advocated a tripartite management of social issues by governments, employers, and unions managed to build a transnational legal system, based first on bilateral reciprocity treaties and then on international conventions. The Treaty of Versailles in 1919 marked their official recognition at the highest level. It included a section devoted to social affairs; created a new legal system, the International Labour Organization; and instituted a new transnational agency, the International Labour Office, as the permanent secretariat of that organization (in this book, the abbreviation ILO is used for both). In the new world order organized around the League of Nations, the ILO had a monopoly on labor and social security issues and implemented an active policy on these matters in the 1920s and 1930s.

Social medicine—a growing political concern and major organizational model during the period—took up the issue of silicosis (chapter 3). At the end of the 1920s, the ILO's Industrial Hygiene Division and the Rand endeavored to have an international convention acknowledge silicosis as an occupational disease, which, by definition, would then pave the way for its recognition through national laws. The first and main step in this process was the convening of an international conference in Johannesburg in 1930. The event was partly subsidized by the Transvaal Chamber of Industry, and it was important symbolically as the first official ILO conference to be held outside Europe. Its aim was no less significant: to gather the best specialists from all industrialized countries and enable them to produce an agreement on the disease—its causes, its effects, its symptoms, its detection, and, consequently, its eligibility for financial compensation. The intent was to produce a medical consensus on the very nature of silicosis, solid enough to serve as a basis for plans offering monetary payments and to allow workers from all over the world—particularly the United States—to take their cases to court with a reasonable chance of success. This goal was achieved, and it allowed the ILO to have an international convention on silicosis signed in 1934.

Silicosis is a striking case of a disease whose medical definition was settled by a transnational compromise that had as its catalysts an international organization and a mining industry (operating, it must be acknowledged, within the constraints of medical knowledge at that time), but also came about through a power struggle between trade unions and employers in the main countries concerned. For a while, this compromise resolved a conflict among medical concepts that had lasted since the early-modern period (chapter 2). At the same time, however, since the agreement had been negotiated with the mining industry, it produced a minimal definition that, in the following decades, brought about new public health problems. The term "silicosis" was far from covering all occupational-dust diseases, not to mention asbestosis. Even today, the difficulties that physicians encounter when dealing with certain pulmonary diseases, and with acknowledging their occupational origin, are the outcome of the negotiated nature of pneumoconioses, that is, the range of chronic lung illnesses and systemic diseases caused by dust, and, most often, by dust in the workplace. These constitute probably the most important and spectacular illustration of Ludwik Fleck's lessons in the sociology of science: most discrepancies between established medical knowledge and clinical observations can be explained, and clarified, by examining the history of how this medical knowledge came to be accepted.[4]

Tolerating Death at Work: New Issues for Social History

Dealing with silicosis requires us to bring history into the picture. But which kind of history? It must undeniably be a sophisticated type that, far from limiting itself to the history of knowledge, needs to take into account economic, social, legal, and political dynamics. Silicosis epitomizes a key issue that is rarely examined, namely, what allows industrialized, democratic countries—where, since the second half of the nineteenth century, social and health policies have been concerned with the value of human life and the fight against death—to knowingly tolerate having a significant fraction of their workforce exposed to potentially deadly materials and activities?

Silicosis exacerbates the ambiguities that have been associated with the notion of occupational disease since Ramazzini published his treatise in 1700.[5] Though the critical reception of this work has been complex and has varied considerably from one period to another, its lasting influence has been assured by Ramazzini's fine, quasi-ethnographic approach to detailing the specifically occupational origin of certain diseases.

Until the second half of the nineteenth century, occupational disease remained a purely medical category. The Industrial Revolution brought about two major changes. First, it simultaneously increased the number of potentially disease-producing products and working environments, the number of workers exposed to health hazards, and the intensity of this exposure. Second, the transformation of workers into what were perceived of as dangerous and, later, revolutionary classes politicized the issue and markedly changed its nature. Whatever their various ideological motivations, the concerns of social hygienists about workers' illnesses were no longer sufficient. As an outcome of elites' social and political fears, and through a transnational dissemination process, legislation on health-related issues in the workplace—which varied nationally[6]— developed all over Europe. Occupational disease thus became a medico-legal category, rather than a purely medical one.

The paradoxical dimension of this legislation must be emphasized. On the one hand, it addressed an unquestionable medical reality and strove to remedy a social injustice: companies, either directly or through private (i.e., commercial) or public (i.e., governmental) insurance provisions, should be held responsible for the degradation of their workers' health, due to their occupations. Yet, on the other hand, it tolerated the existence of occupational diseases, as well as isolating and marginalizing them. While personal ailments, especially infectious diseases, became a major public health concern, occupational diseases tended to become a second-class category of illness, for which, to some extent, financial compensation mattered more than prevention or cure.

No wonder workers' movements were often reluctant to embrace a legislative approach. Trade unions in France would have preferred dangerous products to simply be banned from the production process. In other countries, such as the United Kingdom, a common fear was that employers would sack workers who declared they had an occupational disease. Employers, too, were reluctant to accept any kind of liability for this range of afflictions. In most European countries, legislation on occupational diseases developed from the end of the nineteenth century to the interwar period as an imperfect compromise between labor and capital. This time frame corresponds with the emergence of silicosis as a major health and economic issue. Just when silicosis became the king of occupational diseases, occupational diseases themselves were becoming a major concern, and this coincidence is at the core of the historical prominence of silicosis. The reason why silicosis bears such a heuristic value for historians is not only because it has a high probability of condemning masses of workers to suffer disabilities and death, but also because it was the first occupational disease to raise the issue that is central to the very definition of occupational diseases: temporality.

Most countries built the medico-legal category of occupational diseases as an extension of their previous legislation on work-related injuries, which was generally established a decade or two earlier, at the turn of the century. But this transposition, which is still the basis for most national legislation around the world (and for transnational conventions), rests on an insuperable asymmetry. Whereas the damage caused by workplace injuries is usually immediately apparent, it takes years for most occupational diseases to manifest themselves. This process generally is even longer for silicosis. The same is true for asbestos-linked medical problems and occupational cancers but, historically speaking, silicosis has been the first life-cycle occupational disease to become a cause célèbre for public health, in parallel with the rise of the notion of chronic diseases. In medical terms, the question has not only been *what* but also *when* is silicosis: at what stage can it be detected, when does it become irreversible, when does it justify a worker's claims for compensation, and, most of all, when does it reduce his or her productivity?

This delay, combined with the difficulty of identifying the first signs of the disease, has paved the way for employers, as well as private- and public-insurance companies, to minimize or negate their responsibility. Even if workers demonstrate that they have contracted silicosis, how can they prove at what moment (and, therefore, during their employment with which company) the disease process started? Pernicious effects have resulted from this time lag and complex set of causes. They have allowed employers' medical experts to try to deny, sometimes for decades, the very existence of silicosis as an autonomous disease. Once silicosis was officially recognized, many workers were fired when they were in the early stage of the disease, before declaring that they were experiencing functional problems. In this way, their employers could avoid the burden of financial compensation. The arbitrariness in deciding *when* the disease started also brought about a systematic statistical underregistration that, together with other factors, minimized the gravity of the disease and its visibility to workers' unions and the public. This process of refutation and underestimation was widespread and, to some extent, identical all over the world (chapter 5), but for now, it suffices to stress its implications for current historiographic issues and, in particular, for social history.

Modern social history, transcending deep national variations, developed after World War II as a discussion around Marxian theories on social stratification and class struggle, the centrality of the working class, and its role as a key historical agent of social and political transformation. This initial focus has broken down since the 1980s. The decline of the working class in Western nations, both as a sociological milieu and as a cultural and political force, combined with the demise of revolutionary ideologies, has fragmented the issues of interest to social history, which nowadays extends to minorities, institutions, practices, and numerous other concerns. The current interest in occupational health, which has blossomed in most countries since the 1990s, is probably the first systematic attempt to look afresh at traditional issues in the history of social classes. It very much echoes such present-day concerns as the degradation of the environment, the intensification of the labor process in modern capitalism, and the ascendancy of the major medico-pharmaceutical companies in the arena of public heath. But an examination of workplace health may also be a way to return to classic questions on the constitution of a society, ones that have been neglected or marginalized for roughly a generation.

Occupational health is also a new way of examining working-class history. Instead of focusing on the morphological characteristics of workers as a social group, it looks at them in a complex political and cognitive configuration. This approach not only encompasses actions and choices by employers, but also the role of medical and legal experts, as well as the strategies of the state and other institutions, such as private-insurance companies and social security systems. It can also help us understand the ways public opinion, which has been central to the history of silicosis, has been mobilized at different times and in different places (chapter 5).

This combination is all the more complex, as it simultaneously involves action at a number of levels. While, to a large extent, legislation, public policy, and employers and workers' unions act first and foremost at the national level, the transnational arena—encompassing international organizations, non-governmental organizations (NGOs), scientific exchanges, and international law—has been a determinant in establishing models for action, although they have been taken up differently from one country to another. At the same time, most of the decisive confrontations between labor and capital have taken place at the local level. Creating a history of occupational diseases allows us to reopen the study of trade unions that, in the past, has often unduly privileged central confederations at the national level. Everywhere in the world, recent historiography has challenged the traditional view that trade unions neglected the issue of health or traded it for wage supplements. At the local level, on the contrary, workers have often mobilized actively against unhealthy working conditions. In other words, dealing with the history of a major occupational disease requires us to build a model relating the global to the local arena: a model that does not negate the importance of the national dimension, but allows a rethinking of its relative importance within a world-wide framework.

This book is the outcome of an original question that shaped our collective research. Why is occupational health, which is handled by such different legislative and institutional arrangements from one country to another, always—including in socialist countries—one of the weak links in overall health and social protection? Whatever the history of the struggles and compromises around health in the workplace, whatever the public solutions adopted, whatever the strengths (or weaknesses) of workers' unions and welfare arrangements, a significant number of occupational diseases are not recognized or, when recognized, are statistically undeclared, poorly compensated (or compensated at the expense of social security programs), and addressed by fewer active-prevention policies than is the case for more-regular, private diseases.

Obviously, part of the answer lies in the power of industry: its ability to use economic arguments (productivity, employment) to downplay the protection of its workforce and to hire experts to navigate in a complex judicial and political field where the most sophisticated legal, technological, and medical dimensions converge.[7] But this consideration is only part of the story. What is at stake is an understanding of the difficulty, and often the relative failure, of all reforms that have tried to improve health protections in the workplace, which is confirmed, for instance, by the constant and massive statistical underregistration of occupational diseases in the United States and the European Union, as well as in socialist and emerging countries (concluding chapter).[8]

Comprehending this somewhat frustrating picture demands a conceptual rethinking of the interactions among laws, agencies, and public policies in today's industrialized, democratic countries. Traditional representations tend to treat legal arrangements as rules of the game that define the roles of social actors, their range of action, and the penalty if they violate the law. This viewpoint, which has been taken up by the social sciences since this set of disciplines was first developed at the end of the nineteenth century,[9] analytically distinguishes legal requirements and penalties from social dynamics.

What the story of occupational diseases, and particularly the history of silicosis at a global level, demonstrates is that this perspective neglects an important dimension: the relationship between a legal arrangement and a political regime. Legislation on occupational diseases emerged in 1900, and laws regarding occupational medicine in 1930, both through a transnational process. But this legal framework, however important, was not autonomous. Financial compensation for occupational diseases, as well as the field of occupational medicine, partially contributed to the building of labor laws, social security, and social medicine. The new medico-legal category of occupational diseases was a local application, in a given arena, of a more ambitious aim: to build a new political order designed to regulate class struggle. To do so meant both acknowledging its existence and attempting to settle or, as was hoped in corporatist and fascist regimes, to abolish it. What mattered was to build a political arena in which conflicts between labor and capital would be contained, in order to avoid revolutionary explosions.

There are two ways in which one might approach these arrangements. The first is to accept that they are sufficient: once legislation develops and institutions are built to control its implementation, the protection of workers' health is guaranteed and, if it is not, violators should be punished and reforms undertaken. This is the path that has been followed, but which is far from having achieved its goal. An alternative approach is to return to the political basis for these arrangements and acknowledge that health-related issues in the workplace, because they concern the internal management of industry, are structurally a cause of disagreement and conflict between capital and labor.

This second point of view makes more sense in a historical context than the application of what had been a new model of action: occupational health. This model, which took hold from the 1970s to the 1990s, was also the outcome of a transnational process that did not alter existing legal frameworks but, rather, built on them. Our comparative and transnational study shows that workers' health policies depend on an asymmetric power struggle in which employers, to minimize what they perceive as management costs, constantly try to mold and, if need be, circumscribe—or even bypass—the law. Legal provisions here are not outside the realm of social interplay; they are not rules of the game. Rather, the political order that undergirds the law is based on litigation and conflicts of interest and allows the most powerful players to interpret the rules according to their own constraints. To some extent, bending the rules is part of the implementation of the rules.

This model also affects concepts of the state and public policy. Far from applying some kind of biopower or biopolitics, the state is the often the powerless referee in an unfair game. Only the successful marshaling of civil society, and the use of transnational processes, may, in exceptional and often temporary contexts, counterbalance this asymmetrical power struggle. With this in mind, the concluding chapter of this book goes beyond the case of silicosis or occupational diseases. It argues that public agencies should strive to support the social power of the weakest actors, rather than exclusively pretending to solve any problems through direct institutional regulation.

NOTES

1. Some medical experts have long hoped that aluminum could protect miners against silicosis, and the European Coal and Steel Community vainly funded research on the subject in the 1950s and 1960s. See Sorenson et al., "Aluminum in the Environment," esp. 54–69. See also Penrose, "'So Now They Have.'"

2. See Ramazzini, *Treatise of the Diseases.* For a current case, see Grätz, "Gold-Mining and Risk Management."

3. Markowitz and Rosner, *Deadly Dust: Silicosis and Politics.*

4. Fleck, *Genesis and Development.*
5. Vincent, "Ramazzini n'est pas le précurseur."
6. Moses, "Foreign Workers."
7. See, for example, White and Bero, "Corporate Manipulation of Research," 112, 123.
8. For the United States, see, for example, Pransky et al., "Under-Reporting of Work-Related Disorders"; Azaroff et al., "Occupational Injury and Illness Surveillance"; Stout and Bell, "Effectiveness of Source Documents"; Leigh et al., "Occupational Injury and Illness"; Leigh and Robbins, "Occupational Disease and Workers' Compensation." For the European Union, see Blandin et al., *Survey on Under-Reporting.*
9. Karsenti, "Loi et sanction."

Chapter 1

Why Is Silicosis So Important?

Gerald Markowitz and David Rosner

In the nineteenth century, the growth of urban populations, the changing use of land, and the creation of previously unknown crowding produced conditions in which a variety of infectious diseases flourished, such as tuberculosis, cholera, typhoid, and various airborne and pest vectors. For much of the industrialized world, the twentieth century was marked by a new set of social conditions that produced chronic, long-term illnesses, frequently of long latency (developing without visible symptoms), and a growing awareness that the world we create has a profound impact on such diseases. Heart disease, cancer, and strokes are certainly linked to radically transformed work and commercial environments. Silicosis is, in many ways, the paradigmatic disease of the twentieth century, representing the new world economic order that dominated industrial societies globally. It is linked to the fundamental changes brought about by the development of the world's industrial economies.

Silicosis, we argue, was to twentieth-century chronic, industrially related disease what cholera was to nineteenth-century infectious illness. Neither cholera nor silicosis were the leading causes of death in their respective eras, yet the histories of each reflected the social and scientific assumptions of their time, and both framed the professional and public understandings of the disease. Silicosis's importance was not necessarily its epidemiological significance, for it was not the most widespread or even the most prominent social disease. Nonetheless, many of our most basic ideas regarding the relationship between the human environment and chronic disease were formulated around silicosis. In the interwar period, silicosis emerged as the "king of occupational diseases."[1] In the United States, it caused a national crisis for labor, management, governmental officials, scientists, and medical personnel. For much of the twentieth century, and in many societies around the globe, silicosis caused incredible suffering for people working in gold, silver, lead, copper, and coal mines, as well as for granite cutters, quarrymen, foundry workers, sandblasters, painters, construction workers, sandhogs, and their families. Further, silicosis was equally a product of imperialist dominance outside national borders, as colonial powers imposed new work methods on peoples who were already exploited and oppressed. Silicosis brought growing inequalities in the economic and political power of industrializing nations into sharp relief and sometimes set into motion broadly based struggles over control of both the work environment and the politics of disease.

But its significance also lay in the fact that so many of the medical, as well as the scientific, social, economic, political, and intellectual questions that have dominated the discourse around diseases as diverse as asbestosis, mesothelioma (cancer of the pleura, i.e., the delicate serous membrane that lines each half of the thorax), coal workers' pneumoconiosis, and a variety of industrially based cancers were hashed out around silicosis. Indeed, the very definition of industrial disability, as well as the continuing controversy over what was owed to workers injured on the job and who should bear the financial and societal burden of dependency, family and community trauma, and personal expense, were first debated through the crises that developed around silicosis in country after country.

Silicosis has been at the center of an ongoing dialogue that has raised fundamental questions regarding health risks in a developing industrial society. What are the responsibilities of government, management, and workers for risks in the workplace? What role should government play in regulating the workforce? Can occupational disease be distinguished from diseases of nonindustrial origin? Is industrial disease an acceptable and normal condition of modern society? What are the maximum levels of toxic substances to which workers should be exposed? And who—professionals, governments, labor, or business—should have the predominant say in setting those levels? Finally, and most importantly for the twenty-first century, how should the disease be defined: in terms of a person's ability to work, or as a bodily insult irrespective of its economic impact on workers and their families? These are the questions that societies and professional communities have had to confront throughout the twentieth century in nearly every corner of the world.

Silicosis assumed great importance because professionals and the public alike recognized that it represented a new kind of disease, different from infectious conditions or even other occupational illnesses, such as lead or phosphorus poisoning, that had heretofore posed the major threat to industrial workers. Here was a disease that was chronic and irreversible in nature, that developed years or even decades after a person's first exposure, whose symptoms were often ambiguous, that was rooted in labor and factory production, and that had enormous social and economic implications for industries. No one would argue that silicosis was not an occupational disease: a disease rooted in work, in the experience of workers in factories, mines, mills, foundries, tunnels, and the like. But it was the first industrial disease whose impact was felt outside the factory walls, in the families and communities around them, as well as in the halls of national capitals and international organizations. Here, we see the seeds of current debates over the dangers of environmental pollution, the effects of long-term exposure to synthetic materials, the impact of unrestrained industrialization on the well-being of populations, and the influence of the global economy on the health status of huge numbers of people. The history of silicosis is also the history of the discovery of chronic disease and its relationship to industrial society.

Silicosis and the Transformation of Work

Silicosis brought into question one of the central beliefs of the twentieth century: technological innovation and the growth of industry would produce general improvements in the quality of peoples' lives. The disease was produced by the very machines and technical innovations that were at the root of industrialization, and silicosis thus became a powerful symbol of the potential threat that industrialization posed—and continues to pose—to the quality of life. The questions that emerged as central to environmentalists and social critics in the last third of the twentieth century were first raised in the context of silicosis. What are the health implications of industrial progress? What are the trade-offs for greater national wealth, personal convenience, and comfort: workers' and consumers' health?

Whether in the gold mines of South Africa, the coal mines of Britain, France, or Germany, or the hard-rock and metal mines of the United States and South America, the introduction of new technologies brought about the destruction of workers' health. As power tools replaced handheld devices and scientific management undermined the autonomy and control that the labor force had been able to exercise over the work process, working conditions deteriorated and health suffered. But the introduction of new tools and transformed technologies were, in themselves, just part of a larger struggle over control of the workplace that occurred in different societies during the twentieth century. Speed-ups, de-skilling, and the "scientific management" of the workforce were central to labor/management conflicts during the course of the century, and the changes in labor practices set the stage for the emergence of widespread disease among workers. As control was wrested from the workforce and skilled craftsmen were replaced with unskilled labor in factories and mines, in some countries silicosis became the first industrial, noninfectious epidemic and therefore came to represent an unnatural form of exploitation and oppression. It was as much a symbol of this unfair usage as it was an epidemiological fact.

In pre–World War II Japan, for example, the mining industry was largely organized around small groups of skilled miners whose pace of work and output was subject to decisions made among the team of workers themselves. Similarly, in the United States during the nineteenth and early twentieth centuries, molders in the foundries were skilled artisans who also largely controlled the pace of work and the output. The general work process in a nineteenth-century factory has been characterized as "the manager's brains are under the workman's cap,"[2] meaning that the early factories were dependent on the decisions and skills of the artisans who worked in them. But in many industrializing societies, including Japan and the United States, the twentieth century was a period of intense class conflict over control of the work process. As managers succeeded in introducing new technologies and methods, skilled workers were replaced by the unskilled, and the former's control over the pace of work and the means of production was transferred to management. In the course of this larger labor struggle, both the wages and working conditions of labor deteriorated, resulting in greater instances of accidents and disease. New power tools and speed-ups resulted in massive increases in the workers' exposure to finely ground particles that ultimately resulted in silicosis, tuberculosis, and other industrial diseases. Under various forms, in North America as well as in Europe and Japan, bureaucracies responded to this as a labor/management issue, as well as one of welfare and public health.

Battles to control work paralleled a broader struggle to define disease itself and to assign responsibility for the protection of workers, their families, and communities. Throughout the early 1900s, tussles over working conditions, production speed, and the rate of pay focused attention on the issues of health, disease, and social welfare that were the hallmarks of twentieth-century labor/capital negotiations and conflicts. The struggle by garment workers following the Triangle Shirtwaist Factory fire in 1911 is perhaps the best known example of the growing awareness of safety as a major labor issue in the United States. Conflicts over working conditions also led to widespread consumer awareness of the health conditions in factories and an understanding of the dangers of disease posed by unhealthful factory production methods.[3] Use of the union label was a signal of hygienic conditions that not only protected the worker, but also shielded the consumer from tuberculosis. In South Africa, gold and diamond miners returned to Wales with tuberculosis and silicosis, heightening British awareness of industrial diseases, specifically of silicosis. Japanese industrial hygienists and social reformers believed that dealing with chronic occupational diseases such as silicosis was a key to ameliorating labor unrest. Industrialists embraced the issue of silicosis as an integral part of their rationalization efforts to develop direct organizational capacities and go beyond the labor-intensive model that was at the heart of labor relations in mining until then. In the United States, pressure from skilled Italian-immigrant granite workers, many of whom were anarchists, created an intense political conflict over dust, the use of power tools, and labor/management relationships that led to the acknowledgment of silicosis early in the twentieth century. In contrast to prevalent medical opinion that emphasized the bacterial origins of lung conditions for granite cutters, these workers insisted that it was the dust in the sheds where the granite was cut that was at the root of the scourge. Also in the United States, where silicosis dominated industrial health issues for two decades, labor struggles in mines and foundries across the country forced professionals and governmental agencies to focus on alleviating the working conditions that gave rise to the disease.

Silicosis and Imperialism

Silicosis was not just a problem in particular societies or within the narrow constraints of national history. In addition to the role played by multinational businesses and the sometimes rapid spread of legislation regarding work accidents and occupational diseases,[4] silicosis was also a transnational problem, rooted in changing imperial relationships. As European nations expanded their reach to exploit the resources of Africa and Asia, they exposed their own workers, as well as natives of the countries they colonized, to the ravages of imperial greed. Britain, for example, sent large numbers of Welsh miners to South African gold and diamond mines and found, on these workers' return, that the nation had poisoned its own workforce. Thomas Oliver, the authoritative

British expert on occupational disease, described the fate of "young miners in the bloom of health." After working in the South African goldfields for only a few years, they "returned to Northumberland and elsewhere broken in health."[5] This experience not only shaped attitudes toward the colonial endeavor, but also heightened awareness and social discord about silicosis among British workers and medical observers within the home country.

But the greatest impact of imperialism on health was among the exploited populations, whose societies were destroyed by the demands of colonial powers who reshaped native cultures to the needs of mining interests.[6] This exploitation, which fed the industrializing economies of other societies in the developing world, also led to silicosis (as well as to less prevalent diseases related to industrial processes). As males were drawn from local villages in South Africa and surrounding countries to the gold and diamond mines, the health of both the workers and the villagers was destroyed. The horrendous mining conditions early in the twentieth century produced silicosis and the resultant tuberculosis epidemics that were transported by returning miners to the communities in which they lived. Later, the movements of peoples joined forces with the destruction of traditional society to create conditions in which sexually transmitted diseases and AIDS emerged as pandemics across sub-Saharan Africa.

The imperial origins of silicosis's discovery in South Africa and Great Britain stimulated a transnational acknowledgment of the relationship between industry, especially mining, and disease. From its earliest days, the International Labour Organization, an arm of the League of Nations that was later folded into the United Nations, played a crucial role in making silicosis a truly international concern. It sponsored research and international conferences— the most significant of which occurred in Johannesburg in 1930[7]—that, in the interwar period, brought together leading medical experts and officials from North America, Australia, and Europe to discuss common policies and practices. In the United States, the Johannesburg conference stimulated similar meetings at the US Department of Labor in Washington, DC, in 1936 and 1937, following the discovery that more than 700 African American laborers were killed by acute silicosis while building a tunnel for the Union Carbide Company in Gauley Bridge, West Virginia.[8] Another conference was later held in Joplin, Missouri, in 1940, following the uncovering of a major epidemic of silicosis among hard-rock miners in the tri-state lead belt of Missouri, Oklahoma, and Kansas. At these meetings, American researchers and clinicians adopted the classifications developed in Johannesburg.[9] The American Association of

Industrial Physicians and Surgeons acknowledged the centrality of the Johannesburg meetings in their journal, *Industrial Medicine*, stating that the Johannesburg meeting was "extremely important" in developing an "adequate and correct conception of the pathology of silicosis."[10] In Europe and South Africa, various financial compensation plans regarding silicosis were adopted along a broad time span, ranging from the 1920s to 1963 (in the case of Belgium). But in all cases those programs, which were often presented as social progress, contained legal limitations that paved the way for a massive underrecognition and underregistration of the diseases caused by exposure to silica dust.

The Medico-Legal Implications of Silicosis

The history of the medical diagnosis of silicosis has been fraught with conflict, confusion, and contention. For much of the nineteenth and early twentieth centuries, silicosis was generally understood as a form of consumption that was associated with specific workplaces. In professional as well as popular literature, the disease we would commonly call silicosis today was referred to as "miners' asthma," or "glassblowers' phthisis," or "grinders' consumption." Symptoms were the basis for diagnosis, and no laboratory procedures existed for distinguishing these various lung diseases from tuberculosis. Hence, like many other diseases, what we today define as silicosis was regarded in the nineteenth century as an industry-specific form of consumption.

While the term "silicosis" was coined in 1871 in Italy, medical opinion about the cause of consumption among workers in mines and foundries began to change with the discovery of the tuberculosis bacillus in the 1880s by Robert Koch. If, in the nineteenth century, workers' diseases were thought of as being the product of working conditions and specific personal characteristics that determined an individual's susceptibility, this new understanding of the bacterial sources of tuberculosis led physicians to see disease in a new light. Despite the fact that the industrialization of a nation created a rich environment for growth in the number of silicosis victims, many physicians began to see the symptoms of wasting away, spitting blood, coughing, and losing weight as signs that workers were suffering from bacterial tuberculosis, rather than from poor conditions in an occupational environment. "Miners' rot," "gold miners' phthisis," and other industry-specific nomenclature was replaced by the term "tuberculosis," which was associated with poverty, crowded housing conditions, and poor personal hygiene. Ironically, advances in medical technology led to a better diagnosis for some individuals who suffered from tuberculosis specifically, but also to a mis-understanding of the sources of the disease for those who worked in mines, foundries, and granite sheds. The arguments over silicosis exposed the ways in which bacteriology served different purposes in the context of massive struggles and masked the class and environmental origins of industrially produced diseases.

Silicosis also exposes the ways in which different, and sometimes competing interests within industrializing societies can lead to the uncovering of industrial disease. Despite the intellectual power of bacteriology to "explain" disease in the early twentieth century, the differentiation of silicosis from tuberculosis was accomplished largely by interests outside the field of medicine and without the use of sophisticated medical technology. Ironically, imperial relationships were at the heart of the first recognition of "Rand miners' phthisis" in South Africa, which occurred as early as 1902. By 1912, the disease was understood to be a noninfectious epidemic caused by dust in the mines and was named "silico-sis."[11] Shortly thereafter, American statisticians—such as Frederick Hoffman at the Prudential Life Insurance Company, where the firm's interests were threatened by a tuberculosis epidemic—built on this South African literature and noted that those in the insured workforce claiming benefits for being affected by consumption instead were suffering from an industrial "fibrotic" condition. By the early twentieth century, in the medical mind, consumption had become indistinguishable from tuberculosis and was widely portrayed as being a disease of crowded slum conditions in highly congested environments. But insurance statisticians noted that the benefit claims related to consumption were coming from relatively rural areas within the United States. After many inspections and trips to several of these communities, the insurance industry decided that there were two diseases that were being confused: tuberculosis (a bacterial disease) and silicosis (a fibrotic condition of the lungs that occurred among miners and others in the dusty trades).

Tuberculosis, the disease that is often equated with the great breakthroughs of the bacteriological revolution in the nineteenth century, was used in a scientific/political struggle that clouded the relationship between work and disease. The social perception of what constituted a "serious" health problem also had an important impact on peoples' understanding of silicosis. In a society traditionally wracked by early death from infectious and epidemic diseases, the measure of significance was the rate of age-specific mortality. Chronic conditions that did not result in early death were seen as less serious problems for the medical community. Despite the fact that chronic diseases were disabling and killing more people than acute illnesses, for the most part, public and professional understanding of disease was rooted in this earlier experience and did not change until after World War II.[12] Because silicosis predisposed workers to tuberculosis, and silico-tuberculosis was life threatening, the continuing decline in tuberculosis death rates after World War I affected public and professional perceptions of its severity. As TB was controlled through the aggressive use of antibiotics and became less prevalent, doctors and laypeople alike assumed that silicosis was, at worst, an inconvenient and only partially disabling condition of the elderly. Also, because ventilation and wet drilling in some of the newer work sites reduced the amount of silica dust in the air, for many workers there was probably a longer latency period between exposure to silica and the onset of disease. It is reasonable to assume that the relationship between exposure to silica and labored breathing was obscured even more, and that, in the absence of widespread public and professional attention, silicosis was diagnosed as emphysema, asthma, and other cardiopulmonary conditions.

It is ironic that silicosis—which had helped awaken the public health and medical communities to the problem of chronic industrial disease—was itself masked by the chronic diseases that became the focus of attention in the postwar era.[13] As workers lived longer and as the period of time between exposure and the onset of disease lengthened, the relationship between work and illness receded from view. People were living longer and suffering, but their suffering became most evident in their retirement years, after leaving the workplace.

The shifting epidemiology of tuberculosis during the twentieth century, especially with the development of antibiotic therapies after World War II, transformed silicosis and silico-tuberculosis. This experience paralleled the general decline in the significance of infectious disease as the major public health threat in industrialized societies and the rise of chronic illness as the focus of public health concerns. The link between silicosis and the life-threatening nature of an opportunistic tuberculosis infection was fundamentally altered by experiments with sulfanilamide and diamino-diphenyl-sulfone in the 1930s, which showed that tuberculosis bacilli were effectively controlled in guinea pigs,[14] and, in 1944, by studies on the efficacy of streptomycin in human tuberculosis.[15] By the early 1950s, the use of streptomycin and para-aminosalicylic acid, and, later, isoniazid, were becoming standard elements in the treatment of tuberculosis, despite serious drawbacks with regard to resistance.[16]

Throughout the twentieth century, death rates from tuberculosis in Europe, Japan, and the United States steadily declined.[17] Although some were wary of the enthusiasm over these antibiotics, most clinicians and the public saw the long search for a magic bullet finally paying off. While tuberculosis remained an important disease in the 1950s, it seemed that death could be postponed (and even avoided) with medical intervention.[18] Silico-tuberculosis, while still severely disabling, was no longer viewed by physicians as a life-threatening disease. Its story illuminates the more general history of what scholars have called the "epidemiological transition" in industrial society.

Silicosis brought into focus the ways in which responsibility for disease is a negotiated concept. In every society, workers, and sometimes the physicians aligned with them, have had to fight for silicosis to be recognized as a disease. Some, particularly in industry, saw workers who were coughing, losing weight, and so forth as suffering from tuberculosis, a condition for which industry bore little or no responsibility. The workers themselves often shared this conviction. It was only gradually, from the 1920s on, that an awareness of being afflicted with a specific disease called silicosis spread from qualified, or specially trained, workers (stonecutters) to laborers in the mines. Yet we should be wary of adopting too linear a view: the current underdeclaration of silicosis in industrialized countries is due to the fragile nature of this growth in awareness, a fragility often promoted by industry. The history of silicosis falls into the category of agnotology, a term created by historians of science and epistemology to describe culturally induced ignorance (e.g., through inattention or selectivity) on questions of public health wherever economic concerns predominate. This interpretation leads us to regard the periods of growth in an awareness of the danger of modes of industrial production as exceptional moments, rather than as steps in an irreversible process. This was the case, for example, in the United States during the Great Depression, when laborers who lost their jobs because of poor health believed their affliction to be silicosis, a disease caused by the industry itself and for which industry should be held accountable.[19]

The Medico-Legal Environment and the New Definition of Silicosis

In the very early decades of the twentieth century, our understanding of silicosis as a disease was influenced by the medico-legal environment within which it appeared. The distinction between silicosis and tuberculosis became important as discussions of responsibility for risk emerged. Difficult debates about who should be held accountable for disease surfaced as nation-states sought to apply the tools of government and regulation to the industrial workplace. The difference between these two diseases became extremely cogent within the context of private and social insurance and liability programs. When workers were laid off in the United States in the 1930s, during the Great Depression, many older workers found lawyers who argued that their unemployment was due to their physical condition, which was brought on by the dusty environment of their workplaces. While Europe and Japan progressively introduced social-insurance compensation plans, in the United States, thousands of lawsuits were brought on behalf of unemployed workers, claiming that employers were responsible for the disease that had led to the workers' disabilities. Silicosis gained enormous attention and was soon perceived as the worst industrial epidemic in the nation's history. Laborers across the country sued for damages, and public health officials feared that as many as 500,000 workers might be at risk for the disease.

Within the American context, the courts were the forum through which some of the most basic ideas about accountability for disease were negotiated, ranging from the significance of disability as a marker of communal responsibility to the practical means by which bodily insults could be remedied, either through medical care or financial compensation. The development of a workers' compensation system became the paramount means of defusing politically contentious arguments that often reflected a deep division between labor and capital. By the 1940s, these conflicts continued as industry argued that silicosis was only considered a disease when it led to a permanent disability that forced workers into retirement, while workers claimed that x-ray images and work histories, even without devastating tertiary symptoms, should lead to some sort of compensation for a disease caused by the industrial workplace. The gap between legal recognition of silicosis and growing public awareness of its effects on the bodies and health of workers was just beginning.

In South Africa and Europe, workers' compensation systems also played a crucial role in taking disease out of the public arena and putting it in the hands of experts and commissions that sought to depoliticize the issue of culpability. The authority of experts was reinforced by the use of x-rays, dust-sampling technologies, and highly technical statistical studies that were inaccessible to the general public and had an aura of scientific accuracy and political neutrality. Historically, x-rays symbolized the esoteric and almost magical powers of medical specialists to see into the body and diagnose disease, while enumeration and statistical analysis were part and parcel of scientific discourse. Science, expertise, professionalism, and bureaucratic and technical sophistication legitimated the dominance of the public health sector, medicine, and engineering.[20]

The establishment of standards regulating the amount of dust in the air constituted a concrete symbol of this power. The rising professions of occupational medicine and "industrial hygiene" (the scientific and administrative terminology used at that time) gained authority because of the highly technical problem of measurement. This reinforced the growing dependence on experts to define objective criteria for judging physiological responses to silica dust. On the one hand, this process played a crucial role in hiding the disease from the public and affected workers alike. On the other hand, the establishment of workers' compensation systems also made silicosis an issue of central importance to government, establishing its right to intervene in what was once the private domain of labor and capital, of the worker and the factory owner.

While the recognition of silicosis was worldwide, the specific conditions of capital and labor in different nation-states determined the methods for controlling the disease and the means of addressing its social and economic consequences. In the United States, where the central government was historically very weak and where much power and authority resided in local institutions, state agencies, and private industry, it was not until the 1970s that any significant federal authority was used to limit the debilitating effects of working conditions and toxic exposure on the workforce. Epidemiologically, economic depressions, combined with speed-ups and a general exploitation of labor, created social, legal, and financial crises and forced a widespread recognition of the disease on a state-by-state basis. Workers' compensation, a system run by the individual states, outside of the central government, became the means through which workers found uneven economic remedies that reflected the altered local power relationships between labor and capital.

In many of the European states, where the voice of labor parties and organizations was often more powerful following World War I, compensation systems were organized on a national level. Silicosis was recognized as an occupational disease in England and Germany before a similar acknowledgment occurred in the United States. The push for recognition of the disease arose from different sources in the United States than it did in much of the rest of the world. In America, pressure from rank-and-file workers thrown out of their jobs during the Great Depression forced the disease onto national agendas. Elsewhere, by contrast, physicians, governmental officials, and powerful elites inside and outside labor unions and transnational organizations (such as the International Labour Office) played pivotal roles. The European story is somewhat different, in that unions and other voices of labor were able to force the disease onto the national agenda in times of economic boom, when the demand for coal and other resources increased, particularly after World War II. The growing power of organized labor during a period of severe shortages and massive immigration of foreign workers increased the toll of silicosis in France, but it allowed labor to bring the issue to the political fore.

In Japan, the role of labor and transnational politics emerged in the interwar period and continued after that time. During the occupation of Japan by the United States following World War II, the blossoming of various institutions representing women, labor, and political dissidents promoted a diverse political discourse that, ironically, was often at odds with the American occupation and its goals.[21] This, in turn, led to the growing presence of worker-oriented political organizations, such as the Socialist Party, that came to exercise an important influence in the National Diet and helped pass a bill in 1955 recognizing silicosis as a compensated occupational disease within the framework of the 1947 Workers' Accident Compensation Insurance Law.[22]

The irony in the history of silicosis is that during the 1920s and 1930s, the myopic focus on it as the predominant threat to workers in the dusty trades served to obscure the importance of other dust-related conditions. When, in the postwar era, professionals inside and outside industry declared an end to the silicosis crisis, they were effectively arguing that dust-caused diseases were no longer the responsibility of industry. In the 1960s and 1970s, other dust diseases—coal miners' pneumoconiosis, byssinosis (brown lung disease), and asbestos-related diseases—would become the focus of national attention in the United States. But this was not the result of medical research or scientific discovery. Rather, it was the workforce itself that, in the 1960s, forced consideration of these health risks. Coal dust, cotton dust, and asbestos dust are now acknowledged as causes of life-threatening industrial lung diseases. Just as silicosis achieved notoriety in the 1930s, these other conditions have entered into the popular lexicon as "black lung," "brown lung," and "white lung," respectively— all symbols of the heartlessness of industry. Silicosis served to cloud the recognition of coal workers' pneumoconiosis and underlined the importance of unions and labor politics in establishing dust-related diseases as a national priority in the United States.[23]

Today, few people, aside from workers in selected industries and those in the specialties of occupational medicine and pulmonology, have heard of silicosis. Yet some researchers estimate that there are as many people threatened with the disease now as there were during the 1930s, when it was the king of occupational diseases. In the postwar era, professionals, industry, government, and a conservative labor movement tried to bury silicosis as an issue. The irony is that for decades, silicosis masked the threat other dusts held for American workers, while today it is obscured by the focus on other dusts.

Because of the attention that had been paid to silicosis during the Depression and earlier, researchers generally understood all occupational lung diseases through the prism of their experience with silicosis. Lorin Kerr, the longtime director of occupational health and safety for the United Mine Workers and president of the American Public Health Association, pointed out the inhibiting nature of the silicosis debate for professional acceptance of coal workers' pneumoconiosis: "This lack of concern with coal miners pneumoconiosis has been due in part . . . to the conviction that only silica and dust containing silica are injurious." It was widely accepted that silica posed the most serious threat to workers' health, while coal dust and other organic and inorganic dusts were of far less importance. "So great is the difference in the toxic properties between silica and some others of this group [of mineral dusts] that if silica is represented by 100, the relative danger from coal, silica-free marble, iron, etc., is about 5."[24] A common, almost universal assumption of public health officialdom during the 1930s was that "anthracosis is primarily a silicosis and . . . it occurs not only in hard coal miners but also in workers in soft coals."[25] If silicosis could be controlled, then there was little worry that coal or other dusts would prove to be a problem.

Today a new frontier appears: it is more and more probable that silicosis only covers a fraction of the health damage wrought by the inhalation of silica. Historical conditions from the 1930s still affect present-day epidemiology, which has only recently begun to move out from beneath their shadow.

The study of silicosis thus reveals the interlocking relationship among three sectors: business, government, and public health. In countries like the United States and South Africa, and, to a lesser extent, Europe, it was largely around silicosis that industrial and imperialist societies, and those under their dominion, developed the modern tools of regulation, compensation, and industrial relations regarding working conditions. Over the course of the twentieth century, workers, management, governmental officials, and professional groups have negotiated over fundamentally different approaches to the problems associated with silicosis. Perhaps most importantly, silicosis has been the impetus for national governments to accept a role in the identification and control of chronic diseases in general, and in specific diseases linked to heavy industry. Silicosis, this disabling disease of industrial society, was indeed paradigmatic. It exposed not only the highly political nature of disease identification, but also the impact of industrialization and imperialism on the health of the people who labored to create our current world economic system.

NOTES

1. McCord, "Grindstones."
2. Montgomery, *Fall of the House of Labor.*
3. Chessel, "Consumers' Leagues in France," 53–70; J. Vincent, "La réforme sociale," 29–60.
4. Moses, "Foreign Workers."
5. Oliver, *Diseases of Occupation*, 279.
6. Seibert, "More Continuity than Change?"
7. ILO, *Silicosis: Records* (1930).
8. Cherniack, *Hawk's Nest Incident.*
9. See US Department of Labor, *National Silicosis Conference*; *Proceedings at National Conference on Silicosis*, National Archives and Records Administration; Tri-State Conference, *Proceedings*, National Archives and Records Administration; Metropolitan Life Insurance Company, *Silicosis*, 13–14.
10. "Silicosis Review," 22.
11. See Rosner and Markowitz, *Deadly Dust: Silicosis and the On-Going Struggle*, 32n61.
12. Colgrove, *Epidemic City*; Frieden et al., "Public Health in New York City."
13. On the concept of chronic disease, see Derickson, *Black Lung*, esp. ch. 6; Hartman, "Silicosis," 9; Rosner and Markowitz, *Deadly Dust: Silicosis and the On-Going Struggle*, ch. 6; Weisz, *Chronic Disease.*
14. Dubos and Dubos, *White Plague*, 154.
15. Committee on Chemotherapy and Allied Measures, "Report on Streptomycin."
16. Dubos and Dubos, *White Plague*, 154.
17. Dowling, *Fighting Infection*, 236–237; Benenson, *Control of Communicable Diseases*, 267–268.
18. Dubos and Dubos, *White Plague*, 154. The Duboses were skeptical about the efficacy of these antibiotics, stating that "the 'miracle' drug which made for such exciting headlines and photographs, in the press of mid-February 1952, will probably be regarded as just another treatment when re-evaluated in the light of experienced judgment."
19. See Rosner and Markowitz, *Deadly Dust: Silicosis and the On-Going Struggle.*
20. Baldasseroni et al., "Naissance d'une maladie."

21. Dower, *Embracing Defeat.*
22. Thanks are due to Bernard Thomann for his advice on this point.
23. Derickson, *Black Lung.*
24. McCord, *Silicosis in the Foundry,* 10.
25. "Silico-Anthracosis."

Chapter 2

The Genesis and Development of the Scientific Concept of Pulmonary Silicosis during the Nineteenth Century

Alberto Baldasseroni and Francesco Carnevale

The history of our understanding of pneumoconiosis also reflects our waver-ing ideas: a glimmer of light, an ingenious act of intuition is often followed by a period of regression, of straying from the path already begun, as scholars are influenced by the prejudices of their own time and the mistaken beliefs im-posed on them by the authority of their teachers.

Luigi Carozzi, 1941

"Exposure to silica=silicosis." This equation first appeared in 1871 in Italy, when the term silicosis was coined. Between the 1910s and the 1980s, it progres-sively became a scientific truth, however fragile and disputed. Since then, it has been called into question by new medical observations, which indicate that other kinds of ailments can be brought about by exposure to silica dust. Before that period, lung damage affecting the various kinds of workers exposed to silica dust was attributed to very different causes. The national and trans-national recognition of silicosis as a distinct entity, from South Africa in 1911 to Belgium in 1963, was as much the outcome of a political and economic compromise as an indisputable medical discovery. In this chapter, we demon-strate the difficulty of understanding the origin of a range of symptoms that, throughout history, have afflicted workers engaged in very diverse industrial sectors and for which competing explanations were available. This is crucial to fully understanding the historical, contingent nature of what one could call the triumph of silicosis in the twentieth century: the differentiation of the patho-logical effects of silica dust and, to some extent, other inorganic dusts under the name silicosis, rather than subsuming them under a wider range of diseases.

The history of silicosis invites an examination of the evolving nature of our understanding of this disease and medical knowledge about it. Numerous references in antiquity from doctors such as Hippocrates and Celsus, as well as polymath observers such as Teophrastus and Pliny the Elder, and even anonymous texts like the *Satire of Trades* (from the Egyptian papyrus Sallier II), might give the impression that silicosis and, more generally, dust-related diseases were identified as soon as mining and industrial activity started. But throughout antiquity and the Middle Ages, the role attributed to respiration (seen, at that time, as regulating the temperature of the vital breath animating the body) and the focus on other presumed risk factors diverted medical attention away from dust. For instance, Paracelsus (1493–1541), an itinerant physician who combined a mixture of alchemical, magical, and mystical concepts with mining-town experience, focused on sulphur, mercury, and saltpetre in his treatise on mountain diseases, *Von der Bergsucht und anderen Bergkrankheiten*, which is often cited as the first book-length work dedicated to occupational diseases.

The mining industry was identified early on as a major source of health hazards. Many observations either accumulated without references to one another or remained compartmentalized by country or sector of activity. George Rosen's classic book provides the broadest and most convincing historical framework on this issue and on the evolution of knowledge.[1] He stresses the centrality of German-speaking physicians' observations, beginning with Agricola and Paracelsius, but also credits Bernardino Ramazzini with synthesizing the knowledge available during his lifetime, on the eve of the eighteenth century.[2] In the Germanic world, the various respiratory diseases affecting the miners of deposits located in the hills of Central Europe were lumped together under a specific category: *Bergsucht* ("mountain disease"), which amalgamated (under their current categories) pneumoconioses and various metal intoxications. In the Schneeberg mines to the south of Dresden, for instance, occupational lung cancer due to radiation from uranium was not identified until well into the twentieth century.[3] Thus the definition of the medical condition known today as silicosis is the result of a lengthy process, lasting at least three centuries: from the early anatomopathological (organ- and tissue-based) observations of Isbrand van Diemerbroeck (1609–1674) and Giovanni Battista Morgagni (1682–1771) until almost the present day. In many ways, this definition is still evolving, as is often the case in medicine.[4] Medical observation—detecting signs and symptoms of a physical or psychological disorder—is dependent on the diagnostic methods available at the time. There is also an evident social influence on medical phenomena.[5] Diseases therefore change their apparent nature and characteristics over time.[6] Our understanding of silicosis, more so than many other diseases, has been constantly conditioned throughout its history: scientific knowledge, social and economic factors, and technical measures have all combined in different ways, at various times, to determine epidemiological trends. We outline some of these shifts by locating them, insofar as possible, within the medical understanding of the relevant time and its underlying social context.

Conflicting Causes and Sources of Observations
The Early Development of Clinical Medicine

At the beginning of the nineteenth century, a physician summoned to a patient's sickbed could rely on the expertise of his teachers, as well as his senses of sight, touch, smell, taste, and hearing, but little else, to determine the nature of the ailment confronting him. "Disease" also had a notably different meaning from what we use today, since medicine was based more on systemic theories and philosophical principles than on empirical observations. Bedside medicine, relying on the classification of observed phenomena and the speculative, unitary (i.e., as an organic whole, with no independent components) nature of diseases and the changes created by them, dominated the medical landscape.[7] The medical system developed by Benjamin Rush (1745–1813) in the United States in the early nineteenth century reduced all human illnesses to a single disease, gauged by fever: "The proximate cause of disease is irregular, convulsive, or wrong action in the system affected. This is a concise view of my theory of diseases."[8] John Brown (1736–1788), a Scottish physician from the late eighteenth century, established the theory known as vitalism, which held bleeding to be a panacea for all ailments. Medicine, a late developer compared with the natural sciences, such as physics and chemistry, was still grappling with a store of acquired knowledge that often harked back to a distant past and was largely powerless in the face of human pathology.

The first steps in a new direction were nevertheless being taken. In 1761, Morgagni collected his observations, made from bodies opened up on dissecting tables, in a work destined to become a milestone of modern medicine, *De sedibus et causis morborum per anatomen indagatis*. From then on, ever-greater importance was attached to postmortem examinations of lesions located on internal organs, comparing them with the signs and symptoms present before death: "As opposed to traditional pathology, which was nonspecific, prevalent, and humoral, the pathology envisaged by Morgagni was specific, localized, and structural."[9]

This new approach made it possible to connect the presence of *pulmonalia tubercula* with consumption and to begin to unravel the mystery of respiratory diseases, which shared a small number of similar symptoms. Indeed, early works covering the diseases of miners and those of Sheffield grinders begin by focusing on these two aspects: clinical methods, with awareness and accurate accounts of the physical symptoms; and postmortem examinations, with detailed descriptions of the form and structure of the lungs. There was no third type of approach before the arrival, in the early decades of the nineteenth century, of a new kind medicine, born in revolutionary and Napoleonic France. The basis of this new practice was the observational method. Making use of the "material" available in hospitals, particular symptoms were carefully paid attention to, in an attempt to aggregate them. Examining the patient became separate from collecting a symptomatic profile, with the goal of the former being to identify objective and reproducible signs that might be perceived by the physician, regardless of the patient's description of his or her symptoms.

To facilitate the examination and detection of symptoms, the physician's senses were coupled with the use of early instruments. In 1760, *Inventum Novum*, by the Austrian physician Leopold Auenbrugger (1722–1809), first described the technique of thoracic percussion (tapping on the surface of the body to determine the underlying structure of the lungs) and paved the way for the identification of phthisical (tubercular) cavities and fluid levels in the pleura. His work was continued in France by Jean Nicolas Corvisart (1755–1821) who, in 1808, translated Auenbrugger's text and expanded on his innovations, and, from 1836, by Joseph Škoda (1805–1881), a Bohemian physician and founder—along with Carl von Rokitansky (1804–1878)—of the Vienna School. The stethoscope, invented in 1816 by René Laennec (1781–1826), the greatest exponent of this new type of medicine, augmented what a physician could hear, particularly when listening to heart tones and sounds in the bronchi (divisions in the trachea leading to the lungs) and lungs. Laennec's innovation was a typical product of this new medical school, which was changing the way in which disease was approached. The era of "hospital medicine" was at hand. No longer merely asylums for the poor and underprivileged, modern hospitals were places dedicated to gathering case studies that were subject to investigation and statistical cataloging, practices suggested by Pierre Louis (1787–1872).[10]

The availability of a standardized thoracic exam, the results of which could be compared by several observers, added a key element in distinguishing the various forms of pulmonary changes in living humans. Amphoric sounds in the lungs (similar to those made by blowing across the mouth of an empty bottle), which are a sign of a tubercular cavity, were now audible to physicians, having been sufficiently amplified by a stethoscope; a lack of murmurs and a dullness when a patient's chest area was thumped were signs of the conversion of elastic lung tissue into more fleshlike tissue; diffuse whistling sounds were a sign of irritated and partially obstructed bronchi. This development allowed a new generation of physicians to approach patients with a greater likelihood of discerning the source of their complaints. Catarrh, which was collected through the patient's sputum (matter expectorated from the respiratory system), was among the various signs that were given great importance by physicians. Careful observations focused on its color (yellow; purulent, or puslike; white; mucous; grey or predominantly black; carbonaceous; reddish or decidedly bloody; or, the most feared of all, phthisical), its consistency (hard; like grains of flint; fluid; thick) and its smell, all aimed at deriving indicators of the future progress of the disease and the sufferer's chance of recovery.[11] Empirical comparisons of the inhalation of catarrh-containing materials during the course of work in mining districts and manufacturing cities convinced medical practitioners of the etiology (set of causes) of their patients' respiratory symptoms.[12]

Workers' Pulmonary Diseases at the Dawn of the Nineteenth Century

Extracting minerals and coal, boring into rock, sharpening knives and blades, milling stones to grind corn and press olives—such activities have always been known to cause diseases and premature death. An awareness that emanations given off by processed materials or released into the atmosphere during the stages of production were detrimental to health was already present among earlier writers.[13] Doctors caring for patients in the communities in which these occupations were concentrated noticed the early onset of consumption, the phthisis that afflicted these workers. A dry cough, shortness of breath, and a progressive inability to carry out a manual occupation were the main symptoms that appeared in young men (more so than women) in their thirties and forties. Before Laennec's invention, which allowed doctors to listen to sounds within the body, there were few signs observable by physicians save for a less mobile thorax, respiration using the diaphragm, overexpansion of both lungs, and, occasionally, retraction of the larynx and bronchi when a person was not able to draw in enough air. Rarely was a physician able to compare data from post-mortem examinations with his clinical observations. When he had access to a corpse, dark pigmentation (grey, predominantly black) and a distinctly increased thickness of lung tissue, along with a squeak of the blade in dissecting the pulmonary lobes, signaled that an organ was no longer able to perform its function.

In looking for the cause of these conditions, it was difficult to imagine toxic effects from dust, which was ubiquitous and billowed in great quantities along the poorly surfaced streets of towns and villages. Even recognized authorities on the study of pulmonary changes and diseases were skeptical about the idea that a hardening of the lungs could be caused by dust emanating from certain kinds of work, since many workers exposed to generalized dust clouds, such as coachmen, did not suffer any alteration whatsoever in their lungs.[14] Poison was conceived of in a completely different fashion. Its effect was thought to be acute and instantaneous, as long as the dose was sufficient. Dust was never seen in this light. No one suspected that it could take years, or even decades, to reveal its harmful effects. On the contrary, anatomophysiological research (on the body and its structures), which was leading to a gradual explanation of the functional mechanisms behind the mucosal lining in the upper airways (epithelium), was opposing the very idea that dust particles were able to reach into even the furthest tiny, thin-walled branches of the bronchi. An explanation of the mechanism behind inflammatory irritation, mucous production, the trapping of coarse particles, and, finally, their expulsion through sputum, came many years before the identification of a fine component of dust, which was invisible to the naked eye and capable of passing through the mucous barrier of the primary airways.[15]

In the era preceding the microbiological revolution of the mid-nineteenth century, and in the absence of truly effective therapies, the only way to distinguish among various clinical forms of disease was to observe their progression. Pneumonia was diagnosed if the symptoms evolved in the space of three to four days, resulting in either the spontaneous recovery or the death of the patient. A phthisis victim suffered from consumption and was afflicted with persistent coughing, weight loss, a loss of strength, catarrh, and the spitting up of blood, with alternating periods of improvement (and at least a partial recovery of the ability to work) and deterioration, until the final crisis. Obstruction of the lungs' deep airways through exposure to dust, gas, and irritating vapors could not be distinguished from pulmonary restriction due to an increase in the fibrousness in lung tissue, an abnormal disruption due to a few particular types of dust.[16] Labored breathing (dyspnea) did not differ in either case, and both resulted in the death of the patient. Yet obstruction of the airways almost always coincides with a fibrous transformation of otherwise elastic lung tissue; thus, even on a dissecting table, the structural changes from different types of lung diseases could not be differentiated.

The prevalent theories about disease arising from vapors did not emphasize dust as the central element. Thus what was known as the miasmatic theory, used to explain the cause of epidemic diseases, considered dust to be, at most, a vehicle for poisonous emissions, rather than a hazard in itself. Overcrowding, perspiring bodies, fermenting fecal matter, and rotting material—ever present in mines and, often, workshops—were postulated as potential sources of emissions that were harmful to workers' bodies and health.[17] These theories, indirectly useful for the general improvement of hygiene in the workplace, nonetheless helped divert attention away from the dust problem.

The Contribution of Morbidity and Mortality Statistics to Solving Disease-Classification (Nosological) Problems

The reorganization of hospitals, beginning in the early decades of the nineteenth century, promoted the statistical study of the causes of disease. Data on differential social causes of illnesses began to emerge, although they tended to focus on certain categories of urban artisans, while workers in isolated communities (such as miners) featured less in the statistics. Quantitative information on the latter came from mortality statistics by William Farr (1807–1883) in Great Britain, dating from the early decades of the nineteenth century, and earlier-appearing ones on the continent, by Louis-René Villermé (1782–1863) in France and Henri-Clermond Lombard (1803–1895) in Switzerland.[18]

In an age when morbidity (the incidence of sickness) meant mortality for certain diseases, particularly those involving the lungs, it made little difference whether data from one or the other were used as a basis for generating statistics. There were many sources of bias, however, when it came to handling these data. Hospital case studies suffered from a "selection effect." Access to these institutions was very much related to a person's occupation, because of the growing role of mutual-aid societies in their funding. This objection was tendered to the great industrial hygienist John Thomas Arlidge (1822–1899) during a parliamentary debate on the worrying morbidity statistics among potters in England's Black Country (an area in the West Midlands). Arlidge had to admit that the relatively high proportion of workers in that occupation who were affected by pulmonary changes and diseases might have been over-estimated, because potters had privileged access to his clinic.[19]

The problem was different in the case of mortality statistics. They were not skewed by any kind of selection process, since they referred to the totality of deaths. Rather, the precision with which data on the professions of the deceased were recorded was questionable.[20] Categories used to classify these professions were very broad and would rapidly become outdated, due to the turbulent industrial development that was taking place. The result was a dilution of the harmful effects of certain occupations, which would be confused in the classification system with others that were similar but, for example, did not bear the same risks to the respiratory system.[21] The accuracy with which this information was recorded was also a cause for concern to those who were asked to interpret the resulting data.

Among various comparative techniques, proportional morbidity and mortality rates were frequently used. This was due to the difficulty of estimating a correct denominator for the numerators. The numerators were derived from hospital case studies (morbidity) or from data on recorded causes of death (mortality). The denominators were the result of general population censuses that either included questions related to occupation or were derived from local, ad hoc estimates. In both instances, the approximate classifications were very broad. Morbidity, in particular, lent itself to being analyzed through the use of proportional estimates, due to the availability of equivalent hospital data for other diseases. Series of cases of pulmonary diseases could be easily compared with series of cases of other diseases with regard to features such as age, sex, and occupation.

The proportional-analysis method, however, was open to errors of interpretation. The total number of admissions from a given professional category had to equal 100 percent. Therefore the lack of one particular cause for admission had to be replaced by a relative excess for another cause, even if, in absolute terms, there was no excess. Jobs where workers were less susceptible to a certain type of disease and its symptoms, which would lead to admission, inevitably meant an apparent increase in another type of illness, even in the absence of a heightened risk. Thus, where patients practicing a particular occupation were found to be more likely to suffer from lung diseases than patients employed in another profession (with the proportion of victims expressed as a percentage), this might paradoxically be because the first kind of job had lower risk for other types of disease. This could occur if, for example, the employees who carried out the work in question received a higher salary, with consequently improved dietary and nutritional conditions. In an age in which the primary cause of disease was a shortage of food and a poor diet, it is easy to imagine how a well-paid occupation, even if harmful to the respiratory system, might, in some ways, help prevent other types of diseases.

Another typical method of analyzing the data from these statistics was to compare males (considered in almost all occupations to be the main participants in that type of employment) with females (believed, except in certain occupations, to be protected from the various types of exposure). This typically occurred in mining districts, where women worked in the industry but were not employed in dusty jobs. Differential rates of death, due to pulmonary causes, between males and females from the same locales attested to a specific risk linked to male occupations. This view was confirmed in the attempt to distinguish between infectious pulmonary phthisis and pulmonary phthisis caused by dust inhalation. The former was thought to be hereditary, a form of predisposition where all members of the same family potentially were equally affected. The age group concerned here—namely, the youngest—was also thought to be significant. In the second type of phthisis, the lack of a hereditary and familial link, as well as the older age groups in which the symptoms developed, were seen as indicative signs. (This was measured empirically, through hospital data for old-age cases and familial surveys.).

Alongside the "semiotics of the individual," which was accumulating information from the use of new instruments and describing the objective examination of the thorax in ever-greater detail, the "semiotics of epidemic curves" was increasingly used, first displayed in a comparative tabular form and, toward the end of the century, in graphs and curves. This allowed showing not only the differential characteristics of an individual's disease situation, as had hitherto been the case, but also its incidence and distribution within an entire community.[22]

Understanding the Causes of Diseases

"*Absque causarum cognitione, morbi nec praeservari nec curari possunt* [without knowledge of their causes, diseases can neither be prevented nor cured]."[23] In the absence of extensive knowledge, especially experimental data, it was difficult to understand the varying toxicity of dust produced by different materials. The theory of anticontagionism (which held that diseases did not arise from an agent that could spread from one human to another, but instead were the result of interactions with the environment), which prevailed until at least the mid-nineteenth century, led to the belief that "dust" was generally harmful to the respiratory system, but more for the chronic irritation it could cause in the membrane lining the airways (epithelium) than for its ability to reach the lung's deep airways and air sacs (alveoli).

Around the middle of the century, the "laboratory medicine" phase arrived, which would lead not only to important progress in understanding disease mechanisms that altered bodily functions, but also to a progressive separation of the investigating physician from the populations being studied, in this case, workers exposed to silica dust. It is in this context, perhaps, that we should consider the famous debate over the origin of the black pigmentation found in the lungs of coal miners, with the German pathologist Rudolf Virchow (1821–1902) at its center. Virchow maintained his firm conviction that this coloration was internal in origin, a result of the transformation of blood-based pigments, rather than the inhalation of carbonaceous dust.[24]

Developments in analytical chemistry began to allow explorations about the nature of inhaled dust. In 1867, Friedrich von Zenker (1825–1898) was able to prove beyond all doubt that dust particles present in the lungs of a female worker, who was employed in the production of pigments and had succumbed to respiratory problems, were made of iron.[25] In publishing this case, von Zenker coined the words "siderosis," a lung disease caused by the accumulation of iron dust, and the often-used "pneumoconiosis," which refers to the broad range of diseases caused by dust inhalation.

During that same period, between 1865 and 1870, analyses using a polarized-light microscope allowed Headlam Greenhow (1814–1888) to identify the presence of silica dust in the pulmonary lesions of several categories of workers.[26] A unifying hypothesis was taking shape regarding these abnormal changes and their possible cause. The idea no longer was to lump together various occupations because of exposure to a generic "dust," but to focus on the effect of a particular type, namely, siliceous dust. In this context, Achille Visconti (1836–1911), a pathologist at the Ca' Granda Hospital in Milan, coined the term "silicosis" in 1871, with the help of the scientist Carlo Leopoldo Rovida (1844–1877), who had measured the quantity of free crystalline silica in the lung of a stonecutter's corpse.[27]

Siderosis, pneumoconiosis, silicosis: the birth of terminology used to this day does not mean that medical research has followed a linear trajectory, leading straight to our current understanding of the causes and origins of diseases.

The theory of particle deposition by means of the airways was by no means the only hypothesis regarding the origin of the dust deposits being discovered on the dissecting table. There had also been suggestions of a digestive mechanism that envisaged the swallowing of dust accumulated on the epithelium, the absorption of these particles in the intestine, and their subsequent deposition in the smallest pulmonary capillaries. These tiny capillary clots would explain the mechanism of the onset of fibrosis that surgeons were finding in lung tissue.[28] In the mid-1870s, studies by William Osler (1805–1895) on the engulfing of carbon particles in the lungs of miners by cells in the immune system (macrophagic phagocytosis) established beyond a doubt that a respiratory mode, rather than a digestive one, was the real mechanism behind the penetration of dust into lung tissue. Osler's work helped do away with baseless theories on the blood-related origin of the black pigments commonly found in miners' lungs.[29]

In the same way, the spirometer, an apparatus invented in 1846 by English physician John Hutchinson (1811–1861) for measuring the volume of air inhaled and exhaled by the lungs, was not immediately used for diagnosing the various lung diseases caused by dust.[30] Hutchinson wanted his apparatus to be used in the life insurance sector, in order to identify individuals affected by tuberculosis, whose reduced life expectancy made them a bad investment.[31] The spirometer was thus initially a screening method in medical exams for healthy people, and later was used to evaluate the ability of workers to carry out dangerous occupations. It took several decades before the spirometer and measurements of respiratory function came to play a crucial role in the history of silicosis. This did not occur until around the mid-twentieth century, in the postwar period, and was again closely related to medico-legal insurance evaluations of injuries suffered by workers exposed to silica.

A crucial landmark on the long and twisted path through the nineteenth century, leading eventually to today's understanding of dust-related respiratory diseases, was the discovery that dust particles (particularly the finer types) could reach the lung sacs, the farthest branch of the respiratory tree. For many years, various theories had been in conflict. According to one view, dust particles inhaled through the mouth and nose were largely intercepted by the epithelium. Inducing coughing was thought to enable workers to completely expel what they had inhaled by producing mucous secretions capable of encompassing foreign particles. This optimistic interpretation, however, was confounded by findings of black pigmentation, corpuscles, and tubercles (knobby protuberances having a flintlike consistency) in diseased lungs.

Improved research in the field of inhalation therapy, which developed rapidly during the first half of the nineteenth century, also helped dispel doubts. In medical circles, the inhalation of aerosols and fine emollient powders had been considered beneficial to the health of the airways ever since antiquity.[32] *Atmiatria pulmonalis* (the treatment of disease by gas or vapors) received a substantial boost in the first decades of that century,[33] coinciding with the development of hydrotherapy and studies on the therapeutic benefits of various waters and related treatment techniques. Yet inhalation therapy was only included in the official British pharmacopoeia (the book which sets the national standard in the description of drugs, chemicals, and medical preparations in the United Kingdom) as late as 1867, endorsing the theory that foreign substances might be able to reach even the most peripheral branches of the respiratory tract.[34]

Artisans and Miners: Differential Visibility
Sheffield Grinders' Lung

The events that occurred *in corpore vili* ("in worthless bodies") during everyday activities in workshops, mines, and factories, where thousands of workers suffered harmful effects, influenced the development of medicine. The combination of new techniques associated with the Industrial Revolution and the growing number of medical observations linked to the increased presence of industrial hygienists expanded the scope of what is now known as silicosis. Steam power, for instance, increased the incidence of silicosis in the tin mines of Cornwall (and elsewhere in Britain), because water could be pumped out and deeper veins of ore exploited. Entire industrial sectors, such as pottery manufacturing, were impacted by the disease. Medical knowledge and debates did not follow a linear and systematic process, however, but instead developed in step with "sanitary crises."

The deaths of Cornish gold miners working in South Africa at the turn of the twentieth century,[35] and, a generation later, the illnesses of American workers during the Great Depression,[36] played a role in the growing awareness of dust-induced industrial diseases. The epidemics of silicosis in the years immediately preceding World War II had a similar effect on Italian society.[37] Here, the history of silicosis fits into a more general picture: from the Industrial Revolution, throughout the twentieth century, and to this day, medical attention to and interest in occupational diseases has been heightened by a succession of crises involving workers' health. The infamous silicosis epidemic among the needle grinders in Redditch, England, for instance, gained a great deal of notoriety in the first decades of the nineteenth century.[38] Rather than detailing how these cases varied by industry and region, however, we focus instead on the series of crises that hit the grinders in Sheffield, England, during the early nineteenth century. They received a lot of attention from both the public and the medical community and shed light on the dynamics and outcomes of these health-related crises.

Cutlery and blade production in the Sheffield area had early origins. Their manufacture used water-powered machinery and thus generally took place in cottages outside the city, along rivers and streams. The artisans employed in this type of industry carried out the entire production cycle, from forging the metal (which arrived in ingots), to grinding, polishing, and packaging the final products. The rhythms of nature determined the availability of water power; it was scarce in summer and abundant in winter. This traditional setup, however, was rocked by two revolutions: in business and in power sources. The former brought about a drastic increase in production and, consequently, a new and rudimentary division of labor that separated the task of "hot working" from that of grinding and refining, centered on particular artisans and workshops. Of still greater importance, the latter led to the introduction of steam-powered machinery, including the stone wheels used to grind and refine metallic objects. This offered two main manufacturing advantages. First, it allowed the maximum and most intensive use of working hours, with no need to take breaks to accommodate any seasonal lack of an energy source (such as water) or of sunlight. Second, production could be centralized in the cities, thus saving on costs, such as the transportation of materials and workers' mobility. All this, however, meant a drastic increase in the intensity and specialization of the artisans' work. Exposure to dust increased from a few hours to 10 or 11 hours per day, exacerbated by the abolition of breaks linked to seasonality and transfers into the countryside to reach the workshops. Effects on the health of these unfortunate workers were soon apparent.

A few years after the first application of steam power to grinding machines (in Sheffield, around 1786), the first reports of resultant, very serious respiratory changes began to emerge in medical literature. Arnold Knight (1789–1871) can be credited with having first raised the issue publicly. His appalling descriptions of the unhappy fate of men in their thirties and forties were enough to galvanize public opinion. Word spread, giving rise to newspaper articles, meetings of artisans, and heated debates, both within local communities and at the national level.

The physicians who were operating in Sheffield, visiting the factories in person, realized that they were always met by very young workers. The "old" workers (men in their forties and fifties) seemed to be missing, as though special circumstances were preventing anybody from reaching such an age. Paradoxically, it appeared that only workmen with the most intemperate habits (alcoholics and those given to "keeping Holy Monday," i.e., taking Mondays off), were among the very few who managed to survive a few years longer.[39] Their irregular work periods at the grindstone and their habit of taking breaks of varying lengths in the pursuit of "vice" and alcohol spared them from continuous, maximum-intensity exposure to poisonous dusts. A workplace disease thus claimed the lives of those who were morally healthier. This perceived injustice further outraged a puritanical and bourgeois public, adding to the growing perception that the price for this industry was too high to pay.

The first initiatives to protect workers from dust inhalation were born in this context. On September 1, 1819, Knight had delivered a paper on "grinders' asthma" before members of the Medical and Surgical Society of Sheffield, summarizing for the first time the scant evidence collected to date among workers afflicted with the disease. Two years later, J. H. Abraham was awarded the gold medal of the Royal Society of Arts of London for his invention of an apparatus to protect workers involved in creating points on needles, as well as those in all other sectors concerned with the grinding of metallic objects.[40] Abraham's device, however, was doomed to fail, since it needed constant attention and frequent worker intervention.[41]

On September 11, 1822, in the Cutlers' Hall in Sheffield, a special committee bestowed the Gold Vulcan Medal on John Elliot for making a significant improvement to the emery wheel, aimed at safeguarding the health of its operators. This involved placing a wooden protector on the front and the back of the wheel, exposing only the amount of surface strictly necessary for the job, and connecting the back of the wheel to an aeration funnel, leading to the outside of the building. Through repeated trials, Elliot had finally realized that the airflow caused by the rapid movement of the wheel itself could be used to get rid of both the metallic and siliceous dust particles produced during manufacture. The application of a another airstream, using a ventilator, made the device even more efficient. The Cutlers' Committee of Sheffield, praising the work of Elliot and Knight, recommended publication of the results, in order to promote awareness among those directly concerned: artisan grinders and factory owners. Shortly thereafter, a 16-page booklet was published, devoted entirely to ways of preventing this grinders' disease.[42]

The way in which labor was organized in the Sheffield cutlery factories hindered the distribution of ventilators. Workers employed in grinding were considered true artisans and enjoyed a measure of independence in their work, compared with the owners of the wheels, who did not possess this skill. The grinders, along with their apprentices, would hire the wheels, paying rent for use of a grindstone and occupancy of the premises, which actually belonged to the "masters," the real owners of the factories. The supposed autonomy of the grinders' occupation, coupled with uncertainty over who should bear the cost of installing the ventilation equipment (the owners of the grindstones and the premises, or the people renting them and carrying out the work) meant that the introduction of systems to remove harmful dust was dependent either on the goodwill of the owners or the grinders' concern for their own health.

Thirty years later, in 1865, an important meeting of the National Association for the Promotion of Social Science was held in the city of Sheffield. The senior physician at Sheffield Public Hospital, John Charles Hall (1816–1876), gave a passionate speech on the health conditions of stonegrinders. He lamented that only a small number of the factories he had visited had introduced the readily available and now-perfected ventilators for suctioning dust. This, in his view, was allowing grinders' disease to persist among workers.[43]

The emotional involvement of public opinion in health-related aspects of the affair is well illustrated in a poem by Ebenezer Elliott (1781–1849), known as "the corn-law rhymer," due to his social commitment. The poem is dedicated to the Sheffield grinders, and it mentions the two preventive devices, invented by Abraham and Elliot, that were offered to workers but whose use met with little success.[44]

The academic community was divided on the causes of the disease. In those years, English medical thought was dominated by anticontagionism, or miasmatism, which held that diseases were airborne, rather than contagious, and were spread by miasma, that is, toxic gases carrying rotting particles of organic matter. Yet, despite the preeminence of the miasma theory, at least two distinct positions were maintained within medical opinion. One was represented by Knight, Hall, and George Holland (1801–1865), who maintained that dust produced during work at the grindstones was the principal cause of disease.

Exposure was aggravated both by inadequate workspaces and ill-equipped workshops, as well as by the positions workers assumed as they leaned over the grindstones to apply force to the blades, placing themselves directly in the line of the dust flow.

At the other end of the spectrum, Charles Fox Favell (1806–1846) held that grinders' disease, although undoubtedly caused by dust inhalation, was aggravated at the clinical level by the intemperate and voluptuous habits of the grinders, who were "bent on vice and dissipation." The strong air currents caused by opening windows and doors wherever possible, while partly encouraging air circulation that carried away some of the dust particles, exposed workers to colds through sudden changes in temperature and their unsuitable clothing. Thus Favell attributed responsibility, at least partially, to what could broadly be defined as personal hygiene: factors separate from the working environment and therefore unrelated to production methods.[45]

Echoes of the Sheffield grinders' affair reverberated throughout the nineteenth century in Great Britain, which was known as "the workshop of the world."[46] In 1902, Sinclair White, the longtime medical officer of health for Sheffield, was a contributor to *Dangerous Trades*, a book (edited by Sir Thomas Oliver, 1853–1942) examining the health problems caused by steel grinding. Chapter 26 in that book included the results of White's own experience, gained over many years of inspections and observational visits to the workplaces in Sheffield. He painted a picture of working environments that, in many cases, were still dangerous; in which health-related conditions often remained unchanged since those described more than 70 years previously; and where the death rate among workers, while improved, remained excessively high, due to the effects of dust exposure.[47] By 1908, debate was still lively within the medical profession, as demonstrated by the record of proceedings of the annual meeting of the British Medical Association held that year, once again in Sheffield. The section dedicated to "Industrial Diseases," chaired by Sir Oliver, saw Dr. Scurfield, who at that point was the medical officer of health for Sheffield, take the speakers' stage first. He presented a paper on mortality in the "dusty trades" of Sheffield and a comparison with the situation in Solingen, Germany, which mirrored its English counterpart in both production methods and health problems among its workers. Sir Oliver followed, with a speech that attempted to refute what he saw as an insidious theory, according to which anthracosis in the lungs of coal miners originated in the intestines rather than the lungs, a thesis based on experimental results by eminent biologists and physicians of the time.[48] Oliver also strove to confirm that in the epithelium and the bronchi, a defense mechanism against the inhalation of dust made it possible to spit out much of what had been inhaled but was powerless in combating the smallest particles. He concluded his presentation by offering clear indications on what really mattered in the development of grinders' disease: "According to the nature of the dust that has been inhaled, the physical characters of the dust, the length of daily exposure to it, and the effectiveness of the ventilation, so will be the longevity of the patient. Rock-drillers in South Africa live only five or six years after the symptoms develop, steel grinders probably 15 years, while coal-miners have a still greater longevity."[49]

The next speech, by A. E. Barnes, clinical tutor at the University of Sheffield, caused a sensation. Directly and without hesitation, he denied that dust was the main cause of the lung diseases prevalent among the grinders:

> The view I hold is that the disease that causes the high mortality among Sheffield grinders is tuberculosis, and that pneumonokoniosis plays quite a minor part, practically never reaching such a high degree as to cause serious symptoms. Thus the practical conclusion is to remove the tubercle bacillus by cheap and handy methods rather than to attempt the removal of the dust by expensive and cumbrous methods. Grinders' phthisis is true tuberculosis.[50]

Barnes reaffirmed his views in a letter commenting on the raging debate sparked by his remarks: "Pneumonokoniosis is now rare in Sheffield. I have good reasons to think that formerly it was common, but the present arrangements, bad as they are, seem sufficient to have eliminated pneumonokoniosis or reduced it to narrow limits. The next object should be the elimination of the tuberculosis bacillus."[51]

Thus the bitter dispute between the two schools of medical opinion over whether dust produced by materials used in manufacturing trades was predominantly, or even exclusively, responsible for lung disease flared up again around 80 years after it first broke out. This time, the naysayers attempted to shift the blame onto a microbiological cause, rather than onto the moral conduct of the workers, as Favell had done.[52] The dominant scientific paradigm had changed by that stage. In the first half of the nineteenth century, anticontagionism had attributed the main cause of all diseases to airborne miasmas. Later in the century, bacterial explanations were favored for all types of disease, even, as the case of silicosis so perfectly illustrates, in the face of glaring evidence to the contrary.

The Trouble with Miners' Respiratory Diseases

The Sheffield grinders amounted to a few thousand workers, as did the potters studied by Arlidge,[53] and an article by Thomas Peacock (1812–1882) on French millstone-makers in London concerned no more than a few dozen people.[54] In contrast, miners were a veritable army of workers who, in shifts rotating 24 hours a day, descended into the bowels of the earth to extract rock or coal.[55] It is not surprising, then, that of all the various categories of workers exposed to silica dust, silicosis in miners was undoubtedly the most significant public health issue in terms of the severity of its symptoms and the spread of the disease. Yet it was far from the most visible public health concern in the nineteenth century, as lexicometric analysis (statistically measuring the use of particular terms in a text) demonstrates.[56] To some extent, the difficulties in observing the characteristics of the phenomenon were due to the fact that physicians investigating exposure to silica dust rarely set foot inside the mines to study the miners at work, although they had done so for other professions.

Throughout Europe, doctors in mining communities generally described living conditions on the surface (but not underground), within miners' households, and in the community, yet they were unable, except on rare occasions, to make a connection between the technology used in the mines and the diseases they discovered. Undoubtedly adding to this is the fact that miners were relatively isolated and lived in very particular social conditions. Their daily frame of reference was almost always their home community and the mining village where they worked, if not their native rural environment, far from the temptations of the "corrupting" and "wasteful" city, unlike the urban-dwelling Sheffield grinders and Black Country potters.

This meant that miners did not fit neatly into the dominant hygienist and medical discourses, which emphasized the harmful effects of cities on their inhabitants. This narrative insisted that it was the growth of cities, poorly constructed and ill-equipped to treat sewage and other harmful human wastes, that was contributing significantly to the spread of tuberculosis. Tuberculosis was perceived to be the true scourge of the proletarian masses, whom the Industrial Revolution had impacted so profoundly. From the mid-nineteenth century onward, alarming statistics from France, and later England, highlighted the soaring incidence of tuberculosis in cities, which made the mortality rates in many mining districts appear less serious than those in manufacturing districts.

But this rural/urban opposition did not explain everything. Additionally, what we could call socioenvironmental clusters, closely linking a specific occupation with a raw material and a locality, served as a basis for observations that were compatible with medical categories of the time and, therefore, were relatively easy to promote. This was the case, for instance, with the lung diseases that affected stone-quarry workers and stonemasons, such as the *maladie de Saint Roch* (Saint Roch's disease) described by Clozier toward the end of the eighteenth century,[57] stoneworkers' pulmonary diseases in the Scottish cities of Edinburgh and Aberdeen,[58] and the French millstone-makers' phthisis described by Peacock.[59] Slate-workers' diseases were also well known, from the Italian slate-miners' consumption[60] to the French *maladies des ardoisiers* (slate-workers' schistosis and phthisis) studied by Sejournet at the Saint-Joseph mine near Fumay in the Ardennes in the late nineteenth century.[61]

Identifying the pathological links was not always straightforward. To complicate matters, in the stonecutters' case, much depended on the nature of the processed material. Those who dealt with marble were largely free of pneumoconiosis, yet those who worked with granite were afflicted with it. Once again, it was the presence or absence of silica in the materials involved that made the difference. In the case of miners' disease, it was particularly difficult to gain a general overview, because of the variety of materials extracted and the nature of the working conditions. The inferior status of workers associated with this occupation—which had traditionally been reserved for slaves, prisoners, and forced labor—probably also played a part. When it came to miners, observations were scarce and, where they existed, were sometimes contradictory. In the case of Cornwall, an early map showed the gravity of the situation among miners, who were plagued by an inordinately high death rate from respiratory and cardiac causes.[62]

Internationally, an early divide in this subterranean world could be seen between mineral mining and coal extraction. The former consisted of excavating extremely hard material that would break up into blocks, releasing fine dust particles with acute, "irritating" angles. The latter involved softer material, whose vegetal origin was verifiable in its microscopic structure. Although porous, and therefore considered less irritating, coal-dust particles were easily found in lungs during autopsies. As a result, coal became a preferred object for studying the mechanisms through which dust was being absorbed by the lungs. One difficulty, though, was the realization that city dwellers were also exhibiting a pulmonary buildup of black pigment, with apparently no distinguishable difference from the buildup in coal miners' lungs.

The unspecific nature of these anatomopathological findings, and a reluctance to acknowledge that dust particles could penetrate deep within the lungs, complicated the explanation of a phenomenon that was already encountering strong resistance. Moreover, mortality studies were probably biased, because of "positive confounding" from the environmental isolation of these communities. In other words, compared with the cities, where overcrowding favored contagion, isolation gave mining communities some protection against the spread of tuberculosis. This resulted in lower overall recorded numbers of deaths due to pulmonary disease relative to the figures for urban environments, even though pneumoconiosis, and especially silicosis, was strongly present in these rural communities. Everybody therefore believed that respiratory diseases in coal miners were less widespread and, especially, less severe than those among Cornish miners and all other workers exposed to rock or metal dust. The very severe forms of "black phthisis" found in the first three decades of the nineteenth century, especially in the coalfields of Scotland, were not replicated on the continent. Increased awareness and attempts to promote safety, following progressive developments in aeration systems, probably helped mitigate the effects of pulmonary dust deposits, allowing these disease symptoms to be controlled in Europe, thus drawing attention to the respiratory problems in Great Britain.

Cornish miners, long before the observations by John Scott Haldane (1860–1936) and Arlidge on acute silicosis in those returning from the Transvaal in South Africa, were well known for their inordinately high mortality rate and drastically reduced life expectancy. Yet the causes of this striking phenomenon remained unclear. Speculation arose that the effort of climbing long, steep ladders to the mine exit at the end of shifts caused fatigue and subsequent exhaustion in the heart, as did working in very deep and poorly aerated galleries.

Irritation from the particularly treacherous nature of the dust produced by black-powder blasting did not go unnoticed, either. But the relative importance of the various sources of risk could not be determined. It was even difficult to make progress in the anatomopathological study of lesions, given the reluctance of families to consent to postmortem examinations of affected laborers.[63] Yet public interest in the fate of this group of workers did not wane. Statistics consistently showed (almost to the point of monotony) a reduction in their survival rates and a high incidence of respiratory diseases, which certainly could not be attributed to particularly depraved moral and social conditions.[64]

Potters' Rot

The production of ceramic and porcelain objects underwent important technological developments in the early years of the eighteenth century. The addition of flint particles to make products less porous and thus more usable can be traced back to Thomas Astbury, a manufacturer who, in around 1720, perfected the formula for the industrial production of white porcelain. This process involved the use of finely powdered flint, and, within the space of a few years, the workers involved suffered from very serious respiratory diseases. To this end, between 1726 and 1732, Thomas Benson, a painter interested in developing new machinery for the production of ceramics, devised a different method for wet-grinding flint, using metal "ball" mills that did not give off excessive silica dust. The importance of this improvement was twofold: it provided better health protection for the workers, and it increased production. The patent awarded to Benson recorded the first descriptions of the harmful effects of exposure to the fine dust generated in abundance during the "dry process" used until then. The patent stated that this process had "proved very destructive to mankind, occasioned by the dust sucked into the body, which, being of a ponderous nature, fixes so closely upon the lungs that nothing can remove it, insomuch that it is very difficult to find persons to engage in the said manufacture, to the great detriment and decay of that branch of trade."[65] An early crisis was thus avoided, due to the invention of more-advanced production methods. But while the acute, immediate effects of dust exposure in ceramic production were mitigated, thanks to Benson's device, this was not the case for chronic effects, which were less evident but no less devastating. Ultimately, his invention did not save the respiratory health of the workers in this industry, who were mainly women and children.

While anecdotal descriptions of poor working conditions and dust exposure were collected by various authors in the 1840s, it was not until the early 1860s that the scientific community once again turned its attention to the dangers in the potteries. The situation was somewhat clarified by the publication of a number of studies conducted in Great Britain during those years on the death rates of the various social classes and different groups of workers.[66] Potters were consistently ranked first in the list of occupations with the highest mortality, due to pulmonary causes. Alongside this statistical evidence, important observations were being made by clinical physicians working in the area where the industry was chiefly based. In 1864, for example, Charles Parsons (1833– 1922), the house surgeon at the North Staffordshire Infirmary, noticed that among his patients—for the most part potters, colliers, and ironworkers—the frequency and severity of pulmonary disease among potters was particularly striking. He made it the subject of his thesis, *On a Form of Bronchitis (Simulating Phthisis) Which Is Peculiar to Certain Branches of the Potting Trade*, for which he received an MD degree and was awarded a gold medal.[67]

Parsons left the potteries region a few years later to practice in Dover, but Arlidge dedicated much of his professional life to the diseases of pottery workers. It was Arlidge who most comprehensively identified and described the problem of dust exposure in the ceramics industry. While carrying out his duties as "certifying factory surgeon" in Stoke-on-Trent, at the heart of the ceramics district in England, Arlidge repeatedly observed the deplorable working conditions and their effects on the health of that city's workers, both male and female. His accounts of the potters' work display great familiarity with the subject, gleaned by studying human beings rather than by consulting technical encyclopedias. His accurate and detailed description of the lung disease afflicting the workers was destined to become authoritative:

> The pulmonary mischief from the dust of potters' clay is slow but sure in its occurrence. The siliceous character of the clay lends it more potency for harm than almost any other dust. It is much more irritant than coal dust, and stands on a par with the worst kinds of stone dust. . . . When uncomplicated by tubercles the potters' disease advances imperceptibly. . . . Haemoptysis does not usher in the malady, and more frequently than not, never makes its appearance. . . . There is no febrile reaction, no accelerated pulse, no hectic, and no rapid emaciation. . . . The cough is more paroxysmal and violent than that of phthisis, and the urgency of dyspnoea greater, and out of proportion to the ascertained extent of consolidated lung. The signs of condensation are not so specially limited to the infraclavicular spaces as in tuberculous lesions. . . . Areas of dullness on percussion are often distributed at different parts . . . [and] between these an emphysematous condition is discoverable. . . . Ulceration of the vocal cords and aphonia are wanting.[68]

Arlidge's work sparked controversy. While local medical circles did not take kindly to his philanthropic and supportive attitude toward this class of workers, who were widely considered to be depraved and prone to vice, criticisms were also directed at his initial statistical studies documenting the potters' elevated death rates. Arlidge himself was forced to admit that some of the data, based on hospital case studies, gave an overly negative impression of mortality among ceramic workers that was due to respiratory diseases.[69] Nevertheless, he succeeded in raising interest in the matter, which signified a step forward in recognizing the harmful effects of the silica dust generated by this type of manufacturing.

A Lesser Known Crisis: The Parisian Mouleurs en Cuivre *("Copper Workers"), 1842–1854*

Smelting and then molding metals into the desired forms involve high-temperature processes to bring the metal or alloy to the point where it can be cast in heat-resistant molds. These are made of refractory clay, from which the molded item can be easily removed. Bronze and brass foundries used silica-based clays in this process, as well as carbon dust for foundry facings in the molds. In early nineteenth-century Paris, there were around 2,000 workers and apprentices in this industry, spread across 100 factories.[70] In 1821, a mutual-aid society, founded by these workers, began to record the causes of diseases among its members. It was the society's own physicians who noticed the high rate of lung disease as a cause of workers' absences. The workers themselves were well aware of the risks they were running. They had coined an expression to define the cause of this chronic condition: *quand la poussière s'attache à un homme* ("when the dust sticks to a man"), which signified the start of a period of suffering that might differ in length from person to person but had an inevi-table outcome. Labor unrest and strikes to demand improved health conditions in the workplace had occurred, starting as early as 1842. One of the initial de-mands was to reduce the working day by 2 hours, from the usual 12 to 10.

Carbon dust was the prime suspect in these diseases. Overwhelming clouds of it arose before casting, then again when it was scattered over the walls of the molds, and once more when the molds were opened to remove the objects after the metal had cooled.[71] A few years later, in early 1853, an older founder, named Rouy, had the idea of replacing carbon dust with potato flour as a foundry fac-ing. From a health point of view, success was immediate. Yet several unad-dressed issues remained. Was it possible to proceed with such a replacement without the industry, which was greatly valued and a source of employment for many laborers, being damaged in some way? Did the elimination of carbon dust guarantee a solution to its associated health complications? In response to these questions, the Minister for Trade and Industry decided to place the matter in the hands of a commission, which included the physicians François Magendie (1783–1855), François Mélier (1798–1866), and Auguste Ambroise Tardieu (1818–1879), as well as the chemist Michel Eugène Chevreul (1786–1889). M. Julien, head of the domestic trade division, assisted the commission, which was chaired by M. Heutier, who held the offices of state councillor and ministerial director. In announcing the commission's findings, Tardieu emphasized how replacing coal dust with potato flour had brought about a drastic reduction in the dust levels. He supported this opinion with environmental survey data but overlooked the possibility that silica, abundantly present in the materials that were used, might be the crucial element in the most severe pulmonary symptoms. The authorities' interest in these problems, however, along with pressure exerted by workers, academics, and governmental experts who were taking on the *patrons* ("bosses"), brought about a positive outcome in improving the general workplace health conditions in these foundries. This also indirectly helped control exposure to silica. The example here confirms that when it comes to public health, excellent results in disease prevention can often be achieved without a perfect knowledge of the etiology and pathogenesis (causes and development) of a particular disease.

Dust versus Microbes: An Unequal Fight?
At the Dawn of the New Century

Several crises in the early twentieth century were to play a decisive role in the way in which silicosis came to be classified as a disease. In South Africa, the problem of gold miners and the "acute pulmonary phthisis" that could cause death after only a few working years came to light. Retrospectively, the mines in the Transvaal area would prove to be among the most dangerous in the world, due to the nature and the level of dust they produced. In Australia, accounts emerged about the terrible death rate among workers in the gold mines of Bendigo, due to lung diseases. An epidemic of fatal lung diseases among Cornish miners returning from the mines in South Africa shocked the English-speaking medical and scientific community. The 1904 report by the physiologist John Scott Haldane, in which he discussed the results of his observations, marked a decisive step forward in identifying silica dust as a causative agent in pulmonary fibrosis.[72]

The degree of medical understanding about lung diseases caused by dust was synthesized at the turn of the century by three of the most eminent British experts on occupational diseases: Arlidge, Oliver, and Edgar L. Collis (1870–1957). Arlidge and Oliver, respectively, wrote the chapter on pneumoconiosis for the first and second editions (1898 and 1909) of T. Clifford Allbutt's textbook on general medicine, *A System of Medicine*. In 1915, at the annual meeting of the British Medical Association, Collis was asked to draft a critical analysis summarizing the current state of knowledge for dust-related lung diseases.[73] These reports became a milestone in the recognition of silicosis as a distinct disease, paving the way for the subsequent transnational debates.

Arlidge's 15-page chapter focused on the possibility of distinguishing the two forms of phthisis—tubercular phthisis and phthisis caused by dust—and suggested the best methods for differentiating between them in live humans. With Koch's discovery of the tuberculosis bacillus and his formulation of the general principles of the infectious model of disease (the "Henle-Koch postulates"), medical attention gradually turned toward the bacterial origin of all massive outbreaks of disease, including the various pulmonary illnesses. Arlidge went no further in separating out the roles played by different types of dust, attributing the same harmful properties to all of them.[74] Moreover, he never used the word "silica" to differentiate its potential effects on the lungs from those of other harmful materials. In short, according to him, most types of dust were "benign" in "normal" conditions. Some kinds, however, were directly irritating to the mucous membrane of the bronchioles (thin-walled branches of the bronchi) and to lung tissue, and thus could have more-serious effects. Arlidge concluded his chapter with a strong reminder of the duty employers had toward their employees regarding the health risks associated with dust inhalation.

Ten years later, Oliver revised this chapter and expanded it to roughly 28 pages. He seemed more concerned with establishing the importance of dust in the origin and development of pulmonary fibrosis than with the role played by tubercular infection, although the latter was widespread among workers. His chapter methodically described the occupations that were causing the dreaded pneumoconiosis. He was particularly struck by recent findings of the severe forms of mass silicosis among British miners whom he had personally examined after their return from South Africa. Oliver expressed his belief that coal dust had a different and lesser capability of causing a fibrotic reaction in lung tissue (pulmonary parenchyma), thus lending authority to the opinion that coal dust was inherently less harmful than silica dust.

On the interaction between dust and the tuberculosis bacillus, Oliver was convinced that dust disease preceded the onset of tubercular infection by providing a fertile ground for the implantation of Koch's bacillus. Other physicians maintained that dust disease could implant itself on an existing tubercular infection, aggravating the symptoms but not causing them. This division within the scientific community not only affected medicine, but also was crucial in determining compensation schemes for workers and workplace arrangements. Favoring the microbiological theory meant acting on the factors causing the spread of the bacillus among the population (unsanitary housing; rapid changes in temperature, including sudden cooling due to unsuitable clothing; excessive humidity; high temperatures; the tendency to spread the bacillus by not spitting into designated containers; etc.). It also meant quarantining and excluding consumptives from the workplace, as a means of controlling occupational phthisis.[75]

Oliver's theory, in contrast, focused on the technical prevention of dust diffusion, positing that protecting workers from dust was the best safeguard against the implantation of the tuberculosis bacillus. From this perspective, identifying and keeping out workers suffering from tuberculosis, a measure also proposed by Oliver, acquired a different significance: that of addressing the severe complications that prevented workers from continuing on the job, due to illness caused by dust inhalation. In this way, Oliver laid the foundations for the insurance industry's future recognition of silica-dust-induced diseases. This development, despite its different directions and outcomes in various countries, would be crucially important in the social management of silicosis and the distinct way in which it was handled, compared with other, equally severe respiratory diseases resulting from exposure to inorganic dusts.[76]

Collis's Epicrisis

By 1915, the time was ripe to take stock of the scientific and epidemiological knowledge on dust-related lung diseases accumulated in previous years. Collis, by then medical inspector of factories, assumed the task of summarizing the current state of understanding when he was invited that year to deliver the annual Milroy Lecture before the Royal College of Physicians. Collis was at the peak of his career, and his extensive, direct experience in workplaces, combined with a first-rate scientific and cultural background, made him a true leader in the field of pulmonary illnesses resulting from dust exposure. His professional position gave him firsthand access to official sources, such as reports by governmental commissions and institutional organizations in charge of investigating phenomena detrimental to the health of workers exposed to dust. (At that time, such reports were piling up on desks in the British Parliament and in offices of the Department of Industry.) He was thus able to conduct his task in a memorable fashion, publishing a long article that would mark a shift in thinking in a new age.[77]

At the outset of his lecture, Collis stated his four objectives: (1) to make it clear that dust inhaled by workers in the course of their occupation caused a larger number of lung-related deaths that could not be attributed to other causes; (2) to determine if the amount of dust inhaled by workers exposed to it was so much greater than that inhaled by the general population, in order to explain the excessive ratio of pulmonary symptoms and diseases; (3) to exclude from the category of pneumoconioses (lung diseases caused by dust) those diseases caused by the inhalation of disease-causing biological agents (primarily tuberculosis); and (4) to establish that, just as not all microbes are disease agents, neither are all dust types equally pathogenic, with siliceous dusts being the worst.

Collis thought it necessary to again confirm that inhalation was the origin of dust accumulation in the lungs, ruling out the digestive system route. He then underlined the semantic confusion behind the mistaken idea that common types of dust could cause asthma in workers. Today's definition of asthma, as an acute and sudden onset of bronchial spasms that constrict the air passages in the lungs, was already known when Collis wrote his article. This allowed him to conclude that a type of chronic lung disease, characterized by the gradually worsening, labored breathing (dyspnea) after exertion that was typical of all forms of pneumoconiosis, had little to do with real asthma.

Collis then went on to analyze bronchitis, noting the inaccuracy of the statistics that were available and restating the peculiar situation for coal miners who, in his opinion, were generally spared from the effects of dust-induced lung disease. (Collis's description of the origin, causes, and evolution of bronchitis still remains accurate and up to date.) Once again, he ruled out the possibility of this particular disease mechanism operating in those exposed to coal dust, just as it did not appear to cause the lung diseases related to dusts produced by alabaster, calcium sulfate, limestone, cement, and dusts coming from animals.

In the next part of his speech, Collis concentrated on pneumonia. While he was aware of the bacterial cause of acute pneumonia, Collis was convinced that dusts, as a whole, encouraged the onset of pneumonia, even if not all types of dust were associated with significant increases in the onset of phthisis. He restated that workers in coal mines did not show increased signs of pneumonia following inhalation of the dust types related to this activity. Finally, he explained his theory that fibrosis-inducing dusts could pave the way for the tuberculosis bacillus to settle in the lungs.

Collis then turned to the crucial section of his lecture, in which he argued that silica was especially dangerous in terms of lung diseases. Significantly, he spoke of "dust-phthisis, or pulmonary silicosis." His argument rested on two foundations. The first was an analysis of epidemic curves related to mortality from phthisis in the general population, and those for workers exposed to dust in certain occupations. The second was the observation that dust-phthisis is distinct from infective phthisis, because the former does not display the typical hereditary characteristics attributed at that time to the latter.

In the epidemic curves, phthisis due to dust markedly increased in older age groups, compared with what was seen in the case of infectious phthisis. Collis highlighted the unique role of free crystalline silica in determining dust-phthisis, now defined as "pulmonary silicosis." He argued that the profession of stonemasonry could be useful as a litmus test for this pathogenic peculiarity, because two different types of stone could be treated in exactly the same way by separate groups of workers. Statistical mortality data showed that only those masons who used stone containing high percentages of crystalline silica experienced an increased rate of lung-related deaths. Collis thus employed a methodology that now might be defined as experimental statistics, or as an early form of the epidemiology of chronic diseases. This approach was rooted in the Anglo-Saxon tradition of public health, which had no equivalent in other countries.[78]

On the relationship between tuberculosis and dust, Collis sided unhesitatingly with those who saw pulmonary fibrosis caused by dust inhalation as a precursor to infection by Koch's bacillus, and who stressed the importance of preventing dust exposure as a means of deterring the spread of the bacterial infection. The final part of his lecture was devoted to a clinical description of the patients' disease symptoms and a diagnosis of the chronic, most common form of silicosis. Collis mentioned the use of a spirometer and the initial results of radiographic diagnostics, referring constantly to the South African case.

Conclusion

Almost a hundred years had passed between Knight's discussion of lung disease in Sheffield grinders and Collis's Milroy Lecture. During that time, the link between dust inhalation and a series of lung ailments had been partly revealed, and the idea that silica dust, in particular, could cause a specific disease had spread and increasingly taken hold. The more this disease was medically defined and classified in nosology, the more the term "pulmonary silicosis" began to come into use.[79] Its etiology had also been clarified: not all dusts, but siliceous dust and a small number of other dust types, were capable of causing fibrotic transformations that were devastating to the health of the workers involved. Through this process, after Koch's discovery of the bacterial agent behind tuberculosis in 1882, "infective phthisis" had also acquired a more precise description and a clearer medical classification.

This evolution had by no means been linear or obvious, however. The fact that Collis could paint a picture that is largely considered valid today does not mean that the theory he advocated had decidedly triumphed. First, older understandings of medicine were still active. As late as 1925, Thomas Oliver would feel the need to begin his article on the role of dust in the lung diseases of workers in certain occupations by reiterating how long the mistaken belief had persisted that dust was not able to reach the lung sacs (pulmonary alveoli) because it was blocked by the body's defense mechanisms. He then went on to decry how much space had been given, even at the experimental level, to the theory that dust might reach the lungs by being absorbed in the intestines and transferred through the blood, rather than through a respiratory route.[80]

Second, the efforts to distinguish silicosis from tuberculosis, so actively pursued at the scientific level, were not applied in the same way when it came to diagnosing individual patients. In the majority of cases, changes caused by the two diseases were associated and overlapped, manifesting themselves simultaneously in the same people. This complicated attempts at clear-cut epidemiological descriptions, ideas about their respective causes, and preventive measures. Often it was precisely the greater treatability of tuberculosis that, from a therapeutic point of view, attracted better care by the physicians called upon to assist ill workers.

A century later, although silicosis has been officially recognized internationally as a distinct entity since the 1930s, we should not overlook these difficulties, which still limit medical knowledge about silica dust's pathological effects. To some extent, the great physician Giacomo Mottura (1906–1990) encapsulated this scientific fuzziness in 1950, when he referred to the "silicosis epidemic" that was then striking Italian workers and stated that "the uncertainties with which this progress has been made, the difficulties that have been met in distinguishing between the part played by silicosis in consumption [among miners] and the complicating tuberculosis, the thoughtlessness of so many pseudoscientists, have provided great nourishment for all those who had a tendency, if not an interest in, clinging to the practice of temporizing."[81]

In the first decades of the twentieth century, the greatest uncertainty surrounding the effect of silica dust on pulmonary fibrosis was its correlation with tuberculosis. This helps explain why the etiological hypothesis of a pulmonary disease that was caused by silica dust, which Collis so explicitly described as early as the 1910s, was not accepted without objections, reservations, and shades of interpretation that later affected its practical application in diagnosing the illness. The realization that tuberculosis could be spread by dry dust containing the microorganism that was its disease agent had focused attention on the characteristics of this disease and the long-awaited possibility of preventing its transmission between humans. Physicians employed at the forefront of public health and clinical medicine strongly resisted the notion of dust as an independent and preeminent cause of the fibrotic disease. They argued, on the basis of statistical data, that although there were higher rates of disease and death among those exposed to dust, the real danger came from Koch's bacillus, which attacked patients already weakened by general pulmonary changes caused by dust exposure. In and of itself, therefore, dust was considered much less dangerous; Koch's bacillus was seen as the real culprit.[82]

Industrialists faced practical consequences as a result of these scientific and professional controversies over pulmonary silicosis, which, in turn, made the debates between specialists particularly heated.[83] At stake was the particular means of preventing (or at least protecting against) this disease. Should measures be taken to control exposure by collecting the dust that was generated, meaning increasingly complex and expensive suction and ventilation systems funded by employers? Or should efforts target the personal hygiene of individual workers, who needed be taught correct behavior (no spitting on the floor or in containers other than those provided for the purpose)?

This issue was particularly sensitive on the eve and in the immediate aftermath of World War I. Economic historians have defined this period as "the first phase of the global economy,"[84] in which civil society and national and international public opinion called for adequate measures to protect the health and income of workers exposed to these risks. Although the body of medical knowledge about silicosis had become quite substantial, official recognition of the disease—in the structuring of private- and social-insurance programs, in governmental policies related to its prevention, and in the management of the industrial workforce—was soon to become a battlefield on a global scale.

NOTES

1. Rosen, *History of Miners' Diseases.*
2. Ibid., 118–120.
3. In these two paragraphs, we rely on Rosental, "History of Occupational Lung Diseases."
4. For a classic formulation of this, see Fleck, *Genesis and Development of a Scientific Fact,* ch. 1 ("How the Modern Concept of Syphilis Originated"), 19: "The development of the concept of syphilis as a specific disease is thus incomplete in principle, involved as it is in subsequent discoveries and new features of pathology, microbiology, and epidemiology. In the course of time, the character of the concept has changed from the mystical, through the empirical and generally pathogenical, to the mainly etiological."
5. For a general overview, see Rosenberg, "Disease in History." The situation regarding chlorosis (also known as "green sickness"), a form of anemia named for the greenish tinge of patients' skin, is one example that has been extensively studied. Symptoms included a lack of energy, shortness of breath, dyspepsia (indigestion), headaches, lack of appetite, and amenorrhoea (the absence of menstrual periods in women of childbearing age). This disease reached a height of notoriety during the nineteenth century, before later disappearing from the twentieth-century medical landscape. See Hudson, "Biography of Disease"; Figlio, "Chlorosis and Chronic Disease"; Starobinski, "Sur la chlorose." An example closer to the current topic of discussion is the subject of a 1995 study by Paterson ("From Fever to Digestive Disease") that describes the evolving notion of "factory ill-health" in Britain from 1784 to 1833. It considers the evolution of medical understanding and perception on the part of those directly affected by this condition, namely, textile workers in large factories during the early industrialization period.
6. See Gandevia, "Australian Contribution"; Markowitz and Rosner, "Illusion of Medical Certainty."
7. Jewson, "Disappearance of the Sick-Man."
8. Cited in Shryock, *Development of Modern Medicine,* 4.
9. Ibid., 43.
10. Jewson, "Disappearance of the Sick-Man."
11. Particularly telling is the description by Arlidge of the various transformations catarrh underwent during the development of silicosis in potters (*Hygiene, Diseases, and Mortality,* 313): "The sputa remain for long white and frothy, with specks or streaks of black matter, which is inhaled dust. Later on this mucous expectoration gets purulent, heavy, and forms pellets, but is not green."
12. See an illustration of the prominence of these categorizations at that time in Baldasseroni et al., "Naissance d'une maladie." Their study relies on a body of 200 medical publications, devoted to pulmonary diseases that physicians considered occupational, published in English from 1800 to 1980. It establishes a chronology, based on distinct periods of lexical homogeneity in key journals, indicated by the paired occurrences of key terms. Each of these periods may be characterized by a set of words that, in comparison with the entire time span of the study, are overemployed or underemployed.
13. Consider, for example, this passage by Christophorus Krause from 1688 (cited in Carozzi, "Contributo bibliografico," 419): "*Inter non-naturales [causas] primas obtinet aer . . . Ad talium productionem spectant etiam miasmata pulmonum putrida, exhalationes fumosae, crassae, metallicae aut minerals* [Between the nonnatural [causes], air plays a major role . . . in the case of occupations which bring about a production of putrid miasma to the lungs, as well as fumes from smoke, dense metals, or minerals]."

14. Laennec, *Treatise on the Diseases*, 150: "The ancient pathologists regarded foreign bodies introduced into the bronchi in a state of powder, as the cause of several severe diseases of those canals, as well as of the substance of the lungs; and among others, of phthisis pulmonalis, and the chalky concretions of the lungs, bronchial glands, or bronchial tubes. This opinion appears to me altogether without foundation. It is imagined that stonecutters and lapidaries are particularly subject to formations of this kind, occasioned by the inhalation of the dust amid which they work. It is needless to remark that this dust is entirely unlike the cretaceous formations in the lungs. On this subject it deserves notice that stage coachmen, who spend their life amid much more dust, are usually healthy, or suffer only from diseases produced by intemperance and the inclemency of the weather."

15. Ibid., 150–151: "Everyone is occasionally caught in a cloud of dust and merely experiences while breathing in it an oppression without any inclination to cough. It is well known that when we have been for some time breathing an air loaded with dust or smoke these foreign bodies are after a certain time expectorated with the mucous secretion [of] the bronchi. For these reasons I consider the chalky formations in the bronchi as well as every accidental production in the living body as the result of perverted secretion."

16. The term "pulmonary cirrhosis"—to indicate a chronic inflammation, with a fibrotic transformation of the respiratory system, through its analogy with the term "hepatic cirrhosis" (described a few years earlier by Laennec)—was introduced in 1838 by Dominic John Corrigan. Cited in Carozzi, "Contributo bibliografico," 622–623.

17. Ackerknecht, "Anticontagionism."

18. Farr, "Vital Statistics"; Villermé, *Tableau de l'état physique*; Lombard, "De l'influence des professions."

19. See note 69 for Aldridge's letter to Parliament.

20. For a critique of these types of statistics, see Newsholme, "Occupation and Mortality"; Willoughby, "Some Prevalent Fallacies."

21. Some years later, Vernon provided a precise description of this effect in "Methods of Investigating."

22. See Ward's classic article, "The Effect, as Shown by Statistics." See also a later discussion regarding Collis in Baldasseroni et al., "Naissance d'une maladie," which provides a statistical confirmation of this trend.

23. This phrase is attributed to Jean Fernel (1497–1558), a renowned French physician who introduced the term "physiology." Cited in Putegnat, "Maladies des tailleurs de crystal."

24. Virchow, "Pathology of Miners' Lung."

25. Von Zenker, "Ueber Staubinhalationskrankheiten der Lungen."

26. Greenhow, "Specimen of Diseased Lung."

27. Rovida, "Un caso di silicosi del polmone."

28. Feltz, *Maladies des tailleurs de pierres*.

29. Rosen, "Osler on Miner's Phthisis."

30. The spirometer was actually preceded by Edward Kentish's "pulmometer," perfected in 1814 (see Kentish, *An Account of Baths*), and other, similar instruments. One such device was also used by Charles Thackrah to study workers suffering from lung diseases caused by exposure to flax dust (see Thackrah, *Effects of Arts*, 73–74).

31. Davis, "Life Insurance," 392–406.

32. P. Anderson, "History of Aerosol Therapy."

33. The term is derived from *atmos*, meaning "vapor" or "gas," and *iatreia*, meaning "treatment." See Hoblyn, *Dictionary of Terms Used in Medicine*.

34. Cohen, *Inhalation*, esp. ch. 3.

35. Katz, *White Death*.

62   *Silicosis*

36. Cherniack, *Hawk's Nest Incident*; Rosner and Markowitz, *Deadly Dust: Silicosis and the Politics*.
37. Parmeggiani, "Considerazioni sui casi di silicosi."
38. Johnstone, "Some Account of a Species."
39. "Report on the Preventable Diseases," 409.
40. The Royal Society had offered the prize since 1804, without ever actually awarding it.
41. "Report on the Preventable Diseases," 408.
42. Knight et al., *Committee Appointed for Investigating the Claims*; Davy, "Grinder's Safety Apparatus."
43. J. Hall, "Effect of Certain Sheffield Trades."
44. Elliot, *Poetical Works*.
45. Favell, "Sheffield Medical Society," 151.
46. The case of the Sheffield grinders also gained notoriety beyond Great Britain. At the Fifth Conference of Italian Scientists held in Milan in 1844, attention was drawn to the merits of a technology that "defended the lungs of steel polishers from harmful metallic molecules through use of the magnetic facemask" (the device proposed by Abraham). See "Voto della Commissione," 311.
47. Oliver, *Dangerous Trades*.
48. Calmette et al., "Sur l'anthracose pulmonaire," 548.
49. Oliver, "Etiology and Prevention of Pneumonokoniosis."
50. Barnes, "Pathology of Grinders' Phthisis."
51. Barnes, "Grinders' Phthisis."
52. C. Johnston and Bennett, "Dust Removal"; Owen, "Popular Lecture on Dust."
53. Arlidge, *Hygiene, Diseases, and Mortality*.
54. Peacock, "On French Millstone-Makers' Phthisis."
55. Oliver, *Diseases of Occupation*.
56. Baldasseroni et al., "Naissance d'une maladie."
57. Clozier, "Maladie, dite de Saint Roch."
58. For Edinburgh, see Alison, "Observations on the Pathology," 373. For Aberdeen, see Beveridge, "On the Occurrence of Phthisis."
59. Peacock, "On French Millstone-Makers' Phthisis."
60. Mongiardini, "Osservazioni e riflessioni."
61. Cited in Oliver, *Diseases of Occupation*, 303–305.
62. Weale, "Letter from Mr. Weale." See also Barham, "Some Remarks."
63. See Bloor, "Richard Quiller Couch," for what Dr. Couch reported in this regard.
64. Haldane et al., *Report on the Health*; Middleton, "Etiology of Silicosis."
65. Audley, *Silica and the Silicates*, 180–181.
66. See Greenhow, *Papers Related to the Sanitary State*; Greenhow, *Third Report of the Medical Officer*.
67. Meiklejohn, "Successful Prevention of Silicosis."
68. Arlidge, *Hygiene, Diseases, and Mortality*, 312–313.
69. In a letter sent to a member of Parliament in response to a request for clarification on the reliability of certain mortality figures concerning potters, which had featured in a pamphlet written by Arlidge himself, the physician replied (Bill 55, *Hansard Parliamentary Debates*, 1864): "Then, again, I would not assert that two-thirds of the potters are scrofulous, though probably one-third are. In so saying I was influenced by the vast number of strumous patients which fell under my observation at the date I wrote, at the Infirmary, and from what I then knew I was justified in making the assertion. That so many scrofulous cases fell to my lot at that time was the result of the usage prevailing, to send such cases to the physicians. It

would lead me beyond the limits of a letter to enter into further explanation of similar accidental modifying circumstances to be allowed for in a fair estimate of my letter."

70. Tardieu, "Étude hygiénique."

71. Dupont, "Accidents causés par l'inspiration." Cited in Carozzi, "Contributo bibliografico," 629.

72. Haldane et al., *Report on the Health.*

73. Collis presented his ideas as early as 1913, in a paper delivered at the International Congress of Medicine in London (Collis, "Effects of Dust"), but the publication subsequently cited in scientific literature is the one from 1915 (Collis, "Milroy Lectures").

74. Arlidge, "Pneumoconiosis."

75. Oliver, "Pneumoconiosis."

76. For an account of the situation in the United States, see Rosner and Markowitz, *Deadly Dust: Silicosis and the Politics*, 78–104. The judgment formed by an Italian pathologist regarding the compensation policy for silicosis in Italy is incisive (Mottura, "L'ammalato per contratto di lavoro," 90): "Compulsory indemnity is a great step forward, but the physician cannot but consider its appearance as a mere stopgap in the face of failed therapy and prevention. The application of the indemnity criterion, economically speaking, each time that it turns out to be, as is almost always the case, to the company's advantage compared to the costs of effective prevention, naturally negates the need for prevention, if there ever had been one. Within the limits of current legislation, which directly or indirectly guarantees the continuation of the capitalist regime, the device of indemnity makes perfect theoretical sense. This, if proportionate, is compensation for damage to the machine, paid to the owner of the machine, but with this a certain consideration is removed, which is that if for the management of the company's assets the worker is a replaceable machine, the validity of the worker, for him, is not replaceable, for he is an individual whose validity is an essential part of him."

77. See Collis, "Milroy Lectures."

78. See Schweber, *Disciplining Statistics.*

79. In 1910, the *Oxford English Dictionary* introduced the medical terms "siderosis" and "silicosis" to define the two lung diseases caused, respectively, by a buildup of iron and of silica dust. See "Medical Terms," 2038.

80. Oliver, "Some Dusty Occupations," 224–230.

81. Mottura, "L'ammalato per contratto di lavoro," 80.

82. See, for example, the debate in which Oliver and Hoffman took part, sparked by a 1912 paper by J. M. Beattie ("Hygiene of the Steel Trade"), the health officer for Sheffield, on the health of workers in the manufacture of cutlery in that city.

83. For a conceptual discussion of the relationship between medicine and society, including in the area of disease definition, see Rosenberg, "Disease and Social Order."

84. Berger, *Notre première mondialisation.*

Chapter 3

Johannesburg and Beyond
Silicosis as a Transnational and Imperial Disease, 1900–1940

Jock McCulloch and Paul-André Rosental,
with Joe Melling

The "Practicable" Science of Silicosis

John Draper, in 1856, commented that human history should be read as chapters in the story of physiology.[1] The cultural history of dust throws up evidence about the way people understand their own social order, as well as offering a record of how scientists viewed the physical environment.[2] We wish to reiterate this point on the contribution of physiology to an understanding of particulates in the workplace. In considering the history of mineral dust and its impact on respiratory health in the workplace, most histories of occupational illness suggest that the identification of bacteriological agents in disease encouraged late Victorian science to accentuate a binary division between the hazards posed by microscopic organisms, such as anthrax spores detected in dead animal skins, and hazards presented by inorganic minerals, such as soot, lead, and silica. Historians have shown that the new focus on bacteriology drew attention away from the more familiar threats of inorganic dust, although some scientists, including the celebrated Scottish physiologist John Scott Haldane, followed Draper in seeking an understanding of the physical world that combined close observations of social habits with a model of the human organism.[3]

The purpose of this chapter is not simply to confirm the contention that physiological inquiry is as much a social and cultural exercise as it is a scientific one. It also argues that the human history of silica dust must be understood in relation to the development of the economic order in different countries. We demonstrate that the medical status of silica was fixed historically by transnational networks of scientists who built institutions that sustained their particular view of the hazards presented by dust. Furthermore, we confirm and complexify the idea that the rise of microbiology and the development of more-complex models of human organisms occluded or obscured a scientific concern with mineral dust, noting in particular the contribution of the new physiology, pioneered by Haldane and others, to an understanding of respiratory disease.

Silica became the subject of a remarkably intense, even fixed, scientific gaze in the closing years of the nineteenth century. Studies conducted between the 1870s and 1910 found that silicosis occurred where fine particles of quartz silted up the drainage channels of workers' lungs, gradually forming characteristic nodules: congealed lumps of grit in the lining of this respiratory organ. The causes of this new industrial disease and the most effective means to detect it—clinical diagnosis and prevention—were to remain the subject of intense, if intermittent, debate, culminating in key international conferences in Johannesburg in 1930 and 1959, and Sydney in 1950.

A thorough historical analysis of medical literature and socioinstitutional contexts attests to this chronology. It is also confirmed by a lexicometric analysis of medical publications during the nineteenth and twentieth centuries, measuring the relative overrepresentation (or underrepresentation) of terms in each epoch. The 1890s to 1920s was a crucial period, during which the isolated expert, who publicized localized observations in medical essays, gave way to a more collective, institutionalized way of dealing with knowledge about health. Administrative and political terminology around 1900 reflected these advances ("commission," "committee," "chairman," "member," "law," "bill," "government"), as did the emergence of demographic and economic terms ("industries," "factories," "population," "mortality") as the focus of analysis progressed in the 1920s. The disease we now identify as silicosis was the outcome and expression of this convergence among medical, political, and economic concerns. The word "dust" was relatively little used in medical publications during the nineteenth century and only began to crop up frequently in the 1930s, suggesting that until then, the medical community had not turned its full attention toward the issue.[4] Explaining this transition, however, requires a broader analysis.

This chapter focuses on the political, medical, and economic arena. In the interwar period, this cross-section managed to unite, at the global level, all the dimensions—scientific, financial, and political—involved in the issue of workers' lung diseases. Until 1930, Johannesburg was at the hub of these debates, followed by Geneva until the outbreak of World War II. In this sense, these two cities were the successive world capitals of silicosis-related issues, and they played a vital role in extending the scope of medical understanding and treatment to a global scale. South African preeminence culminated in 1930, when an international conference in Johannesburg durably established the medical and legal fate of silicosis.

South Africa: Coloring Dust in the New World
The British–South African Connection

By the end of the nineteenth century, Britain's metal-mining industry was all but finished. The Cornish mines were expensive to maintain, if not already exhausted, and were unable to compete with new producers in Africa, Asia, Australia, and the Americas. South Africa was on the rise and occupied a unique place in the global mining industry. During the first five decades of the twentieth century, that country produced most of the gold on which the stability of the international financial system rested.[5] South African gold mining saw its most spectacular period of growth when Britain's metal-mining industries went into marked decline during the closing decades of the nineteenth century, with some British operators undertaking global mining operations in overseas colonies.

The competitive pressures on British mineral mining also resulted in a series of technological and organizational changes that exposed labor to both familiar and novel hazards in the mines. The introduction of powered drills led to a significant increase in fine particles of silica quartz, clouds of which surrounded miners and entered their lungs. It was the deleterious impact of such technological changes that Haldane and other investigators exposed in their studies of Cornish miners in both Britain and South Africa during the early twentieth century, though the solutions proposed were generally technical improvements in dust suppressants and ventilation.[6] In comparison with Britain, South Africa's gold mines were models of technological innovation in the extraction of ore and control of the intense dust generated by gold mining. The price of gold was fixed by international treaty, and other elements were constant: the industry's dependence on cheap migrant labor; the cost structure of materials, power, and transport; and the importance of the mines to state revenue. Another important factor that did not change was the threat of occupational disease.

The Rand goldfields employed a huge number of people, drawn mainly from rural communities in South Africa and the surrounding states and colonies. Mine depths and the size of the labor force both increased rapidly at the close of the nineteenth century. The bulk of the manual work was undertaken by black migrants, supervised by whites. In 1910, there were 10,000 white miners overseeing the work of 120,000 black miners. By 1929, there were almost 200,000 black miners and 21,000 whites, establishing a racial balance that was more or less maintained throughout the century.[7] The nature of the health problems facing employees, and the profile of those most affected, reflected the changing pace of technology and the altered composition of the labor force used in the mines during the first three decades of the twentieth century. Black labor from the tropical north was withdrawn from the mines after 1912, lead-ing to dramatic falls in the incidence of viral pneumonia among the workforce. There was also a shift, starting in 1916, in the use of white labor. Instead of imported workers, there was a growing reliance on the "New Rand" miners recruited from rural South Africa, who were believed to have better physiques and greater immunity to disease than their predecessors.[8]

The mines of South Africa, which date from the 1880s, had always been dangerous. Before 1930, the four major statistical causes of morbidity and mortality were accidents, viral pneumonia, silicosis, and tuberculosis. Accidents were recognized as chance episodes with specific causes and, often, practical, cheap remedies. The Transvaal Chamber of Mines had never shied away from talking publicly about such events. After 1913, improved workplace health mea-sures and a change in recruitment patterns saw a rapid fall in the death rate among black migrant workers. In contrast, silicosis and its sequel, tuberculosis, remained intractable. Silicosis (or, for a long time, "miners' phthisis") has been overwhelmingly associated with South Africa's mining industry.[9] The only way to prevent silicosis, and, with it, a propensity for tuberculosis, was to eradicate dust from the workplace. But evidence dating from the period of the Johan-nesburg conference in 1930 indicates the difficulties of dust control and the suspicion among some experts that it was impossible to make the mines safe.

Commercial links between South Africa's goldfields and the United King-dom meant that knowledge about silicosis and an understanding of the means for its prevention were available before mining began in the Transvaal. But that knowledge was not so easily translated into the creation of safe work-places. Gold mining dominated the economy of the Transvaal and was pivotal to national reconstruction in the period following the Second Boer War. The close association between mine management and the Department of Mines was founded on a shared interest in maintaining the industry's profitability. There were also frequent exchanges of personnel between the two sectors.

Horace Weldon, a former mine manager who became a governmental mining engineer and chief inspector of mines in 1899, chaired the first South African commission on silicosis. The mine owners, or "Randlords," were also politically influential, controlling South Africa's press.

It was a transnational dynamic, both bilateral and colonial, since it was the status of South Africa as a colony of the British Empire that led the former to tackle the issue of silicosis. The Rand mines, which had closed during the Second Boer War, reopened in May 1901. Many of the Cornish miners who left for Britain early in the war never returned. They may have been swayed by reading newspaper accounts of their prospects as working miners, for a report by the Transvaal's governmental mining engineer in December 1901 found that in less than four years, over 200 rock drillers had died from silicosis.[10] Adverse publicity in the British press,[11] as well as questions in the House of Commons about the fate of Cornish miners, influenced the decision of the High Commissioner for South Africa, Lord Milner, to appoint the Weldon Commission in November 1902 to study the causes and extent of silicosis. Within six days, Britain's Home Office announced that another deliberative body, the Haldane Commission, would investigate silicosis in Cornwall, a decision that was long overdue, given the death rates among tin miners in the United Kingdom.[12]

Preventing, Monitoring, and Compensating Silicosis: The Racial Roots of South African Preeminence

The Weldon Commission found that silicosis was a major problem among all classes of mine labor, but especially for rock drillers. According to Weldon, rock drillers had an average working life of just seven years, although it was probably closer to four, as the accelerated form of silicosis in South Africa was more severe than elsewhere.[13] Weldon correctly identified the cause as the fine silica dust generated by pneumatic drills and the use of gelignite for blasting.[14] The remedy consisted of wet drilling, the use of ventilation, and water sprays for laying dust. In the United Kingdom, the Weldon Commission's report was used to justify British rule in the Transvaal, but the commission's findings did not lead to any major reduction in dust levels, and silicosis continued unabated. Haldane and Sir Thomas Oliver pressured the British government to implement safer working methods, but conditions only improved after the passage of the Mines and Works Act of 1911.[15]

Nineteenth-century discussions about diseases among the European working classes were quickly absorbed into racial discourses about black labor in colonial Africa. Gold mining was South Africa's most important industry, and the state was dependent on mining revenues. Compensating workers suffering from silicosis was an expense that both the state and industry were reluctant to bear. State regulations, such as the instruments for measuring dust levels and the methods of diagnosing silicosis, changed over time, as did the composition of the labor force and the disease's profile. In public debates about the rights and capabilities of European and African miners, compensation was always the central issue. The South African government recognized phthisis as an occupational disease in 1911. At that time, the first Miners' Phthisis Act introduced compensation for afflicted workers and imposed a levy system on the industry as a whole. Compensation rates were always far more generous for white miners than they were for their black counterparts, however.[16]

The racial bias of the compensation system has to be understood in the wider context of a state provision for social maintenance. There was no general national-insurance program in South Africa. In contrast, in many other countries, miners' chronic illnesses due to work were compensated de facto by social-insurance plans for those with disabilities. Particularly during the interwar period, these were to play a major role in postponing the necessity for instituting a specific compensation system for silicosis. South Africa's progressiveness in the matter of silicosis was thus partly due to its backwardness in terms of social policies, arising, among other causes, from its colonial status and the preeminence of its agricultural sector at the beginning of the century.[17]

The compensation system was designed to provide benefits for white miners and their families. In order to cope with miners' mobility among various employers, compensation was paid from an industry-wide levy, based on the number of men employed at each registered mine. At the 1930 ILO conference, H. W. Sampson, minister of posts and telegraphs, claimed that, as a result, South Africa's mines bore a financial burden of almost £1 million a year.[18] It was a major expense and was cited as such at the 1920 Low-Grade Mines Commission. As G. E. Barry, the legal advisor for the Chamber of Mines, remarked, changes to South African legislation imposed such a heavy burden on the industry that some mines had been forced to close after 1911. "It was impossible to alter the South African legislation without upheaval," he noted, "because any new benefits granted produced thousands of retrospective claimants."[19]

Medical monitoring of the workforce was also conducted along racial lines.[20] In accordance with the Miners' Phthisis and Mines Acts of 1911, 1912, and 1916, white miners were examined by specialists at the Miners' Phthisis

Medical Bureau, and they also had access to private physicians. The screening of whites involved a clinical exam, a chest x-ray, and the taking of medical and work histories. Black miners were examined by mine medical officers or at the Witwatersrand Native Labour Association (WNLA) compound in Johannesburg. The mine medical service consisted of a small number of senior officers, supported by a group of young graduates who used the mines as a stepping stone to a better career. A full-time medical officer on a medium-sized mine could be responsible for 6,000 men.[21] The workload of the five full-time physicians at the WNLA hospital was also crushing. In addition to responsibility for more than 250 hospital patients, each doctor examined between 300 and 1,200 black miners a day.[22] The medical corps' status was such that they were referred to by their Johannesburg colleagues as "kaffir doctors" (native medicine men).[23] No records relating to black miners were kept. X-rays were rarely taken. Medical care, too, was different for white and black workers: white silicotics went to sanatoriums, while black employees were repatriated.

Nevertheless, the geographical concentration of silicosis into a small region, the Rand mines, and its impact on the workforce had fostered the growth of an impressive medical-research community in Johannesburg. South Africa in the 1920s was at the forefront in the recognition of silicosis as an occupational disease. Its monitoring system had allowed it to accumulate a unique body of radiographic evidence, which was a model for the rest of the world. Yet this seemingly advanced position was a product of and biased by the country's racialized labor system. The focus of scientific literature and data generated by medical surveillance was on white miners, who represented less than 10 percent of the workforce. Whites were mainly in supervisory roles and therefore had a lower exposure to dust. Blacks did the bulk of the physical labor, from drilling to loading skips—tasks that involved heavy dust exposure. They also differed from white miners in terms of nutrition; the number of deaths due to accidents; rates of enteric fever, meningitis, and infectious pneumonia; and susceptibility to tuberculosis.

Medical monitoring and compensation had been forced on the industry by the militant, white Mine Workers Union (MWU), founded in 1913, to protect its members, whereas black miners had no trade union representation. These provisions made labor by white miners even more expensive, but their numbers were sufficiently small for the industry to carry the cost. It could not have borne the burden of fully compensating black miners. The fixed price of gold meant that only by minimizing expenses, particularly the cost of black labor, could the industry remain profitable. The recorded silicosis rate among whites was around 14 times higher than that for black workers, even though blacks suffered from greater dust exposure because of their job specializations. In explaining this anomaly, South African scientists dismissed the role of the cursory exams for blacks conducted by mine medical officers, as well as the fact that official silicosis rates were based on successful compensation claims made before the Miners' Phthisis Medical Bureau. Blacks rarely made such claims and were therefore underrepresented in the statistics.[24] Instead, South African experts and officials latched onto the short-term contracts of black miners as the reason for this difference: at some mines, the annual turnover of black labor was as high as 100 percent.[25] The higher-ups claimed that migrant workers, after spending brief periods underground, returned to their villages, where they quickly recovered from the effects of dust exposure.

Conversely, black miners suffered from far higher rates of tuberculosis than whites. The official explanation focused on poor hygiene in rural areas and the greater susceptibility of blacks to infection.[26] No mention was made of the synergy between silicosis and pulmonary tuberculosis, where being afflicted with the former greatly increases an individual's chances of contracting the latter. This connection has been especially visible in southern Africa, where the rural communities from which internal and foreign migrant laborers were drawn had little prior exposure to infection. The Chamber of Mines and the Miners' Phthisis Medical Bureau also ignored rural poverty, malnutrition, and low mine wages, all of which contributed to the spread of infectious disease. In this context, the use of the term miners' phthisis, rather than silicosis, in South African legislation until 1946 was significant.

The migrant labor system weakened the data further. Many black miners came as migrant workers from neighboring states and other colonial empires, notably Portuguese colonies, such as Mozambique. The Department of Health and the Department of Mines in Pretoria took no interest in these miners' health once they returned home. The colonial administrations in Lesotho, Nyasaland, Swaziland, and Mozambique, which all sent laborers to the Rand, had neither the incentive nor the resources to identify the extent of silicosis among workers returning from South Africa. Each Tuesday morning, two trains with special coaches for lying-down cases left Booysens Station in Johannesburg, one bound for Ressano-Garcia in Mozambique, and the other for the Cape. They carried repatriated miners. The trains had a white conductor to look after the patients, but no medical officer. In addition to "ordinary repatriations" of miners who had sustained a traumatic injury, around 20 men suffering from tuberculosis were shipped out each week. The two departments, like the chamber, were uninterested in the migrant workers' health from past employment. Nor did they offer assistance to labor-sending states eager to control the spread of tuberculosis. The only follow-up study from that period looking at black miners compensated for tuberculosis comes from 1926. Of the 110 workers repatriated to the Transkei with tuberculosis in that year, 76 were dead within six months and a further 19 were expected to "possibly die shortly."[27] As late as the mid-1940s, the Chamber of Mines was not notifying the colonial administration in Malawi of the number of miners being repatriated with infective tuberculosis.[28] The Gold Producers Committee regularly faced complaints from the colonial administrations in Malawi and Mozambique about the numbers of returning miners with tuberculosis. Occasionally, protests came from the WNLA's own medical officers.[29] William Gemmill, secretary of the Chamber of Mines, who regularly toured the recruiting stations and handled major negotiations with union officials and colonial administrators, participated in numerous commissions of inquiry into miners' phthisis, where such issues were raised by the Department of Native Affairs.[30]

The South African experience might have had few direct implications for the international understanding of dust-related diseases among mining populations if the close relationship that existed between that country and the United Kingdom had not attracted intense scientific, political, and legal attention after 1918. It was then that the United Kingdom became the first European country to introduce legal provisions to compensate workers suffering from silicosis. In the 1920s, a global arena, constructed by transnational networks and institutions devoted to social medicine, allowed South Africa to promote its struggle against silicosis as a pioneering effort and capitalize on it. This new conjunction transformed South Africa into a world role model and a pivotal country, triggering a process that finally saw silicosis internationally recognized as the major occupational disease of its time. This recognition was enshrined in a 1934 convention held under the auspices of the ILO.

The 1930 Johannesburg conference played a major role in the process. Yet the international delegates who attended were unaware of the extent to which South African medical science and data were derived exclusively from white miners, and thus were heavily influenced by the racial science produced in Johannesburg. The conditions under which black miners contracted silicosis and were repatriated without compensation remained invisible. As Andrew Watt from the Rand Mutual Assurance Company pointed out, neither dust reduction nor medical monitoring effectively eradicated first-stage silicosis (which is difficult to detect clinically and is irreversible); therefore neither removed the considerable risk of pulmonary tuberculosis for black miners, which they brought back to their villages.[31] Given the strong relationship between silicosis and working conditions, this initial medical bias and its concentration on one segment of the workforce had a major effect on the way in which the international recognition of silicosis played out. Significantly, it also affected how the medical characteristics of silicosis came to be defined, and it still weighs heavily on current medical knowledge about the disease.

The World Crusade of Social Medicine against Silicosis

The failure of the League of Nations (LN) to achieve a lasting peace, which was its central purpose, has long dissuaded historians from investigating this organization closely. Only in the past two decades has the growing interest in transnational processes led historians to question this neglect and revisit the role of the technical entities connected to the LN.[32] In particular, its achievements in the field of social and health policy have been reevaluated.[33] Internal departments, such as its Industrial Hygiene Section (IHS), and external organizations, such as the International Labour Office (ILO), which was largely autonomous from the LN, are now considered to have played a major role in the expansion of public policies and the development of social security schemes and labor legislation. The ILO's work in relation to silicosis is no exception: indeed, it exemplifies the success (but also the limitations) of these attempts to institute a new world order.

The Creation of a Transnational Arena

Formally, this story began in 1919, when the negotiators of the Treaty of Versailles decided to dedicate a whole section to the creation of the International Labour Organization. The organization's secretariat, the International Labour Office, was granted a monopoly on work issues. Its purpose was (and remains) to encourage governments to sign international conventions guaranteeing workers' social rights. Its ideological purpose was to arbitrate between the respective interests of capital and labor, in order to promote social justice and remove the threat of revolutionary socialism. To achieve these aims, it operated on an original, tripartite principle that involved national commissions—comprised of representatives of trade unions, employers, and national governments—in negotiations mediated by senior ILO officials.

The Russian Revolution lent this agenda a searing relevance by placing most European countries under pressure of the "Bolshevik threat." Yet the principles behind it dated from the last decades of the nineteenth century, when an informal network of social reformers belonging to the economic, administrative, and academic elites on both sides of the Atlantic had decided to develop transnational networks and associations devoted to the development of labor law and social protection.[34] Long before the creation of the ILO, these prominent figures, organized initially through informal networks and then, at the end of the nineteenth century, in international associations, had assured the signing of the first international conventions at the 1906 congress in Bern. World War I, which had ultimately increased the level of state intervention in economic and social policies, as well as cooperation between unions and employers, had accelerated the access of this select group of social reformers to key political and administrative positions. By 1919, this process had made them influential enough to secure the inclusion of a social section within the Versailles peace treaty; the creation of the ILO was, to a large extent, a way of achieving official recognition for this victory. In a sense, it provided a continuous diplomatic forum devoted to social issues in which governments, employers, and unions committed themselves to participation and dialogue.

In this way, the ILO managed to have 67 international conventions ratified during the interwar period, laying the foundations for the rise of the welfare state in the aftermath of World War II.[35] The organization's scope of action encompassed the fight against occupational diseases, as had also been the case for the reformist network before World War I. Significantly, the ban on white phosphorus in the manufacture of matches had been one of the first two international conventions adopted by the 1906 Bern congress (the other concerned women's and children's night work). This established, from the outset, the idea that occupational diseases were to be discussed at the international level. It was a good illustration of an ideological breakthrough—an attempt to accommodate both the free market and social reform through a series of negotiated compromises. In previous years, the status of occupational diseases had begun to change in many European jurisdictions. Once a strictly medical notion, occupational diseases were becoming a medico-legal category. From then on, an illness contracted in the workplace only officially became an occupational disease if an accord between employers and unions, enshrined in law, had previously agreed to define it as one.

Occupational diseases were negotiated diseases, then as now. The 1906 Bern congress offered the first official international recognition of this transformation, one that the ILO would push further after World War I. In order to understand this agenda and the preeminence it gave to silicosis, we must go back to the turn of the twentieth century and the roots of an organized, transnational network of social medicine. One man embodies this continuity during the first two-thirds of the twentieth century: Luigi Carozzi (1875–1963). As head of the Industrial Hygiene Section created by the ILO in September 1920, he was to take charge of the international crusade against silicosis.

Luigi Carozzi: From Milan to Geneva

Carozzi was the perfect product of the social reform network that grew up at the turn of the twentieth century. Among the multiple associations created by this transnational milieu, one of the most important was the International Permanent Commission on Occupational Diseases (the CIPMT, according to its official French acronym, and currently the International Commission on Occupational Health, or ICOH). Established by a group of reformist Italian physicians who were particularly influential in their country, it was devoted to social medicine in the workplace. The commission was inaugurated on June 13, 1906, following the First International Congress on Work-Related Illnesses, held in Milan at the same time as the Universal Exposition.[36] One of its leaders, Malachia De Cristoforis (1832–1915),[37] was a gynecologist and a free-thinking politician in a country still heavily affected by Roman Catholic values, but where liberal governments were receptive to social reforms in the early years of the century.[38] De Cristoforis supported the pioneering initiatives of Luigi Devoto (1864–1936) to improve workers' health. Devoto, a professor of medicine since 1899, trained in medical pathology and became interested in pellagra (a disease caused by malnutrition) before specializing in occupational diseases and founding a professional journal on the subject in 1901. Devoto's idea of an ambitious "work clinic" for Milan was developed in 1902, and the Clinica del Lavoro finally came into being in 1910. For a few decades, it became a global center for the study of occupational diseases.[39]

Devoto employed Luigi Carozzi, one of his protégés, to carry out surveys of working conditions in partnership with trade unions and voluntary associations, such as the Società Umanitaria. Like Devoto and many other social reformers of his time,[40] Carozzi acted simultaneously at municipal, national, and transnational levels. In 1910, he was elected to the Milan city council, which had continually supported initiatives regarding occupational health. Four years later, he left the Clinica del Lavoro to head the medical work inspectorate of the Ministry of Agriculture, Industry, and Trade. Carozzi was also, from their inception in 1906, the long-serving secretary-general of the three yearly international congresses held by the CIPMT. He only resigned after the 1954 Naples congress, and he became the association's "permanent honorary president" in 1957.[41]

As a result of his international experience, Carozzi joined the ILO in 1921, where he headed the IHS (which had been created just a couple of months earlier) until the outbreak of World War II. This career move was not unusual; most of the senior officers in the ILO combined administrative or academic expertise with a long-standing commitment to the international reform movement, whether at the national level, like the ILO's first director-general (1919–1932), Albert Thomas, a former Socialist politician and French Minister of Armament, or at the municipal level, like Imre Ferenczi and Louis Varlez. Carozzi, however, was to find himself in a unique position within the ILO, a fact that partly explains why he became "the silicosis man."

Silicosis as a Strategic Cause for the ILO

It is important to note the extent to which doctors' positions in the debate about silicosis were often determined along national lines, particularly by the nature of social insurance in each country—its benefits, funding, and relative importance, as compared with private insurance—and the numbers of workers at risk for this disease. Under Carozzi's stewardship, the prime mission of the IHS would be to reconcile these varying national positions, in order to achieve a transnational recognition of silicosis.

Chapter 1 noted the structural factors that had made silicosis "the king of occupational diseases" by this point in time.[42] For the ILO, silicosis offered a relatively protected sector in which it could assert its dominance. Officially, the 1919 Treaty of Versailles had provided the ILO with a monopoly over work-related issues. Occupational diseases fell within its mandate, as did unemployment, retirement schemes, labor contracts, and the protection of migrant workers. But in practice, when it came to health issues, the office was continually subjected to interference from the League of Nations' health section. Formally, the LN's director, Ludwik Rajchman (1881–1965),[43] respected the ILO's prerogatives by avoiding questions specifically related to labor issues. It was tempting, however, for him to argue that a country that disregarded the ILO's social conventions, as Greece did in 1929, threatened the health not only of workers, but also of their families—and, consequently, the population at large, since weakened workers were more sensitive to infectious, contagious diseases. Whenever such failures were highlighted within a given country—by press campaigns, for instance—a joint LN-ILO commission was set up, in which the ILO generally found itself in a subordinate position, because of its limited financial capability to support its operating costs and send delegates.[44]

Rajchman also took advantage of structural issues to force the ILO into a collaboration in which his organization was financially more powerful. In 1927, he was instrumental in the creation of a joint commission with the ILO, which was in charge of coordinating the network of medical institutions devoted to public health with those run by social-insurance bodies. From the standpoint of the ILO's social-insurance section (headed by Adrien Tixier), this was a continuous source of intrusion.[45] This dynamic continued after 1929, with efforts to optimize the resources deployed by both international organizations, in order to prevent that era's economic crisis from wreaking devastating consequences on public health.[46]

Behind this ongoing battle, which the ILO, with its circumscribed mandate and reduced resources, fought mainly on the defensive, was an unspoken struggle over two different ways of organizing social and health actions. The LN advanced a local, voluntary, charitable model, as opposed to the national, tripartite, contributory social-insurance model put forward by the ILO (as required by its bylaws). Professions, too, were involved in this tussle. International associations of private doctors took the side of the LN. They were hostile to the model promoted by the ILO—which championed social medicine, provided by wage-earning physicians in a relationship with social-insurance programs—considering it to be unfair competition. At the core of this conflict was setting prices for medical services, as social insurance (and consequently the ILO) demanded that they be officially regulated.[47]

Against this backdrop, silicosis was a relatively safe and increasingly pressing cause. Unlike Adrien Tixier's social-insurance section, which was vulnerable to interference from the LN, the IHS could get involved in the crusade against a noninfectious disease transmitted by exposure to a substance, rather than by contact with people. There was less risk that the LN's health section would take over the cause as one concerning general public health—on the condition, naturally, that the disease could be proven to be one that could only be contracted in the workplace. In this case, Carozzi's firm medical convictions aligned with his section's interests: silicosis *had* to be recognized internationally as an occupational disease, both because this would guarantee the ILO a broader field of action, and because it was the most serious occupational disease of its time in terms of morbidity and mortality.

The cause that Carozzi had chosen also made sense within the ILO. His section was effectively in competition with the industrial-safety section that had been set up in 1921, a year later than the IHS. A merger of the two had been considered and then dismissed, because the ILO was afraid that this would inevitably lead to the supremacy of an engineering approach over a medical one. The scientific complexity of silicosis provided justification for Carozzi to legitimize the priority of a medical approach: while not overlooking questions of safety engineering (prevention) and social insurance (compensation), the first task was to detail the disease's origins, development, and effects. In practice, research into silicosis in the 1930s extended to other disciplines—such as chemistry, physics, biology, and engineering—as medical consensus advanced; this extension was officially included in the agenda of the 1938 Geneva conference on silicosis.

The legal aspect provided more reasons for prioritizing a medical approach. Medical experts throughout the world had to have confidence in and endorse the scientific foundations of the ILO conventions, in order to guarantee the credibility of these conventions in legislative, judiciary, and other legal proceedings.[48] Avoiding risky causes was part of the ILO's habitus. In 1925, Carozzi had resisted pressure from international stoneworkers' trade unions to include silicosis in the ILO's first international convention on occupational diseases. At the time, he believed that scientific consensus was not solid enough to ensure that a treaty including silicosis would be ratified by member states.[49]

The ILO's position on medical matters was further complicated by its lack of resources. Apart from a few modest subsidies to academics in the 1930s, the IHS could not afford to directly commission research and instead had to rely on evidence that was already accepted. After 1925, the ILO used its power to advance the transnational debate: it garnered support from workers' movements and employers in those countries that had already recognized silicosis, and it fostered a medical (especially a radiological) body of evidence regarding the existence of the disease.

Like other ILO sections, Carozzi's IHS used its possession of centralized documentary evidence from all over the world, provided by the ILO's exceptional network of correspondents, to full advantage. In the case of silicosis, this took the form of impressive bibliographies, which the IHS supplied on request to governmental departments, voluntary associations, and experts, and articles in the ILO's *Encyclopaedia of Occupational Health and Safety*. (First published in 1930, the *Encyclopaedia* was central to the IHS's strategy and its success in the interwar years.) The ILO's activities included the establishment of a network of experts sympathetic to the silicosis "cause." The ILO searched for them around the world and tested their medical convictions, through field missions if necessary;[50] gave them international legitimacy; and appointed them to specialist committees. It is no accident that a substantial portion of the IHS's archives (and those of the ILO in general) is made up of files regarding these selections. By creating commissions of experts, chosen according to their nationality, skill, and scientific position, the IHS, like the ILO, formed a global medical forum on silicosis and managed its own internal structures.[51]

This was a diplomacy of expertise—diplomacy in the true sense, since member states sometimes refused or imposed, against the ILO's will, the appointment of one of their national experts. It involved maintaining a delicate balance of both economic and scientific power and respecting the major industrial countries—while keeping them at a distance if their medical positions were too hostile to the cause. France paid dearly for denying the existence of silicosis by being kept out of the Johannesburg conference. The presence of its experts at the major discussion forums of the 1930s was met with suspicion by ILO officials, and France, along with Belgium and the Netherlands, felt compelled to hold, as it were, counter-congresses in 1936 and 1937. Conversely, South Africa became the crucial partner of the ILO in its crusade against silicosis. That country's legislative precedents, its medical-monitoring procedures, the clinical experience of its physicians, its unique set of 65,000 x-ray photographs,[52] and its readiness to contribute financially to the development of an international forum on silicosis turned South Africa into a powerful lever that the ILO used to achieve transnational recognition of the disease.

Defining Silicosis: Johannesburg, 1930

This artful balancing act reached its peak in the 1930 Johannesburg conference, organized at the initiative of the Transvaal Chamber of Mines, at a time when the ILO's agenda converged with that of the South African gold-mining companies. Industrialists, governmental officials, and scientists in South Africa designed the 1930 event as a monument to the progress made in the investigation of dust-induced illness among mine workers in this crucial industry in the early twentieth century;[53] international trade still depended on gold for secure transactions. The choice of this remote city for the historic conference gave international recognition to South African science and publicized the role of the South African state in addressing an occupational disease. The Johannesburg meeting was all the more visible for being the first ILO conference held outside Europe. This was no accident: a discrete purpose drove the South African mining industry to sponsor the event.

The Transvaal Mining Industry's Hidden Agenda

First, while the Chamber of Mines' interests aligned with those of the South African government, the chamber was also eager to secure access to migrant labor from surrounding colonial states, in particular from the tropical north. Indeed, one of the main reasons for its foundation in 1889 was to ensure a steady flow of black workers to the gold mines. That recruiting market had been closed in 1913, because of the appalling death rates from infectious pneumonia.[54] The mines were labor intensive and had to compete with farmers and manufacturers for workers. Mine wages were low, but the chamber's recruiting arms, the WNLA and the Native Recruiting Corporation, offset this disadvantage by providing cash advances, free travel to Johannesburg, and the repatriation of wages.[55] The tropical areas of Mozambique and Nyasaland (Malawi) offered an untapped pool of workers. In 1928, the chamber began to lobby for expansion into the north. It pressured the United Kingdom's high commission in Pretoria and both the Colonial and Dominions Offices in London for their support. In Geneva, the chamber presented itself to the ILO as a champion of the free movement of labor.[56]

For the ILO, too, the issue was particularly topical, as this organization was striving to expand its reach into the empires. Although it could not impose metropolitan legislation or standards on the colonial world, it did strive to ameliorate the worst features of imperialism, including forced labor, corporal punishment, and hazardous work practices. This led to the adoption of the C29 forced labor convention in 1930.[57] In the late 1920s, the ILO took a particular interest in issues related to migrant workers, including the recruitment of labor, working conditions, and the provision of medical care. One result was its voluminous correspondence with the Transvaal Chamber of Mines, the British Colonial Office, and the administrations of Nyasaland, Mozambique, Southern Rhodesia, and Swaziland, all of which supplied miners to the Rand. The ILO's interest in migrant labor gave South Africa's mining companies all the more reason to publicize the safety of their gold mines.[58]

A second incentive, even less visible, can truly be categorized as biopolitical, in the sense that it relied on a combination of medical constraints and social-insurance procedures. Securing enough workers for the mines did not depend solely on immigration from inside or outside South Africa. It also meant ensuring that, once hired, workers would remain active and physically fit for as long as possible. This was especially true for the skilled positions reserved for whites. It was therefore crucial that workers resisted the onset of silicosis that, particularly in the gold mines, rapidly debilitated those affected by it. As Anthony Mavrogordato (1873–1944), one of the leading experts from the South African Medical Institute, put it, thanks to a series of improvements, including initial medical exams, "ante-primary silicosis [i.e., the first phase of the disease] was made as ever, but it now took thirteen years instead of eight to nine years. . . . If the time taken to produce a clinical silicosis could be pushed up to twenty years, silicosis could be considered as eliminated on the Rand from the social point of view."[59] This particularly blunt formulation labeled a purely economic concern as a social one: silicosis mattered as long as it affected actively working miners, and only them.

By paying close attention to the conference proceedings, especially during the sessions devoted to the issue of financial compensation, and by gathering a series of fragmented workers' claims from the Transvaal mining industry's experts, a more detailed and consistent picture of employers' expectations emerges, which allows us to make sense of Mavrogordato's formulation. The problem facing the industry was that the evolution of legislation since 1912, under pressure from the active white miners' unions,[60] had progressively built a compensation program that was costly and could be seen as particularly generous, according to the international criteria of the time. G. E. Barry, a legal advisor to the Transvaal Chamber of Mines, was not challenged at the conference when, on the basis of a detailed financial analysis, he concluded that the last of these reforms, the 1925 Miners' Phthisis Acts Consolidation Act, "was the most liberal in the world, and the only Act that could be compared with it was in Ontario."[61]

Union demands and a lack of alternative social provisions for sick miners were not the only reasons for South Africa's relatively favorable compensation

program. The government, in a reasoning common at the time across all industrialized countries,[62] expected that high rates of compensation would encourage
employers to invest in prevention. South African representatives to the conference, however, were far from united on this point, which was fiercely opposed
by the mining industry, claiming that such an improvement was utopian,
because the silicosis issue could not be solved. This partly explains why Alexander Jeremiah Orenstein (1879–1972), although head of the medical service of
the Witwatersrand gold mines, adopted a highly critical stance, contesting any
statistics showing that the health-related situation of silicotic miners had improved in South Africa. "Great weight was given in legislation to the necessity
of fixing compensation for silicosis sufficiently high to stimulate prophylactic
measures," Orenstein noted, and added that "the reporters might consider
whether silicosis could be called preventable."[63] One of the main reports discussed during the conference supported this argument, paradoxically concluding
that South Africa's mines were a model of workplace reform that demonstrated
the limits of what could be achieved through technological controls.[64]

The other medical clarification that South African experts sought from the
conference was equally linked to the fate of silicotic miners, particularly whites,
who were generally the most skilled and thus the least replaceable. This concern
was also linked to the compensation system. Although the powerful mining industry lobby had a strong hold on the government, it faced a dilemma that A. B.
Du Toit, chairman of the Miners' Phthisis Board,[65] which was in charge of the
compensation program, expressed in dramatic terms. On the one hand, "no
State could be expected to legalize what amounted to slow suicide" by a ruinous
compensation system.[66] On the other hand, insufficient compensation would
deter silicotic miners from leaving their present jobs since, as Orenstein explained at length, in South Africa no alternative jobs were available for them. As
a result, Du Toit continued, "if silicotics were allowed to remain in their underground occupations without any restrictions, the position might be reached
after a period of years when the gold mining industry would be entirely run
by employees who were silicotics and this in the end was bound to affect
efficiency."[67]

Gathering some of the world's best medical experts in the field of dust
diseases was thus also a way of making progress on a highly complicated issue,
linked both to medical knowledge and the scientific organization of work:
when did silicosis start to impair workers' productivity? How could physicians
and, to a lesser extent, engineers, slow down this debilitating process (i.e., as

Mavrogordato said, postpone it for a few years)? For Orenstein, one priority was to obtain from the conference scientific legitimacy for the solution he proposed: transferring part of the money devoted to compensation to rehabilitation programs, which would contribute to keeping (white, skilled, lifelong) miners active for as long as possible. Whatever the risks, there was no point in prematurely taking these miners away from from underground work: "It was a misconception that removal from work in the earliest possible stage [of silicosis] would prevent further development: if it was true that continued employment was really slow suicide, no man should be allowed to work in any dusty occupation at all."[68]

Observing how the Transvaal Chamber of Mines' motivations aligned with those of the ILO provides a consequential case study in how the twentieth-century welfare state was built in industrialized countries. An examination of the views and statements of South African experts reveals the way in which a combination of the scientific organization of labor, the segmentation of the workforce (here, in terms of skills and race, although this division was not absolute), and actuarial optimization had led mining companies to both develop their own social and health provisions and pressure the state to do the same— the Chamber of Mines having rapidly become the most powerful employers' association in the country. But employers' strategies also had to take into account the powerful white trade unions, under the leadership of the militant Mine Workers' Union. Employers now adopted a less combative approach, endeavoring to find some common ground with the political agenda of the ILO. Yet how could utilitarianism and the search for profit be reconciled with a political model based on social and humanitarian concerns? This equation was at the heart of the creation of the ILO, which fostered a social reconstruction of a market economy.[69] This led directly to the 1930 Johannesburg conference and its outcomes.

Strategic Timing

The period from Carozzi's 1925 refusal to include silicosis in the international convention on occupational diseases to the meeting in Johannesburg in 1930 was significant in the history of this disease. During those years, silicosis became a public health issue and started to attract popular attention. In 1929, Germany had introduced silicosis legislation that covered four occupations. One year earlier, through the Various Industries Act, the United Kingdom had extended the scope of its 1919 compensation legislation to coal miners, or at least those working directly with silica-rich rock.[70] In the late 1920s in the United States, the courts were inundated with claims related to occupational injuries. All dusty industries—including those glass, steel, and iron foundries that used sand, along with asbestos manufacturers—faced the same problems of lung disease and litigation. A turning point in public awareness of the dangers of silica came with the Hawk's Nest hydroelectric project in West Virginia. The construction of its three-mile-long tunnel, undertaken in 1927 by Union Carbide, employed 3,000 workers, many of them African American migrants from the American South. They toiled in clouds of almost pure silica dust, and the deaths of hundreds of men from silicosis eventually led to a congressional inquiry.[71] According to Anthony Lanza, doyen of United States' pneumoconiosis specialists, both silicosis and asbestosis "burst upon the amazed consciousness of American industry" in 1929.[72]

Even for a country as reluctant as France, 1929 proved to be a turning point. In April, the Commission Internationale pour l'Étude des Maladies Profession-nelles (CIMPT, today known as the International Commission on Occupational Health, or ICOH) had organized a congress in Lyons, on the initiative of Albert Thomas, head of the ILO. He and others wanted to exert pressure on France to catch up in the control of occupational diseases.[73] Although the congress failed to achieve immediate results in the recognition of silicosis, the spectacular dem-onstration of South African physicians' knowledge, especially their display of a sample of x-ray radiographs, prompted a number of occupational doctors, such as the Christian unionist Jean Magnin (1876–1952), to develop research in this field. The French collieries reacted negatively. Frightened by the Lyons con-gress, their leaders mustered four university professors to help them develop a medical argument claiming that silicosis was only a condition arising from tuberculosis and could not be considered an occupational disease.[74]

There was a contrast, though, between this growing public awareness of the problem and medical uncertainty. The idea that sustained inhalation of free silica dust could damage workers' lungs was now widely disseminated through-out the world, although not accepted by all lung specialists. But this was not enough to bring about a consensus on the disease and on the policies designed to prevent and offer compensation for it. Carozzi was well aware of this dis-cord, which had already resulted in his decision not to add silicosis to the list of occupational diseases recognized by the 1925 convention. In 1926, he was able to gauge the odds in this international dispute by circulating a letter to a list of prominent experts, asking them to describe how physicians could identify silicosis at an early stage and establish the degree of disability affecting individual workers. Recipients included Edgar Collis and Thomas Legge in the United Kingdom, Franz Koelsch in Germany, Giovanni Loriga in Italy, Duncan G. Robertson in Australia, W. R. H. Kranenburg in the Netherlands, and Ernst Brezina in Austria.[75]

The minutes of the 1930 conference show how unclear the medical picture was for the two dozen experts who gathered in Johannesburg, half of whom were from South Africa and the other half from Europe, North America, and Australia. For all of them, the intrinsic danger of free silica dust was now evident. Yet how could one define the exact type danger it posed, given that free silica dust was not limited to mining, but also existed in many industrial sectors (including grinding, stonemasonry, pottery, glasswork, and the manufacture of firebricks), with concentrations that could range from almost nothing to pure silica and be present under vastly different working conditions, including employee turnovers? Every aspect of the definition of free silica dust was subject to doubt. Britisher Edward L. Middleton, a medical inspector of factories who had firsthand knowledge of silicosis in pottery manufacturing and refractory processes, pointed out that dust counts in and of themselves were of little practical or medical value unless the size, quality, and impact of the particles could be accurately measured and a means of control identified. Some experts feared that such a determination was impossible, because the smallest particles were undetectable, even though research had long established the dangers they posed.[76] Others, adhering to a supposition that had lasted for several decades, wondered whether the presence of other kinds of dusts (coal dust, for instance) could have a protective effect on workers' lungs. Another complicating factor was that silica dust was almost always mixed up with other kinds of dust generated in these industries. In his opening speech, Louis Godfrey Irvine (1892–1946), who was head of the Miners' Phthisis Medical Bureau and chaired the conference, reminded participants of the fact that "certain dusts which contain free silica are phthisis-producing dusts," while "other dusts which also contain free silica are not," a difference that could be attributed to the presence of other "constituents." Even within a given industrial sector, the situation was far from clear. In the mining industry, was there any difference between the silica dust associated with metallic ore and that linked to coal?

Specific cases were puzzling. The South African Mavrogordato wondered how one could explain why "in Great Britain there were two kinds of firebrick with the same silica content, but the incidence of the disease [among the workers who manufactured them] was very different."[77] Another major issue, which was nevertheless kept in the background, concerned how much attention should be devoted to other pneumoconioses. These included asbestosis—many experts had no doubts about its danger, although its medical effects were still far from clear. As Mavrogordato put it, the difficulty "to get at silicosis as a specific occupational disease and define it" came from the ambiguous "distinction between a silicosis and a pneumoconiosis."[78]

Varying laws in a range of jurisdictions added to this uncertainty. Silica-related health problems were monitored and recorded differently in various countries (and within the same country, in the case of federal states), limiting the efficacy of statistical and clinical comparisons. Compensation systems, when they existed, contrasted enormously, depending on factors such as the number of workers at risk, the role of social insurance, and the nature of each state (central or federal). The United Kingdom had passed a bill on silicosis in 1919 that did not extend to collieries. Australian states, such as New South Wales, Victoria, and South Australia, compensated pneumoconiosis sufferers—as long as no silica dust was involved.

This context provided the perfect opportunity for Carozzi to take a more decisive step toward convening an international conference in Johannesburg, a proposal that had been tendered to the ILO's deputy director, Harold Butler, on November 21, 1927, by the Rand mines' superintendent of sanitation, Alexander Orenstein, who had formed the idea during a recent visit to South Africa by Butler.[79] Orenstein worked closely with William Gemmill, secretary of the Chamber of Mines, who had played a key role in this regard. Gemmill, who was to emerge as a brilliant publicist and eventual general manager of the Chamber, had served in 1919 on the Low-Grade Mines Commission, chaired by the governmental mining engineer, Sir Robert Kotze. In that same year, South Africa had sent three delegates to the founding meeting of the ILO in Washington, DC. Gemmill was included in the delegation as the representative for South Africa's employers,[80] which offered him the chance to meet Harold Butler, with whom he remained close.

This connection would prove to be crucial. On March 14, 1929, the board of the ILO agreed that the office would organize and contribute toward financing the Johannesburg conference, along with the South African Chamber of Mines, which, on March 19, 1928, had decided on a £2,000 contribution.[81] Although this sum represented two-thirds of the total estimated cost, the French delegate had voted against the ILO's resolution; the other 19 members had approved it. Carozzi's IHS immediately launched preparations for the conference in a manner typical of the ILO: officially remaining neutral, but setting the agenda and selecting the participants in such a way as to impose its view. During the following months, the choice of experts and the formulation of the conference agenda would illustrate the subtlety of the diplomacy of expertise.

Harmonizing the Agenda: Carozzi and Orenstein, or the ILO–Rand Mines Partnership

The Johannesburg conference, with an agenda that included the objective of defining silicosis, was planned for August 14–27, 1930. The idea was to bring together the most-qualified international experts to reach an agreement on the medical definition and causes of the disease, while not excluding questions of prevention and compensation. Selecting the experts and countries represented, as well as meticulously preparing the conference agenda, were two men who personified the principle of joint national and transnational action: Luigi Carozzi and Alexander Orenstein.

Orenstein had begun his career as a doctor in the US Army in the early twentieth century, during the digging of the Panama Canal. There, he encountered the three topics that would drive his entire career: occupational medicine, infectious diseases, and tropical medicine. An orientation toward public health was not uncommon in the milieu of US military doctors involved in colonial medicine. In 1914, its leading figure, Colonel William C. Gorgas, had directed Orenstein to the mines on the Rand, where the latter tried to develop a "social" approach to workers' health, for which, today, he is considered the father of South African occupational medicine.[82] In South Africa, as in other industrialized countries, the goal of this approach was to combine care for workers' health with maximizing their productivity.

Carozzi's tight-knit alliance with Orenstein was a revealing one. In most areas, the ILO's director, Albert Thomas, was able to closely monitor the daily activities of his senior officials. Nonetheless, Carozzi, who was perpetually in conflict with his superiors, enjoyed some autonomy in a field that was undoubtedly of interest to Thomas but less easily controlled by him, due to the nature of the expertise and the networks involved. Carozzi had gained the upper hand in the appointment of members of the Correspondence Committee on Industrial Hygiene.[83] Nonetheless, his section was, to some extent, restricted to "technical" issues, compared with the social-insurance section, which was in political competition with the LN's health division.

After some hesitation, Carozzi excluded French experts from the conference, because of their refusal to recognize silicosis as an autonomous occupational disease. Combined with the absence of the Belgian delegate, officially due to heath problems,[84] this omission was an important step in the attempt to build international consensus around the disease. The head of the IHS struggled for many months to secure an invitation for Edgar Collis to participate in the conference, with little success. Instead, the British government was determined that a rather different circle of experts, who served on statutory bodies and in recognized research committees, should be selected.[85] In Britain, there were a host of experts, many based in the Home Office (the United Kingdom's interior ministry). These included the elder statesmen of occupational health, Edgar Collis and Thomas Legge, each of whom had served in the factory inspectorate. They were largely self-educated specialists in occupational health, though, by the late 1920s, their expertise was being superseded by laboratory specialists such as E. H. Kettle, who developed the colloidal model of the causes of silicosis. These two men were also relegated to the background by the committees established by Britain's Medical Research Council (MRC) to investigate pulmonary disease among industrial workers, although Collis and Legge were close to Britain's Trade Union Congress (TUC). The TUC, assuming Collis would be invited, pressed the British Labour government to also send Legge, recently appointed as TUC's medical adviser. These efforts were completely unsuccessful.[86] Collis had been a key contributor to the discussions that led to the organization of the ILO conference. He was considered by Carozzi to be "the best private expert" for his role in synthesizing and clarifying medical knowledge on silicosis, and his presence was expected by South African physicians, yet he was effectively sidelined by the British government.[87]

The determination of a Labour government to send Home Office civil servants and medical experts to the conference, but no trade union representatives, can be explained in part by the existing tension between previous British governments and labor organizations over ILO initiatives.[88] These difficulties can be somewhat attributed to the deep suspicion of British Conservatives toward any internationalist bodies claiming to prescribe standards for health and safety in sovereign territories of the Crown. Such frictions eased, but did not disappear, when the Labour Party came into office in 1929 and the incoming mines minister agreed to reappraise the problem of dust in coal mines. Within the scientific community, the continuing struggle over the research agenda and the best avenue for the prevention of dust-related diseases in mining industries was reflected in preparations for the Johannesburg conference. Experts such as Haldane were associated with the "practical" approach of mining engineers and inclined to view dust as a ventilation problem, while pathology researchers such as Kettle, and Carozzi himself, wanted the conference to prioritize the medical aspect of the problem.

Britain was ultimately represented by Arthur J. Hall, a science professor at Sheffield, and by Edward L. Middleton. Other selected experts came from North America, Australia, and Europe. In addition to Orenstein and Irvine, the South African delegation (many of whom had been educated in Scotland) notably included Anthony Mavrogordato, who had worked with Haldane in the United Kingdom and been appointed Fellow in Industrial Hygiene to the South African Institute of Medical Research in 1919.[89] All contributed to a burgeoning international literature on the broader field of pneumoconiosis. The universally close relationship between government and industry is indicated by the fact that all of these men were employed in the public sector, excepting only Andrew Watt and Orenstein.[90]

The Johannesburg conference relied heavily on South African science and data, even though it was evident that the problems facing South Africa's gold mines were very different from those in the United Kingdom, continental Europe, the United States, and Australia. In the United States, silicosis was spread over a range of industries located in dozens of states, involving thousands of individual employers. Industry resolved the emerging dust crisis by focusing its energies on the various state legislatures, where it wielded the most influence.[91] In South Africa, public debate and trade union activity surrounding silicosis was confined to the gold mines, an industry dominated by just a handful of corporations. The mines' importance for employment, foreign exchange, and state revenue gave those companies even greater political influence than their US counterparts. In South Africa there was no federal system and, therefore, no lower jurisdictions on which to devolve the question of industrial hygiene. In addition, white labor unions were well organized and equipped to confront employers and government commissions with compensation claims.[92]

Scientific Agreement on Silicosis

Each conference session was organized around the discussion of one or several papers, which had been distributed beforehand to all the participants and were later published with the minutes. Meticulous preliminary preparation was a hallmark of the ILO, and the Johannesburg conference was no exception. As a senior ILO official would state in a different context, the organization could not afford to "waste time and money" and made a virtue of necessity by consulting experts beforehand in writing, in order for the meetings it convened to reach decisions in a single session.[93] Although prevention and compensation were part of the conference's program, Carozzi deliberately ensured that the medical dimension remained at the center of the debates.[94] The priority was the pathological, clinical, and radiological characterization of silicosis. The implicit goal of the meeting was to lay the basis for a future international convention, which brought the crucial issues of the diagnosis and etiology of silicosis to the fore.

The agenda for the Johannesburg conference was based on responses to a five-page, six-section questionnaire that the ILO had distributed to all participants. The questions were thorough and exhaustive.[95] In his opening speech, Irvine formulated what was at stake:

> Can we agree from the fundamental pathological standpoint upon a definition of what constitutes silicosis regarded as a definite condition of disease, the presence of which renders the affected man capable of being certified as suffering from a specific and identifiable occupational malady, which may constitute a valid basis for a possible claim for compensation in that respect? Can we agree upon a terminology which will render a description of the characteristic lesions and varieties and possibly the "stages" of silicosis mutually intelligible to observers in different countries? Can we agree upon a terminology descriptive of the various types of radiograph found in cases of silicosis, or other conditions of pulmonary fibrosis, which may similarly be intelligible to different observers?[96]

The experts, in other words, were convened to come up with a medical, international, standard definition of silicosis. For this reason, the ILO delegation—which consisted of Edward J. Phelan (the head of the diplomatic division) and Luigi Carozzi—was pleased that the congress took place in Johannesburg. Its participants were, as they saw it, "trapped" in the middle of nowhere for two weeks, with few distractions, other than a Zulu dance performance that was put on in their honor.

To a large extent, these initial goals were achieved, even though the 1930 meeting produced neither a detailed agreement on all the medical issues linked to the hazards of free silica dust nor a scientific revolution. It did not bring to light new, crucial findings on silicosis. To some extent, the conference even circumscribed the limit of available knowledge, as demonstrated by one of the final resolutions, which stated that it was "impossible, under existing conditions, properly to correlate dust determinations made in different countries, in different industries, and for different purposes, as well as for different immediate objects."[97] The reason why the conference was a decisive turning point, however, is that it managed to clarify preexisting knowledge and to refute major hypotheses, and it did so *at the international level.* This international dimension may seem fundamental in science, but it was far from obvious in the case of silicosis. The diversity in geological conditions, types of industry, organization of labor, and legislative and social-insurance arrangements (both among and within countries) hindered the comparability of working conditions. Moreover, economic interests created an additional source of division within the medical community.[98] Thus the ILO, by taking the initiative, became a decisive actor in the evolution of medical knowledge.

The conference reached a definition of silicosis: "Silicosis is a pathological condition of the lungs due to inhalation of silicon dioxide. It can be produced experimentally in animals."[99] Minimal as this statement might appear, it acknowledged, once and for all, the universal danger posed by the inhalation of free silica dust, whatever the geological conditions and occupational context in which it occurred, even though "admixture of other dusts tend[s] to modify the picture in the direction of that of other pneumoconioses, in some relation to the proportion of silica inhaled."[100]

The Johannesburg meeting also definitively dismissed a range of hypotheses, some of which had been predominant and had hindered the recognition of silicosis as an occupational disease. It put an end to the idea that silicosis was not an autonomous disease. More precisely, it explicitly rejected the notion that silicosis merely developed from tuberculosis. Aware of the economic implications of this refutation, Orenstein—probably in solidarity with Carozzi, who faced the opposition of many continental European physicians on this point—insisted on having things spelled out by the participants.[101] The synergy between silicosis and tuberculosis was discussed at length, particularly as it was complicated by the racial factor in South Africa, and final resolutions included a call for the removal of miners suffering from both afflictions simultaneously.[102]

The conference also produced a characterization of the evolution of the disease, divided into three stages.[103] Largely based on the South African approach, it has guided the clinical and radiographic detection of silicosis ever since. By stating that "appropriate action should be taken to inquire into the possibility of establishing an internationally comparable technique of radiography, and terminology of radiographic findings," it also paved the way for further research and negotiations over the following decades. The ILO played a decisive role in the creation of international radiographic standards, although that took a further three decades.

The conference also increased the level of coordination on a series of issues linked to prevention. The decisions adopted at the end of the conference, on August 25 and 26, confirmed that a consensus had been reached on a wide range of points. Most experts now accepted silicosis as a universal, dust-induced occupational disease, despite the diversity of the conditions and professions in which it arose. The medical consensus that emerged from the conference also downplayed the protective role of other dusts and constituents mixed up with free silica dust; cast doubt on the possibility of reliable, standardized measures of dust; and promoted an open but critical attitude toward prevention through ventilation and the use of water, which could neither be entirely dismissed nor treated as universal remedies.

What "Recognition" Means: The Legacy of Johannesburg

Literature on the history of occupational diseases tends to see "recognition" as a turning point. The new medico-legal definition turned "private" diseases, attributed to an individual's personal constitution, habits, and environment, into "social" diseases caused by specific working conditions. In some cases, this shift corresponds to a move from invisibility to visibility.[104]

The history of silicosis followed this logic. The Johannesburg conference was fundamental: it fostered research worldwide,[105] and, in its immediate aftermath, it triggered the recognition process for silicosis by a number of ILO member states, such as Japan, that were eager to demonstrate their rapid adoption of ILO policies in order to garner favor with the major European powers, who were dictating the terms. This was a crucial step that made the June 1934 signing of the C42 ILO international convention possible. As Carozzi would write a couple of weeks before the vote on this convention, "the findings of Johannesburg remain in force and do not fear attack by small patrols of enemies."[106]

At the same time, the story of silicosis throws into doubt a purely legalist vision of history. It is true that official international recognition of the disease was crucial and, on balance, paved the way for an increase in preventive and compensation measures in many countries. Yet recognition may hide as much as it reveals: the attribution of rights to the victims of the disease at times went hand in hand with the legalization of arbitrariness. These points do not stem from any radical stance on our part, but rather from an empirical observation on how the conclusions of Johannesburg and the subsequent 1934 ILO convention were interpreted and implemented. Silicosis is a test case, all the more telling because it is so extreme. It defies a linear vision of the progress of science and social rights and shows how much the social and political balance of power among employers, unions, and states, as well as the interplay of "technical" insurance procedures, perpetually called into question and limited the recognition of silicosis for the workers afflicted with it.

Johannesburg did not mark a sudden leap forward in medical knowledge and in the prevention of and compensation for occupational lung diseases.[107] There were as many limitations as there were achievements in the final resolutions of the conference (which were later carried over into the 1934 ILO convention). This was partly due to the parameters of medical knowledge, as well as to the complexity of grasping the etiology and nosology of silicosis. South African medical science, which was dominant at the meeting, provided much of the evidence that shaped the transnational medical and legal definitions of the disease. But clinical and radiological knowledge of the disease process, the geological conditions, the racial segregation of the workforce and of medical monitoring, and compensation issues were all particular to South African gold mines and created specific epidemiological conditions. The ILO—in one of its trademark, high-risk alliances of convenience—had to rely on South African research to advance its own cause. Orenstein and Carozzi themselves had the opportunity to express their doubts and discuss these limitations between themselves during preparations for a meeting convened in London on July 27, 1932, by the Medical Research Council's Committee on Industrial Pulmonary Diseases. There they met with several British experts, including Edgar Collis, and the American Leroy U. Gardner, director of the Saranac Laboratory, which was the first US laboratory devoted exclusively to research on tuberculosis.[108] As Orenstein acknowledged in a letter to the head of the ILO's Industrial Hygiene Section:[109] "In South Africa they do know what silicosis is. But, and this is a very big 'but' I now think, we only know *our* silicosis, and I am afraid there are quite a number of other varieties." Investigations in different industries, such as the coal and the abrasive-powder-manufacturing sectors, brought to light cases in which Orenstein himself found it "almost impossible to say whether one looked at true silicosis or chronic tuberculosis." In his mind, this made it "hopeless to attempt any international convention on this matter" as long as one could not "definitely say what is silicosis and by which dusts it is produced."

During the July 1932 conference, and then in October of that year in correspondence with the British Home Office, even Carozzi acknowledged the necessity of exercising caution when faced with the diversity of the manifestations of the disease, depending on the industrial sector and local conditions, and confessed that "it must at the present stage of development be left to Governments to interpret silicosis as encountered in their industries and to decide which industries should be covered."[110]

This limitation was carried over into international law. Extraordinarily, the C42 international convention recognized silicosis without clarifying which industrial sectors or work processes were supposed to cause it. In other words, no worker was entitled to rights because of the nature of his or her occupation. Digging, drilling, or indeed any other activities were not automatically associated with silicosis. Whereas the 1934 convention recognized phosphorous poisoning as the outcome of "any process involving the production, liberation, or utilization of phosphorous or its compounds," and anthrax poisoning as, among other things, the consequence of "handling of animal carcasses or parts of such carcasses including hides, hoofs, and horns," silicosis was to be attributed to "industries or processes recognized by national law or regulations as involving exposure to the risk of silicosis."[111] Governments were left with total freedom to accommodate the agreement as they wished (or, rather, managed to negotiate). Silicosis had to be "interpreted," as Carozzi had stated in 1932, both for medical reasons and, probably, because he was perfectly aware of what was politically achievable. Thus the "authoritative" international medico-legal definition was an entirely artificial construction, defining the disease simply as whatever was nationally accepted as silicosis.

Other limitations in what one could call "South African science" left their imprint, still visible to this day, on the international medical understanding of silicosis. One concerned the three-stage classification approved by the 1930 conference. In 1937, in a personal note to Harold Butler, Carozzi admitted that its adoption "represents merely a somewhat arbitrary classification, commonly adopted by medical experts on the subject, exclusively in regard however to clinical study of silicosis and with a view to clinical, radiological, and anatomo-pathological correlation of findings; such a classification has nothing whatever to do with compensation, in regard to which the only element to be considered is reduction of earning capacity or working capacity."[112]

While this classification had not been retained by the 1934 convention, it underpinned medical and radiographic knowledge for decades (and, to some extent, to the present day). While Carozzi's generation was aware of the three-stage classification's shortcomings, physicians soon forgot its rather empirical, unrefined foundations, and it became the frame of reference for individual clinical exams and x-ray photographs. Also forgotten was Carozzi's acknowledgment that this classification was based on a pure correlation (valid for masses of clinical cases, but fragile at the individual level), and that "the reduction of earning capacity or working capacity" was the only valid element to consider for compensation claims, because it was the only reliable, observable criterion. This contrast between scientific legitimization and the practical implications for insurance programs in a compensation system that severely limited workers' ability to exercise any power had devastating consequences, however.

Another flaw was Carozzi's choice to emphasize the "pure" danger posed by free silica dust in isolation from other considerations. This position was compatible with both the medical knowledge of his time and, incidentally, the financial issues at stake. It also served to deliberately minimize a discussion and understanding of the diversity and complexity of occupational dust diseases, which vary not only according to the different kinds of dusts, but also to their combination. The border between silicosis and pneumoconioses was frequently bandied about during the conference, but it was universally agreed that any further discussion on this larger issue should remain closed. To some extent, the choice of silicosis as the most important category was a way to corral the issue and to minimize the scope and focus of medical attention, preventive measures, and compensation plans. In this sense, too, the 1930 conference had long-lasting effects, creating a hierarchy of occupational lung diseases. While it paved the way for the 1934 international convention, the earlier conference simultaneously delayed the recognition of other pneumoconioses. A range of "second-order" diseases were evoked at the 1930 conference, to which the majority of pneumoconioses were relegated. A particularly striking example for the purposes of the present volume is that of anthracosis, caused by the inhalation of coal dust (chapter 6). Asbestosis received substantial attention during the Johannesburg conference, and one of the meeting's resolutions was even devoted to it.[113] Yet it would only take center stage a generation later, at the 1959 Johannesburg conference, which marked a symbolic transition in which asbestosis became the more prominent disease.[114]

ILO experts, who kept silent during most of the Johannesburg conference, could do no more than adopt a pragmatic stance. To be sure, medical knowledge of silicosis was not solid enough to allow a more aggressive strategy against industry's goal of minimizing compensation and prevention costs. Nor was the medical community sufficiently independent from industry. Nevertheless, there were murmurs of dissent. The proceedings of the conference could not completely disguise consistent criticism from some of the participating scientists, as well as from labor organizations, although the voices of organized labor beyond South Africa were generally muted and their views indirectly expressed at the Johannesburg gathering. While the unions continued to advocate a much broader understanding of dust-related diseases and policies compatible with this wider point of view, most of the Johannesburg conference participants affirmed the effectiveness of management policies adopted by industrialists who (in collaboration with leading scientists) had persistently advocated for "practicable" measures to control silicosis.[115]

To a large extent, the conclusions and recommendations produced at the 1930 meeting on the silicosis hazard posed by sandstone reflected the robust consensus formed among industrialists, policy makers, and scientific communities in their different national contexts. Together, these groups forged an institutional framework in which intellectual fraternities established strong relationships with the business community and with political groups eager to find "practical" answers to problems that inhibited efficient production and damaged the functionality of the labor force. The scientific solutions reached during this period were largely framed in accordance with the demands of the global economy and the "protection" of employment for workers in industries such as mining. Limiting the exposure of vulnerable employees to the risks of dangerous dusts was very much a secondary consideration.

Throughout the 1930s, scientific eminence and expertise on silicosis was recognized according to the outcome of international discussions and debates, in which a key priority was to limit the liability imposed on employers for the damage inflicted on their workers by silica dust. We argue that much of the scientific inquiry into the problem of lung disease caused by workplace dust was guided by this reduction in employers' susceptibility to litigation arising from their employees. This preoccupation with narrowing the agreed-upon causes of occupational diseases served to concentrate scientific attention on the "unique" hazard of quartz (pure silica) exposure to lifelong skilled workers and effectively exclude the risks of carbon dust and other dusts.

In every country, the biases underpinning the final medical agreement at Johannesburg remained as the basis for all future debates on the legal recognition of and compensation for silica-dust hazards, methods of prevention, and radiological and medical controversies. The next chapter explains the terms on which this relationship among scientists, business leaders, and governments developed during the decades between 1890 and 1950, as the risks of working with dust were calculated and reassessed country by country. This was a process in which, as ever, transnational debate and international conventions played a pivotal role.

NOTES

1. Cited in Steedman, *Dust*, 163–164. Draper was the author of *Human Physiology* (1856) and *History of Intellectual Development of Europe* (1864). Steedman suggests the influence, or shared assumptions, of Michelet in such texts.

2. Steedman, *Dust*, 69–72, 158–60.

3. Sturdy ("A Co-Ordinated Whole") argues that Haldane's work on the physiology of blood formed part of a teleological model about the functions of an organism within the larger purpose of the needs of the body.

4. Baldasseroni et al., "Naissance d'une maladie."

5. See Ally, *Gold and Empire*.

6. See Burke and Richardson, "Profits of Death"; Burt and Kippen, "Rational Choice."

7. See table 5, "Employment on the Gold Mines," in Yudelman, *Emergence*, 191. In 1929, 193,221 blacks and 21,949 whites were employed.

8. On the making of the workforce in the South African mining industry, see also Jeeves, *Migrant Labour*; F. Wilson, *Labour*. On the crucial role played by health aspects in the management of the labor force, see McCulloch, *South Africa's Gold Mines*.

9. The expression "miners' phthisis" may seem somewhat archaic and paradoxical in a country such as South Africa, which was supposed to lead the medical response to silicosis. Louis G. Irvine, head of the South African Miners' Phthisis Medical Bureau, lamented in 1930 that it remained "entrenched in the titles of the local Acts although it is nowhere mentioned in their substance," which, for him, "has unfortunately acted as a deterrent in the obtaining of employment by beneficiaries and has also, perhaps, in a good many instances, a subtle psychological effect in this and other directions upon the beneficiary himself." See ILO, *Silicosis: Records* (1930), first sitting, August 13, 1930.

10. Katz, *White Death*, 3.

11. Derickson, "Industrial Refugees," 66–89.

12. Katz, *White Death*, 25.

13. Ibid., 4.

14. See *Report of the Miners' Phthisis Commission*, xxi–xxii.

15. Katz, *White Death*, 154.

16. H. W. Sampson (ILO, *Silicosis: Records* [1930], 14) stated: "The enormous burden that the industry has to bear of nearly £1,000,000 per annum, totaling, I believe, some £15,000,000 for compensation claims since 1911 and arising chiefly from an average of 21,000 to 30,000 whites employed underground during that period, will convey to your minds the suffering to the victims and loss to the industry." See also Penrose, "Medical Monitoring and Silicosis."

17. Louis G. Irvine, chairman of ILO's Johannesburg conference, claimed that "in South Africa there was no general national insurance act for invalidity, and there was therefore a tendency to treat the Miners' Phthisis Act as a kind of substitute for the Poor Laws" (ILO, *Silicosis: Records* [1930], tenth sitting, 84–85). In February and March 1932, when Carozzi consulted European medical experts in order to prepare for what would become the 1934 international convention on silicosis, the answers he received from Italy (Biondi) and the Netherlands (Kranenburg) confirmed that, in their opinion, disability plans allowed de facto compensation for silicosis (HY 553/4/34/1, ILO Archives [henceforth A-ILO]). Belgium also chose this path in the mid-1930s, which delayed the recognition of the disease for decades.

18. Devinck and Rosental, " 'Une maladie sociale.' "

19. G. E. Barry, in ILO, *Silicosis: Records* (1930), tenth sitting, 84.

20. For an overview, see McCulloch, "Medicine, Politics, and Disease," 543–556.

21. On occasion, this figure could be as high as 12,000. See Dr. Williams, "Discussion," *Proceedings of the Transvaal Mine Medical Officers' Association* (1935), 81.

22. "Reservations by Mr. W. Boshoff" in *Report of the Miners' Phthisis Commission of Enquiry*, 100.

23. A. Miller, "President's Address," 147.

24. In addition to the deficiencies in medical surveillance, there were more-fundamental problems with the data. Epidemiology played no part in the compilation of the official disease rate, which was based entirely on the number of successful claims made before the Miners' Phthisis Medical Bureau. In other words, the disease rate *was* the compensation rate. There were numerous barriers that prevented black miners, who made up 90 percent of the workforce, from receiving compensation, so they were grossly underrepresented. The chamber's key committees were aware of the data's inadequacy.

25. This explanation was cited routinely by the chamber at select committee inquiries and commissions. Dr. Mavrogordato (ILO, *Silicosis: Records* [1930], fourth sitting, 45) told the 1930 conference that "the smaller incidence of silicosis among natives, as compared with Europeans, was due to intermittent employment; natives who were employed continuously developed silicosis more rapidly than Europeans."

26. See Irvine et al., "Review of the History," 203.

27. "Discussion of Tuberculosis," *Proceedings of the Transvaal Mine Medical Officers' Association* (1926), 4.

28. *Phthisis and Miners Compensation*, Malawi National Archives.

29. In November 1924, Dr. L. Bostock, district manager of the WNLA at Lourenço Marques, wrote in protest to the Gold Producers Committee about the spread of tuberculosis among men returning from the mines. The issue was raised at a Mine Medical Officers' Association meeting in Johannesburg in March the following year. See *Proceedings of the Transvaal Mine Medical Officers' Association* (1925).

30. Little has been written about William Gemmill. The exceptions are Jeeves, "Gemmill"; Yudelman, *Emergence*, esp. 153–155, 204–207.

31. McCulloch, "Air Hunger," 118–137.

32. See, for example, Clavin and Wessel, "Transnationalism"; Cayet, *Rationaliser le travail*.

33. See the pioneering book by Weindling, *International Health Organisations*.

34. Rodgers, *Atlantic Crossings*; Topalov, *Laboratoires du nouveau siècle*.

35. On the reappraisal of the role of the ILO in the rise of the welfare state in the twentieth century, see Rosental, "Géopolitique et État-Providence"; Conrad, "Sozialpolitik transnational"; Haworth and Hughes, *International Labour Organization*; Van Daele, *ILO Histories*; Kott and Droux, *Globalizing Social Rights*.

36. Carnevale et al., "Concerning the First International Congress." On the general development of these international networks and congresses, see Herren-Oesch, *Hintertüren zur Macht*.

37. De Cristoforis, a former military doctor in the voluntary Garibaldian troops, militated for the autonomy of his medical specialty, gynecology—which, in Italy, was under the influence of the Roman Catholic Church, through obstetrics—and for major secular and rationalist causes, such as cremation and secular schooling. An influential Freemason (he was Grand Master of the Italian Grand East), De Cristoforis was also a member of parliament from 1895 to 1904, and he became a senator in 1905. See Forti Messina, *Malachia De Cristoforis*.

38. Bartocci, *Le politiche sociali*.

39. This paragraph is based on information provided by Sergio Iavicoli, Valentina Guastella, and Daniela Fano on the ICOH's website, www.icohweb.org.

40. Payre, *Une science communale?*

41. See note 39.

42. An expression from that period, cited by Rosner and Markowitz throughout *Deadly Dust: Silicosis and the On-Going Struggle*.

43. Balinska, *For the Good of Humanity*.

44. SI 21/2/3, A-ILO. Although the ILO enjoyed some autonomy, the LN had financial control over its activities, since the ILO's budget was approved by the fourth commission of the LN Assembly. See also Cayet, "Le BIT." Concerning the role of the secretariat of the LN, see Clavin and Wessel, "Transnationalism."

45. SI 21/1/1, A-ILO.

46. SI 21/7/0, A-ILO.

47. SI 22/1/1, A-ILO.

48. See Carozzi's letter to Verne A. Zimmer of the Division of Labor Standards, US Department of Labor, March 12, 1937, HY 1000/34/2, A-ILO.

49. In a letter dated March 3, 1926, Carozzi it made clear to Albert Thomas, the head of the ILO, that Carozzi wanted to avoid a "defeat from a technical standpoint" on an issue—pneumoconiosis—that, according to the South African Miners' Phthisis Medical Bureau itself, "is one of the most complicated in medicine." Paul Weindling ("Social Medicine") has demonstrated that the ILO tended to favor well-established issues over adventurous causes. This was both a limitation and a necessity in its complex interaction with nation-states, which were infinitely more powerful.

50. This was done, for instance, in 1932 in Germany, a key country because of its economic importance and because its medical community was one of the most divided on this issue.

51. Silicosis was the only disease to which the IHS devoted a specific structure, with the creation of a specialist subcommittee in 1936.

52. According to A. J. Orenstein, "Memorandum to Harold Butler, 21 November 1927," HY 1000/34/1, A-ILO.

53. On this advanced medical position, with all its racial ambiguities, see Packard, "Tuberculosis"; Penrose, "Medical Monitoring and Silicosis."

54. See Malan, *Quest of Health*, 95–112.

55. See Yudelman, *Emergence.*

56. Jeeves, "Gemmill."

57. Alcock, *History of the International Labour Organization*, 81–98.

58. See, for example, "Employment of Natives," British National Archives.

59. ILO, *Silicosis: Records* (1930), eighth sitting, 79.

60. Alexander, "Race, Class Loyalty."

61. ILO, *Silicosis: Records* (1930), ninth sitting, 84.

62. Viet and Ruffat, *Le choix de la prévention.*

63. ILO, *Silicosis: Records* (1930), tenth sitting, 85.

64. Irvine et al., in their paper on the history of the South African mines ("Review of the History"), concluded that decreases in dust levels after 1910 had reduced disease rates and increased life expectancy. Nevertheless, they acknowledged that silicosis, viral pneumonia, and tuberculosis were no more treatable in 1930 than they had been in 1902. Even Andrew Watt, medical officer for the Rand Mutual Assurance Company and the physician who pioneered the use of x-rays in the Rand, reminded delegates that where dust prevailed, "every man working underground, including shift bosses, samplers, and mine captains, were liable to contract miners' phthisis" ("Personal Experiences," 589–596).

65. The Miners' Phthisis Board was responsible for compensation, whereas the Miners' Phthisis Bureau was in charge of the medical monitoring of silicosis.

66. For instance, Barry (ILO, *Silicosis: Records* [1930], ninth sitting, 84) added that it "was impossible to alter the South African legislation without upheaval, because any new benefits granted produced thousands of retrospective claimants."

67. Ibid., 82.

68. Ibid., 85.

69. See Weindling, *International Health Organizations.*

70. Bufton and Melling, " 'A Mere Matter of Rock.' "

71. This is the subject of Cherniack's *Hawk's Nest Incident.*

72. Lanza, *Silicosis and Asbestosis*, 64, 405–406. The situation with respect to silicosis and asbestosis, arising out of a period of economic depression, became manifest as a medico-legal phenomenon whose scope and intensity were both preposterous and almost unbelievable. For background, see Sayers and Lanza, "History of Silicosis and Asbestosis," 7. By 1916, South Africa's Miners' Phthisis Prevention Committee claimed that "radiographic appearances in cases of silicosis afford the most reliable single piece of evidence in establishing the existence and the actual stage of the disease in any particular case" (quoted in Meiklejohn, "Development of Compensation," 200).

73. Buzzi et al., *La santé au travail.*

74. Devinck and Rosental, " 'Une maladie sociale.' "

75. See Luigi Carozzi's circular letter, March 12, 1926, HY 553, A-ILO.

76. ILO, *Silicosis: Records* (1930), second sitting, 30. Dr. J. McCrae's 1914 study, according to which 70 percent of the dust found in miners' lungs during autopsies measured less than one micron, identified the smaller particles as the most dangerous ones.

77. ILO, *Silicosis: Records* (1930), sixth sitting, 10.

78. Ibid.

79. A. J. Orenstein, "Memorandum to Harold Butler, 21 November 1927," HY 1000/34/1, A-ILO.

80. Kotze was later a director of Anglo-American mining. On Gemmill's role in shaping labor policy, see note 30. Alexander ("Race, Class Loyalty," 128–129) examines how "Gemmill drew on the lessons of his transnational experience by importing American employers' techniques to contain labor movements."

81. Letter by Orenstein to Butler, March 20, 1928, HY 1000/34/1, A-ILO.

82. During a career that spanned the period from 1913 until the 1960s, Orenstein was variously head of sanitation for Rand Mines, Ltd.; chair of the powerful Gold Producers Committee within the Chamber of Mines; and, from 1956 on, the inaugural director of the Pneumoconiosis Research Unit in the Department of Mines. See W. Anderson, *Colonial Pathologies*; Packard, "Invention of the 'Tropical Worker'";" McCulloch, "Air Hunger"; Orenstein's necrology in *Proceedings of the Mine Medical Officers' Association*, 1–2. Orenstein's memory is honored in South Africa today through the A. J. Orenstein Memorial Lecture, organized annually by the University of the Witwaterstrand, and the A. J. Orenstein Library in the National Institute for Occupational Health in Johannesburg.

83. After the war, David Vaage, the new head of the ILO's Industrial Safety Section, reported with great surprise on this practice ("Memorandum, May 16, 1946," HY 1003, A-ILO): "Whereas for the Correspondence Committee on Accident Prevention we have always consulted the governments and asked them to propose candidates for membership on the Committee, I understand that Dr. Carozzi's practice was [for the Correspondence Committee on Industrial Hygiene] to propose and select candidates himself."

84. Letter from the Belgian Ministry of Industry, Labor, and Welfare (*"Prévoyance"*) to Albert Thomas, June 21, 1930, HY 1000/34/1/2/7, A-ILO.

85. Melling and Sellers, "Objective Collectives?," 113.

86. See W. Citrine to J. R. Clynes, March 3, 1930, requesting that Legge be sent as the official representative, since Citrine understood from the ILO that Collis was the unofficial representative funded by the ILO, and Clynes' reply to W. M. Citrine, March 12, 1930, TUC 292C/144.34/1, Modern Record Centre, University of Warwick, Coventry, England. After applying to Trinity (his old college at Cambridge), Legge was told that if Trinity had desired representation, then Mavrogordato would have been their choice. See Legge to Mavrogordato, at the South African Institute for Medical Research, May 21, 1930, TUC 292C/144.34/1, Modern Record Centre.

87. Collis to Butler, April 23, 1928, HY 1000/3H/a, A-ILO; "International Conference on Pneumo-Coniosis [Silicosis], Johannesburg 1930: Correspondence with Great Britain," July 20, 1928, HY 1000/34/1/2/25, A-ILO; Butler to Delevingne, March 26, 1929, HY 1000/34/1/2/25, A-ILO: "What I would like to do, therefore, in our official letter is to suggest Collis and whatever second man you suggest as the experts nominated by the ILO, and to invite the Government to send Dr. Middleton in addition"; Butler to Orenstein, May 24, 1929, HY 1000/34/1/2/25, A-ILO; Butler to Gemmill, November 7, 1929, HY 1000/34/1, A-ILO. See also Teleky, *History*, 87–90, for another individual promoted by Collis.

88. See, for example, Arthur Pugh, of the Iron and Steel Trades Confederation, to C. W. Bowerman, of the TUC Parliamentary Committee, June 7, 1921, TUC 292/935/1, Modern Record Centre.

89. The other main South African experts were A. Sutherland Strachan, F. W. Simson, Spencer Lister, and Andrew Watt of the Rand Mutual Assurance Company, Ltd. W. Watkins Pitchford, the founding chair of the Miners' Phthisis Medical Bureau, had recently

died. On the South African medical community, see McCulloch, "Counting the Cost." The main foreign experts were Leroy U. Gardner (1888–1946), who had been the director of the Saranac Laboratory since 1927, and Albert E. Russell, from the US Public Health Service, for the United States; John Grant Cunningham (1890–1965), head of the Industrial Hygiene Division of the Ontario Board of Health, for Canada; and Keith Moore, head of the Industrial Hygiene Division of the Commonwealth Department of Health, and Charles Badham (1884–1943), medical officer of industrial hygiene in the New South Wales Public Health Department, for Australia. For European countries, the delegates were Franz Koelsch (1876–1970), professor of occupational medicine at the University of Munich, and Dr. Böhme, for Germany; W. R. H. Kranenburg, medical adviser to the labour inspectorate, for the Netherlands; and Giovanni Loriga (1861–1950), first medical inspector for labor, for Italy. Many of them were members of the Correspondence Committee on Industrial Hygiene of the ILO.

90. On the process of selection, see HY 1000/34/1, A-ILO.

91. See Rosner and Markowitz, *Deadly Dust: Silicosis and the On-Going Struggle.*

92. As described in Davies, *Capital, State, and White Labour.*

93. Note by Adrien Tixier, head of the social-insurance section, to ILO's director, Harold Butler, February 21, 1933, SI 21/7/2, A-ILO.

94. This choice had been thoroughly debated in correspondence between Butler and Carozzi for the ILO, and Orenstein for the South African mining industry. They had explicitly decided that the engineering issues could be left aside, particularly as the Empire Mining Congress planned to discuss them a few months before the Johannesburg conference. Indeed, during that mining congress, a "world-famous engineer," whose name is not cited in the proceedings, confirmed the relevance of this choice (ILO, *Silicosis: Records* [1930], 20): "Let the physiologists tell us plainly what they want done, and we shall find ways of doing it for them." See also the letters from Butler to Orenstein on May 24, 1929, and from Carozzi to Butler on August 10, 1929, SI 22/1/1, A-ILO.

95. For instance, section 1, devoted to "the aetiology and course of silicosis," raised questions about the concentration of silica dust necessary to produce silicotic changes; the period and extent of exposure (including intermittency, due to an alternation of occupations); the influence of the presence of other dusts on the occurrence and course of silicosis; the extent to which other dusts (including asbestos) might cause evidence of a lung change similar to silicosis; the variations among the types of silicosis encountered in different industries, such as metal grinding, sandblasting, mining (including for tin and lead), and quarrying and dressing stone, as well as products such as pottery, china, clayware, scouring powders, and the like. The other sections dealt with diagnosis, prognosis, silicosis-producing dusts, prevention, and research. See the appendix to the letter from Butler to Orenstein on May 24, 1929, HY 1000/34/1, A-ILO.

96. ILO, *Silicosis: Records* (1930), first sitting, 24.

97. Ibid., eleventh sitting, 94.

98. In July 1934, a few weeks after the adoption of the C42 international convention on silicosis, Carozzi noted that silicosis had been a unique case of an occupational disease, in that it had brought about national legislation in 23 countries, but not as an international convention (HY 1000/50/1, A-ILO).

99. ILO, *Silicosis: Records* (1930), eleventh sitting, 86. The volume does not explicitly state that the report discussed during this session was adopted; the archival version, however, does (HY 1000/34/1/4, A-ILO), as does the *Supplement* published in 1938 by the ILO to its two-volume encyclopedia, *Occupation and Health.* See Middleton, "Silicosis," 1.

100. ILO, *Silicosis: Records* (1930), eleventh sitting, 86.

101. On August 19, 1930, Orenstein insisted on clarifying the conclusions of the seventh sitting by asking if he "was right in understanding that the Conference had accepted Professor Hall's proposal that in the present state of knowledge of the pathology of the disease, the view was not considered justified that silicosis was essentially tuberculous, at least as seen in South Africa" (ILO, *Silicosis: Records* [1930], 72).

102. Physician Andrew Watt argued that, whereas in Great Britain, miners came from densely populated areas and therefore had some immunity to infection, black miners in South Africa had little prior exposure. In theory (there was no data regarding this question until 1994), this meant that the migrant labor system posed a grave threat to rural communities. It was therefore fortunate, according to Watt ("Personal Experiences," 596) and most of his colleagues, that there was not much silicosis among black miners and little prospect that tuberculosis was being exported from the mines. See also Packard, *White Plague, Black Labor*, 159–193.

103. Final resolutions 18–20, in ILO, *Silicosis: Records* [1930], 88: "In the first stage symptoms referable to the respiratory system may be either slight or even absent. Capacity for work may be slightly impaired. There may be a departure from the normal in percussion [tapping on the surface of the body to determine the underlying structure of the lungs] and in auscultatory signs [sounds within the body], and the radiograph must show an increased density of linear shadows, and the presence of discrete shadows, indicative of nodulation. In the second stage, there is an increase of the physical signs observable in the first stage, and the radiograph shows an increase in the number and size of the discrete shadows indicative of nodulation with a tendency to their confluence. There must be some degree of definite impairment of working capability. In the third stage all of the above conditions are grossly accentuated and indications of areas of massive fibrosis are usual. There is serious or total incapacitation."

104. Hatzfeld, "Les malades du travail."

105. Gallo and Marquez Valderrama, "La silicosis."

106. Note from Carozzi to Phelan and Butler, May 14, 1934, HY 553/0/2, A-ILO. Carozzi was reporting on his journey through Germany and Switzerland, countries in which the medical community had long been divided over the question of whether silicosis simply developed from tuberculosis.

107. Among the numerous reactions after the conference was that of A. Hall, "Some Impressions," 655–666.

108. The conference was organized by Edward Middleton, in the Factory Department of the Home Office, for the centenary of the British Medical Association.

109. Letter from A. J. Orenstein to L. Carozzi, June 10, 1932, HY 1000/50/1, A-ILO.

110. Carozzi, "Presentation to the 1932 Silicosis Meeting," HY 1000/50/1, A-ILO; Carozzi, correspondence with the Home Office, HY 553/5/25, A-ILO.

111. ILO, "Workmen's Compensation." Workmen's compensation convention (revised), in ILO, *International Labour Conference* (1934).

112. Personal note from Carozzi to Butler, March 11, 1937, HY 1000/34/2, A-ILO. Carozzi reacted to fierce criticisms of the use of this three-stage classification by the ILO that were leveled by Verne A. Zimmer, the director of the division of labor standards in the US Department of Labor.

113. Final resolution 23, in ILO, *Silicosis: Records* [1930], 89: "The inhalation of asbestos dust produces a definite pneumoconiosis, which may occur also in association with tuberculosis, and deaths have been recorded. This pneumoconiosis is associated with the presence of "asbestosis bodies", but the mere presence of these bodies in the lungs or sputum does not constitute evidence of the disease. For the diagnosis of this pneumoconiosis the same

criteria as described for silicosis should be applied, *mutatis mutandis* [all things being equal]. There is not at present sufficient evidence to show definitively to what extent tuberculosis and this type of pneumoconiosis react upon one another."

114. See Orenstein, *Proceedings of the Pneumoconiosis Conference.*
115. McCulloch, *South Africa's Gold Mines.*

Chapter 4

The Politics of Recognition and Its Limitations
A Transnational Process?

Martin Lengwiler and Julia Moses, with Bernard Thomann and Joseph Melling

In 1912, the Swiss Trade Union for Stone and Clay Workers submitted a petition to their national parliament. The labor organization demanded that Swiss mining and stonecutting trades be placed under the legal protection of the Factory Law, and thus under the responsibility of the Federal Factory Inspectorate. The petition was partly motivated by the lack of a tradition of governmental control over the mining industry, in contrast to, for example, Prussia and the German Empire.[1] Its authors were also concerned about the health of workers—in particular, widespread (though not officially recognized) occupational illnesses among miners and stonecutters.[2] Over several pages, they cited a series of recent medical investigations showing that, in different European countries, there was an increased incidence of severe lung disease in the mining and stonecutting trades. They referenced, among other things, statistical evidence gathered by industrial hygienists, mutual-aid societies, factory inspectors, statistical offices, and trade unions, as well as legal provisions from Germany, Austria, the Netherlands, Denmark, and Switzerland—but not from the United Kingdom or South Africa.[3] Although the authors were unaware of the concept of silicosis—the term had been coined roughly 40 years earlier and had begun to be used internationally—they nevertheless argued that the mining trade was beset by specific occupational illnesses and had to be specially protected by governmental intervention. They asked for a reduction in the maximum number of working hours and the introduction of water sprinklers for dusty workplaces, in order to inhibit the production of dust.[4] The petition went no further, as the Swiss parliament refused to support it. A few months later, with the outbreak of World War I, the political context and priorities became even more unfavorable. Under the exigencies of the war economy, demands for accident prevention and workplace safety lost their momentum and were sidelined.

This episode represents an important moment in the history of the recognition of silicosis as an occupational illness. It is a reminder that, even before World War I, knowledge about occupational illnesses specifically associated with mining emerged in various European countries, and that interested groups started to make connections among these separate bodies of expertise, thereby ensuring the first steps toward a coherent understanding of what was later called silicosis.

In retrospect, this period marked the start of a transnational discourse on the disease. Initially, the picture was still fragmentary. The Swiss petitioners, for example, were not aware of the fact that South Africa had already introduced a law to compensate victims of silicosis. Such developments continued after World War I, spurred on in part by the United Kingdom, which, in 1918, seven years after South Africa introduced its compensation laws, became the first European state to legally recognize this new occupational illness. In the 1920s, the secretary of the Swiss Trade Union for Stone and Clay Workers, Robert Kolb, became secretary-general of the International Trade Union of Quarrymen and continued, now at an international level, to lobby for the protection of miners. Although Kolb's efforts were unsuccessful, due to the ILO's cautiousness, by the late 1920s and 1930s a number of states began to follow South Africa and the United Kingdom in politically and legally recognizing silicosis as an occupational disease by including sufferers' rights to compensation in national laws.

Closer investigation shows that the path to recognition was a highly complex and multilayered process that reveals much about the difficult relationships among national, international, and transnational actors. Previous chapters examined the transnational aspect of this recognition process. But all the actors—experts, workers, employers, and legislators—involved in coming to a consensus about silicosis were already part of nationally specific institutional contexts, namely, each country's general system of compensation for industrial accidents and occupational illnesses. These institutional, political, and social conditions had important effects on the process of recognition, and each state followed a unique path toward legislation regarding silicosis.

Nonetheless, national experiences were directly intertwined with global processes, both on a small scale (through scientific exchanges, international conferences, and labor migration) and on a large one (through imperial entanglements, as was the case for the United Kingdom and South Africa). Shared histories of industrialization, economic modernization, and technological and scientific development played a crucial role in determining the commonality of developments pertaining to silicosis around the globe. In the first half of the twentieth century, therefore, political recognition of the disease was a global phenomenon, resulting, in part, from simultaneously emerging concepts and models of thinking regarding this health issue. In this respect, what happened with silicosis echoes similar experiences in other areas of occupational health during the same period, such as the notion of "accident-proneness" of particular workers.[5]

This chapter employs a comparative perspective, investigating exemplary national case studies from Western Europe and the wider world in order to reveal the mechanisms that shaped the ways in which silicosis legislation was framed during the early twentieth century. It reflects on the significance of international networks and organizations in this process, complementing a transnational view (chapter 3). Yet its primary aim is to disentangle the complex web of transnational and national dynamics involved in the recognition process. In this way, this chapter uses silicosis as a case study to make this interaction between national and transnational history explicit.

The countries that we have chosen to examine offer a representative variety of paths toward recognizing silicosis as an occupational illness in its own right, thereby meriting measures for its prevention and compensation. The case studies selected include forerunners, like the United Kingdom;[6] countries that enacted relevant legislation in the interwar period, such as Germany, Switzerland, Japan, and the United States; and latecomers, including France, Italy, and Chile, which adopted compensation policies in the 1940s and 1950s. These countries also represent different institutional traditions, namely, social-insurance systems (adopted in the majority of the case studies here) and workers' compensation systems (adopted, for instance, in the United Kingdom).

This chapter therefore seeks to show how silicosis became a political issue around the globe in the first half of the twentieth century by examining both the unique and the common processes involved. It points out the main actors in this story, demonstrating how workers, employers, and politicians took up scientific, legal, and moral arguments in order to make their case about silicosis. Finally, it addresses the paradox of the great degree of commonality in the resulting legislation on this illness. Many countries adopted policies on compensation at different times, and each followed its own legislative path regarding silicosis. Nonetheless, fairly similar systems to address silicosis emerged across the world. In each case, legislation on silicosis ultimately found employers liable for the disease—even though the precise details of compensation systems differed and their timing varied greatly, from a few years to several decades after the process was triggered. Moreover, vastly diverse countries around the globe, with disparate political, economic, and social circumstances, adopted these policies on silicosis within several decades of each other. Nonetheless, legal recognition was not simply an institutional watershed and a point of no return. Instead, the history of silicosis shows how the illness was a source of constant struggle.

Silicosis as an Occupational Illness: Conditions for National Recognition

By the end of the nineteenth century, many states around the globe had adopted a system of compensation to address work-related accidents. Occupational illnesses such as silicosis were generally incorporated into these systems at a later time. Such diseases were addressed by two different legal systems: workers' compensation, adopted, for example, by Britain (1897), Spain (1900), Japan (1911), Chile (1916), and the United States (instituted state by state over the first quarter of the twentieth century); and social insurance for accidents, first developed in Imperial Germany (1884) and later taken up by other nations, such as Italy and France (1898) and Switzerland (1918).[7] Both kinds of systems required employers to pay compensation for occupational injuries, regardless of fault, since these policies assumed that workplace accidents stemmed from activities that were part and parcel of that work, not from the decisions of individual workers. Under these systems, therefore, and in contrast to previous legal rulings, workers could not be held responsible for causing accidents that injured them. Following the same logic, several of these policies were later extended to include occupational illnesses. This usually took place initially through judges' decisions in court cases, and then either by the introduction of a statutory list of compensable diseases—as was the case, for example, in Britain (1906), France (1919), and Germany (1925)—or through the introduction of separate policies focusing specifically on the treatment of occupational diseases—such as in Belgium (1927), Japan (1928), Italy (1928), and Spain (1936). Under these laws, employers were required to offer assistance to their workers, pay damages, and, in some cases, provide medical care. As a result, most employers in countries with a workers' compensation policy chose to cover the financial risk of accident claims by purchasing insurance from a commercial insurance company, though many employers decided to pay for any costs associated with accidents or occupational diseases by forming their own mutual insurance funds or directly assuming financial liability. In countries with a social-insurance system, workers needed to be covered by an accident insurance policy, either through a commercial insurance firm, public fund, or mutual-aid association that would be funded by employers' contributions and, in some instances, subsidies from public funds and workers' contributions. In both systems, injured workers (and, in case of death, their families) received compensation that was based on a portion of their lost salaries. For insurance policies, these payments were provided at regular intervals, while in the case of workers' compensation, they were often granted as a lump sum that could be changed to regular installments upon request. In both systems, doctors played an important role: first in determining the nature of an accidental injury or illness and, later, in ascertaining whether, and to what extent, the condition had subsided.

Like earlier laws on employers' liability and workplace safety, these policies had an indirect but important effect on the later recognition of occupational diseases like silicosis. These policies also marked a turning point for the creation of industrial medicine as a specialized medical discipline that was supposed to reconcile a concern for workers' health with productivity, and they spurred increasingly systematic endeavors toward a medically based understanding and treatment of work-related accidents and diseases. In this sense, they produced a series of actors and organizations responsible for the systematic production of knowledge on work-related health hazards.

An important force in the recognition process was the creation of private accident-prevention organizations that began to flourish in Europe in the middle of the nineteenth century. These groups—such as the Association of Italian Industrialists for the Prevention of Industrial Accidents—were frequently formed by employers. They collected accident statistics and promoted the development of new safety equipment.[8] Similarly, factory inspectorates, institutionalized in Great Britain (1833), Prussia (1839), and other European countries (in the latter part of the nineteenth century), contributed significantly to the body of knowledge about occupational illness.[9] For much of the nineteenth century and into the early part of the twentieth, factory inspectors were rarely trained as physicians, which limited their ability to deal with occupational illnesses. These inspectors, while generally recruited from the ranks of engineers and technicians, or, as in Germany and Italy, from local police bureaus and prefectural agencies, were nevertheless involved in collecting statistics and monitoring hazardous industrial activities.[10]

One of the most significant consequences of the new policies on accident compensation and safety was the development of occupational medicine. In Great Britain, silicosis was known but, for a variety of reasons, remained largely neglected by public health officials throughout the nineteenth century. It was only after that country enacted its legislation on workers' compensation in 1897 that physicians began to concentrate more fully on the issue of work-related illnesses.[11] Factory doctors, physicians employed directly by insurance firms, medical examiners (in the case of deceased workers), and certifying doctors (registered by the state to oversee the implementation of compensation policies) all played a crucial role in administering compensation systems, as well as overseeing occupational health in general at this time.[12]

New hospitals focusing on occupational injuries and illnesses—such as the Bergmannsheil ("miners' well-being") clinic, founded in Bochum, Germany, in 1890; a similar one in Jaén, Spain, established in the late nineteenth century; and the hospital founded in Ikuno, Japan, in 1897—also contributed to a blossoming of new knowledge on work-related health. Not least, the work of the renowned Clinica del Lavoro in Milan led to a greater understanding of work-related diseases.[13] These efforts produced an important set of evidence that would later benefit the first generation of silicosis researchers.

The adoption of compensation and social-insurance legislation from the 1880s on contributed to the vast expansion of the community of specialists dealing with occupational health.[14] The most visible consequence of this development was the emergence of an international network of experts, along with regular international conferences around the topic of industrial accidents and illnesses. There were several landmark congresses in this field: the International Congress on Workplace Injuries[15] began meeting in 1889; the International Congress on Workers' Protection met regularly from 1889 on; and the International Congress on Professional Diseases, where the first congress, in 1906, led to the creation of the Permanent Commission on Occupational Health (PCOH, now known as the International Commission on Occupational Health). The groups responsible for these conferences not only shared information about occupational illnesses, but sometimes also acted as lobbies. In 1889, the International Congress on Workplace Injuries pressed for the extension of compensation systems to all workplace categories, including occupational illnesses, while the International Association for the Legal Protection of Workers, created in 1901, successfully petitioned for an international convention on white lead in 1906. These international organizations, however, were still unable to reach consensus about the most effective way to deal with occupational illness. For example, the International Congress on Occupational Illnesses that met in Brussels in 1910 focused on conceptual questions related to the etiology of industrial diseases and how to offer compensation for them.[16]

On a national level, an increasing awareness of occupational illnesses, fostered by the establishment of social-insurance systems in Germany and other countries, led to the introduction and growth of new medical professions. Among the fields that benefited from these new institutional opportunities were *Gewerbehygiene* ("industrial hygiene"), which had existed since the 1860s but grew substantially after the establishment of social insurance in the 1880s, and *Unfallmedizin* ("accident medicine"), which was associated with the new institutions that grew up around the laws on accident insurance. Professional associations for accident medicine were also established, for example in Switzerland in 1912 and in Germany in 1923.[17]

None of these disciplines focused specifically on silicosis—or even recognized the existence of such an illness. Nevertheless, they generated a field of medical expertise that later became important in the recognition process for silicosis and for occupational diseases more generally. Early compensation systems focused on accidents, which were usually defined as "something that happens" at a particular point in time and "in the course of work." Thus various compensation policies were tested by court cases that questioned whether a worker could be remunerated for an occupational illness. In Italy and Germany, courts debated whether industrial disease could be seen as the consequence of a "series of small accidents"—for example, through repeated exposure to noxious chemicals or loud noises. Thus bladder cancer, a disease caused by aniline and prevalent in the chemical industry, was recognized as an occupational illness in Germany by 1895 and compensated through the associated accident insurance, 30 years before the general inclusion of occupational illnesses in that country's accident insurance system. In Italy, which did not insure workers against occupational illnesses until 1929, few illnesses passed this test. An exception was malaria, as it could be traced to a mosquito bite: a momentary but directly attributable event.[18] The same was true in France for "glassworkers' cataract," which was recognized before the notion of occupational diseases was legalized. Significantly, this ailment affected specially trained workers—who were costly to attract and keep in the workforce.

Apart from these institutional conditions, other factors proved to be important. In particular, the existing traditions for treating occupational illness had a significant influence on the recognition process. Fundamental differences characterized how mining hazards were perceived and legally dealt with in various countries. In continental Europe, especially in the German states and Austria-Hungary, where the mining industry was generally state run, the trade was already highly regulated in the early-modern period. This led to inaugural forms of social protection, such as mutual-aid funds and medical provisions for miners, during the seventeenth and eighteenth centuries. Mining authorities also provided benefits and care when faced with a series of endemic professional illnesses, such as miners' phthisis.[19] Similarly, in Japan, the condition known as *yoroke*, which had been recognized since the eighteenth century by local mining communities, was treated by miners' mutual-aid associations (*tomoko*).[20]

These medical conditions were part of early-modern mining culture, and, by the end of the nineteenth century, they were still not regarded as illnesses of the modern industrial era. Consequently, the statutory accident insurance policies set up in the late nineteenth and early twentieth centuries rarely dealt with conditions associated with mining in the same way as they addressed illnesses associated with other industrial occupations (e.g., bladder cancer in the chemical industry).[21] Occupational diseases in the mines were not prioritized by physicians, either. At least until World War I, silicosis remained in the shadow of "modern" and "industrial" occupational illnesses and was not seen as a political issue. Neither employers, workers, nor the state authorities—much less the medical community—pursued special legislation related to the disease. As a consequence, the process of recognizing silicosis as a workplace disease often started late, since actors had to be convinced that silicosis was neither a byproduct of tuberculosis nor an inevitable outcome of working in particular industries, but rather an occupational risk that could be contained. In this respect, medical experts, employers, workers, and governmental officials needed to agree that silicosis stemmed from an explicitly *industrial* pathology that could and should be dealt with by modern social-insurance institutions.

Moreover, different countries had different approaches to silicosis. In particular, in some states, the rise of the mining industry occurred as part of a more general process of industrialization. The perception of mining hazards, therefore, was shaped by overarching concerns about the new risks of an industrialized era characterized by mechanization (chapter 6). Accordingly, the rapid rise in silicosis cases caused by the introduction of new mining technologies in the late nineteenth century was immediately made public, becoming a scandal that was politicized by trade unions and the medical profession. This was the case in South Africa and, later, in Britain. The early politicization of silicosis did not, however, automatically mean that these countries would also provide a means of social protection. Often, as in the United States and France, the overwhelming power of employers' associations—compared with that of trade unions—inhibited the legal recognition of silicosis, despite widespread public debates about the illness.

The explosion of labor unrest at the turn of the twentieth century cannot be understood without looking to this expansion of technical innovations and their consequences for workers' health. For example, in the early 1900s in the United States, the *Granite Cutters' Journal*, the publication of the granite workers' union, contained numerous articles about "stonecutters' consumption," closely linking its increase to the introduction of power tools and the continuing problem of ventilation in the sheds. In particular, tunneling and bridge-building projects exposed American workers (usually immigrants and minorities) to the dangers of inhaling silica-rich dusts in confined spaces. In July 1905, an article in that journal stressed the importance of better ventilation in the sheds.[22] Similarly, in Australia at the end of the nineteenth century, mutual-aid societies and the Amalgamated Miners Association were the first to draw attention to the large number of sick and injured workers and the need for improved ventilation in the mines. In 1896, they played an important role in convincing the gold-mining city of Bendigo to document the rise in phthisis and recommend legislation regarding it.[23] Moreover, industry spokespeople sometimes accepted the industrial origins of workers' complaints. *Iron Ages*, an American trade journal, asserted that "miners' phthisis is so great an evil" that it was essential to deal effectively with "this most terrible form of tuberculosis."[24] Even in Japan, where *yoroke* had long been seen as an inevitable consequence of working in mines, in the 1930s the primary mining association (*Nihon kôzan kyôkai*) conducted several large-scale surveys on the harmful effects of silica dust.[25]

Along with the introduction of power tools and the continuing problem of ventilation in the sheds, changes in management structures at the turn of the nineteenth century undermined workers' autonomy and health and paved the way for a future mobilization against silicosis. In American foundries—as in other industries—the increase in dust was intimately linked to the decline in status and power of skilled workers. In the first decade of the twentieth century, labor relations in the Joplin District mining region of the United States deteriorated as ownership passed from entrepreneurs working in small teams to corporations. The Western Federation of Miners alleged that this growing corporatization of the mining industry and the increasing number of absentee owners had created a piecework system that amounted to a speed-up and further undermined the health of the operators.[26] Similarly, in Spain, the large size of companies operating in the lead-mining industry facilitated the widespread use of mechanical drilling in the late 1910s. In 1920, Guillermo Sánchez Martín, from the medical staff of the British-owned New Centenillo Silver Lead Mines Company, reported the inevitable onset of a new public health problem in the province of Jaén, where the company was operating.[27]

Countries that had long accepted the inevitability of lung diseases in the "dusty" trades, and those where industrialization went hand in hand with efforts to mitigate conditions such as silicosis, experienced a common impediment to enacting legislation regarding this illness. The dominance of bacteriological paradigms—and, thus, the prevalence of diagnoses of tuberculosis over silicosis—played an important role during the late nineteenth and early twentieth centuries in shaping discussions about how to address these diseases.[28] This was particularly the case in France and Germany, where Louis Pasteur and Robert Koch, respectively, became national icons. Elsewhere, it remained a matter of debate whether silicosis indeed was a disease caused by bacteria associated with the poor living conditions of miners and others working with stone. In part, the popularity of this view was linked to the influence of Koch's ideas, notably in Britain and Japan.[29] Nonetheless, as happened in France, lobbying by the mining industry also played a significant role in promoting the view that silicosis was related to tuberculosis.[30] In any case, these traditions, based on prior modes of thought, persisted as long as medical technologies remained the same. It was only in the 1920s, with the increased prevalence of and clearer standards for radiography, that it became possible for national governments—usually working together with international organizations and the international medical community—to agree on the nature of silicosis.

Mobilization and Legal Recognition

Medical knowledge, compensation and safety policies, governmental structures, management practices, and cultural traditions surrounding work-related illnesses all played a role in determining how silicosis was recognized as a political and legal issue. Nonetheless, social mobilization was the decisive factor within these institutional, political, and cultural contexts. The history of how this came about cannot be written as a simple enumeration of the actors who put the silicosis question on the public-political map; rather, it must show how, in each case, those individuals and groups interacted with a particular set of conditions. There was little agreement among experts as to what effect silicosis had on workers. Medical authorities were unsure about how the disease progressed, whether it could be clearly linked to particular workplaces, whether physical impairment was inevitable, and how much time it would take for initial symptoms to develop after exposure to silica dust. In the face of these uncertainties, social actors—not only the workers themselves, but also industry representatives, public health and social reformers, civil servants, legislators, statisticians, and the representatives of insurance companies—all had the potential, along with researchers and medical experts, to influence whether silicosis was investigated and, ultimately, whether it would become the object of special legislation. The growth of organized labor, which paved the way for collective bargaining in the face of silicosis, and the mass media both played a crucial role in advancing these questions.

Although the countries discussed in this chapter adopted their silicosis policies at different times and across several decades in the first half of the twentieth century, the process of recognition followed a general pattern that included three phases. The first was characterized by local and national upheavals, including court cases, media coverage, and pressure from trade unions, in addition to the investigations of governmental bureaucracies and scientists. The second, which most often took root after World War I, was greatly influenced by the adoption of policies on silicosis in South Africa and the United Kingdom in 1912 and 1918, respectively, and by the emergence of a new international order symbolized by the creation of the ILO in 1919. The transnational connections of trade unions also played an important role during this period. The final stage followed the 1929 and 1930 ILO conferences, which called for the legal recognition of silicosis as a compensable occupational illness and agreed on its main characteristics.

First Phase: Pre–World War I and the Primacy of National Dynamics

The first phase, from the turn of the twentieth century until the beginning of World War I, was influenced more by local factors and knowledge than by international discussions and consensus on the nature of silicosis. The labor movement, which, in the nineteenth century, was already intensively involved in questions related to occupational health, helped make connections among different areas of knowledge.[31] In the foreground were the stoneworkers' and metalworkers' unions, whose members were not only particularly affected by silicosis, but also represented skilled professions. These groups occupied a central position in the international labor movement before World War I. They also had a strong tradition of establishing self-help, or mutual-aid, associations that focused on issues such as disability and illness. Mining unions also became a powerful presence in the new industrial economies of the United States, South Africa, and Australia, achieving an influence already enjoyed by their counterparts in many of the older industrialized economies, where the state had traditionally depended on minerals for strategic and military purposes. The mining unions, which sought to maintain the often-privileged legal status of their workers (in comparison with other workers in the industrial sector), also exerted pressure. The unions most directly concerned with silica dust had a legal rather than an academic interest in the silicosis issue. They sought financial and medical provisions for workers afflicted with the lung diseases associated with their trades, regardless of whether the illness was diagnosed as tuberculosis—as was usually the case at that time—or under the new concept of silicosis. The activities of the Swiss Trade Union for Stone and Clay Workers were representative of this first stage in the process of recognition.

The media, too, played a crucial role during this period. From early on, miners' horrifying working conditions were a recurrent theme in newspapers. Yet the media had a predilection for emphasizing the effects of industrial accidents, rather than illnesses. Thus, for example, "by 1902 there had been six times more deaths from miners' phthisis in Bendigo than from mining accidents, but [these] had not received anything like a proportionate amount of attention."[32] The newspapers' focus on accidents, however, could also garner attention for the plight of miners, resulting in greater coverage of occupational diseases and political mobilization. For example, the impetus for uncovering dust hazards in the foundry industry came from an investigation by New York State that had been prompted by the worst tragedy in its industrial history. In the aftermath of the Triangle Shirtwaist Factory fire on March 25, 1911, which claimed the lives of 143 immigrant women and was covered extensively in the press. New York State established a Factory Investigating Commission to look into industrial working conditions and recommend legislation. In the commission's four years of work, its members pointed to the responsibilities of management in controlling hazards that led to disease and protecting workers from the excesses of industrialization, and they even extended their analysis of accidents and acute diseases to the issue of long-term degenerative lung disorders.[33] This dynamic of public outcry, investigation, and the attribution of fault to employers was to hold true throughout the twentieth century, demonstrated, for instance, by the tragedy at Fouquières-les-Lens in northern France on February 4, 1970. Sixteen miners were killed, prompting Jean-Paul Sartre's subsequent intervention on December 12, in the role of prosecutor of a *tribunal populaire* ("people's tribunal") that symbolically condemned the collieries as being responsible for the catastrophe.[34]

Labor conflicts also provided opportunities for the media to translate medical knowledge into newspaper sales. This was particularly the case in the United States. Publicity relating to working conditions and occupational diseases often resulted in industrial action as well as lobbies to push for improved occupational health.[35] After the anthracite strike of 1902, and during the hearings of the federal commission that followed in November of that year in Scranton, Pennsylvania, newspapers published witnesses' accounts. This helped lead to the recognition of industrial disease by physicians, operators, the miners themselves, and the general public in the anthracite region. The *New York Times* wrote of lungs as "black as coal" and pointed out that older miners could not escape "miners' asthma." The *Chicago Tribune* also seized on vivid descriptions of autopsies in an article subtitled "Few Escape the Asthma." Similarly, the *Pittsburgh Press* ran a front-page story, "Disease and Death Lurk in Coal Mines," which reported that "the avocation of miners usually brings on miners' asthma" and that "complications resulting from miners' asthma were usually fatal."[36]

During this first phrase in the process of recognizing silicosis as a political problem, public health and social reformers played a decisive role by contributing medical expertise that could be used for further social mobilization. In the United Kingdom, the creation of a powerful orthodoxy on the distinctive hazards presented by silica could be traced to a group of Home Office experts on industrial disease, including Thomas Legge and Edgar Collis, as well as scientists such as John Scott Haldane. In 1900, Legge had reported on the high death rates among men who mined ganister, a silica-rich fire clay, and described their lungs as displaying "iron grey nodules" and serious lesions. These symptoms were soon recognized as characteristic of those suffering from the prolonged inhalation of concentrated silica dust. In the UK, as elsewhere, experts in occupational medicine were often cosmopolitan in their outlook and cultivated close ties with other researchers abroad, including in Germany.[37] As a consequence, their findings on silicosis were widely shared and helped to contribute to a fledgling consensus on the condition. Similarly, the government in the state of Western Australia formed a Royal Commission in 1910, directing J. H. L. Cumpston to determine the prevalence of mining-related silicosis and tuberculosis. In doing so, Cumpston charted distinct stages of the disease, which were to have a profound impact on the diagnoses of miners around the world.[38]

Statistics and data collection also became powerful tools to marshal actions during this first stage in the recognition process for silicosis. Both played an important role in forging a consensus about the nature of this disease. In 1914, for example, the US Public Health Service and the US Bureau of Mines initiated the first detailed community study of silicosis at a federal level. This effort was conducted by Anthony J. Lanza in Missouri, Kansas, and Oklahoma, states that were involved in lead and zinc mining. Although public health workers had long accepted that heavy-metal poisoning could cause chronic diseases, the significance of Lanza's study lay in his demonstration that symptoms from toxic exposure could, and did, occur years—and sometimes decades—after exposure.[39] The role of statistics in the process of rallying support depended on the categories that were employed. In Japan, for example, in 1926, Ishihara Osamu, a physician who had become one of the Home Ministry's first labor inspectors, published a new edition of his 1913 study on health conditions in mines. In the updated version, he created the category *Kôhai* ("miners' lung disease") as a cause of death and found that it was the major factor for the mining sector, contributing to almost a quarter of all mortality in that industry.[40]

Statistics and data were not, however, exclusively within the purview of social reformers with ties to government. In the United States around 1910, Frederick Hoffman, a statistician for the Prudential Life Insurance Company, and

Louis Dublin, his counterpart at the Metropolitan Life Insurance Company, were especially receptive to workers' claims that pneumatic tools were a source of disease because workers' experiences using this type of machinery helped explain the morbidity and mortality rates these insurance giants were encountering. Hoffman and Dublin gathered enormous amounts of related evidence, documenting disease, disability, and death rates among every conceivable industrial population.[41]

By the outbreak of World War I, therefore, a number of different sources located in various countries around the globe had contributed to making silicosis a political issue. The major turning point at this time, however, was South Africa's adoption of a policy on silicosis in 1912. After Haldane's 1903 study that confirmed higher death rates among Cornish miners returning from the goldfields of South Africa, silica was recognized as representing a serious danger to the health of workers. For experts in the United Kingdom, the incidence of tuberculosis was a complex etiological question, as well as a complicating factor in advanced silicosis.[42] Herbert Samuel, undersecretary of state for the Home Office, concluded that silicosis was a tangible threat in very dusty trades. He thought, however, that the milder and earlier forms of this illness—with a subsequent loss of earnings if miners were fired when they were identified as being sick—were a significant threat to the overall welfare of the workforce, outweighing the benefits of legislating on compensation for the relatively few advanced cases. Silicosis was not, therefore, added to the prescribed list of diseases attached to the 1906 Workmen's Compensation Act.[43] The debate was shaped by concerns about protecting the earnings of the family breadwinner, rather than by an overriding principle that disease must be prevented at all costs.

The nature of the debate and subsequent legislation in South Africa was rather different. Between 1910 and 1912, a broad consensus was reached that the impact of silicosis should be contained by preventive action and regular screenings of the underground workforce, with periodic exams for miners by a specialized group of physicians, as well as by scientists and technicians in related fields. In contrast to the United Kingdom, the question of tuberculosis was also addressed, not by seeking to link lung disease to the physical proximity of silica rock, but by continuing with the nineteenth-century lexicon of phthisis and by screening for tuberculosis as well as dust-related occupational diseases. In practice, workers were compensated for a loss of employment due to tuberculosis as well as silicosis. This contrasted with the British model for compensation, which was finally extended to silicosis in 1918 but still excluded the mining sector.

The interesting point about the parallel experience of South Africa and Britain is that the growth of scientific and medical knowledge progressed steadily in the first two decades of the twentieth century and made a seminal contribution to an international network of expertise that provided a consensus on the nature of silicosis before the 1930 Johannesburg Congress. Yet the relationship of tuberculosis to silicosis remained unresolved, and the threat posed by other dusts and fibers, including asbestos, was already apparent by 1930. Not least, even though both countries legally recognized silicosis as an occupational illness that merited compensation, they adopted policies that provided minimal solutions to the problem. The fact that miners, who were among the most severely affected, were excluded from the 1918 British policy, and that white workers in South Africa were granted priority treatment, are testaments to this trend.

Despite these broad similarities in and connections between the experiences of both countries, their legislative and legal responses to the hazards of silica remained distinctive. Putting aside the racial and colonial dimensions of the South African situation, as well as the specificities of the gold-mining industry, an important factor in the contrasting experiences of these two countries was the differing size of the mining sector (which was carried out on a larger scale and was more significant to the country's economy in South Africa) and the strategic importance of metal mining in South Africa, compared with the United Kingdom. Another difference was that, in the massive British coal-mining industry, employers rallied to prevent coal dust from coming under similar suspicions. By contrast, their South African counterparts felt the need to deal head on with silicosis but restricted their efforts to the white, numerically inferior part of the workforce. Only through a prolonged struggle in the courts, and political pressure, did British coal-workers' unions finally compel governments to recognize that coal workers could suffer from lung disease, and that such diseases did not always depend on the immediate presence of silica-rich rock in the workplace. Coal workers finally entered the "various industries" compensation plan in 1929, and by 1953, the requirements for awarding compensation had gradually been relaxed. Through the force of such campaigns, and by fostering contact with the ILO, British trade unions in coal and other sectors were, to some degree, able to shift the agenda of international research during these years.

Outside the British Empire, it was only after World War I that occupational illnesses were added to existing accident insurance programs—but these usually excluded silicosis. By 1918, Switzerland was leading the way. The Swiss Institute for Accident Insurance was modeled after German accident insurance institutions. As the Swiss authorities tried to build a state-of-the-art social-insurance system, however, they opted for the modern approach of offering comprehensive coverage, including, for example, accidents associated with leisure activities and occupational illnesses. It certainly helped that the Swiss Institute for Accident Insurance was a tripartite organization, in which trade unions, employer associations, and governmental authorities were equally represented. This contrasts with German professional insurance associations (*Berufsgenossenschaften*), in which employers' interests dominated,[44] and where, therefore, social-insurance authorities were reluctant to provide coverage for occupational illnesses. The driving force here was the Ministry of Labor under the left-wing government of the Weimar Republic, which introduced a list of compensable occupational illnesses in 1925. It classified 11 ailments as occupational illnesses to be insured within the statutory accident insurance program, but—again—silicosis was not on the list. Like Germany and Switzerland, other nations, such as France and Belgium, adopted policies on occupational illness in the 1920s and 1930s, but none included silicosis in their early legislation in this domain.[45]

Although silicosis was not usually covered by social insurance, the introduction of these legal provisions was nevertheless an important step in the recognition process. It increased the authority of physicians as arbiters on the question of whether a specific illness was work related (and therefore counted as an occupational disease). The rise of medical expertise was particularly evident in the new discipline of industrial medicine, which played an important role in shaping discussions about silicosis during this period.[46] Thus, in the 1920s, debates about recognizing silicosis gained momentum, not least because the newly founded ILO and various international trade unions acted as catalysts. As a result, recognition was achieved in a variety of states around the globe during the 1920s and 1930s. Nonetheless, the provisions made for silicosis at this time were generally minimal, either granting compensation to a select group of workers, or ensuring that it was extremely difficult to prove a causal link between one's employment and affliction with the disease.

In this respect, at the outset of its medico-legal recognition, silicosis constituted a test case, due to its severity and the huge numbers of workers exposed to risk. Then, as now, the hazards of silica dust held up a magnifying glass to the ambiguities of the very definition of occupational disease, which was by no means a purely scientific category derived from the most up-to-date medical knowledge of its time. The diagnosis of an occupational disease was, in a way, a disputed social right determined by an economic and political balance of power.

Second Phase: The 1920s and the Expansion of the Transnational Arena

The second phase in the process of recognition began shortly before World War I but took off during the 1920s. It was characterized by intensive transnational and international connections, particularly among scientific experts and trade unions. The starting point was the recognition, within the British Empire, of various kinds of pulmonary ailments that differed from the generic diagnosis of tuberculosis. The 1912 law on silicosis compensation in South Africa, and a similar policy adopted in the United Kingdom in 1918, sparked a new era of transnational and international discussion about the nature of silicosis and possible means to address it politically.

Despite the new policies in the British Empire, the medical community in continental Europe, as elsewhere, was reluctant to fully accept this concept of silicosis. Moreover, governmental authorities saw little room for maneuvering in terms of enacting legislation related to the disease, given that, at the time, and in contrast to the United Kingdom and South Africa, few countries had policies in place for occupational illness. In German-speaking countries, occupational physicians accepted the diagnosis of silicosis relatively early. Nonetheless, the small group researching the illness found little acceptance of their opinion within the broader medical community and, in any case, their views were met with anxiety by social-insurance programs, which recognized the incalculably large costs implicit in the legal recognition of silicosis.[47] In France, as soon as the primary mining firms began to sense international pressure for silicosis compensation, they convened a committee of four prominent university professors, who soon came to act as mouthpieces for the industry's interests.[48] This quartet negated the existence, autonomy, and seriousness of silicosis, making an impression on senior officials in government and sowing confusion in the minds of the occupational physicians who confronted the effects of silicosis on a day-to-day basis. As a result, this group of eminent experts played a major role in postponing legal recognition of the disease in France until as late as 1945.[49]

It was only with the entry of new actors—in particular, international trade union organizations—that the situation began to change. Encouraged by the British and South African examples, the International Stoneworkers' Union—significantly, a skilled-workers' union—advocated for the official recognition of silicosis as a disease distinct from tuberculosis at its 1921 conference in Innsbruck, Austria.[50] In 1922, the organization began lobbying various national governments to recognize pulmonary ailments as occupational illnesses and provide compensation for these conditions under their respective national accident insurance policies. The union provided a range of statistics to make its case but was heavily criticized by the medical community; ultimately, governmental administrators ignored the union's proposal. It was this failure to advance its cause through national channels that, by 1924, pushed the International Stoneworkers' Union to seek an alternative route and contact the ILO to investigate silicosis.[51] The director of the ILO, the former Socialist armaments minister of France, Albert Thomas, personally took up the plight of the stoneworkers' union and transferred the group's file to Luigi Carozzi's Industrial Hygiene Section.[52] It was under such circumstances that the IHS endeavored to have silicosis recognized as an occupational illness, working its way through piles of correspondence and holding numerous meetings, starting in Düsseldorf in 1928.[53]

The ILO's struggle to create an international consensus about silicosis was accompanied by a well-targeted lobbying campaign involving the crucial players from the national level as well as international networks of social reform professionals (in this case, those involved in social medicine, from factory doctors to industrial hygienists). The Permanent Commission on Occupational Health, where Carozzi had gained his international experience before World War I, contributed to shaping this transnational forum, which was of strategic importance for the ILO, partly by trying to link, as much as possible, its thrice-yearly International Congress on Occupational Illnesses with ILO action. In this way, the Clinica del Lavoro, the nerve center of the PCOH, spread its influence far beyond Italy, to the emergent world of occupational medicine. The commission's members not only contributed to the ILO's crucial network of expert advisors, but they also worked as activists and trailblazers by reporting back to their own countries on the state of the transnational debate and by pushing for the adoption of an international convention that would recognize silicosis as a distinct occupational disease. Through these members, the ILO set up a sort of circulatory system, where medical information flowed into the center to be summarized, was then directed out to national and local branches, and subsequently was converted into arguments for political pressure.

The case for the recognition of silicosis benefited from this collaboration when the PCOH placed the illness on the agenda of its 1929 international conference in Lyons[54]—the famous meeting where both British and South African research was presented and debated.[55] For European medicine, this was a major step toward the rejection of the French "Pasteurian" and German "Kochian" views on the bacterial origins of pulmonary illnesses which implied that silicosis was somehow related to tuberculosis. This questioning of the tubercular root of silicosis had a direct influence on how the accident insurance systems would come to treat silicosis itself.[56] Despite this breakthrough, one should not focus exclusively on the accomplishments of the wave of conferences from 1928 to 1930. Limitations of knowledge nonetheless persisted—due, partly, to the objective scientific difficulties of measuring and understanding the health effects of silica dust, as well as to the more-or-less hidden agendas of companies' medical experts.

Third Phase: The 1930s and the Age of International Recognition

In the third phase, the process of recognition was rapid. As it became clear that occupational medicine, both within the ILO and among international conferences of specialists, would accept silicosis as a work-related illness in its own right, various accident insurance programs throughout the world began to follow suit. For example, the Professional Mining Association (*Knappschafts-Berufsgenossenschaft*), which was part of the German accident insurance system, decided as early as 1929 that silicosis and related pulmonary ailments should be seen as occupational illnesses and added to the list of compensable diseases that had been legislated in 1925. The distinction between silicosis and tuberculosis was abandoned, in the sense that the new law saw that dust-related cases of tuberculosis were always linked to some form of silicosis and therefore had to be compensated through social insurance.[57]

In Germany, as elsewhere, the new legislation on silicosis was quite restrictive, echoing the ambiguities and limitations of the conclusions of the Johannesburg conference.[58] In the German case, this law only allowed the most important occupations to be insured under the new program, and only those suffering from severe silicosis were entitled to compensation.[59] In particular, silicosis was understood in a narrow sense. As had been the case in the United Kingdom 10 years earlier, only illnesses caused by stone dust, not coal dust, were to be covered by social insurance—which automatically excluded the sizeable coal industry from the new policy. These limitations reflected the strong influence of the employer-dominated Professional Mining Association in Germany, which lobbied for a watered-down version of the law.[60] Three years later, the Swiss Accident Insurance Board followed suit, again with a narrow definition of silicosis, restricting it to stone-related professions (a distinction that mattered less in Switzerland, a country lacking a substantial coal-mining industry).[61]

These policies emulated those adopted by other countries in the 1920s, before the ILO's involvement in investigating the issue. For example, Chile had already adopted a policy on workplace accidents and occupational illness in 1924, following intensive lobbying by workers in its significant copper industry, but the new law only allowed compensation for silicosis if the disease was reported within one year of contracting it. This provision made it almost impossible to make such a claim, given that the disease took years to develop.[62] Likewise, in 1924 in Japan, the Home Ministry headed an official inquiry into occupational illnesses, including respiratory diseases from mining. An investigation into the Ashio copper mine in 1925 proved to be a critical turning point: the ancient condition known as *yoroke* was recognized by governmental experts as an occupational illness that would require further inspection, prevention, and compensation. By 1927, the government set up a sickness insurance policy that allowed compensation for all illnesses, private and professional alike, and was financed by contributions from employers and employees. In 1930, the Japanese plan permitted compensation for silicosis itself, but additional provisions in the country's general sickness insurance—such as a funeral allowance and a long-term disability pension—were minimal and difficult to obtain.

Similarly, the policy on silicosis adopted in the United Kingdom in 1918 met with repeated opposition, this time in the form of court cases, and therefore it saw revisions in 1928 and again in 1931. Finally, in 1934, a more comprehensive scheme was introduced, foreshadowing the path that other nations would eventually follow.[63] The legal battles continued over how long a worker must have been employed in an industry in order to qualify for compensation and over the eligibility of coal workers to register claims. The Silicosis Medical

Board, established in 1931, continued to reject large numbers of compensation claims in its first decade of existence.

Stagnation and Setbacks: Impact of the 1930s and World War II

From a global perspective, the 1930s and 1940s were an ambivalent period for the development of legal provisions in cases of silicosis. On the one hand, more countries decided to recognize the new occupational illness, even—as in the case of Italy and France—in the strained conditions of the wartime economy after 1939. Moreover, several countries that had already enacted legislation on silicosis, such as Chile and Japan, expanded coverage of the illness under their systems of compensation. On the other hand, countries that had already recognized the illness, such as Germany and Switzerland, experienced serious setbacks in their endeavors against silicosis, both during the Great Depression and World War II. Despite this diversity of experiences, there were some global commonalities in how silicosis was handled during the 1930s and 1940s, and especially during World War II and its aftermath. The war created an intense need for coal, coupled with obstacles to importing it. A lack of workers meant that increasing national production was often difficult: many miners were sent off to war or made prisoners, and immigration suddenly became almost impossible.

As the example of World War II reveals, the legal recognition of silicosis, once achieved, was fragile. The German and Japanese cases are especially revealing in this respect. In Germany, protection for individuals suffering from silicosis deteriorated gradually over the course of the 1930s. Under National Socialism, reducing the costs associated with silicosis was the central motivation for research into the disease. After the seizure of power by the National Socialists, employers began to take greater control of the powerful Professional Mining Association, which was part of the country's accident insurance system.[64] Nonetheless, research into the illness was actually strengthened during this period. The Professional Mining Association supported two silicosis institutes, including Bergmannsheil, the large clinic at Bochum that was a leading international authority in the field. This cost-savings ethos was further reflected in the actions of accident insurance programs, which became more restrictive in their treatment of compensation recipients. Employers, who dominated the accident insurance system, played an important role here. They held their own against the German Workers' Front (*Deutsche Arbeitsfront*), the united trade union under the National Socialist government. With rapid rearmament after the beginning of the first Four Year Plan in 1936, both the government and the Professional Mining Association maintained their strong position against miners. The association even ceased the preventive measure of periodically changing workers' tasks in order to limit their exposure to silica dust, and it also reduced medical exams to the legal minimum. Moreover, the pathological criteria for financial compensation were reevaluated, and only those patients with advanced silicosis were eligible for treatment or compensation.[65]

The longer the war carried on, the more the social and political principles behind Germany's accident insurance policy receded. Only prevention was strengthened. At the same time, however, workers were pressured not to leave their jobs if they were diagnosed with silicosis. In the last years of the war, partly due to the lack of available physicians, mine regulation had almost withered away. As a consequence of National Socialist rearmament policies and World War II, health conditions for German miners seriously deteriorated over the course of the 1930s and 1940s.[66]

The Japanese case, however, was less straightforward. On the one hand, the country's war economy saw a focus on the expansion of heavy industry and the securing of a stable food supply, as well as the widespread use of Korean and Chinese forced labor in mines. Together with the cessation of all collaboration with the ILO in 1938, the result was that industrial hygienists employed by the Japanese government neglected the prevention of silicosis. For instance, Ônishi Seiji, the most prominent expert on silicosis in the Home Ministry Social Bureau, now focused exclusively on food supply and the introduction of a minimum wage.[67] Moreover, the Japanese Society for Industrial Hygiene, which had been the main platform for scientific debates on silicosis before the war, shifted its focus to an epidemic of tuberculosis among female workers, who were increasingly being integrated into the war economy.[68]

On the other hand, the public health policies that were adopted during the war, and their biopolitical implications, prepared the ground for an improved recognition of and screening for silicosis during peacetime. In 1938, the revision of the 1929 Rules for Industrial Hygiene and the Prevention of Workplace Accidents (*Kôjô kigai yôbô oyobi eisei kisoku*) compelled businesses with more than 500 employees to designate a factory physician.[69] In 1942, the Factory Act (*Kôjôhô*) was revised, now requiring workers to undergo a medical exam within the first 30 days of taking up a new job. Most factories had to provide yearly medical exams, while those in "dangerous" trades were required to offer biannual exams. Moreover, examination records had to be kept for at least three years. For small- and medium-sized enterprises without the financial resources necessary to carry out these medical procedures, the 1940 Act on the Physical Condition of the Population (*Kokumin tairyoku hô*) provided health centers. Some of these small businesses, under the umbrella of the Patriotic Committee for Industrial Service (*Sangyô hôkokukai*), an organization modeled on the German Workers' Front, acquired ambulant x-ray equipment for tuberculosis screening that, after the war, allowed a nationwide survey of silicosis to be conducted.[70]

As the examples of wartime Germany and Japan reveal, silicosis was a disease whose legal status, as well as its detection and prevention in the workplace, fluctuated significantly according to economic and political factors. In Spain and France, too, similar dynamics were at play during this period in terms of how silicosis was handled. Nonetheless, each country had a very different experience of World War II.

Spain was not a combatant in World War II, but its Francoist government bore certain similarities to the Vichy regime that had been set up in France during the war, such as their corporatist organization of labor. Spain was a neutral country but, due to the ideology of its regime and the echoes of its civil war, its rulers aimed at an autarkist (self-sufficient) economic policy. Yet this placed the government under pressure, not least to secure an abundant production of coal. In the 1930s, Spain's short-lived Republican government had finally put an end to the fierce resistance of employers toward any law on occupational diseases—and toward any law that would cover more than the three diseases recognized by the 1925 ILO convention (lead and mercury poisoning and anthrax infection). Pressure from organized labor had been intensifying since the 1920s. Its arguments were supported by Spanish physicians, who had closely monitored the ILO conferences on silicosis, even if their country had not participated directly. In 1936, Spain adopted a law on occupational diseases that, in comparative international terms, covered an extensive list of illnesses, including silicosis.[71]

France, too, had been influenced by the findings of the international conferences organized by the ILO between 1928 and 1930, and then by its 1934 international convention. The same year, the popular democrat Henry Meck and the socialist André-Jules-Louis Breton put forward two separate proposals, both calling on government to extend the list of occupational diseases that were eligible for compensation to silicosis or to all pulmonary afflictions linked to silica dust, limestone, or clay dust. After much debate, including resistance from employers' lobbies and the physicians and university researchers representing them, both proposals fell, revealing the weakness of the Popular Front government. The Communist Party, along with the support of Catholic trade unions and the tacit assistance of the ILO, then made the issue its prerogative, pursuing a law on silicosis for the next several years. Economic circumstances in France favored fierce resistance from the mining sector. Coal was a major national industry with a huge workforce, and, since the creation of a social-insurance scheme for occupational diseases in 1919, it had been left entirely up to employers to meet the costs associated with occupational diseases. As a result, employers' medical experts advocated the tubercular origins of silicosis, which meant shifting responsibility for expenses linked with it onto the health insurance systems developed in 1928 and 1930, which were jointly financed by employers and wage earners.[72]

How did the war affect the situation in these two countries? It was only in 1941—five years after its 1936 act—that Spain created a fully functioning silicosis program covering three industrial sectors. The plan had, in part, been influenced by the new Francoist regime's desire to appeal to workers.[73] Compensation for those suffering from silicosis who were employed in the gold mines was comparatively generous, as this industry had a very limited workforce and was a state-run company that, in line with the government's autarkic philosophy, had been created after the nationalization of the country's gold mines. In comparison, the refractory industries, which were spread over tiny family companies, were far less generous in the silicosis compensation they offered. Only 159 refractory workers—out of a much larger labor force, comprising tens of thousands of workers—were granted compensation from 1946 to 1950, a number equivalent to the total of everyone in the gold mines who had applied (all of whose claims were upheld). The third sector, lead mining, was also in private hands and equally hostile to silicosis compensation plans, not only because of the financial burden of compensation, but also because medical exams threatened to drive away skilled workers diagnosed with silicosis. The industry's strategy—slowing down the frequency of such exams—anticipated that of the collieries when they entered the compensation program three years later. Citing large numbers of workers and a shortage of medical instruments and materials as their justification, employers minimized the number of medical exams and, consequently, the recognition of silicosis among coal miners.[74]

France reached a comparable outcome by following a very different path. Pressure from the ILO and progressive international recognition slowly helped change French physicians' minds. This process reached a high point during the war, at a 1943 meeting organized by the collieries in Saint-Étienne. The Vichy government considered the issue of silicosis to be a priority, in light of the alarming miners' strikes of 1941. Further impetus came from the importance of the mining industry to the war effort and the difficulty of securing an adequate workforce. Yet the program still faced opposition from employers. France did not introduce its first law on silicosis until 1945. The new Republican government was quick to herald the policy as a triumph for the miners who had toiled during the war, particularly as the Communist Party was part of the alliance that had helped bring about the new law and nationalize the mining sector. Political propaganda aside, the ordinance was largely the outcome of a compromise that had already been negotiated under the Vichy regime. The new act was shaped by the difficult circumstances of its genesis. It acknowledged the existence of silicosis and made provisions for its compensation, but it set such difficult conditions that, in the following decades, they would prove to be almost arbitrary. In a rather remarkable way, the 1945 ordinance explicitly called on physicians working in the mining sector to balance health considerations with a concern for the economic viability of the sector.[75]

In both Spain and France, therefore, priorities were divided during the 1930s and 1940s between protecting the workforce and heeding employers' objections. This was particularly the case in sectors where labor was badly needed (or, more precisely, where skilled workers were lacking), or where the unions managed, at least for a while, to attract the attention of the public or create a strategic power struggle with employers. This balance often reached its peak in the collieries. The outcome very much depended, often in surprising ways, on the political context. The ideological determinations of the governing political parties were far from the only driving forces, however, particularly when compared with the constraints of political propaganda. Meanwhile, advancements in medical science were never effective per se. International conferences were crucial in increasing the visibility of new knowledge about silicosis and in proving that silica dust itself was a cause of disease. But their lessons had to be carried further in the various countries, usually by individual physicians, who sometimes were marginal actors. The outcome of this intricate web was rarely black and white. Rather than a clear distinction between recognition and nonrecognition of silicosis, its acknowledgment came in a more subtle form, combining restrictive legal provisions with limited control over the implementation of the law.

Like France and Spain, Italy was in no hurry to enact legislation, despite the intensity of international exchanges championed by the ILO from 1928 onward. The Medical Inspectorate of the Office of Labor, whose head, Giovanni Loriga, had attended the conference in Johannesburg, noted that in Italy, many doctors did not "believe in the existence of a pure pneumoconiosis that could in itself be the cause of the inability to work."[76] There was much disagreement among the Italian medical community about the nature of silicosis, because it so often seemed to overlap with other illnesses, especially tuberculosis. As always with silicosis, however, this state-of-the-art diagnosis and these controversies did not originate in purely scientific, abstract considerations. Silicosis was not widespread on the Italian peninsula, which served as a disincentive for action; only discrete areas, especially Veneto in the north of the country, gave grounds for concern.[77] A further barrier was the attitude of the Fascist government under Mussolini, which favored workers with its Charter of Labor of 1927 but also sought to bolster economic growth—to the disadvantage of laborers.[78]

Last but not least, national social-insurance provisions and the economic organization of the workforce played a decisive role in shaping physicians' perceptions. For example, Italy's 1927 adoption of a national social-insurance law regarding tuberculosis further complicated national decisions about how to proceed with the silicosis question. As this insurance was funded by workers, employers, and, indirectly, the state (e.g., through the provision of hospitals and oversight), it was in employers' interests to attribute silicosis cases to tuberculosis. Therefore, Fascist Italy did not adopt a policy on silicosis until 1943. Important actors in the creation of the law were the corporatist trade unions, which helped workers bring their cases to court, in part because they would receive a share of any compensation that was awarded. Yet employers, too, played a key role in bringing about a silicosis compensation policy after a major lawsuit against the Falck steel mill outside Milan proved that paying compensation out of their own pockets—rather than through the Fascist social-insurance programs—was an undesirable and expensive alternative.[79] Despite the ratification of the new law, however, the necessary regulations to implement it were only enacted in 1960.[80]

In Italy, as elsewhere, the numbers of workers thought to be at risk played a decisive role, and the (Fascist) government seized the moment and latched onto silicosis as a means of legitimating its own agendas. Moreover, Italy's recognition of the disease in 1943 did not mean that the law was easily implemented. Particularly striking, too, was the role played by social insurance: the existence of a tuberculosis provision hindered the recognition of silicosis because employers preferred to pass costs on to social-insurance programs, where the burden of funding was shared with wage earners.

This dynamic was widespread and is perhaps most evident in Japan. It legislated on silicosis as early as 1930, partly because the workers' health insurance law of 1927 had diverted most of the financial responsibility for occupational diseases to a new general insurance program. As a result, Japanese employers had no reason to oppose silicosis as a "regular," private disease like tuberculosis. This changed after World War II, when the silicosis issue reemerged in the context of the food shortage crisis that followed Japan's military defeat. In 1946, at the Ashio copper mine, a campaign by locals targeted at food shortages quickly turned into a protest against the social costs for local families afflicted by *yoroke*. After a governmental investigation—along with negotiations on the issue with the US occupying authority—Japan adopted a more comprehensive policy on silicosis in 1955.[81]

Paradoxically, as the case of Japan shows, countries that had adopted a social-insurance program for health issues—a system generally considered more socially advanced and, at a minimum, fitting in with the ILO's standards— were not necessarily the ones most open to acknowledgment of the disease. In the preponderance of countries in which such a program was implemented, lengthy and obstinate resistance by employers delayed the recognition of silicosis. But this process produced a number of surprising national variations.

For example, in 1937 in Belgium, a royal decree recognized different forms of pneumoconiosis as occupational diseases in particular industries, excluding coal mining. Coal miners had to wait until 1963 to see the adoption of a law on silicosis. The reason for this excessive delay (by that time, silicosis was recognized throughout most of the world) is that the 1937 decree resulted from a deal made with the unions which transferred the cost of compensation for silicosis to the social-insurance programs responsible for disabilities. This financial compromise might have lasted longer if it had not failed to address the plight of the many migrant workers (who largely came from Italy) afflicted with the disease. Working in conjunction with the General Federation of Belgian Workers, Italian activists organized two congresses on silicosis in Liège, in January 1960 and March 1963, which ultimately resulted in governmental action on the issue.[82] And, the Italian Communist Party played an important role by organizing underground militant action for the acquisition of political and social rights for Italian workers in Belgium.

In the United States, by contrast, no system of social insurance for healthcare or long-term disability existed during this period, meaning that, in some ways, it was easier to make headway in pushing for the legal recognition of silicosis. In this context, it was largely the opportunities—and the despair—brought about by the Great Depression that resulted in a concerted lobbying for and success with legislation on silicosis. Writing to Eleanor Roosevelt, the secretary of a local trade union offered to send the First Lady "plenty of factual and documentary evidence that men are dying like flies and that 8 out of 10 women in this district are widows; 75 percent of the children orphans."[83] Indeed, during the Depression, workers were thrown out of work and families were forced to support the disabled on little or no income. In this context, arguments about responsibility for occupational illnesses and disability took on a new urgency and meaning. Many unemployed workers in the dusty trades therefore turned to the courts. While employed workers, fearful of losing their jobs during this economic crisis, may have been hesitant to report their symptoms to company physicians, the unemployed had nothing to lose and used any means necessary to survive.

As more and more US workers in the foundries and other silica industries turned to the courts for redress, judges became increasingly likely to hold companies accountable for deaths and disabilities resulting from silicosis. In New York State alone, in 1933 the foundry industry faced lawsuit claims and costs of over $30 million. In 1936, in the midst of the liability crisis, the revelation surfaced that perhaps as many as 1,500 workers had been killed by exposure to silica dust while working on a tunnel project in Gauley Bridge, West Virginia. Newspapers and magazines all over the country ensured that the scandal became a national issue. It was in this context that the foundry industry and their insurance representatives introduced a bill in the New York State legislature to add silicosis to the list of occupational diseases covered by workers' compensation. Ultimately, New York, like many other American states during this period, amended its workers' compensation law to include all occupational diseases, including silicosis, thereby preventing workers from going to court to sue companies and their insurers over liability claims, which could prove to be a much more costly avenue.[84]

By contrast, in Switzerland, the economic conditions of the 1930s and 1940s meant a declining interest in silicosis and its prevention, despite the fact that the illness was newly covered by the Swiss Institute for Accident Insurance, starting in 1932. When the institute first began to compensate victims of silicosis, its governing board significantly underestimated the risk, believing that a country like Switzerland, lacking a substantial coal-mining industry, would not produce more than a few cases per year. The board ignored the fact that the construction of dams and military structures in the Alps, rich in quartzose stones, caused thousands of cases of quartz-related silicosis. Moreover, the institute neglected prevention. During the Great Depression, it had difficulty convincing employers of the advantage of an active prevention policy. With the onset of World War II, prevention was entirely neglected, leading to a sizeable jump in the number of cases of silicosis. This upswing was mainly caused by the war-related expropriation of coal reserves, the intensified construction of electric plants in the Alps and, above all, the erection of military fortifications. The number of silicosis victims in Switzerland increased during the war. Those involved in construction and mining for military purposes were particularly endangered, as, first of all, the military administration was under enormous time pressure and, second, conditions during the wartime economy meant that measures to prevent accidents were not always enforced. Between 1932 and 1937, therefore, the Swiss Institute for Accident Insurance calculated that there were 136 cases of silicosis; around a decade later, between 1943 and 1947, it found nearly 10 times as many (1,225 cases). Moreover, the mortality rate for this generation of silicosis sufferers was particularly high. In 1952, the institute reported that 25 percent of the workers involved in digging tunnels died from silicosis, with a further 25 percent disabled. The majority of these cases stemmed from the war years. It was not until 1944 that the Institute for Accident Insurance was able to compel the Swiss government to institute a new policy on silicosis that would emphasize prevention, as well as provide improved medical assistance that would lead to an earlier diagnosis. But the disaster had already occurred. Silicosis was to become the most expensive of all injuries insured by the national accident insurance program. During the twentieth century, the institute compensated more than 11,000 cases of silicosis, including 4,000 instances of disability and 3,000 deaths.[85]

Conclusion

The process of enacting legislation regarding silicosis in the first half of the twentieth century was both universal and particular. On the one hand, there were a number of common elements that characterized how different countries around the globe recognized silicosis as a medical, insurance, and political problem worthy of both prevention and compensation. Many of these elements were really transnational, in that they crossed and superseded national borders. This is true, first and foremost, of the international medical debates that developed and gathered speed in the late nineteenth century and then grew, especially during the interwar period, which progressively brought about a real change in the spread of knowledge and a relative agreement about silicosis. International organisations such as the ILO and international medical associations also played a crucial role in these developments. What we have shown in this chapter is that near-universal experiences of industrialization and war, along with the entanglements brought about by the expansion of empires and the international migration of workers, also determined the common course of recognizing silicosis as a political problem during this period.

International transfers between national actors such as government authorities, trade unions, and academic communities helped foster the emergence of similar processes in different countries. The first factor, in each case, was that existing systems of compensation and prevention had a major impact. It mattered whether disability, sickness, or tuberculosis insurance was already in place in a country that was considering the enactment of silicosis legislation, and whether occupational diseases were compensated by a specific program exclusively financed by employers. The second factor was what kind of prevention system was in place; whether that system employed inspectors or similar agents who could collect information also played a role. The third decisive factor was the proportion of the workforce believed to be exposed to the risk. Countries with a limited mining sector were often more open to recognizing silicosis, although the extent of its presence in other industries sometimes proved to be a nasty surprise. The shock experienced by Switzerland, with its unexpectedly high (and financially costly) wave of deaths during that country's intense tunneling activity over the course of World War II, is a case in point.

All of these dynamics help us to understand why, despite the diversity of national features, there was a great deal of commonality in the process of recognizing silicosis: from the late nineteenth century until the early 1960s, vastly different countries around the globe were subjected to the same three ranges of factors in debating and enacting legislation on silicosis. It is important, however, not to overstate the commonalities in this global history. Local and national experiences and cultural norms, along with differing legal systems, economies, and scientific traditions, also shaped the ways in which silicosis became a political issue in each country.

Given the multitude of factors involved, it is not surprising that the ambivalent treatment of silicosis continued into the postwar period. On the one hand, a number of countries adopted more comprehensive polices on the disease. The Progressive Popular Front government in Chile, for example, introduced a new silicosis law in 1952. On the other hand, the process of recognition was clearly incomplete. While the efforts of the ILO, international associations of workers and experts, and powerful connections within the British Empire, as well as the common processes of industrialization, shaped experiences with silicosis in the first half of the twentieth century, these developments did not touch all parts of the globe. Today, silicosis continues to wend its way around the world, marking a new era of political recognition as recently developing countries embark on a process of rapid industrialization. In the countries that did recognize the disease, their legislation regarding silicosis was never definitive: court cases would continue to test the compensation policies, which generally made it very difficult for workers or their dependents to gain financial assistance. Moreover, the enduring problem of migrant workers, whose rights to compensation were continually curtailed with respect to silicosis, remains a particularly vexing issue to this day.

In most cases, the difficulties of recognizing silicosis left their traces on the legislation that was meant to address it, creating lasting effects. Of crucial importance has been not only what, from a medical and legal point of view, silicosis *is*, but also what it is *not*. To a great extent, recognition of this illness has been limited or conditional. The following chapter will turn to the effects of these initial loopholes in the regulation of the disease, starting with compensation.

NOTES

1. For the history of German mining regulations in the late nineteenth and early twentieth centuries, see Geyer, *Die Reichsknappschaft.*
2. Kolb, *Die Berufsverhältnisse*, 15–27.

3. Ibid., 17–18, 22–27, 85–102.
4. Ibid., 73–82.
5. Burnham, *Accident Prone.*
6. For South Africa, see chapter 3.
7. For an overview of these systems, see Knowles, "State Control."
8. Romano, *Fabbriche, operai, ingegneri,* 71–74.
9. Teleky, *History,* 22–51.
10. This was particularly the case in Germany. See W. Ewald, *Soziale Medizin,* 2: 661.
11. See Mintz, "Hard Rock Miners' Phthisis," esp. 79–87.
12. Geerkens, "Entre soins et prevention."
13. See chapter 2. Also see Miura, *Rôdô to kenkô no rekishi,* 7: 206–207; Menéndez-Navarro, "Politics of Silicosis."
14. Horstman, "Om het beheer."
15. The organization was later called the International Congress on Workplace Injuries and Social Insurance, and renamed again as the International Congress on Social Insurance.
16. Moses, "Contesting Risk"; Moses, "Policy Communities."
17. Kaufmann, *Handbuch der Unfallmedizin,* 5–7; Horn, "Unfallversicherungsmedizin"; "50 Jahre Schweizerische Gesellschaft."
18. Moses, *The First Modern Risk,* ch. 4.
19. Teleky, *History,* 1–15.
20. Thomann, "L'hygiène nationale"; Thomann, *La naissance.* See also chapter 5.
21. For the Swiss chemical industries in Basel, see Schaad, *Chemische Stoffe,* 189–220.
22. Rosner and Markowitz, *Deadly Dust: Silicosis and the On-Going Struggle,* 22, 39.
23. Kippen, "Social and Political Meaning," 492.
24. Rosner and Markowitz, *Deadly Dust: Silicosis and the On-Going Struggle,* 23.
25. Thomann, "L'hygiène nationale," 158–160.
26. Rosner and Markowitz, *Deadly Dust: Silicosis and the On-Going Struggle,* 53, 143–144.
27. Menéndez-Navarro, "Politics of Silicosis," 81–82.
28. In addition to chapter 2, see Lengwiler, "Internationale Expertennetzwerke."
29. Mintz, "Hard Rock Miners' Phthisis," 59–72; Thomann, "L'hygiène nationale," 145–146.
30. Devinck and Rosental, "'Une maladie sociale.'"
31. On the early efforts of trade unions in lobbying for occupational health measures, see Teleky, *History,* 75–86. On Britain, see McIvor and Johnston, *Miners' Lung,* 188–196, which looks at the actions of the Miners' Federation of Great Britain. In the 1920s and early 1930s, the Miners' Federation sought to put silicosis on the map and seek compensation for it by bringing together medical, governmental, and other reports on silicosis and related illnesses. See also M. Bloor, "South Wales Miners Federation."
32. Kippen, "Social and Political Meaning," 492. For a comparison with the Courrières catastrophe in 1906 in France, see Varaschin and Laloux, *10 mars 1906: Courrières*; Centre Historique Minier. *10 mars 1906: La catastrophe*; Chatriot and Fontaine, "Courrières."
33. Rosner and Markowitz, *Deadly Dust: Silicosis and the On-Going Struggle,* 58.
34. On the profound influence of this disaster on French critical thought in the 1970s, see Behrent, "Accidents Happen."
35. Dale et al., "Kiss of Death." For a comparison with continental Europe, see Gordon, "Ouvrières et maladies professionnelles"; Rainhorn, "Le mouvement ouvrier."
36. Derickson, "United Mine Workers of America," 783.
37. Bufton and Melling, "Coming Up for Air," 64; Melling and Sellers, "Objective Collectives?"

38. Penrose, "Medical Monitoring," 289.
39. Rosner and Markowitz, *Deadly Dust: Silicosis and the On-Going Struggle*, 33.
40. Sumiya, *Shokkô oyobi kôfu chôsa*, 171–204.
41. Rosner and Markowitz, *Deadly Dust: Silicosis and the On-Going Struggle*, 24–25.
42. Mintz, "Hard Rock Miners' Phthisis," 74–77.
43. *Report of the Departmental Committee on Compensation.*
44. Lengwiler, *Risikopolitik im Sozialstaa.*
45. Boyer, *Unfallversicherung*, 31–33; Geyer, *Die Reichsknappschaft*, 41–64; and the articles gathered by Rosental in "La silicose, un cas exemplaire."
46. Buzzi et al., *La santé au travail.*
47. Lengwiler, "Internationale Expertennetzwerke," 208.
48. See the outcome of the 1929 international congress in Lyons, outlined in chapter 3.
49. Devinck and Rosental, " 'Une maladie sociale.' "
50. Kolb, "Staubkrankheit," 187; Kolb, "Was ist Silikose?"
51. Guinand, "Zur Entstehung von IVSS."
52. Kolb, "Staubkrankheit," 188; Kolb, "Was ist Silikose?," 51.
53. Kolb, "Staubkrankheit," 188; ILO, *Silicosis: Records* (1930), 1–2.
54. Kolb, "Staubkrankheit," 188; Koelsch, *Beiträge zur Geschichte*, 218–226.
55. ILO, *Silicosis: Records* (1930), 2–3.
56. Kolb, "Staubkrankheit," 187–189; Commission Internationale Permanente pour l'Étude des Maladies Professionelles, *IVe Réunion de la Commission*; Koelsch, *Beiträge zur Geschichte*, 218–226.
57. Boyer, *Unfallversicherung*, 133.
58. The agenda of the 1930 conference in Johannesburg was to set the parameters for a *minimal* recognition of the disease.
59. ILO, *Silicosis: Records* (1930), 346–347; Boyer, *Unfallversicherung*, 221.
60. Boyer, *Unfallversicherung*, 133.
61. Lang, "Unsere Erfahrungen," 264.
62. Vergara, "Recognition of Silicosis;" Melling, "Beyond a Shadow of a Doubt?"
63. Bufton and Melling, "Coming Up for Air," 80.
64. Boyer, *Unfallversicherung*, 221–235.
65. Ibid., 240–248.
66. Ibid.
67. Kaneko, "Nenkô chinginron."
68. "Dai 15 nendo Nihon."
69. This threshold was reduced to 100 employees in 1940.
70. Miura, *Rôdô to kenkô*, 4: 432.
71. See Menéndez-Navarro, "Politics of Silicosis."
72. Devinck and Rosental, " 'Une maladie sociale avec des aspects médicaux.' "
73. See Menéndez-Navarro, "Politics of Silicosis."
74. Ibid., 97–100.
75. Devinck and Rosental, " 'Une maladie sociale.' "
76. Loriga to Carozzi, 10 June 1926, HY 553/L59/505, A-ILO.
77. Loriga to Carozzi, 8 February 1932, HY 553/4, A-ILO; Biondi to Carozzi, 23 February 1932, HY 553/4, A-ILO.
78. Carnevale and Baldasseroni, "Long-Lasting Pandemic"; Carnevale and Baldasseroni, "Mussolini's Fight."
79. Carnevale and Baldasseroni, *Mal da lavoro*, ch. 6. Many thanks to Manuela Martini for pointing out this issue.

80. De Paoli et al., *L'evoluzione della tutela*.

81. Ebihara, *Shokugyôbyô undôshi*, 46–117.

82. Ghirardelli, "1964: Une victoire," 129–133; Lemaître, "Compagnons de route"; Geerkens, "Quand la silicose."

83. Rosner and Markowitz, *Deadly Dust: Silicosis and the On-Going Struggle*, 73.

84. Ibid., 81, 92–96.

85. Lengwiler, *Risikopolitik im Sozialstaat*, 258.

Chapter 5

Silicosis and "Silicosis"
Minimizing Compensation Costs; or,
Why Occupational Diseases Cost So Little

Paul-André Rosental and Bernard Thomann

In all industrialized countries, whatever their health-related and insurance ar-rangements, occupational diseases are underregistered. This means that de-spite theoretical legal protections, in practice these diseases are compensated on a significantly smaller scale than they would be if such legislation was im-plemented fully.[1] This trend is so striking, with converging evidence showing that it occurs across a range of countries and circumstances, that it should now be treated as an initial question for research: how do we account for such sys-tematic underregistration?

Silicosis provides a perfect testing place in which to research this issue. Like other pulmonary diseases, silicosis takes years, and often decades, to enter a clinical phase that affects a worker. Until then, it is "visible" only to specialists—for most of the twentieth century, this meant well-trained radi-ologists with good equipment. Although the introduction of scanners in the 1980s improved the quality of means to uncover simple forms of silicosis, only more-recent and expensive techniques, which are rarely implemented, allow a systematic detection of the presence of silica dust in the lungs. This delay is critical: during that exposure period, a worker may have been employed by several companies. More generally, in contrast to workplace *injuries*, with im-mediately apparent origins, occupational causes of *diseases* compete with private (i.e., non-work-related) ones. In the first decades of the twentieth century, tu-berculosis was a powerful rival to silicosis.[2] Since the 1980s, when the carcino-genic effect of silica dust began to be discussed, smoking and more generalized environmental pollution have been put forward by companies as the real causes of workers' lung cancers.

This question of temporality is inherent in the medico-legal definition of occupational disease. It was one of the main obstacles to the recognition of occupational diseases at the end of the nineteenth century, because it extended the scope of work-related injuries, which were enshrined in law at that time.[3] Since then, it has also stood in the way of financial compensation for those affected by silicosis, in contrast to payments made for workplace injuries.[4] The question of medical complications also comes into play, which raises the issue of the triggering disease. Workers can inhale different kinds of dust, all at the same time. Each type of dust may cause its own pathological effects, as well as being likely to produce other symptoms when combined with additional dusts. Isolating the "pure" effect of silica dust in this process is even more difficult, because the exposure conditions vary tremendously from one workplace to the next. Moreover, the disease evolves in very different ways, according to how silica-rich the rock is and how effectively preventive measures (such as ventilation) and protective devices (like masks) are used. These factors make it extremely difficult to establish a threshold of exposure that would limit the risk.

In all of these aspects—temporality, multiple causes, and the problem of determining an upper limit for "safe" exposure—silicosis exemplifies the difficulty of advocating for financial compensation for workers. In much of the literature on the subject, the underregistration of occupational diseases is attributed not only to companies' cost-cutting strategies, but also to irrational behavior (i.e., non-rational motives within models of actions) on the part of exposed workers. The argument is that workers are trapped by their masculine culture, which prevents them from acknowledging risks at work and protecting themselves from them. Trade unions, it is sometimes claimed, have systematically traded health for wage supplements. Yet a social history of silicosis paints a more complex picture. It takes a multifaceted approach to understand the under-declaration of the disease and recognize workers' constrained rationality as well as the active attempts of employers to disrupt laborers' strategies.

A Minimal Implementation of the Law
General Legal Obstacles

South Africa, 1912; the United Kingdom, 1921; Japan, 1930; France, 1945; Belgium, 1963—although the chronology of the recognition of silicosis across various countries suggests a hierarchy of "advanced" and "backward" nations, this superficial comparison of laws may be deceptive. As seen in the preceding chapter, the institutional contexts in which silicosis was recognized varied greatly and involved different levels of cost for industry. In those countries in which the recognition of silicosis has had financial implications, employers have tried to anticipate the effects of the law and to reduce its scope.

In some cases, this limitation has been clear and straightforward. As seen earlier, when the United Kingdom classed silicosis as an occupational disease in 1921, it excluded the mining sector from the industries covered under the law. The 1934 ILO international convention on silicosis left each country free to determine the list of sectors eligible for financial compensation: an implicit acknowledgment that this international agreement was a compromise among countries in which the costs of compensation for silicosis were particularly feared by employers. Recognition per se cannot be considered a workers' victory, nor is it uniform from one country to the next. It is the outcome of a bargaining process in which limiting the extent of the law has been as important as the law itself.

The gold mines in the Australian state of Queensland are a good illustration of this phenomenon. In August 1916, Queensland's parliament passed a workers' compensation bill that did not include miners' phthisis. A few months later, in December, compensation for this disease finally passed into law, thanks to an amendment added under pressure from miners and their representatives. This legal provision might have seemed revolutionary at the time, but it established a requirement for a medical exam that would check whether miners were "predisposed towards the disease." Only workers too sick to work would be compensated. In this instance, the word "workers" is to be understood in its legal sense. Far from being a global yet imprecise category, it excluded miners who worked under special types of contracts with the mine owners. Any compensation was also very limited financially: £1 per week, up to a maximum of £400.[5]

Far from being exceptional, the Queensland case illustrates a general pattern that took various forms in different countries but always involved a circumscription of the definition of silicosis and, therefore, the response to it. Screening procedures mandated by law, which offered loopholes for excluding certain workers from compensation, contributed to cost containment. A good example can be found in Japan: the 1955 special law on silicosis and the pneumoconiosis law that replaced it in 1960. What was adopted in the latter was a classification of silicotics in four stages, reflecting the degree to which the disease had advanced. This system involved a study of the worker's professional history, as well as a clinical exam. The sufferer was entitled to compensation, however, only if the disease had reached the fourth stage, thus leaving the company physician and the director of the departmental labor bureau ultimately in charge of the classification. In Japan, as elsewhere in the world, no objective medical or radiological grid was able to provide a definitive relationship among a given x-ray picture, a stage of the disease, and a rate of compensation.

In 1937, Luigi Carozzi had reservations about the internationally accepted, South African–based, three-stage classification of silicosis that, he said, "has nothing whatever to do with compensation, in regard to which the only element to be considered is reduction of earning capacity or working capacity."[6] Indeed, on this issue, as on several others examined in this chapter, the debates in the 1930s proved prophetic and often remain valid today. In many ways, the discussion has not moved forward since this period, when the foremost world experts with an intimate (if partial) knowledge of pneumoconioses demonstrated the difficulties inherent in defining silicosis and delineating its effects. This opened up a significant arena in which the mines' doctors could balance their medical judgment against financial considerations. For instance, most workers classified in the fourth category had to undergo an extra medical exam, and even then they were not automatically entitled to compensation. The employer, informed of the classification decision, was supposed to let workers know about treatments for the disease and tell them of their right to compensation. Many workers, however, were not notified by their employer of the result of their classification and were therefore unable to apply for compensation.[7] Even in cases where workers were informed of their rights, obtaining compensation was still a difficult and lengthy process: victims had to submit their requests to a commission in the departmental bureau of labor standards, which would check with all of their previous employers on the nature of their past dust exposure. This process could be particularly complex for rural migrant workers (*dekasegi rōdōsha*), who constituted the bulk of the workforce in the mining and tunnel-construction industries and moved around frequently, meaning that they had a number of successive employers all over the country.

Administrative requirements also limited the implementation of compensation laws. In many countries, legislation on silicosis was exceptional because, in contrast to laws relating to other occupational diseases, it required a certain length of exposure before compensation could be granted. In France, for example, a miner could only claim financial compensation after five years underground. This constraint may seem negligible, since in most cases, mining is a lifelong occupation. But the material issue of how long careers lasted was soon turned into a legal one: what is meant by "underground," and what constitutes "five years"? French labor law provided a special status for collieries. This economically strategic sector was also a politically touchy one, because of the influence of the Communist Party and the trade union movement among miners. As a reaction against the perception of too generous a social security system within the mining industry, which was nationalized in 1946, the state gave collieries control over the compensation system for workplace injuries and occupational diseases in 1948. The industry drew up a list of occupations that hierarchized the exposure to risk. Only a few activities, such as drilling tunnels, were recognized as placing workers fully at risk. In such cases, one year of work was counted as one year underground. The majority of occupations, however, provided only fractional equivalencies: one year of work could be counted as just a semester, a trimester, or less underground. A 1990 sociological survey demonstrated the significant limitations of these restrictions. In order to be eligible for financial compensation, miners needed to have spent about 20 to 25 years underground—in other words, four times more than the amount of time listed in the 1945 edict.[8]

The progressive introduction of the notion of a threshold of exposure in the second half of the twentieth century potentially should have reduced arbitrariness by objectively defining the dangerousness of each mine or gallery. Far from being straightforward, however, the concept left much room for interpretation, exacerbating the unequal relationship between industry and workers. First, the very definition of an admissible threshold for inhaled dust was questionable, and amounts varied widely from one country to another, more often than not adjusting to the technological constraints of the time rather than to medical knowledge.[9] The Cold War contributed to these inconsistencies, as the opposition between Soviet and American conceptions increased such definitional conflicts. Second, measuring a "safe" level of dust exposure was far from easy. It required instruments, where their availability (or unavailability) further increased international gaps. Third, dust measurements were either directly or indirectly in the hands of the mining industry.[10] The latter situation occurred in socialist Czechoslovakia, where facilities in collieries often substituted for an insufficient number of public occupational health centers and where practitioners could, for instance, use defective measuring instruments without external supervision.[11]

Fourth, and finally, dust concentration was only one indicator of exposure. Actual inhalation depended on how work was organized and what its pace was.

In France, this fact was used by the collieries to argue that it was impossible to determine a threshold level for dust, above which continued work would expose miners to the risk of coniosis (dust-related medical conditions).[12] Instead, in each mine the chief engineer, the occupational health doctor, and the engineer in charge of dust control were left to draw up a list of occupations that they considered harmful to workers—in other words, leaving all margins for compensatory action under the control of the Charbonnages de France ("French National Collieries"). The argument for the variability of danger from one workplace to the next was progressively refined on an epidemiological basis. Not until 1975 did a decree state that thresholds should be established site by site, on the basis of "contradictory evaluations" (independent and generally adverse assessments) by the collieries and the trade unions.

This process of diluting the impact of silicosis legislation is particularly illuminating, as it took place within a nationalized sector that, in theory, was not so much profit- as production-driven. The collieries, led by state engineers and administered by a Ministry for Industrial Production that kept coal mines outside the sphere of the Ministry of Labor, followed this highly industrialist ideology, which was largely shared by the dominant, pro-communist union. These methods for minimizing compensation for silicosis echoed those adopted by socialist Czechoslovakia during the same period. In that country, too, compensation was based on the length of time spent working underground. The list of mining trades was carefully established and frequently redefined. As in France, the gap between actual exposure to risk and entitlement to compensation was so apparent that administrative procedures had to be invented to circumvent the law or, more precisely, its implementation. Ad hoc institutions, acting as medico-legal "courts," were created to examine the files of miners who, although they had spent their entire career underground, were not entitled to compensation.

One may question the rationalities of a system that, in France as in Czechoslovakia, added a contradictory complexity to the law: reducing, in terms of risk exposure, calculations of the length of time miners spent underground, and then giving a second chance to those who had been unduly excluded from financial compensation through the list of eligible occupations. Yet administrative rationality was not the point. The idea of this double and paradoxical procedure was to turn a legal entitlement (based on the number of years spent underground) into a discretionary process, in which the collieries could decide, on a case-by-case basis, who would benefit from silicosis payments. From that perspective, it is a paradigmatic illustration of the way in which industry could circumvent legal provisions.

The need to prove five years—or, indeed, any length of time—underground served to break any automatic connection between suffering from silicosis and entitlement to compensation. In Czechoslovakia, as in France, it was the worker who had to prove the length of time spent underground. The task was extremely difficult in a world where places of work and changes in job status were often numerous. The worker had to keep track of his entire *curriculum laboris* ("work history"), which often could only be documented through the notebooks of the *porion* ("foreman"). Here again, the requirement to document time spent underground mitigated against the legal principle of occupational diseases, which is supposed to free workers from producing proof of the origin of the illness.

To achieve this aim—making silicosis conditional, in order to maximize the gap between being sick (silicotic) and being officially recognized as and compensated for being sick ("silicotic")—each element of the law (whether it was related to diagnosis, prevention, length of exposure, or complications) was contested by the companies, and its cost was minimized. Among its other provisions, the 1945 French edict announced that a list of companies in which the whole workforce was definitely exposed to the risk of silicosis would be published, yet this never occurred. Instead, the edict merely established a list of occupations "likely to cause" silicosis.[13] The distinction is not negligible. Listing the companies where workers were at risk would have provided a clear legal parameter: the workers concerned would not have had to establish any proof that they had been contaminated through the work process. Although making a list of trades, rather than of specific companies, may sound reasonable, it opened the way for litigation rather than an automatic assumption of entitlement, and it made workers responsible for proving that they had held this or that position.

Establishing proof of contamination through the work process was particularly difficult, as silicosis continues to progress even after exposure, and clinical signs can start to manifest themselves when workers are later involved in non-dusty occupations, or even once they have retired. In Europe, the severely ill are often involuntarily retired and accordingly are left out of the industrial medicine system.[14] In Japan, the law explicitly excludes workers from any medical monitoring once they retire or when they leave the most risk-exposed jobs. Starting in 1996, a large longitudinal survey was conducted among elderly homeless people—usually former dayworkers from the public works industry who had mining or tunneling experience. The study revealed that about 30 percent of those who had had x-rays taken suffered from pneumoconiosis. They had breathing problems but tended to attribute them to their advanced age. As these people did not benefit from continued medical exams, they did not know that they were afflicted with pneumoconiosis and thus had not initiated any compensation proceedings.[15]

An Unequal Power Struggle

Why did the implementation of legislation concerning silicosis gave companies so much room to maneuver? And why was there such a degree of collusion, or at least tolerance, from public authorities? These questions are particularly relevant, as we are not building a univocal model that would focus only on employers' agency, presenting workers as powerless victims. Such a model runs contrary to the principles of social history that are the basis for our approach. Rather, we need to understand why the balance of power was clearly in favor of industry, how industry's influence was channeled, and what effects it produced.

Industrialist lobbies could marshal varied and weighty arguments and tools in order to successfully exert pressure on the making and implementation of laws on silicosis. Everywhere in the world, the mining sector, by definition, dealt with the extraction of strategic resources, but it was coal that was particularly valuable as the primary source of energy in the United States until 1950 and, in European countries, until the 1960s (and sometimes later). An examination of the situation in Japan reveals this strategic dimension. In 1949, the first and most generous bill on silicosis compensation drafted by Japanese Labor Ministry experts was dumped by the American occupation authorities. This was due not only to budgetary considerations, but also to the fact that, with the beginning of the Cold War, coal had become the strategic resource on which the recovery of Japan—a rampart against the communist bloc—depended.[16] Incidentally, coal remains the second-most-important source of energy in the world (as it is in the United States), and it is competing to rank as the first by 2020, depending on economic growth in China and India, nations that particularly rely on coal.

Coal was the cornerstone of industrial production; it was also essential for heating individual homes. Its value, therefore, was simultaneously economic and social. Its extraction was a national priority; for a long time, any increase in its cost to consumers and companies was politically sensitive. This made compensation for workers suffering from silicosis a particularly thorny issue. Companies could reasonably claim that minimizing compensation was a matter of the collective good. In this respect, there was little difference between capitalist and planned economies. Profit-oriented strategies from the privately owned mining sector in the former shared many similarities with strategies employed by production-driven companies in the latter. In both cases, the crucial value of coal gave them the power to virtually blackmail the state.

In postwar socialist Czechoslovakia, as well as in France, where collieries were nationalized in 1945, compensation for silicosis amounted to about 5 percent of the entire expenditure on wages. In Czechoslovakia, the union, which was controlled by the Communist Party, was instrumental in advocating for the "general interest" against the reservations of the Ministry of Public Health. It was the union that fought victoriously to keep miners who were suffering from silicosis—by definition, the most experienced ones—still working underground; it also lobbied against too generous a compensation system.

The French case exemplifies the mythologization of miners as heroes, always ready to make the supreme sacrifice. In this sector, at least, no "cultural demobilization" occurred after World Wars I and II.[17] Miners killed by workplace injuries were said by their comrades to have "fallen in work's field of honor." As in other countries, this military ethos was shared by most unions and by many on the Left, particularly those in the communist orbit.[18] Productivist ideology entered into a complex mix in which belief in protection by their patron saint, Saint Barbara (whose statue was omnipresent underground), united miners and gunners.

Institutional elements translated these ideological sensitivities into tangible processes. In socialist Czechoslovakia, the unions were heavily involved in cutting compensation costs, as they were in charge of social insurance. In France, nationalization made the state reluctant to countenance any improvement in compensatory provisions, which would have had a direct impact on its budget.[19]

When it came to compensation for silicosis, whether economies were profit driven or not was, in the end, less important than the ability of workers to exert their will against a minimalist compensation system. From a political and administrative point of view, the ability to do so depended on the structure of a nation's government and the status of its compensation insurance system. In most countries around the world, governments divided their concerns between, on the one hand, a Ministry of Industrial Production or a Ministry of Mines that was in charge of the interests of the extraction industry and, on the other, a Ministry of Labor and a Ministry of Public Health, which were more open to workers' concerns.

In countries that lacked this institutional tension among ministries, miners' cases were particularly difficult to address. In France, the mining sector depended on a special section of labor law and was not covered by the Labor Ministry at all. This lack of institutional protection was all the more detrimental, since the state-owned mining sector was run by the nation's premier engineers, who had graduated from the elite Grandes Écoles, notably the École Polytechnique, which also had ties to the military sector. This special administrative body, the Corps des Ingénieurs des Mines ("Mining Engineers Corps"), which shaped top engineers' careers in French administration and public companies, was at the heart of the French state—increasingly so throughout the twentieth century, as the public industrial sector expanded.[20] The corps was closely connected to the top administration at both the national and local levels (*départements*), leaving little room for workers and their supporters to contest the implementation of the compensation system. An indication of this political and administrative helplessness is that, in the 1950s, the only political group that carried enough weight in parliament to improve the compensation system was the Communist Party, which played an outsider role during the Cold War and could not hold a candle to the lobbies of the Charbonnages de France. The situation was exacerbated by the fact that French trade unions traditionally preferred applying political and administrative pressure to pursuing judicial action, the former being collective and the latter individual, according to the law. Moreover, comparative studies show that in countries where judicial action was more common, such as Australia, workers still hesitated to go to court over compensation issues. Not only did mid-twentieth-century workers fear losing their jobs, but they also balanced the cost and difficulty of the court case with the low "output" of judgments, which often seemed arbitrary and limited: "More often than not, the insurance companies succeeded in convincing the miners to gratefully accept out of court settlements of amounts considerably less than would now be seen to be their due."[21]

The Strategic Use of Medical Ambiguities
When *Is Silicosis?*

Determining eligibility for compensation for silicosis was one thing; deciding on the nature of the disease was another. Reaching professional agreement on the medical classification of the disease had been very difficult. For workers, an important aspect of this discussion was the relationship between the medical definition of the illness and its actual manifestation. The question here is not so much *what* is silicosis, but *when* it is acknowledged. Should the disease be officially recognized as soon as it is identified clinically or radiologically by medical professionals? Or is it to be recognized only when it produces "observable" effects and limits a worker's productive capability? For the mining industry, the answer was the latter. Before discussing the impact of this on compensation, however, we want to emphasize its effect on public health. The gap between being silicotic (having one's lungs affected by the disease) and being "silicotic" (being officially acknowledged as such) was not merely a static categorization between compensated and uncompensated workers. It relied on the tacit choice to exclude from compensation miners whose lungs were affected but who were still capable of continuing to work underground, even though this would obviously give the disease time to develop further. In all industrialized countries, discussions about when compensation should start have been based on the implicit agreement that nothing should be done until a miner's health has deteriorated to the point of clinical dysfunction. A handful of medical experts have denounced this policy, but they have failed to alter it. At any rate, the miners themselves would probably have disagreed with them.

Socialist Czechoslovakia, which disseminated intensive propaganda on the quality of its care for workers, as opposed that in the capitalist system, addressed the issue by announcing an ambitious policy of protecting miners by taking them out of the shafts as soon as they were diagnosed as being unwell. Across the entire country, and in all of its economic sectors, the government required companies to draw up a list of "soft" jobs that would be reserved for ex-miners. Silicotic laborers with no or only a limited disability and who were still able to work would thereby be protected from further lung deterioration, without losing the social status afforded by participation in the workforce in socialist countries.

The contrast with capitalist countries seems absolute. Around 1930, in the Porcupine gold mines in Ontario, miners who exhibited initial signs of silicosis could, in theory, ask to be removed from underground work. It often happened, however, that the early detection of silicosis led management to fire them. As a result, miners "preferred" to keep working underground as long as their health allowed.[22] In big Japanese mining companies, collective agreements that had been negotiated at the end of the 1940s were supposed to compensate for the loss of revenue resulting from a transfer out of the mine. As in Ontario, a lump sum was provided, in order to allow miners time to transition to another job. In practice, however, the sum was not sufficient to achieve this aim. The Japanese Federation of Metal-Mining Labor Unions (*Zen Nihon Kinzoku Kô-zan Rôdô Kumiai Rengôkai*), which negotiated the agreement, was not in a position to bargain for more than two months' salary.[23]

In France and in the United Kingdom, mining companies did not hesitate to muster an argument that came close to explicit institutional blackmail. If legal regulations stated that silicotic workers would have to be taken out of a mine's underground galleries and instead work at the surface, the companies would not guarantee that they could find these workers a job. We are accustomed to thinking of the postwar years as a period of full employment. The threat of losing one's job, however, was still a deterrent—particularly once such threats actually began to be carried out in sectors such as the grinding and polishing industries, and in fine-metals foundries—even for workers without any physical incapabilities.[24] British trade unions had always feared that the implementation of the law on occupational diseases would trigger this kind of pernicious effect. In France, it became a major issue in the 1970s, when there was mass unemployment.

To a large extent, silicosis was a test case for this tragic balancing act between health and employment. As a result, in the 1950s, French collieries hired underground miners whose degree of "partial permanent invalidity" was above 65 percent, which was the threshold for general disabilities. This level, however, was partly arbitrary. Nevertheless, the collieries' aim was to keep miners underground until they had "fully exhausted their working capacity,"[25] which was one of the leading principles of the Johannesburg conference.

Another approach to the same issue was related to insurance. The Swiss National Fund for Injuries exemplified a technique that was primarily developed in Germany and Austria: estimating, on an actuarial basis, life-cycle costs caused by disabilities.[26] In general, the criteria for determining annuities were precise, and the amount awarded for losing a part of the body was determined by the worker's age when the injury occurred. In the case of silicosis, actuaries tried to combine different parameters—such as x-ray images, time spent in various jobs with a risk of dust exposure, the amount of quartz within the kind of stone used, and the type of prevention available—to estimate the degree of disability. Nonetheless, in the mid-twentieth century, despite these sophisticated variables, there was still a consistent margin of error, evaluated then at 10–20 percent. This paved the way for frequent contestations. A portion of these cases concerned workers who were "suspected" of having silicosis but were not medically recognized as suffering from the disease. Being forbidden to work underground, yet deprived of any compensation, the only way they could maintain an equivalent pay level was by moonlighting.

Returning to socialist Czechoslovakia, its generous (and propaganda-driven) intentions were undermined by the same problems that were faced by companies in Western countries. First, there were not enough soft jobs available to employ the tens of thousands of miners potentially covered by the government's policy. Second, the needs of the collieries were too high to allow any workforce losses, especially of trained miners. It was difficult to find enough workers, and, in contrast to most industrialized countries, immigrant labor was not readily available.

The interplay between the "invisible" and "visible" phases of silicosis has therefore had a dramatic impact on public health everywhere and may be considered one of the most spectacular examples of the importance of constructivism in the social sciences. Neither of these aspects could be precisely defined. First, to enter the invisible phase meant that the disease was "diagnosable": such was the adjective used at the important 1950 Sydney International Conference of Experts on Pneumoconiosis.[27] At that time, it referred to a condition apparent on an x-ray or in a respiratory-function test. The Australian physician J. Milne, in the Industrial Hygiene Division of the Victoria Department of Health, insisted on the medical limits of this criterion: "Diagnosis may be impossible in the early stages, [as] changes are microscopic and cellular."[28]

Entry into the diagnosable phase depended less on any functional manifestation of the disease than on the quality of the medical monitoring of miners' health. The frequency of compulsory medical exams varied tremendously among countries, and even among mines, as did the quality of the clinical and radiological procedures. Identifying the appearance of silicosis in a lung demanded good x-ray equipment, good-quality film, and well-trained specialists. It was not until the early 1950s that many European countries were able to meet these criteria.[29] Czechoslovakia was far from being able to do so, even by the 1970s.

Technological apparatus was not the only variable. Such equipment could only be used to its full potential if there were enough occupational health doctors to conduct medical exams,[30] and then only if workers participated in them.

Yet this was far from being the case. In 1950s France, approximately 20 percent of the miners seem to have avoided "compulsory" examinations.[31] This rate may have reached 60–80 percent in socialist Czechoslovakia.[32] Lack of knowledge might explain their absenteeism, as miners may have been unaware of the dangers of silicosis. Conversely, they may have been all too cognizant of its potential harm, fearing they might be found to have an incurable disease that causes terrible suffering in its last phases. Medical monitoring may have also been seen as a tool that could potentially be used by a company against its workers. In Australia, when such monitoring was introduced in 1920 in Broken Hill, the Workers' Industrial Union barred compulsory periodic exams, because it believed that employers could use the information obtained to increase their control over the workforce.[33] Such fears were not unfounded. Before 1918, British governments resisted the introduction of compensation schemes for silicosis, arguing—as did the Samuel Committee in 1907[34]—that an early diagnosis of silicosis in employees would effectively exclude them from the labor market.[35]

But immediate material obstacles were probably the determining factor. Whenever medical exams took place outside of work hours, miners were reluctant to show up. Their workday was not only intensive, but it was often preceded and followed by a long trek between the mine elevator and the gallery, a journey that could last more than an hour each way. Adding on extra time for preventive medical exams was, therefore, not particularly attractive. As a result of these technical and socioeconomic constraints, identification of the invisible phase of silicosis could be delayed by several years.

The same uncertainty surrounded the issue of an inability to work. No medical ranking established a clear relationship between clinical or radiological symptoms and levels of disability. Following the 1930 conference in Johannesburg, Luigi Carozzi anticipated that the ILO would have to develop and promote an international radiological classification related to silicosis. It took almost three decades to accomplish this, not without enormous medical and political difficulties. Yet the classification system, in its final form, was a compromise, in much the same way that the 1934 international convention had been. The international radiological standards presented by the ILO in 1958, and renewed since then, were purely descriptive. They were represented by a set of radiographic images that *showed* the action of silicosis on the lungs and classified it in different stages, but these standards did not define it medically.

Thus the combination of high economic stakes and medical complexity had prevented the ILO from drawing up an international agreement on the development of the disease and its effects on workers.

Rates of financial compensation were determined by the stage to which silicosis had advanced. Yet whether an affected worker was informed of the degree of advancement of the disease was, for the most part, arbitrary. Silicosis and silico-tuberculosis had been recognized in the Porcupine gold mines in Ontario since 1926, and medical experts were in charge of deciding "whether or not an individual worker was 'fit' for work." But, as has been the case in other countries, such as France, Canadian mining corporations managed to give their own medical practitioners a monopoly over these controls: "It seems quite plausible that the term 'fit' was open to varying interpretation. Certainly mine workers complained repeatedly that they were sent back to work while still incapacitated or were prevented from resuming employment while believing themselves physically capable to perform necessary work tasks."[36] Beyond the difficulty of clearly distinguishing between able and disabled workers, which is true of all occupational diseases,[37] a fact that was acknowledged at the time by prominent medical experts, silicosis raised specific issues because of the similarity between its symptoms and those of other pulmonary and cardiac diseases, including tuberculosis, which, in the 1930s, was still—according to mine management—the cause of miners' health problems.

On a global analytical scale, statistics from French collieries between 1945 and 1987 display a vague underlying relationship between the length of exposure to particular risks and the degree of disability, but they are so unstable over time that one can infer that the rates of compensation granted to miners followed a logic that was not strictly medical. In the 1950s, in order to retain their workforce, the employers' priority was to postpone compensation for as long as possible, while still ensuring that the miners would wait patiently for it. This double bind was overcome by the creation of a "blank" category: after a few years underground, a large part of the workforce was recognized as "silicotic at grade 0" and received no compensatory allowances for it. This surprising, apparent catch-22 category made more sense than it seems. It gave workers a signal as to their status and offered them the hope of shortly entering into the compensation system and then progressively rising through it. To some extent, the French collieries used silicosis compensation to encourage workers to remain in their positions longer and stabilize the workforce it needed so badly in those reconstruction years. Miners progressed up the financial compensation levels not so much on the basis of clear medical determinants, but according to time and their obedience to a highly paternalistic and authoritarian system.

The workers' motivation was twofold: not only in anticipating increased wages, but also, as they sometimes said, in "working for their widows." When a miner who was formally recognized as silicotic died, a committee, which was controlled by the collieries, decided whether silicosis could be considered as having caused his death, which entitled his widow to an annuity. A purely customary practice, based neither on legislation nor on a medical ranking, was for these committees to deny compensation for any miner who was less than 50 percent silicotic when he died. Yet even if a husband had reached this level, his widow was not automatically entitled to compensation, as the official cause of death was decided on a case-by-case basis. Many families gave up on the procedure, particularly as an autopsy was often required, which would take place long after the miner's death. Nevertheless, the possibility of reaching the 50-percent level or above gave a miner some hope that his family might escape misery after his death. This lifelong concern may be one of the reasons for the epitaph many miners chose for their graves: "dead from silicosis."[38]

Employers' Maneuvers at the Edges of the Law

The way in which the compensation system was administered was a structural handicap for miners. Far from being neutral and following an abstract bureaucratic ideal, the system was, in most countries, directly or indirectly controlled by the mining industry. At the very least, it favored that industry in its power struggle with workers.

First, purely administrative obstacles hindered the compensation process. Submitting a complete file containing all medical and occupational information concerning risk exposure, and then having it examined by the insurance system in charge of compensation and responsible for initiating the payment of a pension, was a complex task. It raised numerous difficulties for miners and could last a long time: at least a couple of years in most French coal basins, and more if the miner happened to have worked in other coalfields.

Bureaucratic complications were not the only hindrance; management also succeeded in minimizing the cost of compensation through a subtle asymmetry. The employers' ability to have the law work to their advantage was, naturally, disproportionately stronger than that of the miners. Industrialists were familiar with a culture of litigation and could easily ask for assistance from their lawyers. But it was a struggle for miners to even become aware of the silicosis issue, let alone consider it worthwhile to claim compensation.[39] Employers forestalled and then limited the number of claims by calling the miners' personal and workplace conduct into question. In all industrial sectors, propaganda materials, such as posters and leaflets, touted prevention and warned against risky behaviors (such as smoking, drinking, spitting, neglecting to wear protective equipment, or failing to concentrate), implying that miners were responsible for—indeed, guilty of causing—their own occupational injuries and diseases.[40]

By contrast, information on occupational diseases was limited and, in some cases, deliberately obfuscated.[41] In a range of industrialized countries, employers used the similarity between the symptoms of silicosis and tuberculosis, as well as their frequent co-occurrence, to delay any publicity about silicosis for as long as possible. Employers did their best to foster confusion among medical experts, in order to spread doubt among good-faith occupational health doctors about the very existence of silicosis. It must be added that this strategy of promoting ignorance and inaccuracies also had an effect on the miners themselves.[42] Until the 1940s, most miners in France were unaware of the cause of their disease. In Japan, the period that preceded acknowledgment of the existence of silicosis in the 1930s jeopardized older, local medical concepts, which, paradoxically, resulted in less protection for workers. Since the eighteenth century, the notion of *yoroke* had allowed miners to become aware of and identify the lung diseases induced by working in the mining industry.[43] The weakening of this lay epidemiology in the first decades of the twentieth century went hand in hand with its downplaying by workers' charitable associations, which took care of occupational risks. Another pernicious effect surfaced in the Bendigo gold mines in Victoria, Australia, where, since 1850, the concentration of silica dust had been killing miners in their thirties or forties.[44] The introduction of preventive actions (such as ventilating the galleries) in the first decade of the twentieth century had a dangerous corollary: creating an unwarranted sense of safety among workers, a typical "moral hazard" (a term from insurance theory, holding that a person is more likely to engage in a risky action when that behavior is covered by insurance).[45] Although the Bendigo miners were removed from underground work sooner than workers in other places, they still had time to contract silicosis without being aware of it. This failed prevention strategy, and its dramatic social consequences, led to a change in focus from prevention to compensation.

The notion that miners deliberately ignored occupational risks to their health is, to some extent, a positivist illusion, which implies that workers purposely chose not to pay attention to risks that were clearly visible to them. In contrast, as an application of the lay epistemology model, writing the history of silicosis means taking the cognitive aspects that were available to workers into account: miners could be aware of the dangerousness of their workplace, without necessarily having access to all of the medical information that would allow them to determine the exact cause or nature of the risk.[46] This is equally true of the medical profession: what was known by whom, and at what time? The answer is that, due to employers' obstructive strategies, silicosis often did not enter into the consciousness of either miners or medical doctors. The same was true of legal knowledge. As is the case regarding many aspects of social welfare,[47] workers were not always fully aware of their rights and often did not even think of either claiming compensation or contesting its amount.[48]

An additional factor was the way in which the implementation of legislation on silicosis has often resulted in the establishment of ad hoc institutions. Bureaucratic "neutrality" may be a misnomer. As the analogy between Canada and France has suggested, and as is still frequently the case,[49] the mining industry, under the guise of offering "expertise" or engaging in "arbitration," tipped the scales in their own favor. In France, during the immediate aftermath of the war, the initial organization in charge of granting compensatory allowances to silicotic workers was dominated by trade unions and tended to be favorable to miners' claims, even when they did not formally meet the legal requirements. In response, employers in 1950 stopped participating in the paritary committee, where their representatives, together with union delegates, delivered case-by-case arbitration on contested compensation files.[50] Taking advantage of the Cold War context, they formed an alliance with minority unions against the dominant, pro-communist union and reached a compromise: miners who were found to be affected by silicosis but were otherwise not eligible for compensation would submit their request for assistance to a "three-doctor commission" that, in practice, was dominated by the collieries.[51] This solution, which, in essence, was a declaration of war against the pro-communist union,[52] was legalized in 1952 and extended nationally. The mines, however, frequently violated the revised law by using unofficial "two-doctor commissions," despite the explicit— and impotent—denunciations of the Labor Ministry. These commissions became the central actors in the distribution of silicosis indemnities and ensured the Charbonnages de France full control over the compensation system.[53]

New medical bodies were also formed. For instance, after the 1945 edict, French collieries created a category of "comptroller-doctors," whose task was to confirm or invalidate a diagnosis of silicosis established by "regular" doctors from the mines. Physicians in the former group, which became official through a 1959 edict, were explicitly in charge of aligning medical science with the financial priorities of the mining industry—an unconventional role for medical experts that did not make them popular among miners.

The Role and Rationality of Miners' Agency

Social historians have long neglected to analyze the development of occupational health's institutional and ideological framework from the point of view of workers and their practices.[54] Furthermore, historians have often latched onto a reductionist argument averring that throughout the past, trade unions have displayed little interest in workplace safety and have privileged wage supplements over the prevention of occupational injuries and diseases.[55]

What is at stake here is the issue of the rationality of workers' agency when torn between health and financial considerations. The ramifications of those decisions are all the more complex, as an individual's perception of risk is structured by social "filter mechanisms."[56] These mechanisms act as both a selection process and a cognitive framework, determining the possible forms that workers' efforts against occupational diseases might take. For example, present-day northern Benin gold miners still believe that hazards are caused by active evil forces that inhabit the mountains. Some of these miners see the risks and dangers related to their activities as an unavoidable phenomenon—gold and wealth being linked to occult forces that demand a payoff.[57] There is a comparable notion in Japan, where, even today, risk is mediated by numerous small shrines inside and outside the mines, where protection is sought from the divinities (*kami*) who inhabit the mountain. These concepts and fears are by no means exclusive to non-Western miners. Ramazzini, in his famous 1700 treaty, considered mines to be the domain of devils.[58] Although more for cultural than religious reasons, especially for Muslim Moroccan miners in the 1960s and 1970s, Saint Barbara, patron saint of all those exposed to fire hazards (gunners, firemen, etc.) was omnipresent underground in mines in the north of France. This was the case not only in the galleries, but also, initially, in the dressing rooms (where miners changed their clothes), and even in the showers.

The reputation of miners as tough, working-class militants—premised in part on their willingness to confront ongoing dangers—is another filter mechanism that operated in the Porcupine gold mines in Canada, and elsewhere. Fighting for the recognition and prevention of silicosis could pose serious challenges to masculine concepts of physical well-being and self-reliance, as well as to the notion of men as breadwinners.[59] The concept of self-reliance dominated Japanese *tomoko* (traditional miner-friendly organizations). It partly explains why labor's mobilization and confrontation with management around the issue of silicosis did not come about until the 1920s in the Ashio copper mine, and why it did not emerge on a larger scale until the late 1940s, even though miners knew from earlier times that the disease they called *yoroke* was linked to dust produced by the work process.[60]

While miners' accounts must be taken seriously, cultural explanations may be deceiving and need to be used carefully. Notions of working-class masculinity are often simplistic and can be an inadequate, lazy explanation when used uncritically in the social sciences.[61] Far from being unproblematic, definitions of masculinity were, on the one hand, used by managers as they sought to control labor, and, on the other hand, were trotted out by workers when they engaged both in contestation and in accommodation. Promoting an ideology that emphasized the miners' intense masculinity was one way in which companies could keep workers tied to their jobs and increase their productivity. In the Chilean copper mines of El Teniente, the American Bradden Copper Company fostered competition among *cuadrillas* ("work groups"), offering prizes and bonuses to the most productive. Miners also competed within a *cuadrilla* to demonstrate who was the strongest or who could perform a difficult job better. Respect from their fellow laborers and from the foremen depended on a worker's ability to work hard, and the tenets of "manhood" exacerbated health hazards, thus becoming a major issue with regard to working conditions. Furthermore, "a worker who flaunted company control with a boastful manhood expressed in activities like fighting with bosses, stealing, moonshining, drinking, and gambling, also frequently violated the strict discipline and moral codes insisted upon by organized labor and the Left."[62] Similarly, employers and managers in Scottish mines deliberately promoted a "competitive, productivist, masculine work culture" as a way to encourage men to take risks.[63]

Reducing the phenomenon of underregistering occupational diseases to a cultural explanation by blaming masculine bravado is not just a simplistic approach to causal processes; it is also a denial of the means employers used to achieve their ends. This point applies not only to the Chilean copper mines and the asbestos mines in Scotland, but can also be extended to all industrialized countries. If we accept that employers treat the compensation costs for workers in the same way as other management expenses, the deliberate, calculated effort by industry, across a range of countries and socioeconomic systems, to minimize that disbursement comes as no surprise. The issue for historians is to understand how this cost-cutting process operates; how it attempts to optimize or circumvent legal obligations; to what extent it involves complicity, or at least comprehension, by the government; how it succeeds in setting occupational health apart from regular public health considerations; and how it interacts with miners' agency.

Such a transnational, multifaceted approach attempts to reconstruct the asymmetrical and, to some degree, violent relationship that has allowed industry to deliberately damage miners' health and minimize their rights to financial compensation, without falling back on the simplifications derived from the major macroscopic models of domination inspired by the social sciences. In many cases, these simplifications are less the fault of the original proponents of the models than the failings of some of their followers. Nonetheless, we are wary of the one-sided Marxian paradigm in which almighty employers impose their views on accomplice bourgeois governments and manipulated workers; of the caricatured Foucauldian complex of (economic) power and (medical) knowledge that would trap miners in a biopolitical jail; and of lazy culturalist claims that explain peoples' behaviors by their supposed specificities. We are aware that this epistemological position is not an obvious approach to adopt, particularly in any examination of the mining industry, which dauntingly dominates a vastly diverse range of contexts. It is an industry that, of necessity, particularly in remote areas, is often rapidly established. Its workforce is called in quickly, and on a massive scale; disciplined for a tough industrial world; and incorporated into highly paternalistic or authoritarian structures.[64] Yet even in this extreme case, social history offers an alternative approach, in which the complicated set of workers' motivations, as well as their interactions with the powerful companies with which, to varying degrees, they both collaborate and fight, enters the picture.

Global Constraints on the Workforce

To understand the so-called passivity of workers and their unions in asserting their right to silicosis compensation, the institutional framework within which labor relations operate must be taken into account. Subcontracting played a particularly detrimental role in those countries in which it dominated the mining and public works sectors.[65] The Japanese situation is a good illustration of these dynamics. Most tunnel workers there did not apply for compensation, despite the fact that they had been diagnosed as silicotic, because they were involved in a long-term subcontracting relationship of a special type, called *Oyaka-Kokata*. The workers were hired by a recruiting agent (*sewayaku*), who worked for a subcontractor. This subcontractor drew up contracts, either directly with the large public works companies or with a higher-ranking subcontractor. Recruiting channels were generally based on local social networks and individuals' provincial origins. The loftiest social expectation for a worker was to become first a *sewayaku* and then a subcontractor. In order to do so, he needed to draw on the long-term connections of his former direct employers, who could introduce him to client firms or to more-senior subcontractors. Studies have shown that workers were reluctant to raise safety and occupational health issues that could inconvenience their direct employers, fearing that these employers would jeopardize the complainants' careers.[66]

An institutional framework could also exert its influence through more-immediate financial considerations. In France, as in socialist Czechoslovakia, miners—especially the most highly trained ones—often avoided declaring that they were affected by silicosis because, in their view, the various levels of compensation for this illness did not compare favorably with the amount of income they received. The miners' wages were generally high, similar to those of skilled workers in other industries. They also benefited from additional bonuses—some of which were in kind (in France, free coal and housing) and others in cash (in the form of special payments for working underground)—that explain their reluctance to take jobs at the surface. There were also discretionary supplements that collieries could provide at any time, not to mention silicosis allowances that, to some extent, also were arbitrary.

In the most paternalistic systems, such as in France—which one sociologist has characterized as a "free-care-based economy"[67]—failure to claim silicosis compensation was therefore far from irrational or passive. Miners who accepted this quite arbitrary compensation system were rewarded by the managerial staff, who systematically discriminated against anyone who expressed impatience with this system. Miners who dared to show their discontent were dismissed as "neurotic" and might expect to progress along the financial allowance scale much more slowly than their counterparts, since the levels of impairment associated with silicosis were proposed by medical doctors and then accepted or refused by medical controllers, who were attached to the collieries. In other words, the mining industry managed to turn silicosis allowances into a part of its human resources policy. These payments were crucial in keeping skilled workers—who, across a number of countries, constituted both the most valuable and the most hard-to-find portion of the workforce—underground for as long as their health permitted. Nonetheless, *recognizing* the miners' rationality in accepting a discretionary and hardly generous compensation system does not mean *adopting* it as a maximizing economic device.

Little is known about the miners' financial considerations. Far from acting in isolation, they operated within a collective unit (the household) where interactions with their spouses were crucial. The extent to which exposure to risk was discussed between husbands and wives has not been clearly documented in historical literature. In one study about the families of injured Canadian workers, miners' wives—although they may have felt overwhelmed by the physical and emotional demands of ministering to an ill spouse, as well as resentful about running a household on their own—usually remained silent on this issue. This silence can be attributed to gendered expectations about being a miner's wife, which dictated that women take on these additional obligations, but it precluded any emotional space for them to complain about these duties.[68] It is clear, however, that in families where disease or accidents were a constant threat, miners took the protection of their (future) widows into account when making decisions. It is also apparent that living with uncertainty was part of everyday life for miners' wives. Furthermore, the different threats to which miners were exposed did not necessarily involve the same timeframes. On the one hand, Canadian miners followed a life-cycle perspective in which, similar to the French compensation system, increasing levels of disability were a form of guarantee for their families. On the other hand, as one Scottish miner put it, "you didnae think of the future, we just thought from day to day."[69]

Those daily concerns focused on workplace injuries, rather than occupational diseases. Statistically speaking, the former did not cause as many fatalities than the latter. Firedamp explosions, for instance, have killed far fewer miners than has silicosis. Yet sensitivity to the risk of fatal injuries (which were less likely, but instantaneous and obvious) prevailed over concerns about the risk of disease (which was probable, but delayed and with less-visible effects). As interviews with miners' spouses or widows reveal, the fear that their husbands would go to work and never come back was a daily one. Yet death was not the only risk. Injuries, which were far more frequent, could be detrimental, both in terms of health and income. Their impact has been documented among Porcupine gold miners in Ontario, a particularly dangerous workplace, even when compared with other mines in the area.[70] Few alternative jobs were available for wounded miners, and even fewer for wives trying to make up for the loss of their husbands' wages, precisely because soft jobs were reserved for former miners who were removed from underground work.[71] The symbolic cruelty of workplace injuries was no less significant. The reality of the wounded miner, whose very survival depended on his family and environment, was in stark opposition to the social values associated with the mining trade.[72] As a Canadian miner's wife stated: "No man emerges from serious injury to his health. Often than not, he is totally disabled and his capacity to enjoy the most simple things in life are forever lost."[73] Silicosis, too, gradually progresses to a tragic level of disability. In its latter stages, victims cannot even breathe without respiratory assistance. When walking a few meters, or even sleeping, becomes painful, every aspect of family life is affected by a father's disability and suffering.[74] Here again, though, the immediacy of workplace injuries made them of greater concern than the more distant prospect of occupational diseases.

Last, but not least, there is a sociological dimension to the higher visibility of workplace injuries, in comparison with occupational diseases. Collective disasters regularly occur in the mining industry and, in the worst cases, involve the whole community. At times, such catastrophes have resulted in group mobilizations that have been so influential in raising awareness about workplace risks that they have, albeit indirectly, influenced the history of silicosis. Such was the case in 1956 in Belgium (Marcinelle) and in the 1970s in France (Fouquières-les-Lens and Liévin).[75] The collective sharing of such tragic events makes their symbolic expression and commemoration more powerful than the individual sufferings caused by occupational diseases.[76]

History and the social sciences do not need to rely exclusively on culturalist assumptions, which are always at risk of being tautological (people behaving in a certain way because of their unconscious or learned feelings), to understand miners' supposed passivity, indifference, or bravado toward silicosis. An examination of workers' calculations reveals many rational reasons for why they tolerated high levels of risk. Yet avoiding culturalist pitfalls does not necessitate adopting a reductionist *homo economicus* model either. The behavior of miners cannot be treated as the outcome of a process where free, unfettered actors maximize their well-being. On the contrary, all the preceding considerations demonstrate the stringent limitations they had to deal with and their highly circumscribed phenomenological horizon.[77]

Additionally, an important dimension is missing from economic and cultural readings. To understand braving danger and ignoring protection, purely as a default strategy, would be ethnocentric and miss a political aspect. In an analysis of mining in the Ottoman Empire, those miners' resistance to safety measures, particularly safety lamps, and their refusal to use a protective device "might well have represented their refusal to accept the centralizing discipline of the mine administration."[78] For Ottoman miners, as well as for their counterparts in many industrialized countries, health and social regulations imposed from above could be perceived as being, first and foremost, production or profit oriented, as well as representing a confirmation and reinforcement of the industrial order in which they were subsumed. In this respect, expressing indifference to danger could be a demonstration of anarchic, individual disdain toward overwhelming economic forces.[79]

Actually, miners' exposure to high levels of health-related risk and their acceptance of relatively low amounts of financial compensation should be understood as the interaction between their own agency and the active policy of their industry. Some of these aspects have already been mentioned, but until now we have looked at the workforce as a whole. Going further implies moving beyond the mythology of miners. While such traditions tend to insist on the miners' unified front, internal divisions created by the mining industry played a major role in this process of laborers underestimating workplace risks. Here, too, the history of silicosis is a good arena in which to understand present-day issues surrounding the neglect of occupational risks.

The Making of Fragile Groups of Miners

Far from being united, the workforce in the mines was divided along at least two major lines: labor contracts and national origin. Tough, free market arrangements have been instrumental in discouraging miners from claiming compensation for occupational diseases. Wherever productivity-based labor contracts and wages have been used, and whatever legal form they have taken, they have had a devastating effect on risk taking. Miners paid according to their productivity, on the basis of piecework, imposed working rhythms on themselves that were detrimental to their health—a dynamic that is true for any workforce.[80] An intensification of effort came at a cost: increasing the degree of dust inhalation, and minimizing the protection afforded by spare time, such as short breaks from work.

This system also had direct and indirect consequences on compensation for disabilities, such as in the Australian gold mines in Queensland at the beginning of the twentieth century.[81] Their workforce was divided among three types of contracts. At the top of the miners' hierarchy, "tributers" leased the mines. They had to pay for their equipment and give the mine owner a share of the gold that was extracted. "Contractors" did specified work in a designated stope (a steplike excavation) or drive. The rest of the miners were paid by piecework. At that time, "tributers and contractors were more likely than other miners to compromise safety because of their eagerness to get out as much gold as possible." Their attitude toward compensation for occupational diseases was also different from that of the regular miners. These higher-ups generally opposed it, because they were excluded from such benefits. More indirectly, the system affected workers' agency. Since both contractors and regular miners entered unions, "any union call for industrial action over either dust or miners' phthisis would almost certainly have produced a fratricidal conflict. It was far safer to leave the issue to Labour's political wing."

The second source of division among miners was the use of foreign workers by employers. Here, too, what is true for the mining sector and for silicosis would be valid for other industries. Immigrants were in a weaker position, due to their relatively poor knowledge of social rights, their lack of language skills, their lesser participation in the unions (for new immigrants at least), and, in some cases, by the unions' xenophobia and racism—though the latter phenomenon is generally difficult to document in archival material. Migrants' trajectories also made it easier for employers to minimize silicosis compensation. It was convenient for employers to claim that foreign miners had contracted the disease abroad, either in their homeland or in an intermediate country. This happened to Polish miners in France in the 1930s, when they were accused of having been exposed to silicosis while working in the Ruhr in Germany. Migrants also had little chance of receiving compensation if they returned home: either legislation prevented them from receiving annuities, or social-insurance agencies exploited geographical distances in order to cut or contest any compensation. For example, when Polish miners in France returned to their home country during the crisis in the 1930s and immediately after World War II, the collieries denied Polish medical doctors any right to make a diagnosis of silicosis for these workers. It took 14 years (until 1959) for the Polish government to reach a bilateral agreement with France to improve the situation. The pernicious effect of distance was even more pronounced in cases in which the mines used a workforce made up of single male migrants with few kinship ties in their new work environment. Workers affected by severe occupational diseases were also more prone to re-emigrate.[82]

The relationship between migration and occupational health is structural. It was the determining factor in the recognition of a medico-legal concept of occupational disease at the end of the nineteenth century.[83] Since then, employers in most industrialized countries have chosen to import and use foreign manpower in the most dangerous occupations, often with the tacit agreement of the unions. This concentration of hazards in work undertaken by poorly protected foreign employees has had aggregate effects on the general level of health and safety in the workplace by allowing employers to minimize costs related to prevention and compensation. The mining sector provides a perfect example of these dynamics.[84] From the 1930s to the 1980s in French collieries, Polish, Italian, and Moroccan miners, successively, were overexposed to risk and underprotected in terms of financial compensation. This process reached its peak immediately after 1945, with German prisoners of war (who, it might be noted, went to work in the galleries singing Nazi military songs).[85] In the United States, various silicosis court cases involved Mexican workers.[86]

Exposure of the most vulnerable to the greatest risk, systematic in all industrialized countries, is underlined by the Czechoslovakian case. Under that country's socialist regime after World War II, foreign immigration was not an option. Who, then, would take on the most dangerous jobs, such as drilling, where the amount of deadly dust was at its highest? As in other countries, and even under the banner of official working-class ideology, occupational hazards were far from being distributed equally among the workforce. The first set of laborers to be exposed to risk in that nation calls to mind the prior history of the mining sector: forced labor was the structural equivalent of migrant workers. Czechoslovakia—which had no qualms about sending its national hero Emil Zátopek to work in the uranium mines after 1968—used political prisoners, ranging from opponents of the regime to Jehovah's Witnesses. The second group to be sacrificed were young, unskilled agricultural workers, who were sent underground without any real training. The latter were affected by silicosis at a very rapid rate and died on a massive scale after a few years.

Conclusion

In spite of the peculiarities of silicosis and, to some extent, its uncommonness, compensation for this disease raises major issues regarding the links between a free market economy and democracy. First, as has been shown through the extreme case of socialist Czechoslovakia (a planned economy), and through the intermediate situation in France (with a nationalized mining sector), there was not an absolute contrast between profit-oriented and production-oriented economies, at least as far as occupational health was concerned. In both systems, compensation was kept to a minimum, and some of the techniques used by industry were surprisingly similar: taking advantage of the myriad medical and legal ambiguities, postponing the removal of miners from dusty work for as long as possible, turning legal provisions into discretionary ones, and the like. Economic efficiency, however, distinguished the two systems. If the paths and procedures followed by socialist Czechoslovakia resembled those in Western Europe, a time lag of about 10 years or more separated them. As late as the 1970s, for instance, Czechoslovakia still could not conform to ILO radiographic standards, due to a lack of both equipment and trained specialists.

Second, there is a parallel in the workers themselves being potentially able to contest various aspects of the compensation system. All programs left them some margin for action. For example, socialist Czechoslovakia tried to institute special courts where miners could publicly defend their cases and raise issues that were not covered either by the relevant legislation or by regular administrative procedures. Yet in all countries, the influence of the industrialist lobby was so powerful, and miners' options so constrained, that legal provisions often appeared as mere formalities or were simply circumvented.

Trade unions have often been held responsible for this unequal balance of power. We have painted a different picture, exploring the numerous constraints that limited the miners' room to maneuver. The task facing the unions was particularly tricky. The technical complexity of the issues surrounding silicosis, which involved medical, engineering, and legal dimensions; the ability of the industry to spread out procedures among several institutions, the majority of which were under their control; the reluctance or fears of the miners themselves, which cannot be reduced to local beliefs or male bravado—all of these aspects made the disease a particularly tricky issue to tackle. Additionally, unions could not fight on all fronts simultaneously. Should they, for instance, argue for higher salaries? Advocate for safety and prevention? Or pursue compensation for their members?

Neither the judicial approach that was dominant in the Anglo-Saxon world, nor the political administrative channel common in southern Europe and non-Western countries, such as Japan, seem to have guaranteed a decent, or at least a transparent, compensation system for silicosis. The containment of political agency, understood in the broad sense of the term, was clearly instrumental in the minimization of payments to workers.

A general lesson can be drawn from this analysis. Most reforms in the occupational health system try—often in vain—to optimize institutional landscapes and procedures. Accepting the idea that legal provisions are always circumvented by employers, and recognizing the importance of agency, would open a new path for action, in which national authorities would support efforts emanating from civil society to improve occupational health provisions in terms of both prevention and compensation.

NOTES

1. For a global view, see Burger, "Restructuring Workers' Compensation," 198. Statistical underregistration in Europe is documented by Blandin et al., *Survey on Under-Reporting.* For France, official reports consider the global rate of underregistration to be above 70 percent for occupational diseases, including the most severe ones, such as cancers. Huge rates of underregistration are familiar to most industrialized countries. For the situation in the United States, see note 8 in the introduction.

2. Rosner and Markowitz, *Deadly Dust: Silicosis and the On-Going Struggle,* 22. Also see chapters 1, 2, and 3.

3. Moses, "Foreign Workers."

4. P. Rey, "La réparation des accidents"; P. Rey and Bousquet, "Compensation." Annalee Yassi, in a report prepared for the Ministry of Labour of Ontario (*Recent Developments*), stated that during the relevant period, only 2 percent of the compensation claims for workplace injuries were refused, versus over 50 percent for occupational diseases.

5. Bowden and Penrose, "Dust, Contractors, Politics, and Silicosis."

6. Note from Carozzi to Phelan and Butler, May 14, 1934, HY 553/0/2, A-ILO.

7. This information is based on a close study by Bernard Thomann of the archives of the "pneumoconiosis trials" that took place in the Japanese mining district of Fukuoka in the 1980s and 1990s. These archives are stored in the Documentation Center for Coal Research (*Sekitan kenkyû shiryô sentâ*) at the University of Kyushu.

8. In classifying mines according to dust levels, legislation allowed the collieries to take only a very limited list of work sites into account when calculating the duration of a miner's exposure to dust. Annie Thébaud-Mony (*La reconnaissance des maladies professionnelles*) gives an idea of the consequences of such a system, based on information obtained in the late 1980s. Among the files she had access to, only two mention the length of time a miner spent working underground. In the first instance, 29 years of mining work were converted into 7 years, 3 months, and 5 days of exposure. In the second case, 38 years underground became 8 years and 21 days of exposure. Moreover, in 1947, the French National Collieries (Charbonnages de France) stated that if a miner could not precisely outline the details of his career, 20 years in tunnels would be considered equivalent to 5 years doing dangerous jobs underground (Circulaire 341, S No. 329, 8 October 1947, 32 W61, CHML).

9. Markowitz and Rosner, "Limits of Thresholds." On the international debates about the definition of threshold limits, see below and chapter 6.

10. See McIvor and Johnston, *Miners' Lung,* ch. 8, esp. 253.

11. Mackova and Rosental, "Les démocraties populaires." All references to socialist Czechoslovakia in this chapter are taken from this article.

12. *Reclassement des silicotiques*, CHML. An additional difficulty was the variety of galleries where mining activity occurs.

13. Confirming the link between the history of silicosis and illnesses linked to asbestos, the Ordonnance sur la Silicose of August 2, 1945, includes the following activities among the "work likely to trigger the diseases . . . engendered or aggravated by silica dust": "drilling, boring, cutting, or extraction of rocks or minerals containing silica or asbestos; crushing, grinding, sieving, or dry-handling of minerals or rocks containing silica or asbestos, . . . carding, spinning, and weaving of asbestos."

14. Blandin et al., *Survey on Under-Reporting.*

15. Masami, "Homuresu mondai."

16. Ebihara, *Shokugyô byô undôshi*, 33–38.

17. Horne, "Demobilizing the Mind."

18. Lazar, "Damné de la terre."

19. Finance Minister Edgar Faure explicitly used this argument on April 6, 1954, against the favorable opinion by the Finance Commission of the French Parliament.

20. Baruch and Guigueno, *Le choix des X.*

21. Kippen, "Social and Political Meaning," 497. The financial impact of a trip to court in Melbourne (100 miles of travel)—and, often, the medical exams that took place in that city—were significant considerations for miners. The workers were also struck by the major differences in payouts granted by the courts for cases that, to them, looked similar.

22. Forestell, "'I Feel Like I'm Dying.'"

23. Ebihara, *Shokugyô byô undôshi*, 44.

24. Desoille et al., "Problèmes et difficultés pratiques."

25. Quoted by Magnin, "Méditation sur la prophylaxie," 475.

26. Lengwiler, "Rationalisation et tarification."

27. On this conference, see Cayet et al., "How International Organisations Compete."

28. Kippen, "Social and Political Meaning."

29. Concerning the imprecision of x-ray in the Porcupine mining district of Ontario, see Forestell, "'I Feel Like I'm Dying.'"

30. An "inadequate number of industrial doctors" was frequently mentioned as a primary cause in underreporting occupational diseases in Blandin et al., *Survey on Under-Reporting.*

31. Rosental and Devinck, "Statistique et mort industrielle," 83.

32. Mackova and Rosental, "Les démocraties populaires," 251.

33. Penrose, "Medical Monitoring and Silicosis," 290.

34. *Report of the Departmental Committee.*

35. Bufton and Melling, "Coming Up for Air."

36. Both quotations are from Forestell, "'I Feel Like I'm Dying.'"

37. Sellers, *Hazards of the Job*; Omnès and Bruno, *Les mains inutiles.*

38. On all these points, see Rosental and Devinck, "Statistique et mort industrielle."

39. Kippen, "Social and Political Meaning."

40. Blétry, "Ceci n'est pas un risque." The French situation is comparable to the Australian case studied by Bowden and Penrose, "Dust, Contractors, Politics, and Silicosis."

41. Here again, the situation in the mining sector throws light on a more systematic process. In some instances, sociomedical services within a company were in charge of minimizing the information given to workers, as in the case studied by Pitti ("Du rôle des mouvements sociaux").

42. Proctor and Schiebinger, *Agnotology.*

43. Thomann, "L'hygiène nationale."

44. Kippen, "Social and Political Meaning."

45. In a quite different context, Quataert (*Miners and the State*, 201–202) describes how the introduction of safety regulations created untoward effects by making miners lose "a sense of accountability for their actions."

46. See M. Bloor, "South Wales Miners Federation"; Melling, "Beyond a Shadow of a Doubt?"

47. Van Oorschot, "Non-Take-Up of Social Security Benefits."

48. P. Rey ("La réparation des accidents") shows that this limitation is still crucial today with regard to compensation for occupational diseases in general. In particular, he quotes a Canadian study (Walters and Haines, "Workers' Use and Knowledge") showing how, in 1988 in Ontario, most workers only had access to legal information through their foremen. Only unionized workers were knowledgeable about the relevant legislation, and they did not dare to act in favor of safety and health measures at work.

49. Today, similar processes are implemented by companies to dilute and control the perception of psychosocial risks, including occupational suicides. See Benquet et al., "Responsabilités en souffrance."

50. This committee was called the Comité d'Avis sur Rente de l'Union Régionale des Sociétés de Secours Minières ("Compensation Arbitration Committee of the Mining Mutual-Aid Societies' Regional Union").

51. These commissions brought together the chief medical doctor from the collieries, a doctor from the mining social security system (also controlled by the mines), and an academic from a local university, who generally was close to management.

52. *Étude des houillères du Bassin du Nord-Pas-de-Calais*, CAC.

53. Even, "Pneumoconioses (réserves)." Dr. Even was a medical adviser for the mining social security system.

54. Cottereau, "L'usure au travail."

55. Bufton and Melling, "Coming Up for Air."

56. Douglas, *Implicit Meanings*, 216.

57. Grätz, "Gold-Mining and Risk Management," 202.

58. Ramazzini, *Treatise of the Diseases*.

59. The workers' rationale operating here was ultimately designed to maximize the earnings of the household (R. Johnston and McIvor, "Oral History," 243–244): "Men would say, for example, that they were working for the family or to give the kids 'a better chance.' This, however, had the potential to lead to bodily damage—fatigue, injury, disease, disability—representing a sacrifice of sorts by the workmen. In turn, such risk taking provided another important justification for male power and male dominance within society. It gave entitlement to a privileged position." See also Forestell, "'I Feel Like I'm Dying'"; Gorman et al., "Asbestos in Scotland."

60. Nisaburô, *Kôfu dôshoku kumiai*, 35–114.

61. R. Johnston and McIvor, "Oral History," 244: "Masculinity, or machismo, is not a static concept, but one that is constantly changing as society evolves and, equally as important, changing throughout the course of men's lifetimes."

62. Klubock, "Working-Class Masculinity."

63. R. Johnston and McIvor, "Oral History," 248.

64. For a good example of this process, see Klubock, "Working-Class Masculinity." Julia Seibert ("More Continuity than Change?," 369–386) details a case in the mining and plantation sector in the Belgian Congo that, while no doubt an extreme example, demonstrates the difficulty for employers in creating a workforce from scratch—which also often meant introducing wage/labor relationships.

65. See similar observations by Mills ("Hazardous Bargain") regarding occupational hazards and risky behaviors.

66. Hiroshi and Wake, "Zuidôkôji dekasegi rôdôsha."

67. Schwartz, *Le monde privé.*

68. Forestell, "'I Feel Like I'm Dying,'" 83.

69. This statement by a former Scottish miner is quoted in R. Johnston and McIvor, "Oral History," 243.

70. Forestell, "'I Feel Like I'm Dying.'"

71. Prior to 1930, approximately one-third of the labor force in the Porcupine mines sustained some form of workplace injury on an annual basis. In more than half of these cases, the injuries were serious enough to warrant more than a week off of work. After that date, the accident rate declined somewhat, but it still did not drop below 25 percent until the late 1940s. Although the majority of injuries were often temporary, a substantial portion of men were left with some kind of permanent physical impairment: company accident reports regularly noted amputated fingers, fractured limbs, lacerated arms and faces, and wrenched backs. Fatal accidents rarely occurred, yet hundreds of mine workers died in these goldfields in the first half of the twentieth century. From the 1930s on, gold mining actually had a disproportionately higher fatality rate than other sectors of the mining industry in Ontario. Long after other industries became less hazardous, at least with regard to accidents, gold mining remained a "dangerous trade."

72. McIvor and Johnston, "Voices from the Pits," 130.

73. Forestell, "'I Feel Like I'm Dying,'" 90–91.

74. Claude Amoudru, who would later become head of the medical service for the French collieries, gives this description of his interaction with a silicotic miner's daughter in the north of France around 1960 (*Médecine, mines et mineurs*, Bibliothèque de l'Académie Nationale de Médecine, 41): "Late one afternoon, I was called to a miner's cottage at Sallaumines; although it was not part of my duties as a hospital physician, this family could not find any other doctor. I can still picture the scene. In a shabby interior—the income of occupational invalids being terribly meager—was a tearful young girl in the living room, who led me upstairs. There I found a man, still young, sitting up in bed, his scrawny torso struggling with each attempt at breath, and an exhausted woman holding his hand. I quickly wrote a prescription for oxygen therapy to be administered at home. As I made to leave, the young girl said to me: 'It's too frightful. My mother and I are forced to be here all the time. That's my father, but he has no more life: nothing, nothing, nothing at all! I haven't even be able to go to a dance for over a year!' A distress which has become almost banal in the mining cottages." On the effects of silicosis on the economic plight of miners' families deprived of their wage-earning father, see Kippen, "Social and Political Meaning."

75. See Behrent, "Accidents Happen." In 1976, François Ewald edited a special issue of Jean-Paul Sartre's journal, *Les Temps modernes*, entitled "Justice, Discipline, Production," with coverage extending from the December 1974 Liévin catastrophe to a general discussion of safety in the mines and occupational hazards. Ewald, who had personal experience teaching in a mining district, was to devote a groundbreaking book, *L'Etat providence*, to the centrality of workplace accidents in the emergence of the welfare state. See also Fontaine, *Fin d'un monde ouvrier.*

76. On the collective basis of supposedly individual memory, see the classic work by Halbwachs, *On Collective Memory.*

77. See similar considerations in Burt and Kippen, "Rational Choice."

78. Quataert, *Miners and the State*, 201.

79. The attitude of French workers toward occupational medicine has been succinctly and carefully analyzed by Ranc ("Les ouvriers"). Comparable hypotheses are arrived at through a different method by Matoševic ("Industry Forging Masculinity").

80. In her survey of the literature devoted to occupational health, Paule Rey ("La réparation des accidents") reminds us that piecework payment limits risk aversion and increases overwork and fatigue. Among others, she quotes Laflamme and Arsenault ("Wage Modes and Injuries"), as well as Stonecipher and Hyner ("Health Practices").

81. Bowden and Penrose, "Dust, Contractors, Politics, and Silicosis."

82. Derickson, "Industrial Refugees." See also Rennie, "Historical Origins"; Burke, "Disease, Labour Migration."

83. Moses, "Foreign Workers."

84. For a list of references, see Rosental, "De la silicose."

85. Amoudru, *Médecine, mines et mineurs*, 26, Bibliothèque de l'Académie Nationale de Médecine.

86. Rosner and Markowitz, "Trials and Tribulations."

Chapter 6

Silica or Coal?
Design and Implementation of Dust
Prevention in the Collieries in Western
Economies, ca. 1930–1980

Éric Geerkens

Kill the dust and you will get rid of the sickness.

H. E. Muntjewerff, "Stofbestrijding"

Prevention is crucial when it comes to occupational diseases. It is another facet of the close link among productivity, management of the workforce, and social welfare. Prevention connects medical and engineering expertise (although not without tensions), and it also structurally relates to compensation. In most industrialized countries, employers are legally responsible for the various costs of occupational diseases and workplace injuries. This not only acknowledges that the organization of how work is done bears the primary responsibility for employees' health hazards, but also stems from the reasoning that employers' cost-cutting concerns will impel them to take preventive action against such hazards.

History, however, casts doubt on the efficacy of this approach, showing it to be too mechanically targeted to capture the roles played by peoples' agency. In practice, due to constraints on the workforce and the complexity and variety of the medical, legal, and technical issues involved, companies have always managed to advance a different agenda that strove to minimize the costs of both compensation and prevention. In its analysis of these issues, the present chapter contributes to this volume's critique of a purely legal, formal analysis of social regulations in industrialized countries. "Critique" should be understood here in the sense of a historical analysis, rather than in the sense of an ideological statement. It is by no means the outcome of an abstract, a priori political stance, but of thorough, comparative, empirical observations, leading to ex post facto analytical considerations.

This chapter focuses mainly, though not exclusively, on Europe. The Old World played an important role in the rise of prevention as a managerial concern and the implementation of measures such as dust removal. Europe was also central in the definition and dissemination of the so-called exposure thresholds after World War II. What happened in the United States regarding this key issue, which was to play a major role in the drama over asbestos in the second half of the century, has been well documented by historians, but it requires further clarification for Europe. European debates over the implementation of these thresholds took place in the context of Cold War divisions and shed light on the intersection between public health and geopolitical interests, an aspect of the history of silicosis that is touched on here and explored further in the last section of this chapter. Finally, this chapter discusses one of the most perverse effects of the ILO's deal making throughout the 1930s: how its focus on the risks of silica drew attention away from the effects of other types of dust on workers' health. By the 1940s, however, the damaging effects of coal dust had already begun to be recognized, and this chapter examines the emergence of other medically classified entities, called "coal workers' pneumoconiosis" (CWP) in the United Kingdom, and "anthraco-silicosis" (in countries such as Belgium or France).

Both CWP and silicosis have their own distinct identities, which can be determined through a microscopic analysis of histological material (i.e., tissues) and the use of radiology.[1] In practice, though, their respective impacts on miners' health varied significantly from one mine to another, and from one type of job in the mine to another, depending on geological conditions as well as how the work was organized, a parameter that evolved over time. But it is difficult for historians to reconstruct exact proportions for the combination of these two diseases, because even the medical staff had a hard time distinguishing them. These illnesses shared some symptoms and radiographic characteristics, but they could also interfere with one another, as the category anthraco-silicosis suggests. An additional disease that could not be ruled out was tuberculosis, which silicosis might trigger, and which, in turn, made silicosis much more dangerous. Here, too, a mixed category, silico-tuberculosis, captured this effect. While TB cases in Western mines fell following the introduction of antibiotics after World War II, the disease remained a significant factor in one major mining country, South Africa, where it also became enmeshed with and aggravated by HIV, beginning in the 1980s.[2]

Silicosis, Coal Worker's Pneumoconiosis, and the Struggle for Prevention and Compensation

In South Africa during the early decades of the twentieth century, silicosis became the focus of a push for compensation as well as prevention. Prevention strategies were both medical, through the screening and monitoring of workers, and technical, with the adoption of end-of-shift blasting and wet drilling. These technical changes spread beyond the gold mines and improved conditions across this sector, particularly with regard to tunneling in coal mines.

Yet, in the coal-mining industry, tunneling, drilling, and blasting occupied only a limited fraction of the workers toiling underground. At the same time, particularly during the 1920s and 1930s, the organization of work in the coal mines underwent a profound transformation. Mechanization revolutionized the cutting and removal of coal, even more than it did for tunneling, rendering the former processes far unhealthier for the majority of workers. Thus, during this period, two distinct phenomena arose—more-effective prevention of exposure in tunneling work, but an increased dust risk in other aspects of production—with contrasting effects on different sections of the coal-mining labor force.

On the one hand, the adoption of wet drilling and end-of-shift blasting reduced the overall incidence of silicosis. Although wet drilling was known and increasingly employed before World War II, the technique would only become widespread in the postwar years, especially the 1950s. In Belgium, for instance, it was used in 50 percent of the coal-mining operations in the late 1940s, a figure that had risen to 90 percent by 1954. Similarly, in France, wet drilling was in general use by around 1950. Internationally, extensive use of water-injection drills was documented by the mid-1950s.[1]

The complexity of these changes can be seen in their contrasting effects on different categories of workers. As "pure" silicosis (according to the Johannesburg definition), which mainly had an impact on tunnel diggers, began to claim fewer and fewer victims, anthraco-silicosis began to affect larger cohorts of workers, such as cutters, transport workers, and propping laborers.

For both anthraco-silicosis and silico-tuberculosis, the reciprocal effects of the diseases involved were so significant that they created new entities. Their progressive recognition in the official medical classification system proceeded at different paces, however. While anthraco-silicosis became part of the International

Spurred by the international conferences in Johannesburg (1930) and Geneva (1934 and 1938) and the inclusion of silicosis in occupational disease tables and numerous national laws, demands for compensation began to emanate from workers in diverse industrial sectors, including the collieries. But the nature of exposure to the several types of dust in coal mining differed from that in the gold mines. In the second half of the nineteenth century, various attempts to address the former had already been made in different European countries. Back then, doctors had concluded that anthracosis was not a separate disease. Three-quarters of a century later, a familiar situation arose: evidence of the pathological states of workers was clear to doctors and other practitioners on the ground, who worked with miners on a daily basis, but references to classic silicosis (as defined at the Johannesburg conference) were used by medical comptrollers, who were in charge of deciding whether miners suffered from an occupational disease or not, in order to prevent the recognition of pneumoconiosis in miners as a compensable occupational disease.

In the immediate aftermath of World War II, pure silicosis continued to present an obstacle to the recognition of anthraco-silicosis—which, at that time, was the most common mining disease—at the conceptual level. In France, this is explained partly by the absence of scientific information in circulation from foreign countries during the war years. French researchers were notably unaware of the Medical Research Council study that had resulted in legislation in Great Britain in 1943.[2] This can be seen in the French coniotic index (defining allowable dust levels), which was chiefly developed with reference to pure silicosis.

Moreover, the cycle continued. When pneumoconiosis in mine workers was finally recognized and the true magnitude of the problem understood, this acknowledgment would, in turn, become a stumbling block to the recognition of miners' other respiratory diseases, such as emphysema and chronic bronchitis.

1. Houberechts, "L'activité de l'Institut d'Hygiène des Mines," (1951): 333, (1953): 325; Proust, *Les méthodes de lutte*, ECSC.
2. Amoudru, "La silicose et les pneumoconioses dans les houillères," 23.

Classification of Diseases during its sixth revision (in 1948), it took 17 more years for silico-tuberculosis to be included (during the eighth revision in 1965). This chronology, and its time lag, are an indication that medical observations alone were not the only drivers. Once silicosis, and then later CWP, were recognized and compensated for as occupational diseases, the distinction between a pure and a mixed entity started to have economic consequences for the companies, as well as for social- and private-insurance systems. As in the case of "simple silicosis," the medical complexity of the disease and tensions over its financial implications went hand in hand. Thus prevention cannot be treated just as a technical issue. It also involved companies' attempts to make work-related health issues less visible. This chapter tells the multifaceted story by focusing on the crucial coal sector, where silicosis and CWP overlapped.

The Ambiguous Causes and Effects of Prevention

For roughly the first 70 years of the twentieth century, the idea that medical monitoring, combined with technical prevention measures, could solve, or at least reduce, the problem of silicosis was widespread.[3] This phenomenon provides rich material for a comparative and transnational history of prevention, which mirrors the history of the recognition of the disease. In both cases, we see ambiguous policies whose sociomedical applications were constrained by economic factors and varied according to the balance of power among employers, unions, and public authorities. Furthermore, the histories of prevention and recognition not only merit comparison, but are intertwined. While proactive management actions on prevention depended, at least partly, on compensation costs, policies on both prevention and recognition strove to keep silicotic workers without massive clinical symptoms in the mines for as long as possible.

Here, again, are echoes of the 1930 debates in Johannesburg, where the efficiency of prevention was a central concern, but for purely practical reasons that were related to the optimal management of the workforce. Long before any initial consensus was reached as to the nature of silicosis, preventive measures had been introduced in the extractive industries in countries such as Germany, Japan, and South Africa as industrialists sought to avoid the effects of a disease and symptoms they did not wish to recognize as occupational but still feared having to compensate for financially. At least as important was the desire to delay the onset of silicosis, so that the workers' impairments would only occur as they neared retirement. The international recognition of silicosis in 1934 as a compensable occupational disease only strengthened these priorities. The development of technical and medical silicosis prevention policies in the coal industry led to the design of indicators to measure the effectiveness of these practices. The data, however, were both indisputable and incomplete. Four examples illustrate the issues at stake.

In the early 1960s, Dutch coal-mine doctors used an analysis of the periodic x-ray exams given to all miners to show the progress that had been made in fighting silicosis (*silikose* in Dutch, but "coal workers' pneumoconiosis" in a UK publication by the same authors). Their study was based on a calculation of the prevalence of the disease (the total number of cases of compensation divided by the number of miners exposed) according to the duration of exposure to the risk. It showed a decrease of around 13 percent in less than 10 years, although the total for those affected by the disease was still over 46 percent in 1958.[4]

British researchers proposed an alternative measurement, in which prevalence was calculated as a percentage not of the entire mining population, but of a specific age group. The prevalence of the various forms of pneumoconiosis in Britain from 1959 to 1968 fell from 2.7 percent to 0.4 percent in x-rayed men between the ages of 25 and 34.[5] These researchers also focused on incidence (the number of new cases declared) to show how this, too, had fallen in Britain over time, from nearly 6,000 cases a year in 1949 to fewer than 500 in 1974.

In France, the average incidence of pneumoconiosis among all active workers fell from 2.4 percent in 1957 to 0.8 percent in 1978. The progress achieved through prevention was measured, in particular, by the average age at death for pneumoconiosis sufferers. In the Lorraine coal mines, in the eastern part of the country, this rose from age 53 in the early 1950s to nearly 69 in 1973, at which point the life expectancy for miners was barely lower than that of the national average for men. But statistics for France as a whole were less favorable, since the average age at death only rose from 55.5 years old in 1960 to 60.5 in 1970, and 65.4 in 1974. This indicator obviously does not account of the miners' quality of life during their illness (what demographers currently refer to as "disability-free life expectancy").[6] Moreover, there is a risk of underestimating the number of silicosis victims, as has been demonstrated by thorough analyses in the cases of France and socialist Czechoslovakia.[7]

At the end of the period studied, with the introduction of epidemiological techniques in the field of occupational health, various mathematical models of the likely development of the disease as a function of the degree of exposure were used to estimate, from the recent past, the probability of avoiding a serious pneumoconiosis (stage 2 and above, according to the Geneva classification) at the end of a full career in the coal mines. Shortly before coal mining in Belgium ceased (1992), researchers at the Institut d'Hygiène des Mines (IHM)

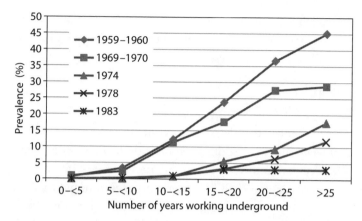

Figure 1. Prevalence of stage 2 (and above) pneumoconiosis in Campine, Belgium. For 1983, only the value for more than 25 years is based on observations; the others are estimated. Minette and Degueldre, "L'importance de l'épidémiologie"; van Sprundel, "Mijnwerkerspneumoconiose."

showed the progress made in the Campine coalfield between the late 1950s and the mid-1980s: the probability of developing a serious pneumoconiosis fell from 45 percent after 30 years underground in 1959–1960, to 12 percent in 1978, and finally to 2–3 percent in 1983 (figure 1).

Although the progress achieved cannot be denied—within the limits of data quality—these differing results raise a number of questions, of which the most obvious is why working conditions improved at so late a date. Any answer must first address the time lag between the refinements in knowledge and the implementation of prevention strategies. The study of health hazards in coal mines covering both classical silicosis, which was internationally recognized in 1934, and CWP is supported by abundant documentation, including the ILO and the European Coal and Steel Community archives, coal-company and employer-association archives, medical and technical literature from various countries, and a vast body of historical literature. The relatively late appearance of data showing the effectiveness of prevention policies also invites us to examine the time lag between the definition of these policies, including regulations and their implementation.

Reflecting the distinctions made by the actors themselves, this chapter first addresses technical and then medical prevention, and subsequently examines the medical contribution to technical prevention. On each of these points, prevention policies are placed in the context of their adoption and then, as far as the available documentation permits, the various obstacles that kept them from being fully effective are described.

Technical Efforts
Silicosis Prevention in Mines

During the first three decades of the twentieth century, various technical means of prevention—wet drilling (mainly with drill bits with an axial water supply), the periodic dampening of broken ground, more-effective ventilation, end-of-shift blasting, and the like[8]—were introduced in industries in South Africa (the first country to do so), Australia, Germany, Japan, and Canada. These measures were not intended primarily for coal mines, however. The information available in the coal industry at that time concerning the etiology of silicosis, in particular the idea that gallery cutters were more exposed to dust than coal hewers, played a major role in the priority given to drilling (wet drilling and drill-dust collection). Before World War II, wet drilling was the most successful means of technical prevention. Chronologically, these initial measures usually were closely associated with the introduction of public-sector compensation policies and, to a lesser extent, with calls for prevention at ILO conferences.

The international recognition of silicosis in 1934 included an appeal for both technical and medical prevention: "Compensation for silicosis should not be considered apart from prophylactic measures. The most important of these is the prevention of dust. Consideration should also be given to the importance of preliminary and periodic examination of employees."[9] The recommendations of the 1938 International Labour Conference stressed technical prevention devices for individuals—in other words, masks. Employers' persistent interest in masks reflected their view of prevention: masks are cheaper than any other form of collective prevention (in the United States, the availability of cheap gas masks following World War I appears to have spurred companies' attraction to their use),[10] and, when they are made compulsory for or merely available to miners, the responsibility for being exposed to dust is shifted onto the workers.[11] The mask issue illustrates how the preferred prevention option for coal-mine owners was the least expensive one, requiring no organizational change.

The results of some surveys—showing more silicosis sufferers among gallery cutters than coal-face workers,[12] leading doctors to distinguish CWP from classical silicosis—helped modify prevention guidelines in the mines, which now focused more on the cutting and removal of coal.

Prevention of Coal Workers' Pneumoconiosis

Paralleling the situation with drilling in metal-ore mines at the turn of the century, the new preventive weapon was water, used in various ways. One of the most effective means of reducing dust in mines was water infusion, or injecting water into the coal seam, a British idea that emerged in 1943 and was developed over the next three decades. Although it was not suitable for all deposits, mine managers adopted infusion with some enthusiasm because, although providing a water supply was expensive, the cost could be outweighed by the prospect of increased output, since infusion "softened" the face. In other words, prevention boosted productivity.[13] While infusion reduced the formation of dust in advance, other methods were added to prevent dust from dispersing during hewing and hauling, such as spraying water near the dust source (using wet-cutting percussive drills, and slicers or breakers fitted with sprays) and along the conveyors (by watering the conveyor belts, ventilating loading points, etc.).[14] Similarly, the technique of fogging to capture dust, inspired by the work of John Scott Haldane's former colleague, Belgian physiologist Lucien Dautrebande, who had used it in the Belgian Congo, was publicized in the early 1950s, although it proved to be an inadequate response. It was intended to prevent the finest, and therefore the most dangerous particles from penetrating deep into the lungs by trapping them in water droplets.[15] More generally, no single technique alone could ensure sufficient dust prevention, and, by the standards of the emerging science of ergonomics, prevention needed to be planned before coal seams were exploited if it was to be fully effective.

The proceedings of the conference held by the ILO in 1952 on the prevention and suppression of dust in mining, tunneling, and quarrying present an extensive collection of techniques known at that time and used over subsequent decades. The ILO periodically circulated reports on the most up-to-date prevention information.[16] These catalogs of techniques used, or at least experimented with, throughout the world should not be confused with the prevention policies actually adopted in the coal-mining industries of the countries studied, however. In practice, the techniques were implemented in a number of ways and came up against a great deal of resistance from both employers and workers.

In mines where employers, willingly or otherwise, implemented preventive measures, they sometimes did the minimum necessary and regularly chose

Coal Mining and Dust-Removal Techniques in the Twentieth Century

In the history of twentieth-century coal mining in Western Europe, two critical practices particularly increased miners' exposure to dust: the adoption of long-wall mining, and the full mechanization of cutting and advancing work, especially after the introduction of pneumatic drills in the galleries (the effects of which had already been reported in several publications).[1]

Major organizational changes in coal mining occurred during the 1920s and increased throughout the 1930s. These were not limited to the mechanization of cutting and transporting coal, which had been taking place since the turn of the century. Work along successive long walls, which mining engineers at that time compared with an assembly line, combined the use of high-volume transporters (shaker loaders and conveyor belts), which could carry off the coal produced by scores, or even hundreds, of coal cutters on the long wall, with block caving, which enabled longer faces to be worked. This change had the consequence of exposing face workers to a continuous draft of dust and packing workers into areas with considerable quantities of dust thrown up by the caving. Safety requirements imposed the use of stronger ventilation for these long walls, which, in turn, threw more dust into the air. The change occurred at a time when silicosis was barely recognized as an occupational disease, and no preventive measures were taken. Furthermore, operating in always-deeper seams makes the atmosphere drier—and, therefore, unhealthier.

In the 1950s, when the concept of prevention was being applied, another organizational change proved to be injurious for miners' health: armored conveyors, carrying slicers and feeder breakers, plus mechanized (self-advancing) support, better known as power-loading machines, enabled the complete mechanization of face work. Although this mechanization considerably reduced the amount of manual labor, the underground workers were more exposed to greater quantities of dust, because the new machines stripped both coal seams and passageways, which explains a brief surge in the silicosis incidence rates. Moreover, since mechanization increased the speed of advancing the face (which now was continuously exploited), it involved a more frequent adaptation of dust-suppression measures, which often limited their effectiveness.

1. See, among others, Lankton, "Machine under the Garden."

the cheapest techniques. For instance, the "Randlords" in South Africa in the early twentieth century initially thought that it would be cheaper to train and employ inexperienced Afrikaners, rather than undertake expensive preventive measures. When forced to adopt prevention, they chose the least effective wet-drilling techniques, which were also the least expensive.[17] Similarly, in the Belgian coal mines in the 1950s and 1960s, there was a definite time lag between the IHM's appeals for prevention and the attitudes of and practical measures taken by the employers who funded the IHM. Every year from 1947 on, this organization, a private body, published a report in its mine-administration journal on progress that was achieved in controlling dust formation underground in Belgian coal mines. The data for 1946–1954 show a preponderant use of individual protection measures (masks), and close analysis reveals that, although 32 percent of the coal mines reported the use of infusion, it was actually only applied on 11 percent of the working faces. Even more instructive is a comparison between these published data and the archives of an organization whose members were all health and safety engineers in a given coalfield (Liège). It shows that the very people who should have been at the forefront of prevention actually hampered it—in the mid-1960s, despite conventional wisdom, they were still promoting masks and criticizing water infusion.[18] Where more-effective prevention techniques were chosen, companies did not always provide enough water to dampen the works. Nor, more generally, did they apply the best methods as efficiently as they could have; sometimes they did not require their suppliers to provide equipment that was already adapted for dust suppression.[19]

In general terms, the coal-mining industry constantly had to juggle economic survival—under threat as early as the 1950s, as the old, exhausted European coalfields faced global competition—with the need to preserve workers' health, if only to continue to attract people to mine work and retain skilled miners pursuing this activity for as long as possible. The productivity policy imposed by the National Coal Board (NCB) on Scottish mines that were threatened with closure was detrimental to workers' health and safety. Local management held diverse attitudes, caught between the imperatives of productivity and the dangers of working above a certain dust threshold.[20]

Resistance to prevention also came from workers. Both before and after World War II, coal cutters complained that wearing a mask interfered with the level of effort demanded of them at that time, a pressure often increased by measures such as incentive pay, which forced workers to make trade-offs between their income levels and their health.[21] The most effective prevention measures—infusion and spraying—were also rejected by the miners, because of the unpleasant nature of work undertaken in such damp surroundings, as well as medical factors, such as a fear of rheumatism. These sorts of objections were reported in Britain, France, Belgium, and socialist Czechoslovakia.[22]

Medical Prevention

On the medical front, preventive thinking about silicosis was adopted early, following the international definition of the disease and recognition of its occupational nature.

Therapeutic Dead Ends

By the early 1950s, it appears to have been widely accepted among physicians that "the treatment of silicosis remains palliative and symptomatic."[23] Consequently, while great attention was given to the relief of acute cases and to complications due to related medical conditions, such as tuberculosis (through preventive BCG vaccination campaigns), cardiovascular insufficiency, bronchitis, and emphysema, the occupational nature of these linked diseases was only recognized much later. Just as exclusive attention to the pathogenic effects of silica hampered the recognition of CWP, the focus on pneumoconiosis appears to have hampered the recognition of miners' other respiratory ailments, a health issue that is still crucial today.[24]

Various dead ends in the medical treatment of silicosis, tried mainly during the postwar period, deserve to be mentioned briefly. The first was aluminum therapy, which was developed in the late 1930s by scientists working for the Canadian McIntyre Porcupine Gold Mine Company and was based on the idea that aluminum powder could protect lungs against silica depositions.[25] In Western Europe, this therapy was widely discussed and criticized in the late 1940s, but by the end of the following decade, it appears to have largely disappeared from medical concerns. Nevertheless, it continued to be used in the gold mines in Ontario until 1979 and was studied by the coal-mining industry in Western Europe, despite the fact that it was designed to guard against problems from quartz rather than coal-mine dust, which contains little quartz.[26] This demonstrates that it was long thought (or hoped) that silicosis could be prevented by pharmacological means. Following this attempt, a similar form of prevention was studied, with support from the European Coal and Steel Community, among others: the use of synthetic polymers (polyvinylpyridine-N-oxide, or PVNO), advanced primarily by two German researchers in 1960.[27]

This therapeutic prospect aroused great enthusiasm in the scientific community, including a 1965 report stating that it would enable a comprehensive set of measures to prevent the development and spread of silicosis.[28] As in the case of aluminum therapy, an initial obstacle to the use of PVNO was uncertainty about the consequences of long-term exposure. At a more basic level, its effectiveness continued to be studied—in the lab and in humans—and discussed for decades, without achieving decisive acceptance.[29]

Another preventive technique was tested in the early 1950s in such countries as Belgium, Germany, and the Netherlands: the collective use of aerosols at the end of the working day to dilate the bronchi and encourage the expectoration of dust. This preventive treatment was abandoned, due to poor results.[30]

Selection as the Primary Tool for Medical Prevention

In all industrial sectors, the main instrument used by occupational health officers since the start of the twentieth century was a medical exam and subsequent selection of the workforce before and/or during employment.[31] The principle objective of prehire efforts was to reject those workers likely to contract an occupational disease. Medical prevention of silicosis before World War II was based on available scientific knowledge about the disease. Because of the connections between tuberculosis and silicosis, medical monitoring was designed to choose new workers by eliminating at the outset those candidates with evidence of lung lesions, primarily caused by tuberculosis.[32] Later, periodic exams attempted to eliminate those workers already suffering from silicosis.[33] One expert at the 1938 Geneva conference stated the matter bluntly: "In most cases, medical examinations on hiring are intended less to safeguard workers' health than to eliminate those who might later become a liability for the relevant compensation funds."[34]

After World War II, this type of medical screening was made compulsory in many industrialized nations; the elimination of sick workers was still the main concern.[35] In some countries, a list was drawn up of medical conditions that made underground work in mines inadvisable. In Europe, these compendiums were used when selecting migrant workers, and the same health officers who created the lists for the mines often employed them in more-general immigration policies. For instance, V. Van Mechelen, a senior medical officer at the Institut d'Hygiène des Mines, took part in an ILO study aimed at determining what medical criteria should be used to screen migrant workers in different professions before they left their countries of origin.[36]

There was no consensus on the value of x-ray exams, which became compulsory in countries such as South Africa (where TB remains a major issue to this day), France, Belgium, and Canada (in the province of Ontario). Nor was there consensus on the optimal frequency of these exams. The United Kingdom, for example, although a leader in combating CWP, only made them systematic in 1959; the question there was the quality of the x-rays produced by the available equipment and the competence of the staff involved in interpreting the results.[37] French hospitals administered by the collieries faced comparable limitations.

As was the case for technical prevention, both the resources available and the effectiveness of the medically based selection of new mine workers deserve examination. Perhaps the reason tuberculosis remained a scourge of mine workers for many years was because the industry's selection processes were not very effective.[38] Some of the Belgian archives that contain information on how medical screening was carried out reveal that when labor was scarce (such as in the immediate postwar years), employers' main concern was not to lose potential workers because of medical exams that were too long or too complicated. In these cases, employers were firmly opposed to film radiography—which was also more expensive—and considered real-time radioscopy to be quite sufficient. Some coal-mine health officers even stated that a clinical exam was still their main tool in selecting workers, who were expected to be productive immediately.[39]

Knowledge, Medico-Legal Recognition, and Medical Screening of the Disease(s)

As knowledge of CWP advanced, periodic exams took on a new significance. After World War II, doctors began to distinguish these medical conditions from those of classical silicosis. For decades, the etiology of silicosis that was determined at the 1930 Johannesburg conference hampered an understanding of and compensation for coal miners' respiratory disease, even though it did formalize a recognition of the risk from silica versus the risk of tuberculosis. Here again, one of this volume's key issues appears: the unintended effects of the minimalist results of the negotiation over the scope of silicosis, concluded in the 1930s under the auspices of the ILO. In the United Kingdom, for example, recognition of CWP had originally been based on criteria similar to those for classical silicosis. The increasing prevalence of pulmonary fibrosis in South Welsh miners spurred the Industrial Pulmonary Diseases Committee of the

Medical Research Council (MRC) to carry out a detailed survey in 1937. This led to the medico-legal recognition of CWP in 1943, and to basic research into its development.[40]

Coal Workers Pneumoconiosis, the Resurgent Former Rival of Silicosis

The coining of a term for this set of conditions was a real "rediscovery of coal dust disease" after a century-long series of questions and debates on the pathological effects of inhaling coal dust.[41] Significantly, CWP progressively replaced the former term anthracosis, which was coined in 1838 by the English physician Thomas Stratton (1816–1886) but had experienced the same difficulties as silicosis (one of its rivals in explaining colliery miners' diseases) in gaining recognition.[42] In practice, the two processes—the accumulation of silica dust and coal dust in the lungs—were difficult to distinguish using clinical, radiological, and breathing tests, all the more so because in most work situations, miners inhaled a mixture of minerals present in dusts. Silicosis and CWP often remained intertwined as risk factors, although it is fair to say that in Western Europe, silicosis was probably most hazardous from 1920 to 1950, while CWP peaked in the ensuing decades. For instance, after World War II, it affected a much larger number of underground workers in France than did silicosis in the narrow sense, whose sole victims were those working in rock-cutting galleries rather than extracting coal.[43] But as always in the case of pneumoconiosis, the combination of medical complexity and high financial stakes made the history of silicosis and CWP far from straightforward. A comparison of the medico-legal treatment of these two diseases in the United Kingdom, France, and United States underscores the importance of social, political, and economic contexts in the history of occupational diseases.[44]

In the United Kingdom, coal-dust hazards were officially recognized following the adoption of the 1943 Pneumoconiosis Compensation Scheme, which expanded the causes of risks attributed to silica and asbestos dusts to "other dusts."[45] World War II played a decisive role in this recognition, which not only involved an acceptance of new medical findings but also marked a form of socioeconomic compromise. Labor shortages at a time of pressing production needs strengthened the hand of miners, who requested the full enforcement of silicosis legislation, which had hitherto been selectively upheld, due to mining's status as a sensitive sector. In 1928, the 1919 law regarding silicosis had finally been extended to the mining sector, but only miners who had worked with ores containing at least 50 percent silica were eligible for compensation.

Like many criteria for recognizing occupational diseases, this clause not only was restrictive, but also placed the burden of proof on the miners at risk, forcing them into an unequal battle with the mining companies' geologists. Instead of lifting these restrictions during the war, the British government extended the range of legally recognized afflictions. This expansion signaled progress, but, by the same token, it diminished the perception of silica risks in the following decades.[46]

In contrast, France only recognized CWP in July 1980, when the category "Occupational silicosis: Diseases resulting from the inhalation of mineral dusts containing free silica," used since 1950, was renamed "Pneumoconioses resulting from the inhalation of mineral dusts containing free silica." In terms of prevention, France certainly lagged behind the United Kingdom, but this gap was closer to 15 years, rather than to 40-year recognition differential between the two countries.[47] Rather than indicating a lower level of generosity in France's compensation plan, this delay reflected two very different institutional ways of interpreting the miners' medical risks. During these four decades, the United Kingdom focused on the hazards of coal itself, leading to a decrease in the perception of silica risk. In France, where physicians often used the term "anthracosilicosis," the legal recognition of silicosis in 1945 was a response by General de Gaulle's National Union government to employers' fierce denial of the very existence of silicosis, an attitude that had prevailed since the end of the 1920s.

The French government, which then included the Communist Party, promoted the recognition of this disease so heavily that "silicosis" became the established diagnostic umbrella covering all miners' ailments. According to Claude Amoudru, former head of the French health service for the national collieries, in the 1950s, employer and worker organizations agreed that compensation for pneumoconiosis linked to coal would be administratively handled through the silicosis system but benefit from more-favorable conditions in terms of length of exposure and time limits for compensation claims.[48] The arrangement's downside was clearly that compensation remained contingent on showing symptoms of silicosis. This continued to be the case, even after France's 1980 recognition of CWP. On June 26, 1986, in written question number 1849, addressed to the Minister for Social Affairs and Employment, the Socialist senator from Moselle, Jean-Pierre Masseret, denounced the fact that CWP, which he claimed accounted for 900 deaths annually, was "most often only recognized if the breathing disorders were related to silicosis,"[49] even though CWP had been legally recognized six years earlier.

The United States presents yet another case that reveals a different history of miners' occupational diseases. The US mining industry refused to recognize CWP after World War II, leading miners and social-rights activists in the 1960s to largely marshal their forces around "black lung." This term, coined by cardiologist and independent activist Isidore Buff (1908–1974), was "the descendant of miners' asthma in the vernacular tradition"[50] and was based on workers' experiences, rather than on conventional scientific knowledge. In 1969, a US federal (as opposed to state-based) Black Lung Benefits compensation plan was established for occupational pneumoconiosis. As was the case in Europe at that time, the recognition of this disease led to a significant reduction in coal miners' deaths, at least until the end of the twentieth century.[51] As in the two other countries, however, the successive recognition of silicosis and CWP left out other diseases, such as chronic obstructive pulmonary disease and emphysema.

Transnational Quarrels on Radiographic Standards

After World War II, Pneumoconiosis Research Unit (PRU) researchers in the United Kingdom reexamined those miners previously checked by the MRC and kept at work, as well as those removed from the workplace because of pneumoconiosis. They were able to distinguish simple pneumoconiosis from progressive massive fibrosis, the latter being truly incapacitating and often fatal. The researchers observed that silicosis became worse if the workers continued to be exposed to dust, but not if they were taken off those jobs, whereas progressive massive fibrosis continued to develop even when the workers were no longer exposed to dust.[52] They revealed a critical stage in the course of the disease, when progressive massive fibrosis overtook simple pneumoconiosis. In the radiological classification they devised, this was the upper limit of stage 2. The results of this research were established by the late 1940s.

As Charles Fletcher, director of the PRU, wrote, the main function of periodic x-ray exams for miners became that of preventing the disease from advancing to a critical stage. Close monitoring was therefore crucial, paying particular attention to the speed at which the first stage of the disease manifested itself. Since the British coal-mining industry—which was short of labor, like its continental competitors—could not agree to remove these workers from underground work immediately, its aim was to keep them at work but away from the dustiest areas before they reached stage 3 of simple pneumoconiosis. This goal, which already was at the heart of the 1930 Johannesburg conference, was shared by various countries. It was the most consistent, strictly medical response to CWP.[53]

The radiological classification of the stages of silicosis, albeit limited and sometimes arbitrary when applied at the individual level, was a key instrument in this preventive policy. Various experts expressed this quite clearly:

> The strongest argument [for an international radiological classification] is that the efficacy of preventive measures against pneumoconiosis must be judged by the disappearance of the disease in men working under reputedly approved conditions. This disappearance can only be assessed radiographically. If those responsible for industrial hygiene in different countries are to obtain a sound appreciation of the effectiveness of control measures used in other countries, they must be satisfied that the diagnostic methods on which the control is assessed are uniform.
>
> Mr. Balgairies [head of the French Centre d'Études Médicales Minières, or Center for Mining Medical Studies] states that classification is carried out mainly with an aim of prevention.[54]

The 1930 Johannesburg conference already called for the establishment of internationally accepted radiographic standards. In 10 years, considerable advances were made in the radiological classification of the stages of silicosis. The Johannesburg (1930)-Geneva (1938) classification was used until the late 1950s in such countries as Sweden, Switzerland, the United States, and the former Soviet Union. In Germany, the Geneva classification continued to be used, because a diagnosis of silicosis was established mainly during compensation proceedings, rather than for preventive reasons.[55] But this classification was subject to international discussion from the outset, and no fewer than 22 classification proposals were made between 1934 and 1951.[56] In 1949, a congress in Lyon adopted a resolution inviting the ILO to examine the definition of new international standards for classifying radiographies for silicosis. That same year, the PRU proposed a new classification, based on greater knowledge about the development of the disease and intended to aid in its prevention. The PRU's innovation was to assess progress within the four stages of simple pneumoconiosis on quantitative criteria, which replaced the qualitative descriptors dating back to the 1930s (reticulation, nodulation, etc.).[57] This classification was welcomed at the ILO's international conference in Sydney in 1950.[58] The PRU was raising an issue that would not go away, namely, the variability of classifications among radiologists, and even between successive

---

Main European Research Centers for Mining Health and Safety Operating after World War II

In 1944, the Belgian federation of coal-mining associations (Fédéchar) created an Institut d'Hygiène des Mines, a private body whose leading staff members were R. Bidlot, A. Houberechts, G. Degueldre, V. Van Mechelen, F. Lavenne, and A. Minette. The IHM published the journal *Communication— Institut d'Hygiène des Mines*, which later became the *Revue de l'Institut d'Hygiène des Mines*.

In 1945, the United Kingdom's Medical Research Council established a Pneumoconiosis Research Unit in Penarth, near Cardiff, under the direction of C. Fletcher. Staff included J. Gilson, A. Cochrane (considered one of the pioneers of evidence-based medicine), and P. D'Arcy Hart. It was the medical department of the National Coal Board, however, that in 1952 initiated wide-ranging epidemiological studies (Pneumoconiosis Field Research) and in 1969 established the Institute of Occupational Medicine in Edinburgh.

In France, the technical and medical aspects of silicosis were addressed by two separate bodies. The Charbonnages de France Study and Research Center (in Verneuil-en-Halatte in northern Paris) was established in 1947 to promote technical progress in coal mining. The center's medical advisor was Professor Albert Policard from Lyon, an eminent specialist in tuberculosis who, in the 1930s, had been instrumental in the success of the collieries' fight against the compensation of silicosis. That same year, the Centre d'Études Médicales Minières (in Sin-le-Noble, near Douai) opened in the northern coalfield, through the initiative of the same nationalized coal mines, with Dr. E. Balgairies as its first director. The center published the *Revue médicale minière*. Research centers were also established in other coalfields: in eastern France, the Centre d'Étude des Pneumoconioses des Houillères du Bassin de Lorraine at

---

interpretations of the same films by the same doctors. Fletcher suggested the use of standard films that radiologists could refer to,[59] a proposal taken up by the ILO. Subsequently, other experts proposed training courses in interpreting batteries of films. Considerable disagreement remained, however, as to how to interpret these radiographic images, even within the same country, such as, in the United Kingdom, between the PRU and the medical department of the NCB.[60] A certain consensus was reached, on the other hand, concerning the use of large-format radiography, rather than small-format

Créhange Hospital, and the Centre d'Étude des Pneumoconioses Lyon-Saint-Étienne for the Loire coalfield, also advised by Professor Policard.

The West German miners' social-insurance funds (Bergbau-Berufsgenossenschaften) established the Silikose-Forschungsinstitut in Bochum, under Dr. Ir. M. Landwehr. It was located near the silicosis clinic in the Bergmannsheil, which had been operating since 1890, and which, in 1955, shifted from a teaching hospital to a practicing clinic. The new institute hosted pioneering work by Drs. V. Reichmann, W. Di Biasi, and O. Zorn; the latter created a European radio-histology research institute in Bochum, with support from the ECSC. The Silikose-Forschungsinstitut published the *Beiträge zur Silikoseforschung (Pneumokoniose)*. The Staatsintitut für Staublungenforschung und Gewerbehygiene, a public institute, was also active in the field of pneumoconiosis. It was attached to the University of Münster (in Westphalia), which published the *Fortschritte der Staublungenforschung*. Since 1958, the Bergbau-Forschung GmbH Forschungsinstitut des Steinkohlenbergbauvereins (in Essen) has contributed to the study of the more technical aspects of silicosis prevention. Within this association, the Hauptstelle für Staub- und Silikosebekämpfung published a series called *Berichte der Hauptstelle für Staub- und Silikosebekämpfung*.

In the Netherlands, in 1949 the Gezamenlijke Steenkolenmijnen in Limburg (GSL) set up the Instituut voor Longonderzoek (in Treebeek-Heerlen) within the medical departments of the Dutch mines, under Dr. A. V. M. Mey. A dust laboratory (*stoflaboratorium*) had been established as early as 1936 within the same medical departments, under the direction of chemical engineer W. P. M. Matla; in 1954 it became the Stofinstituut van GSL (in Heerlen).

In Italy, the ECSC's main partner in silicosis research was the Clinica del Lavoro "Luigi Devoto" of the University of Milan, headed by Professor E. Vigliani. The clinic publishes *La Medicina del Lavoro*.

radiography (7×7 or 10×12 centimeters) or radioscopy, to diagnose first-stage pneumoconiosis.[61]

As a result of cooperation between the United Kingdom and France, the British classification was refined and, in June 1951, new standards (known as Cardiff-Douai standards) were presented, which were later augmented by collections of standard films.[62] This classification was not unanimously accepted internationally, but it provided a basis for the ILO's 1958 Geneva classification. The new ILO classification won out, although adaptations to it were made after laborious negotiations.[63] Its main feature was that it was based on a set of films that gave a purely visual characterization of silicosis but was by no means a medical one. This radiographic standardization was a perfect indication of the economic stakes of the disease. Its great diversity from one country to another demonstrated that the actual medical bases of the disease were to be disregarded. "It did not take account of diseases, but only described lesions,"[64] with a table classifying tissue anomalies according to their visual aspect (e.g., "multiple small pulmonary opacities disseminated in both lung zones, with virtually complete disappearance of the bronchial wall"[65]).

Medical Contribution to Technical Prevention and the Definition of Exposure Thresholds

In the early 1950s, medical experts were given a new mission: to assess the effects of technical prevention, mainly with epidemiological studies. As Charles Fletcher wrote to A. Grut, then chief of the ILO's Industrial Hygiene Division, "the only ultimate criterion for the effectiveness of their [engineers'] work is the disappearance of the disease and that requires that doctors testify to that disappearance."[66] This correspondence occurred at a time when the influence of doctors in the ILO was declining with respect to that of engineers.

Stage One: Setting Admissible Exposure Thresholds

The apparently purely technical question of setting thresholds for the level of exposure to toxic substances or dust in the workplace had a certain political dimension in the bipolar world of the Cold War. The Soviets adopted maximal protection standards: ceiling values that must never be exceeded, but that were set independently of the practical conditions of their implementation. This contributed to them being largely ignored. In the United States, on the other hand, the publication of standards was subject to the technical possibility of implementing them. These standards corresponded to average concentrations over time, and they could be exceeded if they were later compensated for by a lower degree of exposure.[67] It would, however, be illusory to suppose that membership in either of the two blocs was enough to account for national standards. Among the Western economies (and the same was no doubt true in the East, as the Czechoslovakian case tends to indicate), divergences among and within nations were significant, although some convergence was achieved in the end.

In the Western coal-mining sector, the definition of acceptable exposure standards appeared to follow a three-stage pattern, characterized throughout by a dialectic among national and international authorities, the mining industry, and centers for the study of mining health and safety. For Western European countries, the ECSC now mattered more than the ILO. This brand-new economic alliance, which, by definition, gave particular prominence to coal, supported member countries' efforts rather than having the resources to unify their policies.

In the first stage, governments adopted provisional standards, which were based on insufficient data, by a process frequently described as arbitrary.[68] These standards, by emphasizing the quartz content of dust, were intended to protect coal miners and aligned with the classical signs and causes of silicosis. They were sometimes based on the findings of the first surveys ever held on the matter, especially those from the statistical study by physicians T. Bedford and C. G. Warner, used in Great Britain and Belgium.[69] Too often, however, these provisional findings long remained the only basis for the standards.

In 1941, the US Bureau of Mines issued recommendations that had been formulated some years before for anthracite miners by the Public Health Service and adopted by the National Conference on Silicosis in 1936.[70] These recommendations focused mainly on silica and were based on a state of knowledge that did not include any of the results of British research into CWP.[71] They were more protective than UK standards for rock workers, but much less so for coal hewers (1,750 particles per cubic centimeter, compared with 650–850 in the UK standards). From the mid-1930s to the mid-1960s, these standards went unchallenged.[72]

The UK standard of 450/650/850 particles per cubic centimeter (450 for rock workers, 650 for anthracite miners, and 850 for miners of other types of coal), adopted in 1948, was based on the first results of a survey carried out during the war by Bedford and Warner. The two physicians proposed provisional figures as an initial practical objective to be achieved in the short term.[73] These remained the standard until the early 1970s. The first Belgian standards (1954), explicitly called "arbitrary admissible rate of dust," were based on the British standards but were less strict (650 particles per cubic centimeter for rock workers).[74] In 1957, the German mining authorities (*Bergbehörden*) made the classification of mining areas, based on the number and harmfulness of particles recorded, compulsory.[75]

As for French standards, from 1952 on (officially, since 1956), they were expressed as a "coniotic index," calculated on the basis of environmental parameters (a particle concentration of 0.5–5 microns per cubic centimeter and quartz content, "because only quartz is involved in the genesis of silicotic fibrosis") on the one hand, and on individual parameters (lung capacity, and a comparison of vital capacity—the maximum amount of air that can be expelled from the lungs after a full inhalation—with the effort required to do so) on the other. The supporters of this index acknowledged that it was "fairly arbitrary": its value was set at 5 by adding 1 to the measurement of particle concentration in an industrial town (in this case, Douai). In places where the index was lower than 5, the working area could be considered safe; if it was higher than 6, the working area was clearly dangerous; and if it was somewhere between 5 and 6, the situation was uncertain.[76] This index was designed to prevent "classical silicosis" and was superseded by new standards intended to prevent CWP. The standards were calculated from a percentage of the prevalence (taken to be the "residual risk") of silicosis in workers after 10 years for a given level of dust that was observed in a coalfield, and they required the amount of dust to be reduced so that that this degree of prevalence would be reached in 30 years instead of 10.[77]

These various standards were thought of as a means of compelling employers to make arrangements for preventive measures, or at least of bringing the need for prevention policies to their attention.[78] But this type of regulation might also be seen as a way to justify continued extraction in virtually unchanged conditions. Indeed, all of these standards were soon criticized for their lack of a scientific basis—not least because they did not protect miners. Those who had worked in areas that were considered to be healthy were also subject to silicosis, and the disease continued to strike men down.[79] In Belgium, there was a kind of competition between the Mines Administration and the Institut d'Hygiène des Mines (which had different standards from the Mines Administration, based on the French standards). The central value was also set at 5, and the goal was to split up the classification of working areas into four categories, as was done in Germany and the Netherlands, in order to reduce the proportion of the dustiest ones.[80] The employer-backed IHM most likely was raising the stakes to gain the upper hand and retain control over prevention objectives.

Stage Two: Epidemiological Studies

In the second stage, studies looking at the incidence of and factors contributing to silicosis were undertaken, with the goal of establishing "safe" dust levels. They were intended to determine exposure thresholds below which only a very low percentage of mine workers would develop simple pneumoconiosis (below stage 2) after 30 or 35 years of work.

The first set of epidemiological studies, following the pattern of some prewar surveys, compared workers' radiological images and occupational careers.[81] This type of research was carried out in the United Kingdom and Belgium, among other countries.[82] These first studies were based on a strong implicit hypothesis, namely, that the dust level remained constant throughout the exposure periods.

After the pioneering work of Edgar Collis in 1915 and the MRC survey on the eve of World War II, British researchers were innovative once again, creating the PRU's Pneumoconiosis Field Research (PFR, also called the "25-pit scheme"), the first epidemiological survey of that magnitude carried out in the field of occupational health. The survey involved a multidisciplinary team of generally 115 (and sometimes up to 137) full-time staff.[83] It ran from 1953 to 1978 and, in one mine, was extended until 1991.[84] The PFR was launched by the NCB in 1953 and headed by J. M. Rogan, with A. Cochrane as its scientific advisor. It originally covered some 31,000 miners, roughly 5 percent of the men then employed in the mines, selected from 25 representative pits in British coalfields. Medical teams with x-ray vans were to visit each pit, with the goal of obtaining lung x-rays every five years (from 1953 to 1978) of all miners in the 25 pits. In the third survey, 47 percent of the miners in the initial sample were x-rayed, but in the fourth and fifth surveys, only 13 and 8 percent (respectively) of the original group were seen (still meaning that for 2,600 miners working in 10 pits, x-ray files and dust measurements were kept for 20 years).

Beginning with the second survey, the exam was also functional, seeking to establish the relationships among dust exposure, the x-ray images, and respiratory failure. At the same time as the x-rays were taken, dust levels were measured in the places where these miners worked. For the first 15 years, the concentration of dust in the air (dust count) was measured with a thermal precipitator, and then with a gravimetric sampler. The data that were collected significantly improved the correlation between the standardized distribution of radiological changes and the average dust concentration for the particle sizes chosen for the survey (with a conversion of particle number counts to weights).[85] The survey was noteworthy for its size, its concern for the quality of the information gathered, and the substantial use of probabilistic statistics (made possible by computers).[86] The main finding of the study, presented in the early 1960s, was the validity of its research hypothesis: the relationship between the total mass of dust plus the duration of exposure and the probability of developing pneumoconiosis.[87] The role of quartz, and the nature of the coal being mined (bituminous, anthracitic, etc.) remained uncertain, as did that of factors other than cumulative exposure to dust in explaining the variability of results among the different pits.[88] These unknowns gave rise to further research in Europe.

A similar but smaller survey was carried out in a major Belgian mine (Houthalen, in the Limburg coalfield) from 1957 to 1966, with financial support from the ECSC. Every two weeks, the dust level in each working area (approximately 2,000–3,000 samples per year) was measured and recorded on each individual worker's file. In 1958, 2,665 miners were being monitored. These data were correlated with medical information from the exams the miners had to undergo every two years (consisting of an x-ray, functional respiratory test, and brief clinical exam).[89] This study established a statistical relationship between the appearance of the first radiological stage of pneumoconiosis and a "harmfulness index," constructed along the lines of the French coniotic index. The Belgian researchers were drawing on the work of their British and French colleagues. The values recorded year after year in Houthalen were directly compared with the preventive measures adopted by this mine (particularly the deep injection of water into the seam beyond the macrofissured zone); they were also compared with the results recorded in a mine in the nearby Liège coalfield, where workers were also periodically monitored by the IHM but where prevention was less systematic.[90]

In Germany there was no systematic survey. Nonetheless, data from a compulsory file kept for each worker from 1954—a combination of the number of days spent in a mine and the average fine dust content to which the worker was exposed—were correlated with individual medical data.[91] Initial results for 9,000 miners working in 10 representative mines in the Ruhr, published in 1960, confirmed a high correlation between radiological images and the total quantity of dust to which the miners had been exposed. They also showed the impact of the total period of exposure to dust: controlling for the quantity of dust inhaled, the percentage of miners suffering from the first stage of the Johannesburg classification for silicosis increased with the length of time of exposure. This result led to protection against excessive exposure for young miners during their first working years. The German survey paid close attention to the composition of the dust, but, as in Britain, quartz was not found to be a significant factor in CWP.[92] A review of recent medical literature confirms this hypothesis, but older articles defend another point of view. It seems that after a period during which attention was focused on the total amount of dust, researchers again turned to its quartz content, with quartz exposure being "an important factor in the development and rapid progression of CWP."[93]

Unlike what was done in Britain, Belgium, and Germany, where studies compared radiological images and dust measurements at the individual level, in the early 1960s, researchers at the French Centre d'Études Médicales Minières began to compare the radiological images of a population of miners "as a whole without individualizing the subjects" with dust records considered to be homogenous throughout a coalfield (Nord-Pas-de-Calais) and stable over time (at least at the start of the study, when systematic dust records were not available). The data were collected from each worker's annual radiological film, with its Geneva classification. In studying tens of thousands of films, the researchers established probability transition matrices from one radiological pattern to another as a function of the time spent working underground. They, like their British and German colleagues, showed that the probability of pneumoconiosis appearing in workers was a cumulative function of their exposure to dust.[94]

The ECSC did not play much of coordinating role in these epidemiological studies, although it did fund some of them (such as the Houthalen study). The ECSC also failed to standardize the dust-sampling devices (the konimeter, the thermal precipitator, the PRU hand pump, the gravimetric sampler, and the "German" tyndalloscope for photometric determination of breathable dust concentrations) and the methods for comparing fine dust concentrations. It did, however, support the development of comparisons of the results obtained by the various sampling methods.[95]

Stage Three: New Admissible Exposure Thresholds

On the basis of the results of these epidemiological studies, the third stage was the revision of official standards. In the United Kingdom, the main results of the PFR survey, published in *Nature* and elsewhere in 1970,[96] proposed using a new dust-measurement device (the gravimetric sampler) and new standards, adopted voluntarily in 1971 and made compulsory in 1975. The German epidemiological studies provided an estimate of the total quantity of dust associated with the probability of developing a limited degree of pneumoconiosis (1958 Geneva-classification stage 2). On the basis of a 35-year career (with 200 shifts per year), it was possible to define an acceptable daily level of exposure. The maximum concentration allowed in French mines followed the same principles as in Germany. The main difference was the way of estimating the total quantity of dust (known as "historical concentrations") a miner could be exposed to for 30 years without reaching Geneva-classification stage 2. Since the sampling devices had changed (first taking discontinuous, and then continuous samples) and their results could not be correlated, historical concentrations had to be extrapolated for the early 1970s. In Belgium, the new public standards imposed by royal decree in 1965 were based on the results of the IHM's survey in Houthalen.[97]

The fact that dust standards were defined says nothing about their enforcement in the coal mines. There was resistance to this aspect of prevention, too. A publication based on oral sources reported that workers in Scotland sometimes impeded the operation of the dust measurement devices; similar statements were collected in the United States. In Belgium, nearly four years after the adoption of the first dust standards, some mines in the Liège coalfield were still not equipped with measurement devices and could not, in practice, monitor the dust levels in the mines—even if the managers were already implementing certain preventive measures. The argument of a lack of dust-sampling equipment was still being reiterated 10 years later by the IHM representative, in order to postpone the enforcement of new standards.[98]

The consistency of these prevention standards may also be gauged by the nature of the monitoring—who did it and whether it could be challenged—and the associated sanctions. This differed, depending on whether mines were nationalized enterprises, in which case standards were set and monitored by the same body, or were in private hands, such as in Belgium and the United States, where employers were trusted to monitor dust exposure in their own mines.[99] In Belgium, where dust monitoring was the task of the Corps des Mines from 1954 on, if samples showed excessive levels, the mine engineers were allowed only to report this to their superiors; they could not stop the jobs in the affected workplace. These superiors, in turn, could make the use of masks compulsory, a preventive measure widely recognized as being ineffective. The Belgian civil servants who drafted the 1954 standards admitted that at that time, the choice of a mask as a preventive device signaled that the Mines Administration did not want to close down too many workplaces. In 1958, it took four successive negative results in an eight-month period for the Mines Administration to close down a site that was too dusty.[100] Mine inspectors in the United States had little more authority to force owners to reduce dust concentrations than those in Belgium did.[101] All these situations meant that monitoring most likely was weakened, whether the mines were nationalized or privately owned.

Conclusion

Prevention, in both its medical and technical dimensions, became a necessity as soon as silicosis contracted in the coal industry became a compensable occupational disease. Once the magnitude of the risk could no longer be denied, coal mines could only continue operating if they addressed prevention. It was also an imperative in workforce management. During the entire period under study here, it was essential to reduce workers' exposure to risk and improve their working environment, in order to be able to employ skilled labor for as long as possible and recruit new workers.[102]

Achieving its practical, effective implementation took longer. The initial decisions were often subject to cost considerations. On the technical side, the mask option was a good illustration of this. On the medical side, radioscopy offered a prime example: for a long time, medical exams for new recruits were designed primarily to protect mine operators. Local resistance from both employers and workers hampered efforts undertaken in the spirit of prevention, and, in the particular economic context of a predictable point when mining would end, because it no longer would be viable, the choice between productivity and health was often made to the detriment of workers.

Using scientific foundations that were still unsure, authorities adopted standards to make employers reduce dust levels in the mines. Later, but in a largely isolated fashion—although organizations such as the ILO and ECSC circulated information and, in the latter case, even helped fund research studies—they began to examine more closely the conditions leading to the development of CWP as a function of exposure to dust and, ultimately, to define "safe" exposure thresholds. The desire to establish a sound scientific basis for these thresholds sometimes delayed the adoption of protection standards. The NCB, for example, waited until 1975 to impose new standards, 22 years after the start of the epidemiological studies it had funded; it could certainly have acted 10 years earlier.[103] While prevention was a necessary part of the discourse by employers and authorities, both nationally and internationally, its implementation was not particularly proactive. The goal was less to protect labor than to set dust standards that, while not exposing workers too much, had as little effect as possible on the profitability of the mines and, consequently, their existence.

Without a doubt, the incidence of pneumoconiosis declined in the 30 years after World War II, but this was not due solely to prevention. Successive reductions in the amount of time spent working (both in weekly hours and in retirement age), thus decreasing workers' total exposure time, contributed to the decline, as did mine closures. As one study has pointed out, "it is sad and somewhat ironic to reflect that the NCB's most significant contribution to protecting miners from respiratory disease may have been its closure program."[104]

NOTES

1. According to current medical knowledge (Baxter et al., *Diseases of Occupations*, 1014–1032): "The histology lesions of silicosis in the lung are nodules made of concentric layers of dense collagen tissue with a core containing birefringent quartz particles. The nodules first form in the centrilobular area and then along the lymphatics both to the pleura and the hilar nodes with lines of less organized fibrous tissue linking them together. The radiograph shows shadows of small, rounded opacities either distributed or more frequent in the upper zones. Hilar node enlargement is common." In contrast, "the features of simple coalworkers' pneumoconiosis result from accumulation of dust in the lung parenchyma and the tissue reaction to that dust. Typically, the chest radiograph shows small, rounded opacities scattered through the lung fields. In the early stages, there is little or no impairment of lung function. Pathologically, there are simple coal macules: collections of dust-laden macrophages around the terminal bronchioles in the centre of the acinus, with a little surrounding centrilobular emphysema ('focal' emphysema)." As Laney and Weissman ("Respiratory Diseases") add: "A more severe form called progressive massive fibrosis (FMP) is characterised by coalescence of small opacities into large (≥1 cm) opacities."

2. On the complexity of statistically recording miners' occupational diseases in South Africa, in addition to Packard (*White Plague, Black Labor*), see Chatgidakis, "Autopsy Survey"; Leger, "Occupational Diseases"; Rees et al., "Oscillating Migration."

3. McIvor and Johnston, "Medical Knowledge," 69.

4. Hendriks, "Frequentie en preventie," 1553; Hendriks and Claus, "Effect of Dust Suppression Measures."

5. See Rae, "Pneumoconiosis and Coal Dust Exposure," 53; McLintock, "Changing Prevalence."

6. McLintock, "Current Views," 9–10; Amoudru, "Les pneumoconioses du houilleur, données épidémiologiques," 61; Dechoux, "Données actuelles," 252–256; Amoudru, "Les pneumoconioses du houilleur dans les mines," 1089.

7. Rosental and Devinck, "Statistique et mort industrielle"; Mackova and Rosental, "Les démocraties populaires," 252.

8. See ILO, *Silicosis: Records* (1930), particularly Irvine et al., "Review of the History"; Moore, "Silicosis in Australia"; Böhme, "Silicosis in Germany"; Cunningham, "Silicosis in Canada." See also Orenstein, "History of Pneumoconiosis"; Katz, *White Death*, 147–176; Foster, "Western Miners and Silicosis," 375; Kippen, "Social and Political Meaning," 494–495. Information on Japan was kindly provided by Bernard Thomann.

9. ILO, *International Labour Conference* (1934), eighteenth session, 664.

10. Foster, "Western Miners and Silicosis," 376.

11. For Germany, see Morhenn, "Regulations to Protect Health." For Belgium, see *Engineers' Report of 5 August 1937*, SAICOM; *Hygiène des mines* (1937–1944), 155, ACCB-S, Écomusée Régional du Centre, Bois-du-Luc, Belgium.

12. For Belgium, see Langelez, "Silicose des mineurs en Belgique." For the Netherlands, see Muntjewerff, "Stofbestrijding," 87. For the United States, see Derickson, *Black Lung*, 95–97. On the trimmers, see D'Arcy Hart, "MRC Pneumoconiosis Research," 5–6; M. Bloor, "South Wales Miners Federation," 130–131; McIvor and Johnston, *Miners' Lung*, 85.

13. McIvor and Johnston, *Miners' Lung*, 167–170; Muntjewerff, "Stofbestrijding," 86.

14. McIvor and Johnston, *Miners' Lung*, 165, 175; Comité Permanent, Conseil Supérieur d'Hygiène des Mines, Administration des Mines, "Minutes of the meeting of the legislative section held in Brussels on September 28, 1961," 6, Minutes 1956–1962, Fonds M. Mainjot, Directeurs divisionnaires, CLADIC.

15. Dautrebande et al., *Essai de prévention*. For the coal industry, see Boucher, "Essais pratiques."

16. ILO, *Prevention and Suppression of Dust* [six international reports].

17. Katz, "Underground Route to Mining," 486; Katz, *White Death*, 163–170.

18. Bidlot, "L'activité de l'Institut d'Hygiène des Mines," 518; *Poussières*, CLADIC; "Survey of Dust Content of Faces," ACPL; "Meeting of December 10, 1952," meetings of chief safety officers, ACPL; "Meeting of September 11, 1963," meetings of chief safety officers, Archives ACPL, IHOES.

19. McIvor and Johnston, *Miners' Lung*, 166; Mackova and Rosental, "Les démocraties populaires," 250; Morrison, *Silicosis Experience*, 284.

20. Perchard, "Mine Management Professions."

21. "Lutte contre les accidents," SAICOM; Commission Nationale Mixte des Mines, "Minutes of the meeting of March 1, 1957," *Maladies professionnelles Fédéchar 1955–1957*, AHCM 1077, SAICOM; Morrison, *Silicosis Experience*, 282; Peet, "Mijnarbeid, veiligheid and gezondheid," 255.

22. McIvor and Johnston, *Miners' Lung*, 164–165; Mackova and Rosental, "Les démocraties populaires," 251; *Lutte contre les poussières: Enquêtes*, AEL.

23. Lambin and Van Mechelen, "Le traitement de la silicose," 7.

24. Menger, *Traitement de la silicose*, ECSC; McIvor and Johnston, *Miners' Lung*, 310. Also see the concluding chapter of the present volume.

25. Penrose, "'So Now They Have'"; Rosner and Markowitz, *Deadly Dust: Silicosis and the On-Going Struggle*, 192–194. This therapy was presented by Denny et al. ("Prevention of Silicosis by Metallic Aluminium") at the ILO's 1938 Geneva conference.

26. Brull, "Enquête sur le problème"; Van Mechelen, "Les lacunes de nos connaissances"; Lambin and Van Mechelen, "Le traitement de la silicose," 1–2; Brown and Van Winkle, "Present Status of Aluminium"; King et al., "Inhibitory Action of Aluminium"; Marcel Robert to J. L. Nicod, February 28, 1958 (with a selected bibliography), CEAB 11-1024, ESCS; Vigliani, *Recherches fondamentales*, ECSC; Policard, *Rapport sur les recherches*, ECSC; Muntjewerff, "Stofbestrijding," 88; Le Bouffant and Froger, "Les pneumoconioses dans les mines"; Le Bouffant et al., "Experimental Results and Possibilities."

27. Schlipköter and Brockhaus, "Effects of Polyvinylpyridine."

28. Vigliani and Cavagna, *Progrès des recherches*, ECSC; "Compte rendu de la réunion," ECSC.

29. Zhao et al., "Long-Term Follow-Up"; Prügger et al., "Polyvinylpyridine N-Oxide"; Banks et al., "Strategies."

30. See Houberechts, "L'activité de l'Institut," (1953): 333–334; Houberechts, "L'activité de l'Institut," (1955): 374; Houberechts, "L'activité de l'Institut," (1956): 382–392; Rosenthal, "New Treatment of Silicosis"; Beckmann, "Contribution aux méthodes thérapeutiques."

31. Nugent, "Fit for Work." For medical exams as occupational medicine's main practice in France, see Buzzi et al., "L'examen médical."

32. Penrose, "Medical Monitoring and Silicosis."

33. Derickson, "'On the Dump Heap,'" 664; Derickson, "Industrial Refugees," 85; Vergara, "Recognition of Silicosis," 741.

34. ILO, *Silicosis: Proceedings of the International Conference*, 74.

35. ILO, *Third International Conference of Experts*, 103–105; *Inquiry of the International Miners Federation*, 37–42, A-ILO.

36. Institut d'Hygiène des Mines, *Contrôle sanitaire*, 3–4.

37. Meiklejohn, "Doctor and Workman"; Cochrane et al., "Role of Periodic Examination"; Reiser, *Medicine*; Melling, "Beyond a Shadow of a Doubt?," 429.

38. Rosner and Markowitz, *Deadly Dust: Silicosis and the On-Going*, 112n17.

39. Commission de Sécurité et d'Hygiène, "Meeting of March 18, 1948," *Examens d'embauche*, Archives ACPL, IHOES; Fédéchar, *Services médicaux du travail*, 9, IHOES.

40. Bufton and Melling, "'A Mere Matter of Rock,'" 172–175; Melling, "Beyond a Shadow of a Doubt?," 458–459.

41. McIvor and Johnston, *Miners' Lung*, 82.

42. Meiklejohn, "Origin of the Term."

43. Amoudru and Quinot, "La lutte contre les poussières," 153; Amoudru, "La silicose et les pneumoconioses dans les houillères," 23–26. In the early 1950s in West Germany, miners suffering from pneumoconiosis were considered to have silicosis, since only silica was recognized as a pathogen. See King et al., *Pneumoconiosis in Germany*, 5.

44. The following comparative analysis is based on Rosental et al., "Contextualiser la reconnaissance internationale."

45. McIvor and Johnston, *Miners' Lung*, 86.

46. McIvor and Johnston, *Miners' Lung*, 86; Morrison, *Silicosis Experience in Scotland*, 161–170.

47. Amoudru, *Médecine, mines et mineurs*, 2: 21, Bibliothèque de l'Académie Nationale de Médecine; Amoudru, *Souvenirs d'outre-médecine*, 1: 72, Bibliothèque de l'Académie Nationale de Médecine.

48. Amoudru, *Médecine, mines et mineurs*, 2: 7, Bibliothèque de l'Académie Nationale de Médecine.

49. Masseret, "Pneumoconiose du mineur du charbon."

50. Derickson, *Black Lung*, 147.

51. Laney and Weissman, "Respiratory Diseases," S18–S22.

52. Fletcher, "Pneumoconiosis of Coal-Miners"; Stewart, "Pneumoconiosis of Coal-Miners"; Fletcher and Gough, "Coalminers' Pneumoconiosis."

53. Fletcher, "Screening for Pneumoconiosis"; Fletcher, "Coalworkers Pneumoconiosis," cited in Lavenne, "Diagnostic radiologique"; *L'évolution des pneumoconioses*, AGR. This goal had been stated in France immediately after the war, but with no precise formalization of the stages of the disease. See Cazamian, "La prévention médicale," 2.

54. C. M. Fletcher to A. Grut, February 9, 1952, *Summary of Information*, A-ILO; Advisory Commission of Experts, "Minutes of the 29 September 1955 meeting," 5, CEAB 11-710, ECSC.

55. Dickmans and Zorn, *Observations critiques*, ECSC.

56. "Appendix A: List of Classification," *Summary of Information*, A-ILO.
57. Fletcher et al., "Classification of Radiographic Appearances."
58. Cayet et al., "How International Organisations Compete," 184–186.
59. Fletcher and Oldham, "Use of Standard Films."
60. Rae, "Pneumoconiosis," 55.
61. Lavenne and Patigny, "Valeur comparée."
62. Cochrane et al., "Entente radiologique."
63. Van Mechelen, "Évolution des idées"; Liddell, "Experiment in Film Reading."
64. Catilina, *Médecine et risque au travail*, 244–245.
65. Quoted from the most recent ILO classification (1980).
66. C. M. Fletcher to A. Grut, June 30, 1951, *Summary of Information*, A-ILO. A comparable analysis can be found in Van Mechelen, "Critères médicaux"; Cayet et al., "How International Organisations Compete," 187.
67. Article in *Cahiers de notes documentaires*, 681, quoted in Devinck, "Les racines historiques," 247.
68. On the lack of a scientific basis for the standards regarding silicosis, see Markowitz and Rosner, "Limits of Thresholds," 255; Rosner and Markowitz, *Deadly Dust: Silicosis and the On-Going Struggle*, 117, 237; Hicks, "Sampling and Analysis," 7; McIvor and Johnston, *Miners' Lung*, 85, 117.
69. Bedford and Warner, *Physical Studies of the Dust Hazard*, 64.
70. Matla, "Concentrations-limites," 262.
71. Derickson, *Black Lung*, 168–169.
72. Rosner and Markowitz, *Deadly Dust: Silicosis and the On-Going Struggle*, 243.
73. McIvor and Johnston, *Miners' Lung*, 84–85.
74. Stassen et al., *Code des mines, minières et carrières*, 221–224; Stassen, *L'après-Marcinelle*, 83; Matla, "Concentrations-limites," 275–276.
75. Landwehr, "Determination of the Silicosis Risk," 198–199; Matla, "Concentrations-limites," 265–270.
76. Jarry et al., "Essai d'indice koniotique," 3–24; F. Rey, "Les mesures d'empoussiérage."
77. Quinot, "Définition des critères"; Ganier, "Méthode pour la détermination" [1974], 268.
78. Berger and Drouard, *Meeting of Experts*, ESCS; *ILO [Second] Meeting of Experts*, ESCS.
79. See, for example, Rosner and Markowitz, *Deadly Dust: Silicosis and the On-Going Struggle*, 242.
80. Houberechts, *L'activité de l'Institut . . . 1960*, 28–30; Houberechts, *L'activité de l'Institut . . . 1961*, 10–12; Houberechts, *L'activité de l'Institut . . . 1963*, 10–12.
81. Derickson, *Black Lung*, 94–95; Geerkens, "Quand la silicose," 138.
82. Belayew, *Rapport sur l'examen médical*, AGR; Houberechts, "L'activité de l'Institut," (1951): 316–317; McIvor and Johnston, *Miners' Lung*, 111–112.
83. Fay, "National Coal Board's Pneumoconiosis Field Research," 310; Attfield and Kuempel, "Commentary," 526.
84. Jacobsen, "Vingt-six ans de recherches," 207; Soutar et al., "Dust Concentrations," 477.
85. Jacobsen, "Vingt-six ans de recherches," 209.
86. Attfield and Kuempel, "Commentary"; Ashford, "Use of Computers."
87. Hicks and Fay, *Study of Respirable Dust*, 11, ECSC.
88. Jacobsen, "La pneumoconiose des houilleurs"; McIvor and Johnston, *Miners' Lung*, 111–119. As early as 1962, Cochrane ("Attack Rate," 61) showed that silica does not play a more central role in the development of progressive massive fibrosis.

89. Degueldre, *Prélèvements de poussières*, ECSC; Houberechts, "L'activité de l'Institut," (1957): 388–389; Degueldre, "Recherche d'un critère," 71–75.

90. Houberechts, *L'activité de l'Institut . . . 1962*, 12.

91. Reisner, "Pneumokoniose und Staubexposition"; Reisner, "Results of Epidemiological Studies"; Reisner, "Les pneumoconioses et l'exposition"; Reisner, "Erkenntnisse epidemiologischer."

92. Breuer, *Hygiène dans les mines*, 5, 9, 19.

93. McCunney et al., "What Component of Coal"; Buchanan et al., "Quantitative Relations"; B. Miller et al., "Risks of Silicosis"; Morrison, *Silicosis Experience*, 286.

94. Quinot, "Définition des critères." Quinot's seminal study, "Épidémiologie des pneumoconioses," inspired British researchers processing PFR data to use a Markov model.

95. McIvor and Johnston, *Miners' Lung*, 152–153; Demelenne et al., "La lutte contre les poussières"; CECA, *Lutte technique contre la poussière*, 36; Breuer, *Hygiène dans les mines*.

96. Jacobsen et al., "New Dust Standards."

97. McIvor and Johnston, *Miners' Lung*, 118, 160; Reisner, "Pneumokoniose und Staubexposition," 55–59; Ganier, "Méthode pour la détermination," [1973], 224–225; J.-J. Stassen, *L'après-Marcinelle*, 88.

98. R. Johnston and McIvor, "Oral History," 239–240; Weeks, "Fox Guarding the Chicken Coop," 1237; *Lutte contre les poussières: Enquêtes*, AEL; Conseil Supérieur d'Hygiène des Mines, "Meeting of September 22, 1964," 5, Centrale Générale, 1964–1965, doc. R64/02-D32, Amsab-Instituut voor Sociale Geschiedenis. A lack of measuring devices was also noted in Czechoslovakia. See Mackova and Rosental, "Les démocraties populaires," 256.

99. Weeks, "Tampering with Dust Samples."

100. Comité Permanent, "Minutes, no. 20, June 27, 1961," 5, and "Minutes, no. 17, February 2, 1961," 7–9, Minutes 1956–1962, Fonds M. Mainjot, Directeurs divisionnaires, CLADIC; L. Pasquazy, Ingénieur en chef–Directeur to R. Dessart, Directeur-gérant des Charbonnages de Wérister, 10 October 1958, *Lutte contre les poussières: Enquêtes*, AEL.

101. Derickson, *Black Lung*, 166.

102. Callut et al., *Lutte contre les poussières*, 22, AEL: "If we wish to keep the current workforce in the mine, we must improve health and safety in the workplace"; Goddard, "Review," 586: "The future of the coal industry lies . . . in the numbers who are willing to go underground."

103. McIvor and Johnston, *Miners' Lung*, 162.

104. Ibid., 176.

Silica, Silicosis, and Occupational Health in the Globalized World of the Twenty-First Century

Francesco Carnevale, Paul-André Rosental,
and Bernard Thomann

As elsewhere in Algeria, carved stone is used as a facade ornamentation in the Tkout district in the Aurès. Over 700 stone carvers cut, sand, and polish with the help of advanced tools, such as electric saws. The downside to this mechanization is that it generates dust. The rock—sandstone mixed with quartz—quickly starts to damage the lungs of stone carvers; in only three years, between 2005 and 2008, 28 died, mostly at a young age (31 years old, on average). During this period, masons, who do the finishing work using hammers and set the stones, had higher survival rates. Young workers were predominantly affected: 15 died before the age of 30. A study identified the source and incidence of the disease,[1] and x-rays revealed that out of 321 stone carvers examined in 2008, 161 had silicosis—a prevalence of 50 percent.

Tkout's "epidemic" of silicosis, which is obviously an environmental disease and not a contagious ailment, illustrates the direct implications of the story we have told in this book: the old and new dangers of occupational pneumoconiosis in the globalized industrial world of the twenty-first century. Silicosis has become a more pressing global-health problem than ever before because of the massive impacts it can have, both at the local level and in particular sectors. A joint WHO-ILO program has focused on the disease since 1995,[2] and in 2002, the WHO's World Health Report estimated that pneumoconiosis results in 30,000 deaths every year, as well as the loss of close to 1.3 million years of disability-free life expectancy. If all diseases caused or aggravated by exposure to dust in the workplace were included, these figures would total 386,000 deaths and the loss of 6.6 million disability-free years.

Silicosis had a devastating impact on the mining sector in the twentieth century, and now this disease affects workers from a wide variety of industries in all countries. The stone-carving case, of which there are many similar examples in very different contexts,[3] tells a familiar story that includes an essential element we have explored: the role of national and international unions, such as the one the federation of stone carvers played in the 1920s in triggering the movement to recognize silicosis (chapters 3, 4). Even earlier, in the nineteenth century, hygienists were at least as concerned about masons' exposure to dust as they were about underground miners.[4] Stone carving, however, is far from the only traditional sector plagued by this disease, which presumably also affects half of the workers manufacturing slate pencils in India and one-third of the pit diggers in Fortaleza, Brazil.[5]

The Tkout example also raises the issue of working conditions and disease treatments. Stone carvers are employed by individuals and operate in small groups. Their work is mobile and precarious, and they have no respiratory protection or any form of social insurance. Furthermore, 80 percent are smokers. In addition to the specific effects of silicosis, they often suffer complications from their use of tobacco: pulmonary tuberculosis in 5.6 percent of the cases, as well as pneumothorax (partial lung collapse) and scleroderma (here, scarring in the lungs). This brings us to the social aspect of silicosis,[6] as well as to the complexity of its nosology (medical classification), which is often muddied by the presence of various lung diseases.[7] Here again, history can aid our understanding of the current global situation.

Having established that silicosis is primarily a modern disease, the challenge is to avoid reducing it to a single sector, such as the mining industry, or to particular nations, such as Western countries (in the past) and China (today and in the future). A complete picture not only includes mines, but also other traditional occupations, heavy industry, and activities that have only recently been found to put workers at risk. The present situation in China is reminiscent of that described in chapter 1: the country depends on coal for 80 percent of its electricity and 65 percent of its energy supply and is predicted to account for two-thirds of the growth in global coal consumption between now and 2030.

Finally, a comprehensive perspective needs to take into account the situations of emerging countries, as well as industrialized and poor countries. Our approach recognizes these economic categorizations, but seeks to incorporate them into a broader framework and highlight the common aspects of what might be called the politics of silicosis and its implications for medicine today. The experience of many emerging and developing countries provides an entry point for exploring little-known aspects of the disease's relevance today.

The Politics of Silicosis: Emerging versus Industrialized Countries?
The Current State of Affairs

Emerging countries confront particular challenges surrounding the disease's development that are not faced by industrialized countries. For example, research has revealed a form of environmental pneumoconiosis in a vast region stretching from the Himalaya-Karakoram in the south to the Tian Shan range in the north, and from the Pamir Mountains in the west to the Qinling Mountains in the east.[8] The significance of this situation reinforces comparable observations made by French doctors over half a century ago about the environmental exposure risks to the inhabitants of the Sahara.[9] In the semiarid northwestern region of China, 24 million people are at risk. Indeed, this area of High Asia is swept by winds that carry silica dust picked up from loess after it is carried out and deposited by the area's major rivers, primarily the Yellow River. Radiological exams of 9,591 inhabitants in the Gansu region in China showed an overall silicosis rate of just above 1 percent, rising to 10 percent for subjects over the age of 70. Cases of silico-tuberculosis among the region's farmers have also been recorded.[10]

Geological peculiarities aside, silicosis has become significant in certain major emerging countries, due to the development of industry in general, and the mining sector in particular. In terms of the number of workers exposed to silica dust, Asia is the most fertile ground for the spread of the disease. The Indian state of Rajasthan, where 65 types of minerals are extracted, has two million miners. In 1996, the Jodhpur-based nongovernmental organization Gramin Vikas Vigyan Samiti, together with the Delhi-based Society for Participatory Research in Asia, conducted an independent medical study of Jodhpur's sandstone miners.[11] Out of the 288 workers who underwent a lung-function test and a radiological exam, 14 percent suffered from advanced silicosis, and 28 percent had silicosis at a less advanced stage. If these figures are representative of the health of the state's miners in general, then Rajasthan alone might have a staggering 800,000 cases of silicosis.[12]

Even the official statistics from the largest Asian countries, notorious for their underreporting, display alarming figures.[13] According to the Chinese health ministry's figures, 10 million workers were occupationally exposed to the inhalation of silica dust between 1949 and 1986.[14] The ministry estimates that there were 665,043 cases of pneumoconiosis between 1950 and 2006. The disease has caused 143,000 deaths and currently afflicts 522,000 people; every year it affects between 15,000 and 20,000 more and leads to 5,000 new deaths. A 2006 report showed that registered cases of pneumoconiosis came from large state mines, but it completely ignored the situation in the smaller provincial and township mines. Yet the latter employ around half of the country's miners.

Silicosis not only has become an important public health issue for economic and mining giants India and China, but it also affects smaller, emerging economies. The number of recorded cases is increasing considerably in countries like Thailand, which is experiencing a boom in industries linked to construction and public works. While only 35 cases of silicosis were recorded between 1973 and 1977, mostly in miners, more-recent studies have shown that, in some industries, more than 20 percent of the workforce is affected. Over 180,000 Thai workers are currently at risk of developing silicosis.[15] A 1995 study conducted across 33 stone-grinding factories in Saraburi Province, north of Bangkok, is revealing in this respect. In 93.6 percent of the workplaces, dust levels in the air were dangerously high, and 676 cases of the disease were diagnosed, a prevalence of 9 percent.[16]

The spread of silicosis in emerging countries is often the devastating price paid for the rising demands for energy and housing that are inherent in rapid economic growth, but it is also linked to desires of the consumerist societies in most developed countries. Some of the highest risks come from gemstone polishing for the jewelry industry and the sandblasting of jeans to give them the prewashed look preferred by many customers. A study published in 2006 looked at 16 young men, with an average age of 23, who had worked in small Turkish denim-sandblasting workshops for three years and had decided to be checked over at the hospital. Of these, 14 exhibited respiratory difficulties, and the remaining two, worried about their colleagues' symptoms, proved to be affected by severe forms of silicosis.[17]

The strictly political aspect of the issue, however, has even deeper roots that are directly tied to occupational health in industrialized countries. In a perfect illustration of the international division of labor, the minimization of production costs goes beyond salaries and affects expenditures arising from occupational risk prevention and compensation. An investigative journalism report, impressive enough to win a Daniel Pearl Award, clearly pointed out the interdependence among occupational problems in new and older industrial countries.[18] One example is the use of rainbow quartz in jewelry manufacturing. In the 1980s, after Japan discovered that rainbow quartz created dust that was likely to cause silicosis, it outsourced most of this activity to China. Another illustration is the debacle in 2005 over asbestos removal from France's iconic *Clemenceau* aircraft carrier. As the *Clemenceau* was en route to India for dismantlement, environmental NGOs raised an outcry in the French and international media over what they claimed was France's willingness to expose Indian shipyard workers to massive asbestos inhalation. After several days, the French government was forced to back down and decided to repatriate the ship, without having found an alternative solution. This outsourcing of risk, which demonstrated how "some foreign companies produce and use in China [and other emerging countries] chemical materials and production technology that are prohibited abroad,"[19] can only be fully understood, however, through an analysis of the factors behind the pervasiveness of silicosis in developing nations.

The Impotence of the Law

One of the peculiarities of the current situation in emerging countries is that the gravity of the spread of this disease is not attributable to a lack of legislation: silicosis is often legally recognized as an occupational disease, thus theoretically conferring the right for compensation to workers. The most extreme case is undoubtedly that of South Africa, where the application of what was once pioneering legislation (chapter 3) has, a century later, and despite the end of apartheid, led to a genuine "epidemic of occupational lung disease,"[20] complicated by interactions with HIV since the 1980s.[21] While the situation of immigrant workers remains the key factor behind the poor workplace health conditions experienced by miners, in many countries the primary constraint on the effectiveness of legislation is the paltry implementation of bureaucratic provisions, illustrated by what happened in Rajasthan. In 1965, 10 years after silicosis was tacked onto the Workman Compensation Act of 1923, this Indian state decided to create a Pneumoconiosis Medical Board to conduct medical exams, submit medical reports, and issue health certificates for salaried miners. But Rajasthan's Labour Department did not actually establish this board until 1993–28 years after its legal creation. Since then, not a single silicosis victim has received compensation. This is due not only to miners' lack of or insufficient knowledge about the disease's existence, but also to the institution's complicated administrative procedures. In 2003, the Health, Environment, and Development Consortium (an NGO) condemned the Pneumoconiosis Medical Board's failure to fill the positions necessary for it to function, resulting in its virtual inability to issue any certificates.[22]

China has also experienced many obstacles in implementing legislation to compensate workers suffering from silicosis. A recent report in the *China Labour Bulletin* highlighted the extreme difficulty employees face in trying to secure financial compensation once they have left their employer. In practice, the ease with which an employer can dismiss a worker suspected of the disease, or offer only a small indemnity and force him or her to quit, precludes most workers from obtaining financial compensation.[23] The migrant status of most workers and the long latency period of the disease compound this problem. Corporate responsibility is also difficult to establish, since many businesses regularly change their legal identities to escape indemnity obligations they might have incurred under the previous company name.

Public health institutes dedicated to disease prevention and treatment tend to refuse to accept patients who show up more than two years after they have left their jobs. The doctors in these centers are often bought off by local businesses and falsify or withhold the results of medical exams. Corruption also affects the administrative chain. Authorities tend to recognize only those diagnoses made by their area's public prevention-and-treatment centers, as well as to refuse to consider applications on the grounds of insufficient documentation. The desire to retain businesses that are located within their jurisdiction can also push local political authorities to dissuade workers from seeking compensation. Even when a worker is granted the indemnity spelled out in the administrative procedures, the aid is of limited duration and the amount is insufficient. The worker often has little choice but to turn to the courts, a process that is expensive and subject to delaying tactics by companies. Furthermore, judges are not always immune to corruption.[24]

Businesses, too, have means of circumventing legislation. Rapid and systematic workforce turnover is a typical example of a strategy that does not technically break the law but betrays its spirit. In addition to being a threat to and creating a penalty for workers, this pattern can serve as a personnel management practice that dilutes companies' legal responsibilities. In Turkey, recent studies have chronicled a reduction in the cumulative length of employment in high-risk companies: for instance, an average of five years in any single quartz-crushing plant, combined with high mobility within that industrial sector. This example can be generalized to any extremely dangerous industry.[25] Here again, history looms large. The "savage capitalism" practiced by emerging countries is reminiscent of the tactics used by private-sector companies in the West at the turn of the twentieth century, as well as by nationalized companies and by states from the former socialist bloc. The same approach had also been used in financial compensation for occupational pneumoconiosis (chapter 5).[26]

One World or Two?

Avoidance and circumvention of silicosis legislation are so widespread that the transfer of high-risk industries from industrialized to emerging countries indicates a difference of degree, rather than kind, between the two worlds. All of the research on workplace health in Western countries highlights businesses' attempts to weaken health laws protecting workers. These efforts have largely succeeded. In the case of France, official reports and budgetary practices explicitly recognize the magnitude of the underreporting of occupational diseases in that country, the cost of which is, for a large part, shouldered by the social security system.[27] The cross-national comparison of the policies towards silicosis, a particularly costly disease because of its gravity and the number of people exposed to its risks, reflects all the aspects this book has explored thus far: (1) bureaucratic obstacles narrowing the scope of the law;[28] (2) employers blackmailing elected officials by arguing that greater regulation and better labor protection would force companies to close, thereby generating stagnation and unemployment; (3) immigrants with temporary work contracts constituting a precarious workforce; and (4) groups that are directly controlled by the mines medically monitoring the workers, resulting in an apparent (though not actual) minimization of occupational diseases and deaths. Moreover, studies in the United States have exposed industry's ability to push medical research toward the denial of occupational hazards—a mechanism that played a large part in delaying the recognition of silicosis in France in the 1930s and 1940s.[29] American researchers have also detailed the methods used by employers to confuse the assessment of health conditions, such as by producing biased dust-level measurements.[30] Again, this directly echoes the structural weakness that plagued public silicosis prevention and monitoring efforts throughout the twentieth century (chapter 6).

In this context, there is not an absolute dualism between an "old world" that respects occupational health law and an emerging world that only is familiar with window-dressing legislation. Rather, conditions in emerging countries can be seen as exacerbating and magnifying the mechanisms that limit the protection of the workforce in the industrialized world. Chapters 4 and 5 addressed the history of an issue that is one of this book's major themes: the need to consider laws not as an end point, where their mere application would suffice to regulate practices, but as a resource whose mobilization depends on a social and economic balance of power that is continuously being renegotiated. The terms of this simultaneously local, national, and transnational balance depend on the political organization of states and the place of civil society and economic actors within these countries. Beyond the modus operandi of what is sometimes called social citizenship, the increasing exposure of emerging nations' populations to the risk of silicosis is mediated by purely industrial factors. Primary among them are the structure of capital and the relative position of small- and medium-sized businesses, which dominate sectors such as the mining industry. For example, India officially has 572 coal mines and 2,500 metal mines of all sizes and equipment levels; some, regardless of whether they are underground or open, have remained entirely manual. Yet an estimated 6,000 metal mines escape all regulation because of their small size or the seasonality of their operations.[31] Overall, a million workers are employed in this sector daily.

Series of local studies in India and elsewhere have revealed loopholes that undermine the protection of occupational health in these emerging countries. First, to a large extent, "informal sector industries escape the protection afforded by labor law provisions intended to protect workforce health and safety."[32] Limited financial resources impede preventive measures, if employers are inclined to apply them at all. A case in point is Turkey, where increased privatization and subcontracting have reduced the average size of companies and, therefore, their means of protecting their workforce.[33] The same applies to the agate industry in India: a detailed study highlights the economic hurdles to installing equipment that might prevent the risk of pneumoconiosis.[34]

Systematic shortcomings—across all sectors—in ventilation, the amount of lighting, and individual protection equipment are also attributable to weak monitoring by official labor and health departments. The damage is all the greater because the "workers (generally unorganized) have no knowledge of basic occupational safety procedures, or do not apply them," as well as because they often enter these jobs at a very young age: as adolescents, or even as children.[35] They are subjected to consistently harmful working conditions, but their shifting among companies hampers any attempts they might make to exercise their right to financial compensation if they suffer from an occupational illness, while also complicating epidemiological studies.

Western small businesses have a "downstream" impact as well. The *American Imports, Chinese Deaths* study emphasizes the prominent role of North American small- and medium-sized enterprises (SMEs) in the importation of Chinese products; these SMEs are not set up to monitor the labor conditions of their suppliers. Even the bigger companies are somewhat limited in their ability to carry out effective inspections, given that their Chinese partners have become adept at creating small-sized model workshops to serve as showcases.

Another structural difference between industrialized and emerging countries is the role, scope, and nature of the labor movement in each. The International Labour Organization—a key actor in recognizing the occupational nature of silicosis during the interwar period (chapter 3)[36]—is fully aware of the gravity of the situation and the need to address it, as demonstrated by its joint action with WHO on the Global Program for the Elimination of Silicosis in the World by the year 2030. Faced with the weakness, or even absence, of union organizations in the countries most affected by the silicosis epidemic, however, the ILO has embraced a form of accommodation of its principle of tripartite representation (unions, employers, and government), which historically has been the organization's driving force. Thus the ILO/WHO eradication plan, although global in nature, calls for each country to develop a program tailored to its needs, after acquiring the necessary know-how. This action is unique in that it does not seek to exclusively target workers—who are mostly males, working in industries where they are particularly exposed to silicosis, such as mining, metallurgy, and the construction industry—but, rather, to join forces with other movements focused on the fight against child labor, the advancement of women, and, more generally, the defense of human rights, such as the Impulse NGO's Network on Mining and Child Labor.[37]

Such programs are supported by international NGO networks like Red Internacional Mujeres y Mineria, whose international secretariat is located in India's Andhra Pradesh state. The organization has established itself in worker communities in developing countries through a network of regional representatives. It is also worth noting, however, that this type of initiative—denouncing occupational health violations through a defense of human rights—is most often supported by NGOs from the most developed industrial countries. When an organization as venerable as British-based Anti-Slavery International denounces silicosis as part of its fight against forced labor,[38] it is expressing an agenda that has long been ingrained in British social reform. This makes it difficult at times to determine to what extent the social actors supported by NGOs from the richest countries have interiorized the discourse on human rights, especially since local debates in other nations on citizenship and social rights might be framed differently. Yet history demonstrates a key lesson of this book: the powerful flow of socially reforming ideas should not be underestimated, whether they come about through scientific networks, NGOs, federations of international unions, and/or international organizations. It is especially important not to underrate their ability to shape local debates on developing social citizenship, even if a country's political, social, economic, and cultural conditions may, at first, seem far removed from their aims.

The case of Japan is of great comparative value here. In the interwar years, when the debate on the recognition of silicosis was just beginning, Japanese political and social citizenship was far less developed than it was in more-industrialized states. Before the country joined the ILO in 1919, except in a few isolated scientific publications, silicosis was considered to be a working-class matter, and a discussion of the disease was confined to the peripheral world of miners and professional associations. It was precisely the emerging Japanese social movement's exposure to the ILO's discourse on the relationship between occupational health conditions and social rights, and Japanese hygienists' contacts with that organization's experts, that brought an awareness of silicosis to the Japanese public. These emerging social forces also contributed to transforming the issue into both a matter of public health that was worthy of judicial regulation and a factor in the political and social integration of the working class. Similarly, today human rights can serve as a means to legitimize local actors in the eyes of their own government, which itself faces international pressures on this topic.[39]

The intersection between promoting human rights and improving working conditions often draws social movements into battles that also touch on political and even geopolitical issues. One of the most active organizations in exposing the fate of workers who have fallen victim to silicosis is the China Labour Bulletin (CLB). The CLB was founded in 1994 by union activist Han Dongfang to defend and promote workers' rights in the People's Republic of China. Dongfang also serves on the board of the Human Rights in China Association and contributes to Radio Free Asia, which is funded by the US Congress. His path illustrates the labor movement's difficult development in certain emerging countries. Dongfang was a railway worker in Beijing who became famous during the 1989 Tiananmen Square events by participating in the creation of the first union independent of the Chinese government, the Beijing Workers' Autonomous Federation. He was expelled to Hong Kong four years later, however.

In this context of union weakness in emerging countries, mobilization movements can capitalize on geopolitical issues to gain support from them, as well as draw on help from international labor movements. One example is the commitment of the International Federation of Chemical, Energy, Mine, and General Workers' Unions (ICEM), which (in November 2007) included over 20 million members affiliated with 467 industry federations in 132 countries. During one of its international conferences in Brussels, on November 17 and 18, 2005, union delegates from the materials sector—including the cement, glass, and ceramics industries—adopted a resolution calling on multinationals in this sector to play a more responsible role in health, security, and environmental issues, especially for silicosis and asbestos. ICEM did not just make a statement of principle, but also participated in campaigns against silicosis for migrant workers in the jewelry industry, who are often involved in the polishing of gemstones, which have become major exports for China and India. More concretely, in 2005, the ICEM was instrumental in sending four workers from these two countries to the Baselworld jewelry show (regularly held in Basel, Switzerland), in order to draw attention to the occupation's deadly consequences.[40]

There is no doubt that this rallying of international union organizations, such as the Global Program for the Elimination of Silicosis in the World, has contributed to restoring the fight against silicosis to its former place as a major objective of international organizations. While parallels could be drawn with past initiatives and the success of the international federations of stone carvers in placing silicosis on the WHO/ILO agenda, over the past two decades strategies to marshal support for this issue have diversified, following the pace of the development of the Internet. Alongside the traditional ILO lever, workers' organizations can now employ more-direct and immediate pressure tactics with a global reach, particularly by using threats to a firm's corporate image as a means of securing commitments to certain goals. Denim sandblasting highlights the complexity of these dynamics. Under international pressure, in April 2009, Turkey announced a ban on this practice, in conjunction with an action plan against illegal factories. Many of the country's companies responded by outsourcing their production to China, India, Bangladesh, and Egypt. This counterstrategy ran up against a public-relations campaign mounted against the major textile brands by the Clean Clothes Campaign network and the International Textile, Garment, and Leather Workers' Federation. Levi's and H&M were gradually joined by 10 additional brands in instituting a ban on sandblasting and other fabric treatments based on abrasive silica, aluminum silicate, silica carbonate, and garnet.[41]

Given the difficulties that traditional unions can experience in gaining a foothold in emerging countries, international networks to defend silicosis victims still depend more on nongovernmental organizations, whose limited means often seem ridiculously small in relation to the magnitude of the problem. For example, the Asia Monitor Resource Centre, a regional NGO founded in Hong Kong in 1976, has been a very active player in campaigns to denounce poor working conditions in jewelry and gemstone-treatment workshops that belong to large Hong Kong firms. It has endeavored to build ties among local NGOs, for example through the silicosis meeting it organized in October 2006 in Baroda, an Indian city in the state of Gujarat. Two Chinese victims of silicosis who participated in this initiative made a memorable visit to the village of Shakarpur, 80 kilometers from Baroda, where many workers who polish agates suffer from silicosis, what the region's stone crushers also call *Godharawali Bimari*.[42] Another network, the Asian Network for the Rights of Occupational and Environmental Victims, was founded in 1997 and currently includes 13 Asian countries. It offers support to the widows and orphans of victims, establishes mutual-aid groups, organizes training courses to help workers exposed to dangerous conditions change jobs, advises and strengthens local victims' associations, organizes conferences and demonstrations, and arranges for lawyers to bring claims to the courts.[43]

In many emerging countries, NGOs involved in the defense of workers have made silicosis a priority, but the engagement of large Western NGOs seems more problematic. The latter sometimes gloss over the silicosis issue and instead emphasize awareness-raising campaigns that are more in tune with environmental concerns the public in these older industrial countries consider topical. Thus one poison can hide another. One of the most revealing examples is the campaign that Greenpeace, together with the Sherpa Association and the Commission de Recherche et d'Information Indépendantes sur la Radio-activité [Commission for Independent Research and Information about Radiation] (CRIIRAD), mounted against the French company Areva. According to these organizations' investigations, Areva's uranium mines in Niger had polluted the environment by contaminating and exhausting limited water resources, as well as exposed its miners to radiation that increased their risk of cancer. The 64 dense pages of Greenpeace's investigative report describe the occupational health problems of the miners at length but only refer to silicosis once, and that just indirectly, through an interview with a local activist.[44] The media coverage following the report's publication in May 2010 only referred to the miners' exposure to radiation. Furthermore, in June 2009, the Sherpa Association, along with Médecins du Monde [Doctors of the World], launched a study on the potential impact of Areva's uranium activities on the health of both the workers and neighboring populations in Niger and Gabon. This joint survey focused on the sole consequences of workers' exposure to uranium, even though there is no evidence to suggest that its effects on the health of workers employed in Areva's mining activities are any more deleterious than those that result from exposure to silica dust.[45]

New Medical Frontiers: Silicosis after the Mines Close
Industry Sectors at Risk: A "Mobile" Disease

The distinction between emerging and industrialized countries also remains relevant in another sense, since silicosis now appears to be only a minor public health problem in the latter. The mass closure of mines over the past four decades of the twentieth century has been accompanied by a decreasing number of new cases reported, with silicosis progressively becoming a disease of retirees in Western countries and Japan.

Yet the number of people at risk remains considerable. In 1991, the National Institute for Occupational Safety and Health (NIOSH) estimated that 1.9 million workers were exposed to the inhalation of silica dust in the United States.[46] Official sources in America show that, since then, the prevalence of silica dust exposure in coal mines has increased,[47] due to a combination of limits in the implementation of regulations and controls and the depletion of thicker coal seams,[48] a pattern that was particularly visible in the smallest mining companies.[49]

Silicosis is also significant in sectors where its dangers have long been known: in smelting operations (especially for workers involved in casting, unmolding, and polishing); public-works projects (drilling siliceous rock); all industries using silica as a raw material (glassworks and ceramics factories, and in the production of fine clay, firebricks, paint, plastic, etc.); and in crushing and grinding plants for siliceous rock (roller mills).[50] Two unexpected categories of workers who are at risk of death from silicosis are dental technicians and farmers, with the latter drawing increased attention in general with regard to health risks.[51]

Abrasive blasting with silica sand has also remained a major problem in the United States. In 1974, the Occupational Health and Safety Administration (OSHA) proposed reducing the permissible exposure limits for silica by half and banning the use of silica in abrasive blasting. Since the 1980s, starting with the election of Ronald Reagan, along with profound resistance by industry, OSHA had been unable to either ban the use of silica in abrasive blasting or drastically reduce the standard for permissible levels of silica.[52] In 2013, however, OSHA proposed a new standard that would dramatically cut exposure to silica in a wide variety of older and new industries. The final rule was published on March 25, 2016, with the new standard taking effect on June 23, 2016. But this standard will still permit sandblasting to be used by industry. Furthermore, new additions to the list of high-risk occupations are appearing, which may be due to the development of new work methods and materials, or to the fact that they have received increased epidemiological attention.

The importance of the new OSHA standard is immense, as it will affect older silica-using industries, such as sandblasting, drilling, and construction. It will also limit more-recent industries that have emerged. Surface-mining procedures, such as mountain-top removal and open-pit excavation, have created additional methods of exposure to silica-containing rock that have led to new epidemics of silicosis in the remaining coal-mining regions of the United States. Similarly, sand is part of the hydraulic fracturing process, and the use of fracking in the rapidly growing oil and natural gas fields in the United States has also led to potential exposures to silica, which have only begun to be publicized. The new US silica standard also promises to protect vulnerable workers in other emerging industries.

As always, controlling the spread of silicosis and heightening perceptions of its risks are complicated by two factors: its cross-sectorial nature and, even more basically, the medical difficulties in identifying the disease. As was the case in the twentieth century (chapters 2, 3, 4), the current diagnosis of silicosis is based on radiological identification, which, according to one specialist, requires the respective talents of "Sherlock Holmes, Albrecht Dürer, and Socrates."[53] A boilerplate definition, developed by the ILO at the end of the 1950s and periodically revised since, describes the effects of the disease more than it does its medical basis.[54] Over the past two to three decades, computed tomography (a CT scan) has made it possible to detect nodular changes that are invisible on conventional x-rays, especially in less-advanced cases of pneumoconiosis. The blending of various types of medical imagery for lung diseases is still in its infancy, however.[55] The most precise methods of analysis to characterize the effect of silica dusts on lung tissue are electron microscopy and microanalysis, but their complexity and cost limit their widespread use. France, for instance, only has two laboratories with such capabilities.

These medical difficulties are compounded by the spread of the disease throughout a variety of production processes. Particular industries are at risk, but so are practices that can be disseminated across very different sectors. For instance, sandblasting, which is the most dangerous form of exposure, affects employees in the construction industry, as well as autobody-shop workers, oil-tank cleaners, and bluejean sandblasters. This can make it hard to see silicosis as a global risk. The medical literature is limited to collecting local observations that allow its authors to identify epidemiological risks, but also hinder a broader awareness of the problem. This fragmentation is further accentuated by different levels of regulation, especially on sandblasting, with significant differences between Europe and the United States. As in most other social issues, Europeans have recourse in their central governments, while the United States has turned to the courts for redress in the silicosis issue. During the 1980s and 1990s, in the absence of federal action, US workers brought numerous lawsuits to court against companies that employed sandblasting, leading to victories of many millions of dollars and massive financial losses for some firms. In the wake of this litigation, many companies abandoned the use of silica as an abrasive.

In England and other European nations, stronger enforcement of silicosis legislation and more-accurate records have led to an about-face, since sectors that had previously appeared to be statistically safe, due to underreporting, turned out to be massively affected by the disease. This can give the misleading impression that the disease is resurfacing. In Italy, for instance, a "reappearance of silicosis" was identified as a factor in the "extension of the monitoring of occupational health conditions to areas that were previously inadequately covered, such as small and family companies, and businesses employing immigrant, illegal, and nonunionized labor from developing countries."[56]

There is less awareness of silicosis risk in the construction sector than in the public-works sector. In the former, risk is dispersed, since workers in the building trades who contract silicosis are usually hired as individuals, or in small groups. In public-works projects, laborers are collectively exposed to major risks when they drill siliceous rock, but they are also most often employed by large companies, which are more cognizant of the dangers.[57] In this latter sector, the development of preventive strategies came as a reaction to major health catastrophes in the twentieth century that struck workers involved in the excavation of large tunnels in Italy, the United States, Japan, Switzerland, and elsewhere. As is the case for mines, collective tragedies are more conducive to effectively raising awareness and taking action.[58] This work-related disease problem is all the more serious, however, since it is a constantly evolving social and economic issue. For example, after the era of major road projects that characterized a large part of the twentieth century, the maintenance of existing networks brought forth less-visible health threats, and research has only recently taken notice of the new risks they pose with regard to pneumoconiosis.[59]

Conversely, the level of prevention does not exclusively depend on occupational health policies, especially in the least protected sectors. Improved construction techniques and materials often result from pressures to protect consumers, which often yield a more rapid response than from lobbying efforts by trade unions—and, more recently, from environmental concerns.[60] This does not, however, mean that private individuals are systematically shielded from silicosis risks. In addition to environmental conditions that mostly affect developing countries today,[61] studies in the 1990s uncovered a serious risk linked to the intensive inhalation of household products by women overusing them in cleaning their homes, and by thrill-seeking adolescents looking for cheap products to huff.[62] Beyond the anecdotal—including incidents that have cost the lives of very young women—it is important to note the dynamic aspect of silicosis. Its traditional portrayal as a mining disease masks its quasi-universal character, as well as the possibility of its resurgence in modern manufacturing processes.

One might think that the underreporting of silicosis is a problem primarily in developing countries, rather than industrialized ones. In the former, the overriding concern is that legislation is poorly enforced (as was the case in the West, in Japan, and in socialist countries in the twentieth century). Yet the primary issue in Western nations is the gap between the perception of silicosis as a mining disease, even among medical specialists, and its actual manifestations, which are more complex, both because of the diversity of the affected economic sectors and the suspected effects of exposure to crystalline silica dust. First, however, it is worth examining the principal terms of the present-day medical debate on silicosis.

Silica, Silicosis, and Other Diseases

One of the major contributions history can make to medicine is to consider the nosological entity known as silicosis as the fragile outcome of a longue durée history: it took centuries to establish current knowledge about the disease, which was shaped by an international compromise negotiated in 1930. This does not mean that the whys and wherefores of silicosis are artifacts. Rather, by thoroughly focusing on silicosis as a *disease*, medical research turned a blind eye to a range of possible alternative effects of exposure to silica dust. From the 1930s onward, silica hazards have been agglomerated and reduced to just one illness, silicosis. This equation only started to fall apart in the 1980s, under the combined effects of new detection techniques, new observations, and a new approach to inflammatory diseases. The uncertainties and doubts about the processes leading to and the importance of these recently identified health hazards are the result of a half-century of almost exclusively focusing on silicosis.[63]

These new investigations into crystalline silica dust hazards in wealthy countries have their roots in a medical debate that has, for the past 20 years, focused on the carcinogenic character of silica (or silicosis), on the one hand, and the "systemic" ailments it is suspected of causing, on the other.[64] Silica or silicosis, that is the question—whether to define the problem as dealing with the complications of silicosis, or as the direct effects of exposure to silica. This predicament is undoubtedly less familiar for medical researchers than it is for historians. The state of knowledge described in chapters 2 and 3 has changed with the development of more-sophisticated techniques to detect silica dust in the lungs, as well as with the twentieth-century advent of the notion of chronic disease, which revisited the causal links between risk factors and the outbreak and evolution of a disease.[65] Current uncertainties, however, simply replay the questions that arose during the nineteenth century (chapter 2) and the compromise solution reached during the interwar period (chapters 3, 4). The wrong-headed effects of this minimal compromise have reemerged today, in both new and familiar forms (such as deaths from a combination of silicosis and tuberculosis, where these mortality rates are higher than ever in emerging countries).[66]

Silicosis—as it has been broadly defined in successive phases since the international convention of 1934, and documented by ILO-certified radiological images since the end of the 1950s—is a blanket term that is too narrow to cover the extent of lung (and probably systemic) diseases that prolonged or intensive inhalation of silica dust is likely to trigger or, at least, to facilitate or aggravate.

The perpetually changing state of knowledge about silicosis is obscured by causative categories, the creation of which requires socioeconomic compromises that are always difficult to renegotiate. This is reflected in the way that silicosis, understood in a deliberately narrow sense, impeded the recognition of coal miners' pneumoconiosis (chapter 6), which is now seen as specific to the inhalation of coal dusts.[67] We need to take a long view if we are to understanding the intensity of the medical debate on potential links between exposure to silica dust and lung cancer, which began over a quarter of a century ago.

The medical profession generally agrees that silicosis has a carcinogenic effect: legislation has been put in place in a number of countries to compensate current and former workers who suffered from pneumoconiosis and then developed lung cancer.[68] In contrast, the effect of exposure to and inhalation of free crystalline silica dust remains controversial.[69] In 1987, the International Agency for Research on Cancer (IARC) officially classified this type of dust as a probable carcinogen. A decade later, in 1997, after a review of new scientific literature, the IARC reassessed the risk level by classifying silica (in the form of quartz and cristobalite) as a group-1 carcinogen for humans. The agency determined that cohort and case-control studies had permitted a determination of the relative effects of other lung-cancer risk factors, such as exposure to tobacco smoke and various occupational carcinogens. Moreover, all else being equal, the IARC considers the carcinogenicity of silica to be an established fact, with its danger increasing according to various indicators of the amount inhaled, such as accumulated exposure, the length of exposure, the maximum level of exposure, and a radiological diagnosis of silicosis. As a caveat, the IARC maintains that proof of carcinogenicity has only been established in certain industrial sectors, such as mining, quarrying, processes using refractory materials, ceramics, and stone carving.

The same evaluation was subsequently repeated by other organizations, such as NIOSH and the National Toxicology Program in the United States, as well as the American Conference of Governmental Industrial Hygienists (ACGIH). In 2009, a new working group established by the IARC confirmed the carcinogenic character of crystalline silica per se. In light of epidemiological developments since 1997, the conclusions of the IARC study, released in 2012, generalized the assertion that the presence of silica in all industrial activities is carcinogenic.[70] It is not certain, however, that this new publication will be sufficient to raise awareness about the dangers of the risk. By proposing a drastic reduction in the threshold-limit value that was previously allocated to free silica (the ACGIH has a threshold of 0.025 milligrams per cubic meter), the IARC is making it extremely difficult to monitor employees' exposure to a diffuse and universal risk, somewhat akin to UV radiation from sunshine.

For the moment, and probably due in part to this very difficulty, protection issues are of secondary importance in a debate whose terms remain predominantly medical.[71] The dichotomy between silica and silicosis does not preclude more-complex causalities, perhaps where only those workers affected by pneumoconiosis might be sensitive to the effect of "dusts."[72] Yet even the precise measurement of each of these two primary relations—a direct carcinogenic consequence from silica, and/or one from silicosis—is not straightforward. The demonstration of a specific effect from the inhalation of silica dusts is hindered by the omnipresence of mixed dusts, where silica is combined with hazardous materials (such as polycyclic aromatic hydrocarbons), radioactive products (such as radon), asbestos, or arsenic. A disease as widespread as lung cancer also requires consideration of other behaviors, such as smoking, which, in turn, are statistically linked to sociocultural background. A careful examination of the composition of samples tracked by epidemiologists further complicates the picture. Some authors believe that the underreporting of silicosis produces selection effects that distort the data, since the population of silicosis victims is composed of workers who qualified for financial compensation.[73] This population is not defined by medical criteria alone, but also by insurance-related criteria and their effective implementation. Also, employees are assumed either to know or to suspect that they have silicosis—but this should not be taken for granted, given that awareness of the disease has varied among sectors.[74]

These question marks regarding factors linking silica, silicosis, and lung cancer are not unrelated to the controversies of the interwar period over the existence of silicosis as an independent occupational disease, producing specific and measurable effects.[75] The debate continues, in the sense that the disease remains hard to identify. In addition to this fundamental difficulty, a detailed examination of the cases that were studied brings to light numerous uncertainties; here again, different trigger conditions for silicosis interfere with epidemiology. Even assuming that the scales are increasingly tipping in favor of recognizing the carcinogenic effects of exposure to silicosis, too many necessary facts are still missing to be able to measure the minimum level and duration of exposure, or to assess the latency period between the beginning of exposure and early manifestations of the disease. The old question of thresholds, for which silicosis has historically served as an important testing ground,[76] is discussed no less now than in the past. Many authors thus seek to attribute the heterogeneous risk of silicosis from one occupation to another to different exposure conditions. For example, brief exposures to very high concentrations of silica dust are particularly dangerous, but these would not necessarily be detectable by standard dust measurements.

A second major area of medical research questions the supposition of an exclusive relationship between long-term exposure to the inhalation of silica dust and silicosis. Recent studies on chronic obstructive bronchopneumopathy suggest that prolonged exposure to *low* levels of silica may lead to the development of emphysema, chronic bronchitis, and respiratory diseases from mineral dusts. Despite the absence of radiological signs of silicosis, silica still causes, or at least aggravates, obstructive respiratory problems. Such diseases generally are not correlated with occupational activity, because they do not line up with the criteria of insurance compensation systems. These criteria, which vary over time and across geographical areas, determine the recording of data on occupational diseases.[77]

In the collieries, long-standing questions on the respective roles of silica and coal dusts are far from being answered. In an attempt to capture the complex uncertainties in how they are medically classified, new semantic categories have been created, such as "mixed-dust pneumoconiosis,"[78] or "coal mine dust lung disease." The latter is supposed to cover classic interstitial lung diseases, including "CWP, silicosis, and mixed dust pneumoconiosis, but also the more recently described entity of dust-related diffuse fibrosis (DDF) . . . which may be clinically indistinguishable from idiopathic pulmonary fibrosis absent the exposure history or pathologic evidence."[79] The probable association between exposure to coal-mine dust and chronic obstructive pulmonary disease is particularly at stake here.[80]

New questions on the exclusive tie between silica and silicosis extend to extrapulmonary symptoms that can be correlated with exposure to silica. Since the pioneering work of Enrico Vigliani at Milan's Clinica del Lavoro in the 1950s, specialized literature has focused on the possible role of silicosis in systemic diseases.[81] New detection techniques have increased the number of observations supporting this hypothesis by using analyses of lung tissue to retrospectively identify contact with silica dusts in unexpected situations. Reported cases include a range of autoimmune diseases in workers or patients exposed to crystalline silica: systemic scleroderma (systemic sclerosis, or hardening of tissues), systemic lupus erythematosus (inflammatory connective-tissue disease), sarcoidosis (collections of inflammatory cells in different parts of the body, including the lungs), rheumatoid polyarthritis (arthritis in the joints), autoimmune hemolytic anemia (antibodies directed against a person's own red blood cells), dermatomyositis (a skin rash with muscle inflammation and weakness), and dermatopolymyositis (inflammation of the muscles and skin).[82] Certain classifications of occupational diseases recognize these types of health effects.[83] Some research also mentions the statistically significant association of exposure to crystalline silica with a higher incidence of and deaths from kidney diseases, Wegener's granulomatosis (a multisystem autoimmune disease), and subclinical kidney disorders (not detectable by the usual clinical tests).

Conclusion: History and Epidemiology
The Legacy of the 1930s

Why, for most of the twentieth century, did silicosis virtually monopolize the attention of doctors seeking to unravel the hidden dangers of silica dusts? Only history can help answer this question, by providing insights that might guide future epidemiological research.

To this day, the underreporting of silicosis, not only in emerging countries but also in Europe and other industrialized countries, stems from its history as the disease of coal workers, who supplied what was the primary strategic energy source until the 1950s in the United States, and the 1960s in Europe and Japan. Because coal served as the basis for generating electricity, its value affected both conditions for economic growth (by determining the production costs for electrical power) and social peace (by constituting the main energy source for households). Since coal mining requires an abundant workforce, the price of coal directly depends on that industry's expenditures for financial compensation for silicosis. Too high a cost would have seriously jeopardized the already vulnerable competitiveness of European deposits, so this led to an underrecognition and undercompensation of silicosis in both privately owned and nationalized coal mines.

This twentieth-century economic constraint fundamentally shaped medico-legal provisions, whose effects still reverberate today. This book has shown how profoundly national laws were influenced by the transnational recognition of the disease. To a large extent, the conditions for indemnification and the medical definition of silicosis were negotiated under the auspices of the International Labour Organization, whose influence in the interwar period was considerable.[84] This official definition was in no way a neutral translation of international medical knowledge. On the contrary, the positions of international experts, who were often directly or indirectly linked to the mining industry, were, for the most part, determined by the size of the at-risk workforce and the funding structure for social insurance in their respective countries. In the vast majority of cases, the higher the number of workers exposed to risk, and the greater the employers' share of compensation costs, the more medical experts sought to restrict recognition of the disease.

At the international level, the ILO dealt with this heterogeneity by negotiating a default medical definition of silicosis in the early 1930s. The 1934 international convention represented both immediate progress and a long-term stalemate. While it officially recognized the existence and universality of silicosis, which was still denied by countries like France and Belgium, it also severely curtailed the medical scope of definitions of the disease. Indeed, the financially significant distinction between chronic lung diseases of occupational origin and those of "private" origin was largely drawn in accordance with the power relations of the day, rather than according to strictly medical criteria. An American doctor summarized this dynamic, referring to silicosis ironically as a "social disease with medical aspects."[85]

Yet these contextual elements, of which all the actors were aware in the 1930s, quickly faded from scholarly memory. The minimalist definition of silicosis, once negotiated, was then ingrained in medical teaching. While some of the occupational diseases this definition left out later were progressively recognized, such as coal miner's disease in France in 1992, the truncated base category continues to have a significant impact to this day. Without a historical perspective, present-day lung specialists—not to mention occupational health doctors and generalists—lack the tools to understand the gap between accepted medical knowledge, as reflected by social-insurance institutions and their coverage (or not) of a particular disease, and the clinical observations that they are likely to make.

A Cluster and Life-Cycle Disease

An empirical examination of the geographical distribution of deaths from silicosis in a country like France in the second half of the twentieth century is revealing. Although the data are both biased and approximate—and are only available at the broader administrative level of *départements* (approximately equivalent to a county in the United States), not the smaller divisions of the 36.000 *municipalités*—statistical observations on the causes of death show the localized nature of silicosis, as if it were specific to a handful of industrial centers. Alongside the giant administrative regions of Nord-Pas-de-Calais and Lorraine (35.000 km^2 in the northeast part of the country) are small local ones, including mining towns in places such as Gard, and nonmining areas such as Haute-Vienne (with its Limoges porcelain) and Maine-et-Loire (with its Trélazé slate). The distribution is not surprising, in light of the classic image of silicosis: porcelain and slate have long been known to be at-risk industries.

Yet perhaps the real question raised by this geographical distribution is the ability of the medical corps (generalists, radiologists, occupational health doctors, pathologists, and even pulmonologists) in other regions to identify silicosis in patients who suffer and die from chronic lung diseases. By the end of the nineteenth century, medical personnel in these old centers of industrial production had started to develop a local vocabulary and specific procedures for addressing occupational pneumoconiosis. It therefore comes as no surprise that a century later, practitioners in these areas knew how to recognize silicosis and record it on death certificates. Silicosis therefore essentially appears to be a cluster disease that absorbed the various local forms of occupational pneumoconiosis throughout the first half of the twentieth century, rather than a general disease that was likely to strike across industrial sectors.

The transmission of medical knowledge, which leaves very little space for teaching about silicosis in the medical curriculum, is also affected by the conditions through which this learning is acquired: traditionally, through prolonged and quasi-epidemiological contacts with silicosis patients. Expertise obtained in this way is circumscribed by time and space. It is retained and passed on by medical personnel and the institutions that employ them. Thus one can only wonder about the implications of the rapid disappearance of the research centers that were built alongside European coalfields with the ECSC's financial support. Granted, today's practitioners have managed to conduct research and enrich the field of pulmonology. But their expertise, built on a long history of visiting numerous silicosis victims at various stages of the disease, has, at best, continued to be developed through the clinical observation of elderly miners affected by the disease. It is therefore likely that a great deal of professional knowledge has dissipated and disappeared. In any case, it does not seem to be available for the regions of the world that are currently experiencing the ravages of silicosis.

A comparison with asbestos reveals a paradox. Geologically, silica is far more widespread, making it arguably integral to industrial activity. From a sociological perspective, silica lacks the factors that eventually raised public awareness about the dangers of asbestos: a very specific disease (mesothelioma); risks to highly skilled workers in the service industry; and, through construction materials, risks to consumers.[86] This contextual difference between the two deadliest occupational diseases of the twentieth century—which were long grouped together in the same medico-legal category—has not just affected laypeople. Mine doctors, the practitioners who are best able to diagnose silicosis, have mostly been unable to play an influential role, because they remain confined to industrial islands and systems controlled by coal-mining companies, which have acted to limit recognition of the disease. The failure of unions, and of political pressure, to permanently break what strongly resembles a closed circuit, as well as the lack of active research strategies from the pharmaceutical industry, meant that silicosis never became a truly national cause. The issue only took hold in the economically crucial but socially isolated and regionally circumscribed mining sector. A key consequence is the global underestimation and underreporting of silicosis. The same disease yields different treatments for patients and varying medical diagnoses, depending on the region of residence and sector of work.

There is also a historical reason for the current limited awareness of other diseases caused by prolonged exposure to silica dusts. In the 1930s, medical experts with close ties to the mining industry, particularly the South African gold mines, heavily influenced the nature of the international recognition of silicosis that was achieved under ILO auspices. Their perspective emphasized the economic interests of mining companies, which lay in production levels and returns on investment. At stake was the employability of miners, often a scarce labor force that gains its qualifications on the job. The goal during that period was to discover how much time it would take before the visible manifestations of silicosis appeared, and then to learn to what degree and at what pace the disease would affect the productivity of workers, including to the point of unemployability. From this perspective, other symptomatic cases—such as workers who fell ill with systemic diseases after moving to another industrial sector—were considered irrelevant. For laborers who found themselves in this situation, the fact of their working in a different industrial environment, and not suffering from any lung diseases, meant that it was difficult for the practitioners who treated them to make a link between previous exposure to silica dust and the systemic diseases that were later diagnosed. Such cases, therefore, fell into a void that studies of the origins and causes of silicosis are only now attempting to fill. A historical perspective provides valuable insights into the shortcomings of present-day medical research and breaks the vicious cycle of a circumscribed awareness of silica hazards: the smaller the amount of factors that are recognized as dangers and diagnosed as illnesses, the lower the number of physicians who are sensitive to them. The convergence of history and medicine—a true collaboration between the two disciplines—may well be the way out of this impasse.

NOTES

1. Hamizi, "La silicose chez les artisans." All of the information in this chapter about silicosis in Tkout is taken from this presentation.

2. Fedotov, "ILO/WHO Joint International Program," 3–5; Lehtinen and Goldstein, "Elimination of Silicosis."

3. Cavalcanti dos Santos Antão et al. ("High Prevalence of Silicosis," 194–201) find a comparable prevalence of silicosis (53 percent) in the city of Petrópolis in Brazil. In each instance, local conditions play an important role in the activity's level of danger. Yingratanasuk et al. ("Stone Carvers in Thailand," 301–308), while recognizing that their results might be underevaluations, find a much lower prevalence (2 percent) in Chonburi Province in Thailand.

4. Baldasseroni et al., "Naissance d'une maladie."

5. Kulkarni, "Prevention and Control," 95; Holanda et al., "Silicosis in Brazilian Pit Diggers," 367–378.

6. For more on industry efforts to separate the scientific and social aspects of the onset of occupational diseases, see the asbestos case explored by Braun, "Structuring Silence."

7. This complexity is reflected in a study conducted from 1992 to 1994 on 458 sandstone-quarry workers in Jodhpur (a total of 50,000 workers covering 15,000 quarries). Their premature deaths (46 years old on average, with a variance of 10 years) most often result from a variety of chronic respiratory diseases: not only silicosis, but also chronic obstructive lung disease, lung cancer, and tuberculosis. The inherent dangers of the work, since dry drilling generates dust, are compounded by the use of explosives, the lack of protection, residence close to the work sites, smoking, and opiate addiction. See Mathur, "Pattern and Predictors."

8. Norboo et al., "Silicosis in a Himalayan Village," 341–343.

9. Policard and Collet, "Deposition of Silicosis Dust."

10. Derbyshire, "Natural Dust," 15–18; Xu et al., "Study of Siliceous Pneumoconiosis," 21–22.

11. Mathur, "Pattern and Predictors."

12. Malik, "Silicosis."

13. For a detailed analysis on these underreporting phenomena in Brazil, see Castro et al., "Mortality Due to Pneumoconioses."

14. The official Chinese government report, *National Pneumoconiosis Epidemiology Investigation from 1949 to 1986*, is cited in Chen et al., "Exposure to Silica and Silicosis," 31–37.

15. Juengprasert, "Toward Elimination of Silicosis."

16. Aungkasuvapala et al., "Silicosis and Pulmonary Tuberculosis."

17. Akgun et al., "Silicosis in Turkish Denim Sandblasters," 554–558.

18. Tofani, "American Imports, Chinese Deaths."

19. Zongzhi, "Les maladies professionnelles."

20. Murray et al., "Occupational Lung Disease."

21. Rees et al., "Oscillating Migration."

22. Malik, "Silicosis."

23. This detrimental effect on the recognition of occupational diseases replays dynamics in Western countries from both the past (for the United Kingdom, see Bufton and Melling, "'A Mere Matter of Rock'") and the present (Rosental, "Expertise").

24. "The Hard Road," *China Labour Bulletin*.

25. See Cimrin and Erdut, "General Aspect of Pneumoconiosis." Comparable phenomena occur in sandblasting activities. See Akgun et al., "Silicosis in Turkish Denim Sandblasters."

26. For more on worker turnover in the jobs most exposed to risk in nationalized French coal mines, see Rosental and Devinck, "Statistique et mort industrielle," 89–90.

27. Rosental, "Expertise."

28. For the United States, Monaghan ("Law Students") notes: "When afflicted miners seek the modest benefits permitted under the federal system—medical care plus $574 a month per primary beneficiary—they invariably run into frustrating, byzantine regulations and pitched resistance from the mining companies for which they worked, often for decades. Only 7 percent of sufferers who pursue claims without legal assistance are victorious."

29. Markowitz and Rosner, *Deadly Dust: Silicosis and the Politics*; Devinck and Rosental, "'Une maladie sociale.'" For a global sociology of these techniques, see White and Bero, "Corporate Manipulation of Research," 105.

30. Weeks, "Fox Guarding the Chicken Coop." These practices have a cross-national character, for which we were able to find equivalents in former socialist Czechoslovakia. See Mackova and Rosental, "Les démocraties populaires."

31. Mine Health and Safety Council, *Silicosis Elimination Programme*, 35.

32. Kulkarni, "Prevention and Control."

33. Cimrin and Erdut, "General Aspect of Pneumoconiosis."

34. Bhagia and Sadhu, "Cost-Benefit Analysis," 128–131.

35. Carel et al., "Souvenir Casting Silicosis."

36. Cayet et al., "How International Organisations Compete."

37. To take but one example, an estimated 70,000 Nepalese and Bangladeshi children are forced to work in the coal mines of the Jaintia Hills District in northeastern India. See "70,000 child workers."

38. Kaye, *Forced Labour*.

39. For more on the ways in which the transnational discourse on human rights is used and transformed in various cultural contexts, see R. Wilson, *Human Rights*.

40. Chung, "Hong Kong–China Solidarity."

41. Cappuccio and Toti, *Jeans da morire*.

42. See Chaudhury et al., "Silicosis among Agate Workers"; and Patel, *Stone Crusher of Gohara*.

43. Peoples Training and Research Centre, "Struggle of Silicosis Victims."

44. Dixon, *Abandonnés dans la poussière*.

45. For a more detailed account, see Moussa et al., "Mesures de l'empoussiérage." For a broader context, see Hecht, *Being Nuclear*.

46. National Institute for Occupation Safety and Health, *Work-Related Lung Diseases Surveillance Report*, cited in Chen et al., "Exposure to Silica."

47. National Institute for Occupation Safety and Health, *Work-Related Lung Disease Surveillance Report 2007*, 42. The latest data (www.cdc.gov/niosh/data/) reframe the data

from 2007, which were presented in five-year increments: prevalence increased annually in the 1990s and then stabilized, ending the trend that had characterized the preceding decades. See also Petsonk et al., "Coal Mine Dust Lung Disease," 1179–1180.

48. Weeks, "Mine Safety"; Pollock et al., "Investigation into Dust Exposures"; Laney et al., "Pneumoconiosis."

49. Laney et al., "Potential Determinants"; Suarthana et al., "Coal Workers' Pneumoconiosis."

50. For an overall view of the dissemination of silicosis risk throughout the economy, see Capacci et al., *Silice libera cristallina*. See also Lemen and Hammond, "Silicosis Kills."

51. See Choudat et al., "Respiratory Symptoms"; Radi et al., "Respiratory Morbidity." For farmers, see Schenker et al., "Pneumoconiosis." For an attempt to synthesize the emerging literature on this topic, see Innocenti et al., "Il rischio SLC," 102–105.

52. See Markowitz and Rosner, "Limits of Thresholds."

53. A. Miller, "Sherlock Holmes." The original citation is from Morgan, "Epidemiology."

54. Cayet et al., "How International Organisations Compete."

55. Sherson, "Silicosis."

56. Cocco, "Long and Winding Road," 157.

57. See Linch, "Respirable Concrete Dust"; Nij et al., "Dust Control Measures."

58. Fontaine, *Fin d'un monde ouvrier.*

59. See Valiante et al., "Highway Repair." Technological changes obviously play a part in the emergence of what might be described as a "mobile" risk. As Valiante notes, this risk increased with the introduction of new maintenance procedures in the mid-1980s, requiring the use of "large teams to cut, break, and remove large sections of concrete road," operations that release "great quantities of dust."

60. Tibbetts, "Under Construction."

61. In India, the dispersal of the agate industry into small family workshops produced collateral effects on the residents, according to Bhagia and Sadhu, "Cost-Benefit Analysis."

62. Dumontet et al., "Silicosis Due to Inhalation," 1085.

63. See Rosental et al., "From Silicosis to Silica Hazards."

64. Cocco provides a good summary of recent developments in medical research ("Long and Winding Road," 157): "The progressive clearing of the dark and thick cloud of silicosis cases has been accompanied by the emergence of other diseases, such as lung cancer, kidney failure, and immune system disorders, which has rekindled the interest in silica research."

65. Weisz, *Chronic Disease.*

66. See Rees and Murray, "Silica, Silicosis, and Tuberculosis"; Khurana and Singh, "Silicosis"; Barboza et al., "Tuberculosis and Silicosis"; Murray et al., "Occupational Lung Disease." Some of these articles show that the combined effects of tuberculosis and silicosis are compounded by a significant risk from the inclusion of HIV.

67. Cocco, "Long and Winding Road," 157.

68. Takahashi, "Silica Carcinogenicity Issue."

69. Takahashi, "Silica Carcinogenicity Issue." See also Cocco, "Multifactorial Aetiology"; Hessel et al., "Silica, Silicosis, and Lung Cancer."

70. International Agency for Research on Cancer, *Silica Dust.*

71. For a good overview, see Lacasse et al., *Silicose, silice et cancer du poumon.*

72. In addition to silicosis, there is now evidence that heavy and prolonged workplace exposure to dust containing crystalline silica can lead to an increased risk of lung cancer. The evidence suggests that this greater risk is likely to occur only in those workers who have developed silicosis. See "Hazardous Substances," 13.

73. Carta et al., "Mortality from Lung Cancer."

74. To give but one example (cited in Lemen and Hammond, "Silicosis Kills," 22–23), in January 1992, NIOSH investigated an industrial sandblasting site where a worker had just died of silicosis at the age of 55, and their inquiry revealed that several of his colleagues had the disease. One of them was 37 years old and, despite his suffering from symptoms for a year, he had not consulted a doctor. He stated: "I had never heard of silicosis. Someone died, but the boss told us it was from tuberculosis. We never thought of silicosis."

75. The question is also applicable in determining the specific role exposure to silica dust has in the onset of tuberculosis. See Linch, "Respirable Concrete Dust"; Nij et al., "Dust Control Measures"; Tiwari et al., "Tuberculosis."

76. Markowitz and Rosner, "Limits of Thresholds."

77. Rice, "Silica-Related Disease," 7. See also Occupational Safety and Health Administration, *OSHA's Final Rule.*

78. Honma et al. "Proposed Criteria."

79. Petsonk et al., "Coal Mine Dust Lung Disease," 1179, 1185.

80. Coggon and Taylor, "Coal Mining"; Kuempel et al., "Contributions of Dust Exposure"; Wang et al., "Prospective Cohort Study"; Wang et al., "Lung-Function Impairment."

81. See Vigliani and Pernis, "Immunological Aspects of Silicosis"; Pernis and Vigliani, "Role of Macrophages."

82. For an overview, see Steenland and Goldsmith, "Silica Exposure"; Sherson, "Silicosis." For an analysis of the various diseases concerned, see Rafnsson et al., "Association between Exposure"; M. Vincent and Lièvre, "Sarcoïdose et empoussièrement pulmonaire"; Costallat et al., "Pulmonary Silicosis"; Finckh et al., "Occupational Silica and Solvent Exposures."

83. In France, progressive systemic scleroderma and systemic lupus erythematosus are officially mentioned among the diseases caused by the inhalation of mineral dusts containing crystalline silicosis. The former is included in table 25 of the general list of occupational diseases and table 22 of the agricultural list; the latter appears solely in the agricultural list.

84. Cayet et al., "How International Organisations Compete."

85. Irving Selikoff, cited by Rosner and Markowitz, *Deadly Dust: Silicosis and the Politics,* 4.

86. Henry, *Amiante.*

Bibliography

Unpublished Reports in Archival Sources

This list includes only unpublished reports. Other archival materials (letters, board meeting minutes, and so forth) are cited in the end-of-chapter notes.

ACPL (Association Charbonnière de la Province de Liège [Coal Association of the Province of Liège]). Archives conserved by IHOES (see below).
  "Survey of Dust Content of Faces," Memorandum for Directeur-Divisionnaire Thonnart, 26 June 1953.
AEL (Archives de l'État à Liège [State Archives in Liège]), Liège, Belgium
  Callut, H., F. Fripiat, and J. Stassen. *Lutte contre les poussières dans le bassin houiller de Liège* [Dust control in the Liège coal basin], s.d. [1952], AAdM, 672.
  Lutte contre les poussières: Enquêtes 1947–1958 [Dust control: Studies, 1947–1958], AAdm, 674.
AGR (Archives Générales du Royaume [National Archives]), Brussels
  Belayew, D. *Rapport sur l'examen médical de la totalité de la population du fond des charbonnages de l'Espérance et Bonne Fortune* [Report on medical exams for the entire underground workforce at Espérance and Bonne Fortune collieries], 1950, Coppée, 2670.
  L'évolution des pneumoconioses et l'influence que nous pouvons avoir sur cette évolution [The development of pneumoconiosis and how we can influence this development], confidential doc., 15 December 1956, Coppée, 2633.
Bibliothèque de l'Académie Nationale de Médecine [Library of the National Academy of Medicine], Archives and Manuscripts collection, Paris
  Amoudru, Claude. *Médecine, mines et mineurs* [Medicine, mines, and miners], Ms 874 (1745)c, 2009, 2 vols.
  ———. *Souvenirs d'outre-médecine 1923–1947* [Memories beyond medicine, 1923–1947], Ms 874 (1745)a, 2000, 3 vols.
British National Archives, Kew
  Employment of Natives on the Witwatersrand Gold Mines, CO 525/173/2.
CAC (Centre des Archives Contemporaines [Center for Contemporary Archives]), Fontainebleau, France
  Étude des houillères du Bassin du Nord-Pas-de-Calais sur les mesures susceptibles d'assurer l'équilibre financier du régime spécial de la sécurité sociale dans les mines [Study of the collieries of the Nord-Pas-de-Calais Basin on measures to ensure the financial stability of the special social security regime in the mines], 8 May 1951, CAC 19770398, art. 7.
CHML (Centre Historique Minier de Lewarde [Mine Historical Center of Lewarde]), Lewarde, France
  Reclassement des silicotiques dans les travaux du fond des mines [Reclassification of silicotic miners working underground], 15 January 1951, 32 W 61.
CLADIC (Centre Liégeois d'Archives et de Documentation de l'Industrie Charbonnière [Liège Coal Industry Archives and Documentation Center]), Blégny, Belgium
  Poussières [Dusts], Fonds Stassen [1948–1960].

ECSC (European Coal and Steel Community) Archives, in the Historical Archives of the EU, Florence

Advisory Commission of Experts for the Diagnosis of Pneumoconiosis, "Minutes of the 29 September 1955 Meeting," CEAB 11-710.

Berger, L. B., and C. R. Drouard. *Meeting of Experts on the Prevention and Suppression of Dust in Mining, Tunnelling, and Quarrying*, Geneva, 26 November 1955, CEAB 11-717.

"Compte rendu de la réunion du groupe de travail 'Recherches Fondamentales sur la Silicose'" [Minutes of the meeting of the "Basic Research on Silicosis" working group], Milan, 4–6 July 1962, CEAB 11-026.

Degueldre, G. *Prélèvements de poussières sur une longue période dans un charbonnage témoin* [A control mine's dust samples over a long period of time], 30 November 1956, CEAB 1-713.

Dickmans, Gerhardt, and Otto Zorn. *Observations critiques sur la classification internationale* [Critical observations on international classification], CEAB 11-712.

Hicks, D., and J. W. J. Fay. *The Study of Respirable Dust in the Pneumoconiosis Field Research*, London, 19 December 1960, CEAB 11-714.

ILO [Second] Meeting of Experts on the Prevention and Suppression of Dust in Mining, Tunnelling, and Quarrying, Geneva, 21–26 November 1955, Exp. Pouss/1955/D12, CEAB 11-717.

Menger, H. *Traitement de la silicose et de la silico-tuberculose* [Treatment of silicosis and silico-tuberculosis], doc. no. 4947/59f, CEAB 11-689.

Policard, A. *Rapport sur les recherches poursuivies au cours du second plan au titre des "recherches fondamentales": I. Épuration pulmonaire et anatomie pathologique* [Report on research conducted during the second plan under "basic research": I. Lung clearance and pathological anatomy], doc. no. 775/64f, CEAB 11-1024.

Proust, P. *Les méthodes de lutte contre les empoussiérages miniers* [Controlling dusts in mines], CEAB 11-717.

Vigliani, E. *Recherches fondamentales sur la silicose* [Basic research on silicosis], doc. no. 832/63, CEAB 11-024.

Vigliani, E., and G. Cavagna. *Progrès des recherches fondamentales sur les pneumoconioses dans le cadre du deuxième programme de travail subventionné par la CECA (1960–1963)* [Advances in basic research on pneumoconiosis under the second work program funded by the ECSC (1960–1963)], doc. no. 1333/65f, CEAB 11-1024.

IHOES (Institut d'Histoire Ouvrière, Économique et Sociale [Institute for Labor, Economic, and Social History]), Seraing, Belgium

Fédéchar (Fédération Charbonnière de Belgique [Coal Federation of Belgium]). *Examens médicaux d'embauche* [Preemployment medical exams], 1946, Archives ACPL.

———. *Services médicaux du travail* [Occupational health services], note "Santé et sécurité," 18 March 1946, Archives ACPL.

"Survey of Dust Content of Faces," Memorandum for Directeur-Divisionnaire Thonnart, 26 June 1953, Archives ACPL.

ILO (International Labour Organization) Archives, Geneva

Carozzi, Luigi. "Presentation to the 1932 Silicosis Meeting in London," HY 1000/50/1.

Inquiry of the International Miners Federation, 30 June 1953, SH 5-6.

Orenstein, A. J. "Memorandum to Harold Butler," 21 November 1927, HY 1000/34/1.

Summary of Information: The International Scheme for Classification of Radiographs, SH 24-3-1-1.

Vaage, David. "Memorandum," 16 May 1946, HY 1003.

Malawi National Archives, Zomba, Malawi

Phthisis and Miners Compensation, Medical Department, M2/3/27.

National Archives and Records Administration, Washington, DC
  Proceedings at National Conference on Silicosis and Similar Dust Diseases, April 14, 1936, Record Group 100, 7-0-4(1).
  Tri-State Conference, *Proceedings*, April 23, 1940, Record Group 100, 7-0-4(3).
SAICOM (Sauvegarde des Archives Industrielles du Couchant de Mons [Safeguard for the Industrial Archives of Couchant de Mons]), Bois-du-Luc, Belgium
  "Lutte contre les accidents et les poussières" [Combating accidents and dust], in *Études et statistiques sur les accidents du travail, 1937–1938*, AHCM 666.
  "Various Studies by Engineers of the Charbonnages d'Hensies-Pommerœul," in *Engineers' Report of 5 August 1937*, Archives de la S[ociété] A[nonyme] des Charbonnages d'Hensies-Pommerœul, no. 382.

Published Sources

Ackerknecht, Erwin H. "Anticontagionism between 1821 and 1867." *Bulletin of the History of Medicine* 22 (1948): 562–593.
Akgun, Metin, Arzu Mirici, Elif Yilmazel Ucar, Mecit Kantarci, Omer Araz, and Metin Gorguner. "Silicosis in Turkish Denim Sandblasters." *Occupational Medicine* 56, 8 (2006): 554–558.
Alcock, A. *History of the International Labour Organization*. London: Macmillan, 1971.
Alexander, Peter. "Race, Class Loyalty, and the Structure of Capitalism: Coal Miners in Alabama and the Transvaal, 1918–1922." *Journal of Southern African Studies* 30, 1 (2004): 115–132.
Alison, W. P. "Observations on the Pathology of Scrofulous Diseases." *Transactions of the Medico-Chirurgical Society of Edinburgh*, 1824: 365–438.
Ally, Russell. *Gold and Empire: The Bank of England and South Africa's Gold Producers, 1886–1926*. Johannesburg: Witwatersrand University Press, 1994.
Amoudru, Claude. "Les pneumoconioses du houilleur dans les mines de charbon françaises: Rappel épidémiologique" [Coal workers' pneumoconiosis in French collieries: An epidemiological reminder]. *Lille médical* 17, 8 (1972): 1082–1089.
———. "Les pneumoconioses du houilleur, données épidémiologiques" [Coal workers' pneumoconiosis, epidemiological data]. *Annales des mines* (January–February 1978) 184 (1978): 59–62.
———. "La silicose et les pneumoconioses dans les houillères: Le cas du Nord-Pas-de-Calais." [Silicosis and pneumoconioses in collieries: The Nord-Pas-de-Calais case]. *Mines et carrières* 86, 164 (2009): 22–30.
Amoudru, C., and E. Quinot, "La lutte contre les poussières dans le Bassin du Nord et du Pas-de-Calais" [Dust control in the Nord and Pas-de-Calais Basins]. *Archives des maladies professionnelles* 28, 1 (1967): 153–155.
Anderson, Paula J. "History of Aerosol Therapy: Liquid Nebulization to MDIs to DPIs." *Respiratory Care* 50 (2005): 1139–1150.
Anderson, Warwick. *Colonial Pathologies: American Tropical Medicine, Race, and Hygiene in the Philippines*. Durham, NC: Duke University Press, 2006.
Arlidge J. T. *The Hygiene, Diseases, and Mortality of Occupations*. London: Percival, 1892.
———. "Pneumoconiosis." In C. Allbutt (ed.), *A System of Medicine*, vol. 5: 241–255. London: Macmillan, 1898.
Ashford, J. R. "The Use of Computers in Pneumoconiosis Field Research." *Journal of the Leeds University Mining Society* 34 (1964): 69–79.
Attfield, M. D., and E. D. Kuempel. "Commentary: Pneumoconiosis, Coalmine Dust, and the PFR." *Annals of Occupational Hygiene* 47, 7 (2003): 525–529.

Audley, James A. *Silica and the Silicates.* London: Forgotten Books, 2013 [first published 1921].

Aungkasuvapala, Narongsakdi, Wilawan Juengprasert, and Nareerat Obhasi. "Silicosis and Pulmonary Tuberculosis in Stone-Grinding Factories in Saraburi, Thailand." *Journal of the Medical Association of Thailand/Chotmaihet Thangphaet* 78, 12 (1995): 662–669.

Azaroff, Lenore S., Charles Levenstein, and David H. Wegman. "Occupational Injury and Illness Surveillance: Conceptual Filters Explain Underreporting." *American Journal of Public Health* 92, 9 (2002): 1421–1429.

Baldasseroni, Alberto, William Martinez, and Paul-André Rosental. "Naissance d'une maladie: Lexicométrie historique de la 'silicose' dans les traités médicaux britanniques (1800–1980)" [Birth of a disease: Historical lexicometry of "silicosis" in British medical treatises (1800–1980)]. In Catherine Courbet and Michel Gollac (eds.), *Risques du travail: La santé négociée,* 65–81. Paris: La Découverte, 2012.

Balinska, Marta A. *For the Good of Humanity: Ludwik Rajchman, Medical Statesman.* Budapest and New York: Central European University Press, 1998.

Banks, D. E., Y. H. Cheng, S. L. Weber, and J. K. Ma. "Strategies for the Treatment of Pneumoconiosis." *Occupational Medicine* (Philadelphia) 8, 1 (1992): 205–232.

Barboza, Carlos Eduardo Galvão, Daniel Hugo Winter, Márcia Seiscento, Ubiratan de Paula Santos, and Mário Terra Filho. "Tuberculosis and Silicosis: Epidemiology, Diagnosis, and Chemoprophylaxis." *Jornal brasileiro de pneumologia* 34, 11 (2008): 959–966.

Barham, C. "Some Remarks on the Diseases of Miners." *Twenty-Second Annual Report of the Royal Institution of Cornwall* (1840): 67–73.

Barnes, A. E. "Grinders' Phthisis" [Letter]. *British Medical Journal* 22 (August 1908): 534.

———. "The Pathology of Grinders' Phthisis." *British Medical Journal* 22 (August 1908): 483–484.

Bartocci, Enzo. *Le politiche sociali nell'Italia liberale (1861–1919)* [Social policies in liberal Italy (1861–1919)]. Rome: Donzelli, 1999.

Baruch, Marc Olivier, and Vincent Guigueno, eds. *Le choix des X: L'École polytechnique et les polytechniciens 1939–1945* [The Xs' choice: The French polytechnical school and the polytechnicians, 1939–1945]. Paris: Fayard, 2000.

Baxter, Peter J., Tar-Ching Aw, Anne Cockcroft, Paul Durrington, and J. Malcolm Harrington, eds. *Hunter's Diseases of Occupations,* 10th ed. London: Hodder Education, 2010.

Beattie, J. M. "Hygiene of the Steel Trade." *Journal of the Royal Society for the Promotion of Health* 33, 10 (1912): 501–506.

Beckmann, H. "Contribution aux méthodes thérapeutiques de la silicose" [Contribution to therapeutic methods for silicosis]. *Mines* 3 (1955): 229–238.

Bedford, T., and C. G. Warner, *Physical Studies of the Dust Hazard and of the Thermal Environment in Certain Coalmines.* Chronic Pulmonary Disease in South Wales Coalminers' Special Report Series 244. London: Medical Research Council, 1943.

Behrent, Michael C. "Accidents Happen: François Ewald, the 'Antirevolutionary' Foucault, and the Intellectual Politics of the French Welfare State." *Journal of Modern History* 82, 3 (2010): 585–624.

Benenson, Abram S. *Control of Communicable Diseases in Man,* 17th ed., 5th printing. Washington, DC: American Public Health Association, 1973.

Benquet, Marlène, Pascal Marichalar, and Emmanuel Martin. "Responsabilités en souffrance: Les conflits autour de la souffrance psychique des salariés d'EDF-GDF [Électricité de France-Gaz de France] (1985–2008)" [Outstanding responsibilities: Conflicts around the psychological distress of EDF-GDF employees (1985–2008)]. *Sociétés contemporaines* 3 (2010): 121–143.

Berger, Susan. *Notre première mondialisation: Leçons d'un échec oublié* [Our first globalization: Lessons from a forgotten failure]. Paris: Seuil, 2003.

Beveridge, R. "On the Occurrence of Phthisis among Granite-Masons." *British Medical Journal* (October 14, 1876): 489–490.

Bhagia, Lakho, and H. G. Sadhu, "Cost-Benefit Analysis of Installing Dust Control Devices in the Agate Industry, Khambhat (Gujarat)." *Indian Journal of Occupational and Environmental Medicine* 12, 3 (2008): 128–131.

Bidlot, R. "L'activité de l'Institut d'Hygiène des Mines jusqu'en fin 1947" [Activity of the Institute of Mine Hygiene until the end of 1947]. *Annales des mines de Belgique* 2 (1948): 518.

Blandin, Marie-Christine, et al. *Survey on Under-Reporting of Occupational Diseases in Europe.* Report Eurogip-03/E. EUROGIP [Groupement de l'Institution Prévention de la Sécurité Sociale pour l'Europe]: Paris, 2002.

Blétry, Nadia. "Ceci n'est pas un risque: Les affiches de prévention des risques professionnels et sanitaires en France au XXe siècle" [This is not a risk: Occupational and health risk-prevention posters in twentieth-century France]. In Omnès and Pitti (eds.), *Cultures du risque au travail*, 155–172.

Bloor, D. U. "Richard Quiller Couch: An Outstanding Nineteenth-Century General Practitioner." *Journal of the Royal College of General Practitioners* 28 (1978): 97–101.

Bloor, Michael. "The South Wales Miners Federation, Miners' Lung, and the Instrumental Use of Expertise, 1900–1950." *Social Studies of Science* 30, 1 (2000): 125–140.

Böhme, A. "Silicosis in Germany: Present State of the Silicosis Problem in Germany." In ILO, *Silicosis: Records* (1930), 339–368.

Boucher, R. M. G. "Essais pratiques entrepris au groupe de Béthune pour l'application de la méthode de floculation par micro-brouillards mouillants" [Field tests conducted by the Bethune group on the application of the flocculation method using micro-wetting mist]. *Mines* 6 (1954): 516–520.

Bowden, Bradley, and Beris Penrose. "Dust, Contractors, Politics, and Silicosis: Conflicting Narratives and the Queensland Royal Commission into Miners' Phthisis, 1911." *Australian Historical Studies* 37, 128 (2006): 89–107.

Boyer, Josef. *Unfallversicherung und Unternehmer im Bergbau: Die Knappschafts-Berufsgenossenschaft 1885–1945* [Injury insurance and employers in the mining industry: Occupational social security, 1885–1945]. Munich: Beck, 1995.

Braun, Lundy. "Structuring Silence: Asbestos and Biomedical Research in Britain and South Africa." *Race & Class* 50, 1 (2008): 59–78.

Breuer, H. *Hygiène dans les mines: Rapport de synthèse sur les recherches du 3e programme 1971–1976* [Hygiene in mines: Summary report on the 3rd research program, 1971–1976]. Luxembourg: Direction Générale, Emploi et Affaires Sociales, 1978.

Brown, E. W., and W. Van Winkle. "Present Status of Aluminium in the Therapy and Prophylaxis of Silicosis." *Journal of the American Medical Association* 140, 12 (1949): 1024–1029.

Brull, L. "Enquête sur le problème de la silicose" [Survey on the silicosis issue]. *Communications de l'Institut d'Hygiène des Mines* 9 (October 1946): 2–12.

Bruno, Anne-Sophie, Éric Geerkens, Nicolas Hatzfeld, and Catherine Omnès, eds. *La santé au travail, entre savoirs et pouvoirs (XIXe–XXe siècles)* [Occupational health, between knowledge and power (19th–20th centuries)]. Rennes, France: Presses Universitaires de Rennes, 2011.

Buchanan, D., B. G. Miller, and C. A. Soutar. "Quantitative Relations between Exposure to Respirable Quartz and Risk of Silicosis." *Occupational and Environmental Medicine* 60, 3 (2003): 159–164.

Bufton, Mark W., and Joseph Melling. "Coming Up for Air: Experts, Employers, and Workers in Campaigns to Compensate Silicosis Sufferers in Britain, 1918–1939." *Social History of Medicine* 18, 1 (2005): 63–86.

———. "'A Mere Matter of Rock': Organized Labor, Scientific Evidence, and British Government Schemes for Compensating Silicosis and Pneumoconiosis among Coalminers, 1926–1940." *Medical History* 49, 2 (2005): 155–178.

Burger, E. J. "Restructuring Workers' Compensation to Prevent Occupational Disease." *Annals of the New York Academy of Sciences* 572 (1989): 282–283.

Burke, Gill[ian]. "Disease, Labour Migration, and Technological Change: The Case of the Cornish Miners." In Paul Weindling (ed.), *The Social History of Occupational Health*, 78–88. Kent, UK: Croom Helm, 1985.

Burke, Gillian, and Peter Richardson. "The Profits of Death: A Comparative Study of Miners' Phthisis in Cornwall and the Transvaal, 1876–1918." *Journal of Southern African Studies* 4, 2 (1978): 147–171.

Burnham, John C. *Accident Prone: A History of Technology, Psychology, and Misfits of the Machine Age.* Chicago: University of Chicago Press, 2009.

Burt, Roger, and Sandra Kippen. "Rational Choice and a Lifetime in Metal Mining: Employment Decisions by Nineteenth-Century Cornish Miners." *International Review of Social History* 46, 1 (2001): 45–75.

Buzzi, Stéphane, Jean-Claude Devinck, and Paul-André Rosental. "L'examen médical en milieu de travail, 1914–1979" [Workplace medical exams, 1914–1979]. *Archives des maladies professionnelles* 63, 5 (2002): 355–363.

———. *La santé au travail, 1880–2006* [Occupational health, 1880–2006]. Paris: La Découverte, 2006.

Calmette, Albert, P. Vansteenberghe, and V. Grysez. "Sur l'anthracose pulmonaire physiologique d'origine intestinale" [Physiological pulmonary anthracosis of intestinal origin]. *Comptes rendus des séances et mémoires de la Société de Biologie* 41 (1906): 548–550.

Capacci, Fabio, Franco Carnevale, and Francesco Di Benedetto, eds. *Silice libera cristallina nei luoghi di lavoro* [Free crystalline silica in the workplace]. Florence: Azienda Sanitaria, 2010.

Cappuccio, Silvana, and Martina Toti, eds. *Jeans da morire/Jeans to Die For: From Genoa to Istanbul; Sandblasting Jeans in Turkey.* Rome: Ediesse, 2011.

Carel, Rafael S., Herzl Salman, and Jacob Bar-Ziv. "Souvenir Casting Silicosis." *Chest Journal* 106 (1994): 1272–1274.

Carnevale, Francesco, and Alberto Baldasseroni. "A Long-Lasting Pandemic: Diseases Caused by Dust Containing Silica: Italy within the International Context." *La Medicina del lavoro* 96, 2 (2005): 169–176.

———. *Mal da lavoro: Storia della salute dei lavoratori* [Occupational disease: History of workers' health]. Bari: Laterza, 1999.

———. "Mussolini's Fight against Occupational Diseases (1922–1943): Italian Leadership in the Production of Artificial Silk." *Epidemiological Preview* 27, 2 (2003): 114–20.

Carnevale, Francesco, Alberto Baldasseroni, V. Guastella, and L. Tomassini. "Concerning the First International Congress on Work-Related Illnesses, Milan, 9–14 June 1906: Success—News—Reports—Motions." *La Medicina del lavoro* 97, 2 (2005): 100–113.

Carozzi, Luigi. "Contributo bibliografico alla storia della pneumoconiosi 'Silicosi' dall'27o. secolo avanti Cristo al 1871" [Bibliographical contribution to the history of pneumoconiosis (silicosis) from the 27th century BC to 1871]. *Rassegna di medicina industriale* 12, 10 (1941) to 13, 5 (1942) [seven articles].

Carta, Plinio, Pier Luigi Cocco, and Duilio Casula. "Mortality from Lung Cancer among Sardinian Patients with Silicosis." *British Journal of Industrial Medicine* 48, 2 (1991): 122–129.

Castro, Hermano Albuquerque de, Genésio Vicentin, and Kellen Cristina Xavier Pereira. "Mortality Due to Pneumoconioses in Macro-Regions of Brazil from 1979 to 1998." *Jornal de Pneumologia* 29, 2 (2003): 82–88.

Catilina, P. *Médecine et risque au travail: Guide du médecin en milieu de travail* [Medicine and risk at work: The physician's guide to the workplace]. Paris: Masson, 2009.

Cavalcanti dos Santos Antão, Vinícius, Germania Araujo Pinheiro, Jorge Kavakama, and Mário Terra-Filho. "High Prevalence of Silicosis among Stone Carvers in Brazil." *American Journal of Industrial Medicine* 45, 2 (2004): 194–201.

Cayet, Thomas. "Le BIT [Bureau International du Travail] et la modernisation économique dans les années 1920: Esquisse d'une dynamique institutionnelle" [The ILO and economic modernization in the 1920s: Outline of an institutional dynamic]. *Travail et emploi* 110, 2 (2007): 15–25.

———. *Rationaliser le travail, organiser la production: Le Bureau International du Travail et la modernisation économique durant l'entre-deux-guerres* [Streamlining work and organizing production: The International Labour Office and economic modernization during the interwar period]. Rennes, France: Presses Universitaires de Rennes, 2010.

Cayet, Thomas, Paul-André Rosental, and Marie Thébaud-Sorger. "How International Organisations Compete: Occupational Safety and Health at the ILO, a Diplomacy of Expertise." *Journal of Modern European History* 7, 2 (2009): 173–194.

Cazamian, P. "La prévention médicale des pneumoconioses dans les houillères: De l'importance d'une collaboration médico-technique" [Medical prevention of pneumoconiosis in collieries: The importance of medico-technical collaboration]. *Note technique, Charbonnages de France*, vol. 2. Paris: Charbonnages de France, 1947.

CECA [ECSC]. *Lutte technique contre la poussière dans les mines: État des travaux de recherche dans les domaines de la médecine, de la sécurité et de l'hygiène du travail (au 1er janvier 1967)* [The technical fight against dust in the mines: State of research in the areas of occupational medicine, security, and hygiene (as of January 1st, 1967)]. Luxembourg: Service des Publications des Communautés Européennes, 1967.

Centre Historique Minier. *10 mars 1906: La catastrophe des mines de Courrières, et après?* [10 March 1906: The Courrières mines catastrophe, and after?]. Lewarde, Belgium: Centre Historique Minier, 2007.

Chatgidakis, C. B. "An Autopsy Survey of Bantu South African Coal-Miners." *British Journal of Industrial Medicine* 20, 3 (1963): 236–242.

Chatriot, Alain, and Marion Fontaine. "Courrières: Histoires et représentations" [Courrières: Stories and representations]. *Cahiers Jaurès* 186, 4 (2007): 56–59.

Chaudhury, Nayanjeet, Ajay Phatak, Rajiv Paliwal, and Chandra Raichaudhari. "Silicosis among Agate Workers at Shakarpur: An Analysis of Clinic-Based Data." *Lung India: Official Organ of Indian Chest Society* 27, 4 (2010): 221.

Chen, W., Z. Zhuang, M. D. Attfield, B. T. Chen, Pi Gao, J. C. Harrison, C. Fu, J. Q. Chen, and W. E. Wallace. "Exposure to Silica and Silicosis among Tin Miners in China: Exposure-Response Analyses and Risk Assessment." *Occupational and Environmental Medicine* 58, 1 (2001): 31–37.

Cherniack, Martin. *The Hawk's Nest Incident: America's Worst Industrial Disaster*. New Haven, CT: Yale University Press, 1986.

Chessel, Marie. "Consumers' Leagues in France: A Transatlantic Perspective." In Alain Chatriot, Marie-Emmanuelle Chessel, and Matthew Hilton (eds.), *The Expert Consumer: Associations and Professionals in the Consumer Society*, 53–70. London: Ashgate, 2006.

Choudat, D., S. Triem, B. Weill, C. Vicrey, J. Ameille, P. Brochard, M. Letourneux, and C. Rossignol. "Respiratory Symptoms, Lung Function, and Pneumoconiosis among

Self-Employed Dental Technicians." *British Journal of Industrial Medicine* 50, 5 (1993): 443–449.

Chung, Suki Ming-lai. "Hong Kong–China Solidarity: Reflections on the Past 10 Years of Supporting Workers' Advocacy in China." *Asian Labour Update* 75 (29 November 2010).

Cimrin, Arif, and Zeki Erdut. "General Aspect of Pneumoconiosis in Turkey." *Indian Journal of Occupational and Environmental Medicine* 11, 2 (2007): 50.

Clavin, Patricia, and Jens-Wilhelm Wessel. "Transnationalism and the League of Nations: Understanding the Work of its Economic and Financial Organisation." *Contemporary European History* 14, 4 (2005): 465–492.

Clozier, M. "Maladie, dite de Saint Roch, à laquelle sont sujets les ouvriers qui travaillent le grais" [Saint Roch's, a disease affecting stone workers]. In *Mémoires de l'Académie des sciences, arts et belles lettres de Dijon*, vol. 2: 60–62. Dijon-Paris: Lejay Libraire, 1774.

Cocco, Pierluigi. "The Long and Winding Road from Silica Exposure to Silicosis and Other Health Effects: Silicosis Is Still a Major Threat for Workers in Developing Countries." *Occupational and Environmental Medicine* 60, 3 (2003): 157–158.

———. "Multifactorial Aetiology of Lung Cancer among Silica-Exposed Workers." *Annals of the Academy of Medicine, Singapore* 30, 6 (2001): 468–474.

Cochrane, A. L. "The Attack Rate of Progressive Massive Fibrosis." *British Journal of Industrial Medicine* 19, 1 (1962): 52–64.

Cochrane, A. L., I. Davies, and Charles Montague Fletcher. ""Entente Radiologique: A Step towards International Agreement on the Classification of Radiographs in Pneumoconiosis." *British Journal of Industrial Medicine* 8, 4 (1951): 244–255.

Cochrane, A. L., Charles Montague Fletcher, John Cary Gilson, and Philip Hugh-Jones. "The Role of Periodic Examination in the Prevention of Coalworkers' Pneumoconiosis." *British Journal of Industrial Medicine* 8, 2 (1951): 53–61.

Coggon D., and A. N. Taylor. "Coal Mining and Chronic Obstructive Pulmonary Disease: A Review of the Evidence." *Thorax* 53 (1998): 398–407.

Cohen, J. Solis. *Inhalation: Its Therapeutics and Practice*. Philadelphia: Lindsay & Blakiston, 1867.

Colgrove, James. *Epidemic City: The Politics of Public Health in New York*. New York: Russell Sage Foundation, 2011.

Collis, E. L. "The Effects of Dust in Producing Diseases of the Lungs." *Seventeenth International Congress of Medicine, London, 1913*, sect. 18, pt. 1: 1–34. London: W. Frowde, 1913.

———. "Milroy Lectures: Industrial Pneumoconiosis with Special Reference to Dust-Phthisis." *Public Health* (August 1915): 252–264; (September 1915): 292–305; (October 1915): 11–20; (November 1915): 37–44.

Commission Internationale Permanente pour l'Étude des Maladies Professionnelles [Permanent International Committee on the Study of Occupational Diseases]. "IVe réunion de la Commission, Lyon, 3–6 avril 1929" [4th committee meeting, Lyon, 3–6 April 1929]. Lyon: CIPEMP, 1929.

Committee on Chemotherapy and Allied Measures, "Report on Streptomycin in Tuberculosis by the Committee on Chemotherapy." *Diseases of the Chest* 13 (March 1947): 169–170.

Compte rendu des journées d'information sur la lutte technique contre les poussières dans les mines (Luxembourg, 11–13 octobre 1972) [Report on the information days about the technical fight against dusts in mines (Luxembourg, 11–13 October 1972)]. Luxembourg: CID [Centre d'Information et de Documentation], 1973.

Conrad, Christoph, ed. "Sozialpolitik transnational" [Transnational social policy]. Special issue, *Geschichte und Gesellschaft* 32, 4 (2006).

Costallat, Lilian Tereza Lavras, Eduardo Mello De Capitani, and Lair Zambon. "Pulmonary Silicosis and Systemic Lupus Erythematosus in Men: A Report of Two Cases." *Joint, Bone, Spine* 69, 1 (2002): 68–71.

Cottereau, Alain. "L'usure au travail: Interrogations et refoulements" [Occupational wear and tear: Questions and repressions]. *Le Mouvement social* 124, 3 (1983): 3.

Cunningham, J. G. "Silicosis in Canada." In ILO, *Silicosis: Records* (1930), 317–337.

"Dai 15 nendo Nihon sangyô eisei kyôkai sôkai kiroku." *Rôdô kagaku* 8 (1941): 59–88.

Dale, Pamela, Janet Greenlees, and Joseph Melling. "The Kiss of Death or a Flight of Fancy? Workers' Health and the Campaign to regulate Shuttle Kissing in the British Cotton Industry, 1900–1952." *Social History* 32, 1 (2007): 54–75.

D'Arcy Hart, P. "MRC Pneumoconiosis Research, 1937–1960." In A. R. Ness, L. A. Reynolds, and E. M. Tansey (eds.), *Population-Based Research in South Wales: The MRC Pneumoconiosis Research Unit and the MRC Epidemiology Unit*. Wellcome Witnesses to Twentieth-Century Medicine, vol. 13. London: Wellcome Trust for the History of Medicine, 2002.

Dautrebande, Lucien, D. Cartry, J. Van Kerkom, and A. Cereghetti. *Essai de prévention de la silicose* [An attempt at silicosis prevention]. Katanga, "Belgian Congo": Union Minière du Haut Katanga, 1954.

Davies, Robert H. *Capital, State, and White Labour in South Africa, 1900–1960*. Atlantic Highlands, NJ: Humanities Press, 1979.

Davis, A. B. "Life Insurance and the Physical Examination: A Chapter in the Rise of American Medical Technology." *Bulletin of the History of Medicine* 55 (1981): 392–406.

Davy, E. "Grinder's Safety Apparatus." *Mechanics' Magazine of London* 15 (1831): 250–251.

Dechoux, J. "Données actuelles sur la pneumoconiose des mineurs de charbon lorrains" [Current data on Lorraine coal workers' pneumoconiosis]. *Archives des maladies professionnelles, de médecine du travail et de sécurité sociale* 38, 4–5 (1975): 252–256.

Degueldre, G. "Recherche d'un critère d'appréciation de la nocivité des empoussiérages miniers" [The search for a criterion for assessing the harmfulness of dusts levels in mines]. In *Compte rendu des journées d'information*, 71–75.

Demelenne, E., A. Houberechts, and J. Stassen. "La lutte contre les poussières [Dust control]: Expert Meeting Held in Geneva, 1–17 December 1952." *Annales des mines de Belgique* 52 (March 1953): 219–225.

Denny, J. J., W. D. Robson, and Dudley A. Irwin, "Prevention of Silicosis by Metallic Aluminium." In ILO, *Silicosis: Proceedings* (1938), 208–210.

De Paoli, D., G. De Campo, A. Papale, and M. G. Magliocchi. "L'evoluzione della tutela delle malattie professionali in Italia" [The evolution of administrative control over occupational diseases in Italy]. Istituto Superiore per la Prevenzione e la Sicurezza del Lavoro (ISPESL), Dipartimento Processi Organizzativi, Rome, 2010.

Deprez, Marcel, Michel Hannotte, Lily Rochette-Russe, and Micheline Zanatta, eds. *Siamo tutti neri! Des hommes contre du charbon; Études et témoignages sur l'immigration italienne en Wallonie* [We're all black! Men against coal; Studies and testimonies about the Italian immigration in Wallonia]. Seraing, Belgium: IHOES, 1998.

Derbyshire, Edward. "Natural Dust and Pneumoconiosis in High Asia." In H. Catherine W. Skinner and Antony R. Berger (eds.), *Geology and Health: Closing the Gap*, 15–18. Oxford: Oxford University Press, 2003.

Derickson, Alan. *Black Lung: Anatomy of a Public Health Disaster*. Ithaca, NY: Cornell University Press, 1998.

———. "Industrial Refugees: The Migration of Silicotics from the Mines of North America and South Africa in the Early 20th Century." *Labor History* 29, 1 (1988): 66–89.

———. "'On the Dump Heap': Employee Medical Screening in the Tri-State Zinc-Lead Industry, 1924–1932." *Business History Review* 62, 4 (1988): 656–677.

———. "The United Mine Workers of America and the Recognition of Occupational Respiratory Diseases, 1902–1968." *American Journal of Public Health* 81, 6 (1991): 782–790.

Desoille, Henri, M. Gaultier, and A. Hadengue. "Problèmes et difficultés pratiques soulevés par la réparation de la silicose" [Problems and practical difficulties raised by compensation for silicosis]. *Archives des maladies professionnelles* 5 (1954): 486.

Devinck, Jean-Claude. "Les racines historiques de l'usage contrôlé de l'amiante (1947–1997)" [Historical roots of the controlled used of asbestos (1947–1997)]. In Bruno et al. (eds.), *La santé au travail*, 243–254.

Devinck, Jean-Claude, and Paul-André Rosental. "'Une maladie sociale avec des aspects médicaux': la difficile reconnaissance de la silicose comme maladie professionnelle dans la France du premier XXe siècle" ["A social disease with medical aspects": The difficult recognition of silicosis as an occupational disease in 20th century France]. *Revue d'histoire moderne et contemporaine* 1 (2009): 99–126.

"Discussion of Tuberculosis." *Proceedings of the Transvaal Mine Medical Officers' Association* 5, 7 (26 January 1926): 4.

Dixon, Andrea A., with Romain Chabrol, Bruno Chareyron, Alexandra Dawe, Nina Schulz, Rianne Teule, and Aslihan Tu. *Abandonnés dans la poussière: L'héritage radioactif d'Areva dans les villes du désert nigérien* [Left in the dust: Areva's radioactive legacy in the desert towns of Niger]. Amsterdam: Greenpeace, 2010.

Douglas, Mary. *Implicit Meanings: Selected Essays in Anthropology*. London: Routledge, 1999.

Dower, John. *Embracing Defeat: Japan in the Wake of World War II*. New York: W. W. Norton/New Press, 1999.

Dowling, Harry F. *Fighting Infection*. Cambridge, MA: Harvard University Press, 1977.

Dubos, René, and Jean Dubos. *The White Plague: Tuberculosis, Man, and Society*. New Brunswick, NJ: Rutgers University Press, 1987 [first published 1952].

Dumontet, Charles, Michel Vincent, Eric Laennec, Bruno Girodet, Danièle Vitrey, Dalith Meram, and Louis Van Straaten. "Silicosis Due to Inhalation of Domestic Cleaning Powder." *Lancet* 338, 774 (1991): 1085.

Dupont, Ferdinand. "Accidents causés par l'inspiration de la poussière de charbon" [Accidents caused by the inhalation of coal dust]. *Gazette des hôpitaux*, ser. 2, 82, 9 (1902) 351–352.

Ebihara, Isamu. *Shokugyôbyô undôshi: Jinpai sengohen* [History of the occupational health movement: Pneumoconiosis in the postwar period]. Tokyo: Iryôtosho Shuppansha, 1976.

Elliot, Ebenezer. *Poetical Works*. Edinburgh: William Tait, 1840.

Even, Dr. "Pneumoconioses (réserves)" [Pneumoconioses (reservations)]. *Revue française des maladies respiratoires* 3, 3 (1975): 281.

Ewald, François. *L'État providence*. Paris: Grasset, 1986.

———, ed. "Justice, Discipline, Production." Special issue, *Les Temps modernes* 354 (1976).

Ewald, Walter. *Soziale Medizin: Ein Lehrbuch für Ärzte, Medizinal- und Verwaltungsbeamte, Sozialpolitiker, Behörden und Kommunen* [Social medicine: A textbook for physicians, medical and administrative officials, social policy experts, authorities, and municipalities]. 2 vols. Berlin: Springer, 1911–1914.

Farr, William. "Vital Statistics; or, The Statistics of Health, Sickness, Diseases, and Death." In John Ramsay MacCulloch (ed.), *A Statistical Account of the British Empire: Exhibiting Its Extent, Physical Capacities, Population, Industry, and Civil and Religious Institutions*, 567–601. London: C. Knight, 1837.

Favell, Charles Fox. "Sheffield Medical Society: Class II. Respiratory System." *Provincial Medical & Surgical Journal*, ser. 2, 8, 11 (1844): 151.

Fay, J. W. J. "The National Coal Board's Pneumoconiosis Field Research." *Nature* 180, 4581 (1957): 309–311.

Fedotov, I. "The ILO/WHO Joint International Program on the Global Elimination of Silicosis." *WHO Global Occupational Health Network (GOHNET)* 5 (2003): 3–5.

Feltz, M. *Maladies des tailleurs de pierres* [Stonecutter diseases]. Strasbourg: G. Silbermann, 1865.

Figlio, K. "Chlorosis and Chronic Disease in Nineteenth-Century Britain: The Social Constitution of Somatic Illness in a Capitalist Society." *Social History* 3, 2 (1978): 167–197.

Finckh, Axel, Glinda S. Cooper, Lori B. Chibnik, Karen H. Costenbader, Julie Watts, Helen Pankey, Patricia A. Fraser, and Elizabeth W. Karlson. "Occupational Silica and Solvent Exposures and Risk of Systemic Lupus Erythematosus in Urban Women." *Arthritis & Rheumatism* 54, 11 (2006): 3648–3654.

Fleck, Ludwik. *Genesis and Development of a Scientific Fact*. Chicago: University of Chicago Press, 1979 [first published 1935].

Fletcher, Charles Montague. "Coalworkers' Pneumoconiosis: So-Called 'Anthraco-Silicosis.'" In *Beiträge zur Silikose-Forschung: Bericht über die medizinisch-wissenschaftliche Arbeitstagung über Silikose, 18–20 Oktober 1951, Bochum* [Report of the Medico-Scientific Working Group on Silicosis, 18–20 October 1951)], 119–138. Hamm, Germany: E. Griebsch, 1951.

———. "Pneumoconiosis of Coal-Miners." *British Medical Journal* 1, 4561 (1948): 1065–1075.

———. "Screening for Pneumoconiosis in Coalmine Workers by Periodic Radiological Examinations." In ILO, *Third International Conference of Experts*, 187.

Fletcher, C. M., and J. Cough. "Coalminers' Pneumoconiosis." *British Medical Bulletin* 7, 1–2 (1950): 42–46.

Fletcher, C. M., K. J. Mann, I. Davies, A. L. Cochrane, J. C. Gilson, and P. Hugh-Jones. "The Classification of Radiographic Appearances in Coalminers' Pneumoconiosis." *Journal of the Faculty of Radiologists* 1, 1 (1949): 40–60.

Fletcher C. M., and P. D. Oldham, "The Use of Standard Films in the Radiological Diagnosis of Coalworkers' Pneumoconiosis." *British Journal of Industrial Medicine* 8, 3 (1951): 138–148.

Fontaine, Marion. *Fin d'un monde ouvrier: Liévin, 1974* [End of a workers' world: Liévin, 1974]. Paris: Éditions de l'EHESS [École des Hautes Études en Sciences Sociales], 2014.

Forestell, Nancy M. "'And I Feel Like I'm Dying from Mining for Gold': Disability, Gender, and the Mining Community, 1920–1950." *Labor Studies in Working-Class History of the Americas* 3, 3 (2006): 77–93.

Forti Messina, Annalucia. *Malachia De Cristoforis: Un medico democratico nell'Italia liberale* [Malachia De Cristoforis: A democratic physician in liberal Italy]. Rome: Franco Angeli, 2003.

Foster, James C. "Western Miners and Silicosis: 'The Scourge of the Underground Toiler,' 1890–1943." *Industrial and Labor Relations Review* 37, 3 (1984): 371–385.

Frieden, Thomas R., Mary T. Bassett, Lorna E. Thorpe, and Thomas A. Farley, "Public Health in New York City, 2002–2007: Confronting Epidemics of the Modern Era." *International Journal of Epidemiology* 237 (2008): 966–977.

"50 Jahre Schweizerische Gesellschaft für Unfallmedizin und Berufskrankheiten" [Fifty years of the Swiss Society for Injury Medicine and Occupational Diseases]. *Schweizerische Zeitschrift für Unfallmedizin und Berufskrankheiten* (1964): 1–185.

Gallo, Óscar, and Jorge Marquez Valderrama. "La silicosis o tisis de los mineros en Colombia, 1910–1960" [Silicosis, or miners' phthisis, in Colombia, 1910–1960]. *Salud colectiva* 7, 1 (2011): 35–51.

Gandevia, Bryan. "The Australian Contribution to the History of the Pneumoconioses." *Medical History* 17, 4 (1973): 368–379.

Ganier, M. "Méthode pour la détermination d'un seuil d'empoussiérage" [Method for determining a dust-level threshold]. In *Compte rendu des journées d'information*, 217–248.

———. "Méthode pour la détermination d'un seuil d'empoussiérage" [Method for determining a dust-level threshold]. *Industrie minérale—Mine*, supplement, December (1974): 264–272.

Geerkens, Éric. "Entre soins et prévention: Le rôle du médecin dans les entreprises belges (c. 1900–c. 1970)" [Between care and prevention: The doctor's role in Belgian companies (c. 1900–c. 1970)]. In Bruno et al. (eds.), *La santé au travail*, 193–212.

———. "Quand la silicose n'était pas une maladie professionnelle: Genèse de la réparation des pathologies respiratoires des mineurs en Belgique (1927–1940)" [When silicosis was not an occupational disease: Genesis of the compensation for miners' lung diseases in Belgium (1927–1940)]. *Revue d'histoire moderne et contemporaine* 56, 1 (2009): 127–141.

Geyer, Martin H. *Die Reichsknappschaft: Versicherungsreformen und Sozialpolitik im Bergbau 1900–1945* [German mining mutual societies: Insurance reforms and social policy in the mine, 1900–1945]. Munich: Beck, 1987.

Ghirardelli, Gino. "1964: Une victoire après deux colloques et cinq années de luttes" [1964: Victory after two conferences and five years of struggle]. In Deprez et al. (eds.), *Siamo tutti neri*, 129–133.

Goddard, B. "A Review of the Prevention and Control of Dust in British Coal Mines." *Mining Engineer* (July 1977): 586.

Gordon, Bonnie. "Ouvrières et maladies professionnelles sous la IIIe République: La victoire des allumettiers français sur la nécrose phosphorée de la mâchoire" [Female workers and occupational diseases during the 3rd Republic: The victory of French match-makers over phosphorus necrosis of the jaw]. *Le Mouvement social* 3, 164 (1993): 77–93.

Gorman, Thomas, Ronnie Johnston, Arthur McIvor, and Andrew Watterson. "Asbestos in Scotland." *International Journal of Occupational and Environmental Health* 10, 2 (2004): 183–192.

Grätz, Tilo. "Gold-Mining and Risk Management: A Case Study from Northern Benin." *Ethnos* 68, 2 (2003): 192–208.

Greenhow, Edward Headlam. *Papers Related to the Sanitary State of the People of England: Being the Results of an Inquiry into the Different Proportions of Death Produced by Certain Diseases in Different Districts in England*. London: George E. Eyre and William Spottiswoode, 1858.

———. "Specimen of Diseased Lung from a Case of Grinders' Asthma." *Transactions of the Pathological Society in London* 16 (1865): 59–61.

———. *Third Report of the Medical Officer of the Privy Council, Sir John Simon*. London: Her Majesty's Stationery Office, 1860.

Guinand, Cédric. "Zur Entstehung von IVSS und IAO" [Genesis of the International Social Security Association and ILO]. *Revue für soziale Sicherheit* 61 (2008) 93–111.

Halbwachs, Maurice. *On Collective Memory*. Chicago: University of Chicago Press, 1992 [first published 1925].

Haldane, J. S., J. S. Martin, and R. A. Thomas. *Report on the Health of Cornish Miners*. London: His Majesty's Stationery Office, 1904.

Hall, Arthur J. "Some Impressions of the International Conference on Silicosis, Held at Johannesburg, August 1930." *Lancet* 216, 5586 (1930): 655–658.

Hall, J. C. "The Effect of Certain Sheffield Trades on Life and Health." *Transactions of the National Association for the Promotion of Social Science* 21 (1866): 382–402.

Hamizi, A. "La silicose chez les artisans tailleurs de pierre algériens [Silicosis in Algerian stonecutters]. Presentation at the 6th Conference of the Association Franco-Algérienne de Pneumologie [Franco-Algerian Association of Pulmonology], Algiers, 27–30 May 2010.

The Hard Road: Seeking Justice for Victims of Pneumoconiosis in China. China Labour Bulletin Research Report. Hong Kong, 2010.

Hartman, Eugene. "Silicosis." *Mine-Mill Union,* March 14, 1949.

Hatzfeld, Nicolas, "Les malades du travail face au déni administratif: La longue bataille des affections périarticulaires (1919–1972)" [Occupational diseases in the face of bureaucratic denial: The long struggle for periarticular diseases (1919–1972)]. *Revue d'histoire moderne et contemporaine* 56, 1 (2009): 177–196.

Haworth, Nigel, and Steve Hughes. *The International Labour Organization (ILO): Coming In from the Cold.* Abingdon, UK: Routledge, 2010.

"Hazardous Substances: Stone-Workers Exposed to Five Times the Safe Level of Silica Dust." *Safety & Health Practitioner* (25 November 2007): 13.

Hecht, Gabrielle. *Being Nuclear: Africans and the Global Uranium Trade.* Cambridge, MA: MIT Press, 2012.

Hendriks, Ch. A. M. "Frequentie en preventie van silikose in de Nederlandse steenkolenmijnen" [The frequency and prevention of silicosis in Dutch collieries]. *Nederlandse Tijdschrift voor Geneeskunde* 104, 2 (1960): 1552–1565.

Hendriks, Ch. A.M., and H. Claus. "Effect of Dust Suppression Measures on the Prevalence of Coal-Workers' Pneumoconiosis in the Dutch Coal Mines." *British Journal of Industrial Medicine* 20, 4 (1963): 288–292.

Henry, Emmanuel. *Amiante: Un scandale improbable; Sociologie d'un problème public* [Asbestos: An unlikely scandal; Sociology of a public problem]. Rennes, France: Presses Universitaires de Rennes, 2007.

Herren-Oesch, Madeleine. *Hintertüren zur Macht: Internationalismus und modernisierungsorientierte Außenpolitik in Belgien, der Schweiz und den USA, 1865–1914* [Backdoors to power: Internationalism and modernization-oriented foreign policy in Belgium, Switzerland, and the USA, 1865–1914]. Munich: Oldenbourg, 2000.

Hessel, Patrick A., John F. Gamble, Bernard L. Gee, Graham Gibbs, Francis H. Green, W. Keith Morgan, and Brooke T. Mossman. "Silica, Silicosis, and Lung Cancer: A Response to a Recent Working Group Report." *Journal of Occupational and Environmental Medicine* 42, 7 (2000): 704–720.

Hicks, D. "The Sampling and Analysis of Airborne Dust for Control Purposes." In ILO, *Report of the Meeting of Experts,* vol. 3: 7.

Hiroshi, Une, and Kenzo Wake. "Zuidôkôji dekasegi rôdôsha no jinpaishô ni kan suru shakai igakuteki kenkyû" [A social medicine study on the pneumoconiosis of migrant laborers working in tunnel construction]. *Rôdô kagaku* 60, 1 (1984), 27–33.

Hoblyn, R. D. *A Dictionary of Terms Used in Medicine and the Collateral Sciences,* New American ed. Philadelphia: H. C. Lea, 1865.

Holanda, Márcia Alcântara, Marcelo Alcăntara Holanda, Pedro Henrique Felismino, and Valéria Góes Ferreira Pinheiro. "Silicosis in Brazilian Pit Diggers: Relationship between Dust Exposure and Radiologic Findings." *American Journal of Industrial Medicine* 27, 3 (1995): 367–378.

Honma, Koichi, et al. "Proposed Criteria for Mixed-Dust Pneumoconiosis: Definition, Descriptions, and Guidelines for Pathologic Diagnosis and Clinical Correlation." *Human Pathology* 35, 12 (2004): 1515–1523.

Horn, Paul. "Unfallversicherungsmedizin 1900–1924" [Medical insurance for injuries, 1900–1924]. *Zeitschrift für die gesamte Versicherungswissenschaft* 25 (1925): 52–66.

Horne, John. "Demobilizing the Mind: France and the Legacy of the Great War, 1919–1939." *French History and Civilization* 2 (2009): 101–119.

Horstman, Klasien. "Om het beheer van de arbeidsongeschiktheid: Het politieke debat over de Ongevallenwet en het wel en wee van een medische markt" [The management of labor disability: The political debate on the Workmen's Compensation Act and the development of the medical market]. *Tijdschrift voor sociale geschiedenis* 4 (1999): 383–406.

Houberechts, A. "L'activité de l'Institut d'Hygiène des Mines" [Activity of Institute for Mine Hygiene]. *Annales des mines de Belgique* [yearly reports]. Reports quoted are (May 1951): 316–333; (January 1953): 325–360; (January 1955): 374–410; (February 1956): 375–402; (May 1957): 373–406.

———. *L'activité de l'Institut d'Hygiène des Mines au cours de l'année 1960*. Brussels: R. Louis, 1961.

———. *L'activité de l'Institut d'Hygiène des Mines au cours de l'année 1961*. Brussels: R. Louis, 1962.

———. *L'activité de l'Institut d'Hygiène des Mines au cours de l'année 1962*. Brussels: R. Louis, 1963.

Hudson, Robert P. "The Biography of Disease: Lessons from Chlorosis." *Bulletin of the History of Medicine* 51, 3 (1977): 448–463.

ILO. *International Labour Conference, Eighteenth Session, Geneva 1934: Record of Proceedings.* Geneva: ILO, 1934.

———. *The Prevention and Suppression of Dust in Mining, Tunnelling, and Quarrying.* Geneva: ILO [six successive international reports, published between 1957 and 1983].

———. *Report of the Meeting of Experts on the Prevention and Suppression of Dust in Mining, Tunnelling, and Quarrying: Geneva, December 1952*, 3 vols. Geneva: ILO, 1954.

———. *Silicosis: Proceedings of the International Conference Held in Geneva from 29 August to 9 September 1938.* Collection Études et Documents, ser. F, no. 17. Geneva: [ILO], 1940.

———. *Silicosis: Records of the International Congress Held at Johannesburg, 13–27 August 1930.* Collection Études et Documents, ser. F, no. 13. Geneva: ILO, 1930.

———. *Third International Conference of Experts on Pneumoconiosis, Sydney, February–March 1950: Record of Proceedings*, 2 vols. Geneva: ILO, 1953.

———. "Workmen's Compensation (Occupational Diseases) Convention (Revised), 1934 (No. 42)," www.ilo.org/dyn/normlex/en/f?p=NORMLEXPUB:12100:0::NO::P12100 _ILO_CODE:C042.

Innocenti, Andrea, Gianfranco Sciarra, and Giuseppina Scancarello. "Il rischio SLC in agricoltura" [The crystalline silica hazard in agriculture]. In Capacci et al. (eds.), *Silice libera cristallina*, 102–105.

Institut d'Hygiène des Mines. *Contrôle sanitaire du personnel des charbonnages belges* [Health check of workers in Belgian collieries]. Hasselt, Belgium: Institut d'Hygiène des Mines, 1962.

International Agency for Research on Cancer, *Silica Dust, Crystalline, in the form of Quartz or Cristobalite*. Monograph 100C, 2012, http://monographs.iarc.fr/ENG/Monographs /vol100C/mono100C-14.pdf.

Irvine, A. G., A. Mavrogordato, and H. Pirow. "A Review of the History of Silicosis on the Witwatersrand Goldfields." In ILO, *Silicosis: Records* (1930), 178–208.

Jacobsen, M. "La pneumoconiose des houilleurs en Grande-Bretagne en relation avec l'environnement minier" [Coal workers' pneumoconiosis in Great Britain in relation to the mining environment]. In *Compte rendu des journées d'information*, 83–89.

———. "Vingt-six ans de recherches sur les pneumoconioses sur le terrain dans les charbonnages britanniques: Contribution de ces recherches à l'épidémiologie des affections pulmonaires des mineurs" [Twenty-six years of field research on pneumoconiosis in British collieries: The contribution of this research to the epidemiology of lung disease in miners]. *Revue de l'Institut d'Hygiène des Mines* 34, 4 (1979): 207.

Jacobsen, M., S. Rae, W. H. Walton, and J. M. Rogan. "New Dust Standards for British Coal Mines." *Nature* 227 (1971): 445–447.

Jarry, J.-J., A. Avy, E. Balgairies, and E. Quinot. "Essai d'indice koniotique" [An attempt at a coniotic index]. *Revue médicale minière* 23 (1953): 3–24.

Jeeves, Alan H. *Migrant Labour in South Africa's Mining Economy: The Struggle for the Gold Mines' Labour Supply, 1890–1920.* Kingston, ON: McGill-Queen's University Press, 1985.

———. "William Gemmill and South African Expansion, 1920–1950." Paper presented at "The Making of Class," history workshop, University of the Witwatersrand, 14 February 1987.

Jewson, N. D. "The Disappearance of the Sick-Man from Medical Cosmology, 1770–1870." *Sociology* 10, 2 (1976): 225–244.

Johnston, C., and R. S. Bennett. "Dust Removal in the Grinding Trades." *British Medical Journal* 22 (August 1908): 485–486.

Johnston, Ronald, and Arthur McIvor. "Oral History, Subjectivity, and Environmental Reality: Occupational Health Histories in Twentieth-Century Scotland." *Osiris* 19 (2004): 234–249.

Johnstone, J. "Some Account of a Species of Phthisis Pulmonalis, Peculiar to Persons Employed in Pointing Needles in the Needle Manufacture." *Memoirs of the Medical Society of London* 5 (1799): 89–93.

Juengprasert, Wilawan. "Toward Elimination of Silicosis in Thailand: Mineral Dusts and Prevention of Silicosis." *Asian-Pacific Newsletter on Occupational Health and Safety* 4, 2 (1997).

Kaneko, Yôji. "Nenkô chinginron ni okeru nôritsu to seikatsu no shisôteki keifu" [The ideological genealogy of efficiency and livelihood in seniority-based wage theory]. *Nihon rôdô kenkyû zasshi* 560 (2007): 89–95.

Karsenti, Bruno. "Loi et sanction [Law and Sanction]." In Paolo Napoli (ed.), *Aux origines des cultures juridiques européennes: Yan Thomas entre droit et sciences sociales* [The origins of European juridical cultures: Yan Thomas between law and social sciences] 235–248. Rome: École Française de Rome, 2013.

Katz, Elaine. "The Underground Route to Mining: Afrikaners and the Witwatersrand Gold Mining Industry from 1902 to the 1907 Miners' Strike." *Journal of African History* 36, 3 (1995): 467–489.

———. *The White Death: Silicosis on the Witwatersrand Gold Mines, 1885–1910.* Johannesburg: Witwatersrand University Press, 1994.

Kaufmann, Constantin. *Handbuch der Unfallmedizin* [Handbook of injury medicine]. Stuttgart: Enke, 1919.

Kaye, Mike. *Forced Labour in the 21st Century.* London and Brussels: Antislavery International and International Confederation of Free Trade Unions (ICFTU), 2001, www.antislavery.org/includes/documents/cm_docs/2009/f/forcedlabour.pdf.

Kentish, E. *An Account of Baths and of a Madeira-House at Bristol, with a Drawing and Description of a Pulmometer and Cases Shewing Its Utility in Ascertaining the State of the Lungs in Diseases of the Chest.* London: Longman, Hurst, Rees, Orme, and Browne, 1814.

Khurana, Alkesh Kumar, and Anup Kumar Singh. "Silicosis: Hidden Behind TB?" *Chest Journal* 139, 4 (2011): 967–968.

King, E. J., S. C. Ray, and C. V. Harrison. "Inhibitory Action of Aluminium on Quartz in Experimental Silicosis." In ILO, *Third International Conference of Experts*, 159–165.

King, E. J., A. H. A. Wynn, G. Nagelschmidt, and A. L. Cochrane. *Pneumoconiosis in Germany*. Research Report 10. Ministry of Fuel and Power, Safety in Mines Research & Testing Branch, May 1950.

Kippen, Sandra. "The Social and Political Meaning of the Silent Epidemic of Miners' Phthisis, Bendigo, 1860–1960." *Social Science and Medicine* 41, 4 (1995): 491–499.

Klubock, Thomas Miller. "Working-Class Masculinity, Middle-Class Morality, and Labor Politics in the Chilean Copper Mines." *Journal of Social History* 30, 2 (1996): 436–440.

Knight, Arnold, S. Roberts, and Company of Cutlers (Sheffield, Yorkshire). *Committee Appointed for Investigating the Claims Made to the Merit of the New Grinder's Health Preservative: Observations on the Grinder's Asthma*. Montgomery, Sheffield, UK: printed and published by order of the Committee, 1822.

Knowles, C. M. "State Control of Industrial Accident Insurance." *Journal of Comparative Legislation and International Law*, 2 (1920): 29–50.

Koelsch, Franz. *Beiträge zur Geschichte der Arbeitsmedizin* [Contributions to the history of occupational medicine]. Munich: Bayerische Landesärztekammer, 1968.

Kolb, Robert. *Die Berufsverhältnisse der Steinarbeiter in der Schweiz und deren Gefahren in Bezug auf Unfall- und Krankheitshäufigkeit: Eingabe an die Mitglieder der Bundesversammlung* [The professional relationships of stoneworkers in Switzerland and their risks in terms of injury and disease incidence: Report to the members of the Federal Assembly]. Zurich: Genossenschaftsdruckerei, 1912.

———"Staubkrankheit (Silikose) als unfallentschädigungsberechtigte Berufskrankheit" [Dust disease (silicosis) as an occupational disease deserving financial compensation]. *Gewerkschaftliche Rundschau* 26 (1934): 187–191.

———. "Was ist Silikose?" [What is silicosis?]. *Gewerkschaftliche Rundschau* 35 (1943): 50–52.

Kott, Sandrine, and Joëlle Droux, eds. *Globalizing Social Rights: The ILO and Beyond*. London: Palgrave Macmillan, 2013.

Kuempel E. D., M. W. Wheeler, R. J. Smith, V. Vallyathan, and F. H. Green. "Contributions of Dust Exposure and Cigarette Smoking to Emphysema Severity in Coal Miners in the United States." *American Journal of Respiratory and Critical Care Medicine* 180 (2009): 257–264.

Kulkarni, Ganesh. "Prevention and Control of Silicosis: A National Challenge." *Indian Journal of Occupational and Environmental Medicine* 11, 3 (2007): 95.

Lacasse, Yves, Sylvie Martin, and Marc Desmeules. *Silicose, silice et cancer du poumon: Méta-analyse de la littérature médicale* [Silicosis, silica, and lung cancer: Meta-analysis of the medical literature]. Montreal: IRSST [Institut de Recherche Robert-Sauvé en Santé et en Sécurité du Travail], 2005.

Laennec, R. T. H. *A Treatise on the Diseases of the Chest and on Mediate Auscultation*, trans. John Forbes. Philadelphia: Thomas, Cowperthwaite, 1838.

Laflamme, L., and A. Arsenault. "Wage Modes and Injuries at the Workplace." *Industrial Relations Journal* 39 (1984): 509–525.

Lambin, P., and V. Van Mechelen. "Le traitement de la silicose et ses complications" [The treatment of silicosis and its complications]. *Communications de l'Institut d'Hygiène des Mines* 73 (15 June 1950): 7.

Landwehr, M. "The Determination of the Silicosis Risk of Rock, Drilling Dust, and Airborne Dust on the Basis of Mineralogical Investigation." In ILO, *Report of the Meeting of Experts*, vol. 1: 198–199.

Laney, A. S., E. L. Petsonk, and M. D. Attfield. "Pneumoconiosis among Underground Bituminous Coal Miners in the United States: Is Silicosis Becoming More Frequent?" *Occupational and Environmental Medicine* 67 (2009): 652–656.

Laney A. S., E. L. Petsonk, J. M. Hale, A. L. Wolfe, and M. D. Attfield. "Potential Determinants of Coal Workers' Pneumoconiosis, Advanced Pneumoconiosis, and Progressive Massive Fibrosis among Underground Coal Miners in the United States, 2005–2009." *American Journal of Public Health* 102 (2012): S279–S283.

Laney, A. S., and D. N. Weissman, "Respiratory Diseases Caused by Coal Mine Dust." *Journal of Occupational and Environmental Medicine* 56, Suppl. 10 (2014): S18–S22.

Lang, Fritz. "Unsere Erfahrungen mit der Silikose" [Our experience with silicosis]. *Schweizerische Zeitschrift für Unfallmedizin und Berufskrankheiten* 31 (1937): 264–276.

Langelez, A. "Silicose des mineurs en Belgique" [Miners' silicosis in Belgium]. In ILO, *Silicosis: Proceedings* (1938), 143–145.

Lankton, Larry D. "The Machine under the Garden: Rock Drills Arrive at the Lake Superior Copper Mines, 1868–1883." *Technology and Culture* 24, 1 (1983): 1–37.

Lanza, Anthony, ed. *Silicosis and Asbestosis.* London: Oxford University Press, 1938.

Lavenne, F. "Diagnostic radiologique des pneumoconioses" [Radiological diagnosis of pneumoconioses]. *Cahiers de médecine du travail* 1, 1 (1963): 25–34.

Lavenne, F., and J. Patigny. "Valeur comparée de la radiographie et de la radiophotographie pour le diagnostic de la pneumoconiose des houilleurs: Étude expérimentale" [Comparison of the value of radiography and radiophotography for the diagnosis of coal miners' pneumoconiosis: An experimental study]. *Revue de l'Institut d'Hygiène des Mines* 15, 1 (1960): 115–135.

Lazar, Marc. "Damné de la terre et homme de marbre: L'ouvrier dans l'imaginaire du PCF du milieu des années trente à la fin des années cinquante" [Damned of the earth and man of marble: The French Communist Party's image of the worker from the 1930s to the end of the 1950s]. *Annales: Économies, sociétés, civilisations* 45, 5 (1990): 1071–1096.

Le Bouffant, L., H. Daniel, and J.-C. Martin. "Experimental Results and Possibilities for Practical Applications of Aluminium Salts in the Prophylaxis and Treatment of Coal Miners Pneumoconiosis." *6th International Pneumoconiosis Conference, Bochum, 1983*, vol. 1: 460–466. Geneva: ILO, 1984.

Le Bouffant, L., and C. Froger. "Les pneumoconioses dans les mines et leur prévention" [Pneumoconiosis in mines and its prevention]. *Annales des mines* (January–February 1978): 66–68.

Leger, J.-P. "Occupational Diseases in South African Mines: A Neglected Epidemic?" *South African Medical Journal* 81, 4 (1992): 197–201.

Lehtinen, Suvi, and Greg Goldstein. "Elimination of Silicosis from the World." *Occupational Safety and Health & Development* 4 (2002): 31–33.

Leigh J. P., S. B. Markowitz, M. Fahs, C. Shin, and P. J. Landrigan. "Occupational Injury and Illness in the United States: Estimates of Costs, Morbidity, and Mortality." *Archives of Internal Medicine* 157, 14 (1997): 1557–1568.

Leigh J. P., and J. A. Robbins, "Occupational Disease and Workers' Compensation: Coverage, Costs, and Consequences." *Milbank Quarterly* 82, 4 (2004): 689–721.

Lemaître, Jacques. "Compagnons de route du PCI à La Louvière" [The PCI's travel companions at La Louvière]. In Deprez et al., *Siamo tutti neri*, 135–145.

Lemen, Richard A., and Terry P. Hammond, "Silicosis Kills." *World Health* (1992): 22–23.

Lengwiler, Martin. "Internationale Expertennetzwerke und nationale Sozialstaatsgeschichte: Versicherung der Silikose in Deutschland und der Schweiz (1900–1945)"

[International expert networks and national welfare-state history: Silicosis insurance in Germany and Switzerland (1900–1945)]. *Journal of Modern European History* 7, 2 (2009): 197–218.

———. "Rationalisation et tarification des accidents du travail: Le cas de la CAN et de la silicose" [Processing and pricing occupational accidents: The case of the Mining Social Security and silicosis]. *Cahiers d'histoire du mouvement ouvrier* 20 (2004): 94–103.

———. *Risikopolitik im Sozialstaa: Die schweizerische Unfallversicherung 1870–1970* [Risk policy in a social state: Swiss injury insurance, 1870–1970]. Cologne: Böhlau, 2006.

Liddell, F. D. K. "An Experiment in Film Reading." *British Journal of Industrial Medicine* 20, 4 (1963): 300–312.

Linch, Kenneth D. "Respirable Concrete Dust: Silicosis Hazard in the Construction Industry." *Applied Occupational and Environmental Hygiene* 17, 3 (2002): 209–221.

Lombard, Henri. "De l'influence des professions sur la phtisie pulmonaire" [The influence of occupations on pulmonary consumption]. *Annales d'hygiène publique et de médecine légale* 11, 27 (1834): 5–131.

Mackova, Emanuela, and Paul-André Rosental. "Les démocraties populaires d'Europe de l'Est ont-elles protégé la santé de leurs travailleurs? La Tchécoslovaquie socialiste face à la silicose" [Did Eastern European peoples' democracies protect the health of their workers? Socialist Czechoslovakia's approach to silicosis]. *Journal of Modern European History* 2 (2009): 237–260.

Magnin, Jean. "Méditation sur la prophylaxie de la silicose dans les mines" [Reflection on the prophylaxis of silicosis in mines]. *Archives des maladies professionnelles* 7, 6 (1946): 475.

Malan, Marais. *The Quest of Health: The South African Institute of Medical Research, 1912–1973.* Johannesburg: Lowry, 1988.

Malik, Deepak. "Silicosis. A 'Dusty' Tale in Rajastan." *Boloji*, 16 April 2006, www.boloji.com/index.cfm?md=Content&sd=Articles&ArticleID=2672/.

Markowitz, Gerald, and David Rosner. "The Illusion of Medical Certainty: Silicosis and the Politics of Industrial Disability, 1930–1960." *Milbank Quarterly* 67, Suppl. 2 (1989): 228–253.

———. "The Limits of Thresholds: Silica and the Politics of Science, 1935 to 1990." *American Journal of Public Health* 85, 2 (1995): 253–262.

Masami, Fujii. "Homuresu mondai no ichisokumen-rôjô seikatsusha kara hakken sareta jinpaishô no 5 rei" [One aspect of the homeless problem: Five cases of pneumoconiosis discovered among people living in the street]. *Rôdô no kagaku* 59, 1 (2004): 39–42.

Masseret, Jean-Pierre. "Pneumoconiose du mineur du charbon: Inscription au tableau des maladies professionnelle," question écrite no. 01849, www.senat.fr/questions/base/1986/qSEQ860601849.html.

Mathur, M. L. "Pattern and Predictors of Mortality in Sandstone Quarry Workers." *Indian Journal of Occupational and Environmental Medicine* 9, 2 (2005): 80–85.

Matla, W. P. M. "Concentrations-limites: Seuils d'empoussiérage" [Concentration limits: Dust-level thresholds]. *Revue de l'Institut d'Hygiène des Mines* 17, 4 (1962): 262.

Matošević, Andrea. "Industry Forging Masculinity: 'Tough Men,' Hard Labor, and Identity." *Narodna umjetnost/Croatian Journal of Ethnology and Folklore Research* 35, 1 (2010): 29–47.

McCord, Carey Pratt. "Grindstones." *Hygeia* 18 (August 1940): 744.

———. *Silicosis in the Foundry.* Chicago: National Founders Association, 1932.

McCulloch, Jock. "Air Hunger: The 1930 Johannesburg Conference and the Politics of Silicosis." *History Workshop Journal* 72, 1 (2011): 118–137.

———. "Counting the Cost: Gold Mining and Occupational Disease in Contemporary South Africa." *African Affairs* 108, 431 (2009): 221–240.

———. "Medicine, Politics, and Disease in South Africa's Gold Mines." *Journal of Southern African Studies* 39, 3 (2013): 543–556.

———. *South Africa's Gold Mines and the Politics of Silicosis.* Woodbridge, UK: James Currey, 2012.

McCunney, Robert J., Peter Morfeld, and Stephen Payne. "What Component of Coal Causes Coal Workers' Pneumoconiosis?" *Journal of Occupational and Environmental Medicine* 51, 4 (2009): 462–471.

McIvor, Arthur, and Ronald Johnston. "Medical Knowledge and the Worker: Occupational Lung Diseases in the United Kingdom, c. 1920–1975." *Labor* 2, 4 (2005): 63–86.

———. *Miners' Lung: A History of Dust Disease in British Coal Mining.* Aldershot, UK: Ashgate, 2007.

———. "Voices from the Pits: Health and Safety in Scottish Coal Mining since 1945." *Scottish Economic and Social History* 22, 2 (2002): 111–133.

McLintock J. S. "The Changing Prevalence of Coal Workers' Pneumoconiosis in Great Britain." *Annals of the New York Academy of Sciences* 200, 1 (1972): 278–291.

———. "Current Views on Coal-Workers' Pneumoconiosis." *Journal of the Royal Society of Medicine* 69, 1 (1979): 9–10.

"Medical Terms in the New English Dictionary." *British Medical Journal* 2, 2609 (31 December 1910): 2038.

Meiklejohn, Andrew. "The Development of Compensation for Occupational Diseases of the Lungs." *British Journal for Industrial Medicine* 11, 3 (1954): 198–212.

———. "Doctor and Workman." *British Journal of Industrial Medicine* 7, 3 (1950): 105–116.

———. "The Origin of the Term Anthracosis." *British Journal of Industrial Medicine* 16 (1959): 324–325.

———. "The Successful Prevention of Silicosis among China Biscuit Workers in the North Staffordshire Potteries." *British Journal of Industrial Medicine* 20, 4 (1963): 255–263.

Melling, Joseph. "Beyond a Shadow of a Doubt? Experts, Lay Knowledge, and the Role of Radiography in the Diagnosis of Silicosis in Britain, 1919–1945." *Bulletin of the History of Medicine* 84, 3 (2010): 424–466.

Melling, Joseph, and Christopher Sellers. "Objective Collectives? Transnationalism and 'Invisible Colleges' in Occupational and Environmental Health from Collis to Selikoff." In Joseph Melling and Christopher Sellers (eds.), *Dangerous Trade: Histories of Industrial Hazard across a Globalizing World,* 113–125. Philadelphia: Temple University Press, 2012.

Menéndez-Navarro, Alfredo. "The Politics of Silicosis in Interwar Spain: Republican and Francoist Approaches to Occupational Health." *Dynamis* 28 (2008): 77–102.

Metropolitan Life Insurance Company, Industrial Health Section. *Silicosis.* San Francisco: Metropolitan Life Insurance Company, 1948.

Middleton, E. L. "The Etiology of Silicosis." *Tubercle* 1 (1919–1920): 257–262.

———. "Silicosis." In ILO, *Supplement to Occupation and Health: Encyclopaedia of Hygiene, Pathology, and Social Welfare* [2 vols., 1930–1934], 1938: 261–287.

Miller, A. "President's Address." *Proceedings of the Transvaal Mine Medical Officers' Association* 18, 206 (April 1939).

Miller, Albert. "Sherlock Holmes, Albrecht Dürer, and Socrates: The International Labour Office Radiographic Classification of Pneumoconioses Reassessed for Asbestosis." *Chest Journal* 113, 6 (1998): 1439–1442.

Miller, Brian G., Suzanne Hagen, Richard G. Love, Colin A. Soutar, Hilary A. Cowie, Malcolm W. Kidd, and Alastair Robertson. "Risks of Silicosis in Coalworkers Exposed to Unusual Concentrations of Respirable Quartz." *Occupational and Environmental Medicine* 55, 1 (1998): 52–58.

Mills, Catherine. "A Hazardous Bargain: Occupational Risk in Cornish Mining, 1875–1914." *Labour History Review* 70, 1 (2005): 53–71.

Mine Health and Safety Council, Safety in Mines Research Advisory Committee. *Silicosis Elimination Programme: Report on Inspection and Enforcement around the World with Regard to Silicosis Prevention.* Johannesburg, 2006.

Minette, A., and Degueldre, G. "L'importance de l'épidémiologie pour la recherche sur les pneumoconioses en Belgique" [The importance of epidemiology for research on pneumoconiosis in Belgium]. *Revue de l'Institut d'Hygiène des Mines* 33, 3 (1978): 154–166.

Mintz, Fredric. "Hard Rock Miners' Phthisis in 19th and Early 20th Century Britain: From Diagnosis to Compensation." PhD dissertation, University of California, Berkeley (2009).

Miura, Toyohiko. *Rôdô to kenkô no rekishi* [History of labor and health], 7 vols. Kawasaki, Japan: Rôdô Kagaku Kenkyûjo Shuppanbu, 1978–1992.

Monaghan, Peter. "Law Students Take On the Coal Industry." *Chronicle of Higher Education*, November 16, 2007.

Mongiardini, G. "Osservazioni e riflessioni sulle Ardesie di Lavagna" [Observations and reflections on slate in Lavagna]. *Giornale Pisano di Letteratura, scienze ed arti* (1809): 333–339.

Montgomery, David. *The Fall of the House of Labor: The Workplace, the State, and American Labor Activism, 1865–1925.* Cambridge: Cambridge University Press, 1989.

Moore, K. R. "Silicosis in Australia." In ILO, *Silicosis: Records* (1930), 295–312.

Morgan, W. K. C. "Epidemiology and Occupational Lung Disease." In W. K. C. Morgan and A. Seaton (eds.), *Occupational Lung Diseases*, 82–110. Philadelphia: W. B. Saunders, 1975.

Morhenn, E. "Regulations to Protect Health against Injurious Dust in Mines." In ILO, *Report of the Meeting of Experts*, vol. 1: 288.

Morrison, Sue. *The Silicosis Experience in Scotland: Causality, Recognition, and the Impact of Legislation during the Twentieth Century.* Saarbrücken, Germany: Lambert Academic Publishing, 2010.

Moses, Julia. "Contesting Risk: Specialist Knowledge and Workplace Accidents in Britain, Germany, and Italy, 1870–1920." In Kerstin Brückweh, Dirk Schumann, Richard Wetzell, and Benjamin Ziemann (eds.), *Engineering Society: The Role of the Human and Social Sciences in Modern Societies, 1880–1990.* Basingstoke, UK: Palgrave, 2012.

———. "Foreign Workers and the Emergence of Minimum International Standards for the Compensation of Workplace Accidents, 1880–1914." *Journal of Modern European History* 7 (2009): 59–78, 219–239.

———. *Legalising Risk: Workplace Accidents and the Making of European Welfare States.* Forthcoming.

———. "Policy Communities and Exchanges across Borders: The Case of Workplace Accidents at the Turn of the Twentieth Century." In Davide Rodogno, Bernard Struck, and Jakob Vogel (eds.), *Shaping the Transnational Sphere: Experts, Networks, and Issues, 1830–1950*, 60–81. New York and Oxford: Berghahn, 2011.

Mottura, G. "L'ammalato per contratto di lavoro: Considerazioni indotte dallo studio delle malattie polmonari da polveri industriali" [Fallen sick by labour contract: Considerations induced by the study of the lung diseases from industrial dust]. *Cultura e realtà* 1 (1950): 69–90.

Moussa, F., S. Saadé, and H. Sékou, "Mesures de l'empoussiérage à la mine d'Akouta (Niger)" [Dust levels in the Akouta mine (Niger)]. *Médecine d'Afrique noire* 44, 7 (1997): 428–430.

Muntjewerff, H. E. "Stofbestrijding in de Nederlandse Steenkolenmijnindustrie, 1920–1956" [Dust control in the Dutch coal-mine industry, 1920–1956]. In J. Massard (ed.), *L'homme et la terre/Mensch und Erde*, 73–101. Luxembourg: Courrier de l'Éducation Nationale, 1996.

Murray, Jill, Tony Davies, and David Rees, "Occupational Lung Disease in the South African Mining Industry: Research and Policy Implementation." *Journal of Public Health Policy* 32 (2011): S65–S79.

National Institute for Occupation Safety and Health (NIOSH). *The Work-Related Lung Diseases Surveillance Report.* Cincinnati, OH: Department of Health and Human Services, NIOSH, 1991.

———. *The Work-Related Lung Disease Surveillance Report 2007.* Cincinnati, OH: Department of Health and Human Services, NIOSH, 2008, www.cdc.gov/niosh/docs/2008-143/.

Newsholme, B. "Occupation and Mortality." *Journal of the Royal Society for the Promotion of Health* 14 (1893): 81–101.

Nij, Evelyn Tjoe, Simone Hilhorst, Ton Spee, Judith Spierings, Friso Steffens, Mieke Lumens, and Dick Heederik. "Dust Control Measures in the Construction Industry." *Annals of Occupational Hygiene* 47, 3 (2003): 211–218.

Nisaburô, Murakushi. *Kôfu dôshoku kumiai "tomoko" seido* [Miners, labor unions, and the "tomoko" system]. Tokyo: Jikôsha, 2006.

Norboo, T., P. T. Angchuk, M. Yahya, S. R. Kamat, F. D. Pooley, B. Corrin, I. H. Kerr, N. Bruce, and K. P. Ball. "Silicosis in a Himalayan Village Population: Role of Environmental Dust." *Thorax* 46, 5 (1991): 341–343.

Nugent, A. "Fit for Work: The Introduction of Physical Examinations." *Bulletin of the History of Medicine* 57, 4 (1983): 578–595.

Occupational Safety and Health Administration. *OSHA's Final Rule to Protect Workers from Exposure to Respirable Crystalline Silica.* Occupational Safety and Health Administration, US Department of Labor, 2016, https://www.osha.gov/silica/index.html.

Oliver, Thomas, ed. *Dangerous Trades: The Historical, Social, and Legal Aspects of Industrial Occupations as Affecting Health, by a Number of Experts.* London: John Murray, 1902.

———. *Diseases of Occupation: From the Legislative, Social, and Medical Points of View.* New York: E. P. Dutton, 1908.

———. "The Etiology and Prevention of Pneumonokoniosis." *British Medical Journal* 2 (August 22, 1908): 481–483.

———. "Pneumoconiosis." In C. Allbutt and H. D. Rollestone (eds.), *A System of Medicine,* 2nd ed., vol. 5: 447–473. London: Macmillan, 1909.

———. "Some Dusty Occupations and Their Effects upon the Lungs." *Journal of the Royal Society for the Promotion of Health* 46, 6 (1925): 224–230.

Omnès, Catherine and Anne-Sophie Bruno, eds. *Les mains inutiles: Inaptitude au travail et emploi en Europe* [Useless hands: Unemployability in Europe]. Paris: Belin, 2004.

Omnès, Catherine, and Laure Pitti, eds. *Cultures du risque au travail et pratiques de prévention au XXe siècle* [Knowledge of occupational risks and preventive practices in the 20th century]. Rennes, France: Presses Universitaires de Rennes, 2009.

Orenstein, A. J. "The History of Pneumoconiosis: A Brief Review." *Journal of the Mine Ventilation Society of South Africa* (1957): 16–23.

———, ed. *Proceedings of the Pneumoconiosis Conference held at the University of the Witwatersrand, Johannesburg, 9–24 February 1959.* London: J. & A. Churchill, 1960.

Owen, E. "The Popular Lecture on Dust and Disease, Delivered at the Annual Meeting of the British Medical Association Held at Sheffield, July 31st, 1908." *British Medical Journal* 8 (1908): 321–326.

Packard, Randall M. "The Invention of the 'Tropical Worker': Medical Research and the Quest for Central African Labor on the South African Gold Mines, 1903–1936." *Journal of African History* 34, 2 (1993): 271–292.

———. "Tuberculosis and the Development of Industrial Health Policies on the Witwa-tersrand, 1902–1932." *Journal of Southern African Studies* 13, 2 (1987): 187–209.

———. *White Plague, Black Labor: Tuberculosis and the Political Economy of Health and Disease in South Africa.* Berkeley: University of California Press, 1989.

Parmeggiani, L. "Considerazioni sui casi di silicosi oggetto di controversie giudiziarie nella provincia di Milano prima dell'assicurazione obbligatoria" [Observations on silicosis cases subject of litigation in the province of Milan before compulsory insurance]. *Medicina del lavoro* 37 (1946): 249–264.

Patel, Jaddish. *Stone Crusher of Gohara.* Asia Monitor Resource Centre, 28 September 2007, www.amrc.org.hk.

Paterson, C. S. "From Fever to Digestive Disease: Approaches to the Problem of Factory Ill-Health in Britain, 1784–1833." PhD dissertation, University of British Columbia, 1995.

Payre, Renaud. *Une science communale? Réseaux réformateurs et municipalité providence* [A municipal science? Reformer networks and welfare municipality], Paris: Éditions du CNRS [Centre National de la Recherche Scientifique], 2007.

Peacock, T. B. "On French Millstone-Makers' Phthisis." *British Foreign and Medico-Chirurgical Review* 25 (1860): 155–162.

Peet, J. "Mijnarbeid, veiligheid and gezondheid" [Mine labor, safety, and health]. In Ad Knotter (ed.), *Mijnwerkers in Limburg: Een sociale geschiedenis* [Mineworkers in Limburg: A social history]. Nijmegen, the Netherlands: Vantilt, 2012.

Penrose, Beris. "Medical Monitoring and Silicosis in Metal Miners, 1910–1940." *Labor History Review* 69, 3 (2004): 285–303.

———. " 'So Now They Have Some Human Guinea Pigs': Aluminium Therapy and Occupational Silicosis." *Health & History* 9 (2007): 56–79.

Peoples Training and Research Centre. "Struggle of Silicosis Victims in Agate Industry of Gujarat." Asian Network for the Rights of Occupational and Environmental Victims, 19 March 2006, www.anroev.org/2006/03/09/struggle-of-silicosis-victims-in-agate -industry-of-gujarat/.

Perchard, A. "The Mine Management Professions and the Dust Problem in the Scottish Coal Mining Industry, c. 1930–1966." *Scottish Labor History* 40 (2005): 87–109.

Pernis, Benvenuto, and Enrico C. Vigliani. "The Role of Macrophages and Immunocytes in the Pathogenesis of Pulmonary Diseases Due to Mineral Dusts." *American Journal of Industrial Medicine* 3, 2 (1982): 133–137.

Petsonk, E. L., C. Rose, and R. Cohen, "Coal Mine Dust Lung Disease: New Lessons from Old Exposure." *American Journal of Respiratory and Critical Care Medicine* 187, 11 (2013): 1178–1185.

Pitti, Laure. "Du rôle des mouvements sociaux dans la prévention et la réparation des risques professionnels: L'exemple de Penarroya, 1971–1988" [The role of social movements in occupational risk prevention and compensation: The example of Penarroya, 1971–1988]. In Omnès and Pitti (eds.), *Cultures du risque au travail*, 217–232.

Policard A., and A. Collet. "Deposition of Silicosis Dust in the Lungs of the Inhabitants of the Sahara Regions." *Archives of Industrial Hygiene and Occupational Medicine* 5 (1952): 527–534.

Pollock D. E., J. D. Potts, and G. J. Joy. "Investigation into Dust Exposures and Mining Practices in Mines in the Southern Appalachian Region." *Minerals Engineering* 2 (2010): 44–49.

Pransky, G., T. Snyder, A. Dembe, and J. Himmelstein. "Under-Reporting of Work-Related Disorders in the Workplace: A case study and review of the literature." *Ergonomics* 42, 1 (1999): 171–182.

Proceedings of the Mine Medical Officers' Association of South Africa 52, 2 (1972): 1–2.
Proceedings of the Transvaal Mine Medical Officers' Association 4, 11 (1925).
Proceedings of the Transvaal Mine Medical Officers' Association 156, 164 (1935).
Proceedings of the Transvaal Mine Medical Officers' Association 18, 206 (1939).
Proctor, Robert N., and Londa Schiebinger, eds. *Agnotology: The Making and Unmaking of Ignorance.* Palo Alto, CA: Stanford University Press, 2008.
Prügger, F., B. Mallner, and H. W. Schlipköter. "Polyvinylpyridine N-Oxide (Bay 3504, P-204, PVNO) in the Treatment of Human Silicosis." *Wiener klinische Wochenschrift* 96, 23 (1984): 848–853.
Putegnat, Ernest. "Maladies des tailleurs de crystal et de verre: Monographie d'une gingivite non décrite, recherches sur une cause non connue de la phthisie pulmonaire" [Diseases of crystal and glass cutters: A monograph on unspecified gingivitis, research on an unknown cause of pulmonary consumption]. *Journal de médecine, de chirurgie et de pharmacologie* 30, 18 (1860): 11–33.
Quataert, Donald. *Miners and the State in the Ottoman Empire: The Zonguldak Coalfield, 1822–1920.* New York and Oxford: Berghahn Books, 2006.
Quinot, E. "Définition des critères permettant de mesurer le degré de nocivité des empoussiérages: Essai de détermination de l'empoussiérage admissible et application au Bassin Nord et Pas-de-Calais" [Definition of criteria to measure the harmfulness of dust levels: An attempt to determine admissible dust levels and application in the Nord and Pas-de-Calais Basin]. *Revue médicale minière* 2 (1970): 89–99.
———. "Épidémiologie des pneumoconioses: Proposition d'une méthode d'étude" [Epidemiology of pneumoconiosis: Proposal for a study method]. *Revue médicale minière* 44 (1962): 91–95.
Radi, S., J. C. Dalphin, P. Manzoni, D. Pernet, M. P. Leboube, and J. F. Viel. "Respiratory Morbidity in a Population of French Dental Technicians." *Occupational and Environmental Medicine* 59, 6 (2002): 398–404.
Rae, Stewart. "Pneumoconiosis and Coal Dust Exposure." *British Medical Bulletin* 27, 1 (1971): 53–58.
Rafnsson, Vilhjalmur, Olafur Ingimarsson, Ingimar Hjalmarsson, and Holmfridur Gunnarsdottir. "Association between Exposure to Crystalline Silica and Risk of Sarcoidosis." *Occupational and Environmental Medicine* 55, 10 (1998): 657–660.
Rainhorn, Judith. "Le mouvement ouvrier contre la peinture au plomb: Stratégie syndicale, expérience locale et transgression du discours dominant au début du XXe siècle" [The workers' movement against lead paint: Union strategy, local experience, and overturning the dominant narrative at the beginning of the 20th century]. *Politix* 23, 91 (2010): 9–26.
———, ed. *Santé et travail à la mine, XIXe–XXIe siècles* [Health and work in the mines, 19th–21st centuries]. Lille, France: Presses Universitaires du Septentrion, 2014.
Ramazzini, Bernardino. *A Treatise of the Diseases of Tradesmen.* London: Andrew Bell, 1705 [first published 1700].
Ranc, L. "Les ouvriers et la médecine d'usine" [Workers and industrial medicine]. In Marcel Eck (ed.), *La médecine sociale: Bilan et perspectives d'avenir.* Collection Droit Social, fasc. 22, 10–13. Paris: Librairie Sociale et Économique, 1944.
Rees, David, and Jill Murray, "Silica, Silicosis, and Tuberculosis." *International Journal of Tuberculosis and Lung Disease* 11, 5 (2007): 474–484.
Rees, David, Jill Murray, G. Nelson, and P. Sonnenberg, "Oscillating Migration and the Epidemics of Silicosis, Tuberculosis, and HIV Infection in South African Gold Miners." *American Journal of Industrial Medicine* 53, 4 (2010): 398–404.

Reiser, Stanley Joel. *Medicine and the Reign of Technology*. Cambridge: Cambridge University Press, 1978.

Reisner, M. "Erkenntnisse epidemiologischer Untersuchungen für den Schutz vor Stauber-krankungen" [Findings of epidemiological studies on protection against dust diseases]. *Glückhauf*, 6 January 1977, 21–26.

———. "Les pneumoconioses et l'exposition aux poussières dans les mines de charbon de la République Fédérale d'Allemagne" [Pneumoconioses and dust exposure in the coal mines of the Federal Republic of Germany]. In *Compte rendu des journées d'information*, 51–69.

——— "Pneumokoniose und Staubexposition." *Silikosebericht Nordrhein-Westfalen* 8 (1972): 221–231.

———. "Results of Epidemiological Studies of Pneumoconiosis in West German Coal Mines." *Inhaled Particles* 2 (1970): 921–931.

Rennie, Richard. "The Historical Origins of an Industrial Disaster: Occupational Health and Labour Relations at the Fluorspar Mines, St. Lawrence, Newfoundland, 1933–1945." *Labour/Le Travail* (2005): 107–142.

Report of the Departmental Committee on Compensation for Industrial Diseases: Report Presented to Both Houses of Parliament by Command of His Majesty. [British] Parliamentary Papers 1907, cd. 3495, 34: 1045. London: His Majesty's Stationery Office, 1907.

Report of the Miners' Phthisis Commission of Enquiry, 1902–1903. Pretoria: Government Printing and Stationery Office, 1903.

"Report on the Preventable Diseases of the Industrial Classes: IV. Workers among Dust." *British Medical Journal* (April 25, 1868): 408–409.

Rey, F. "Les mesures d'empoussiérage dans les houillères françaises et l'état actuel des procédés techniques de lutte contre les poussières" [Measuring dust levels in French collieries and current state of procedures and techniques to combat dust]. In *Journée d'étude consacrée à l'hygiène des mines*, 57–59. Brussels: Union des Ingénieurs Sortis des Écoles Spéciales de l'Université Catholique de Louvain, 1958.

Rey, Paule. "La réparation des accidents du travail et des maladies professionnelles: Tendances et perspectives" [Compensation of occupational accidents and diseases: Trends and outlook]. In Jeanne Mager Stellman (ed.), *Encyclopédie de sécurité et de santé au travail*, 3rd French ed., sect. 26-6. Geneva: Bureau International du Travail, 2000.

Rey, Paule, and A. Bousquet. "Compensation for Occupational Injuries and Diseases: Its Effect upon Prevention at the Workplace." *Ergonomics* 38 (1995): 475–486.

Rice, Faye L. "Silica-Related Disease: It's Not Just Silicosis." *WHO Global Occupational Health Network (GOHNET) Newsletter*, 12 (2007): 6–7, www.who.int/occupational_health/publications/newsletter/gohnet12e.pdf.

Rodgers, Daniel T. *Atlantic Crossings: Social Politics in a Progressive Age*. Cambridge, MA: Harvard University Press, 1998.

Romano, Roberto. *Fabbriche, operai, ingegneri: Studi di storia del lavoro in Italia tra '800 e '900* [Factories, workers, engineers: Studies of labor history in Italy between the end of the 19th and beginning of the 20th centuries]. Milan: Franco Angeli, 2000.

Rosen, George. *The History of Miners' Diseases*. New York: Schuman's, 1943.

———. "Osler on Miner's Phthisis." *Journal of the History of Medicine and Allied Sciences* 4 (1949): 259–266.

Rosenberg, Charles E. "Disease and Social Order in America: Perceptions and Expectations." *Milbank Quarterly* 1 (1986): 34–55.

———. "Disease in History: Frames and Framers." *Milbank Quarterly* 67, 1 (1989): 1–15.

Rosental, Paul-André. "De la silicose et des ambiguïtés de la notion de 'maladie profession-nelle'" [Silicosis and the ambiguities of the concept of "occupational disease"]. *Revue d'histoire moderne et contemporaine* 1 (2009): 83–98.

———. "Expertise and the Evolution of Private Law: The Case of Occupational Illness in Twentieth-Century France." In Michael Lobban and Julia Moses (eds.), *The Impact of Ideas on Legal Development*, 244–264. Cambridge: Cambridge University Press (2012).

———. "Géopolitique et État-Providence: Le Bureau International du Travail et la poli-tique mondiale des migrations dans l'entre-deux-guerres" [Geopolitics and the welfare state: The International Labour Office and the global politics of migration in the inter-war period]. *Annales: Histoire, sciences sociales* 61, 1 (2006): 99–134.

———, ed. "Health and Safety at Work." Special issue, *Journal of Modern European History* 7, 2 (2009).

———. "The History of Occupational Lung Disease: A Long View." In Anthony Newman Taylor, Paul Cullinan, Paul Blanc, and Anthony Pickering (eds.), *Parkes' Occupational Lung Disorders*, 4th ed. Boca Raton, FL: CRC Press (2016).

——— "La silicose, un cas exemplaire" [Silicosis, an exemplary case]. *Revue d'histoire mod-erne et contemporaine* 56, 1 (2009): 83–176.

Rosental, Paul-André, Catherine Cavalin, and Michel Vincent, "Contextualiser la recon-naissance internationale de la 'silicose' dans les années 1930: Une hybridation historico-médicale pour mesurer les effets de la silice dans le monde contemporain" [Contextual-izing the international recognition of "silicosis" in the 1930s: A medical-historical hybridization to measure the effects of silica in the world today]. In Florent Brayard (ed.), *Des contextes en histoire*, 181–205. Paris: Jouve, 2014.

Rosental, Paul-André, and Jean-Claude Devinck. "Statistique et mort industrielle: La fabri-cation du nombre de victimes de la silicose dans les houillères en France de 1946 à nos jours" [Statistics and industrial death: Manufacturing the number of silicosis victims in French collieries from 1946 to today]. *Vingtième siècle* 95, 3 (2007): 75–91.

Rosental, Paul-André, and Catherine Omnès, eds. "Les maladies professionnelles: Genèse d'une question sociale." Special issue, *Revue d'histoire moderne et contemporaine* 56, 1 (2009).

Rosental, Paul-André, David Rosner, and Paul D. Blanc, eds. "From Silicosis to Silica Haz-ards: An Experiment in Medicine, History, and the Social Sciences." Special issue, *American Journal of Industrial Medicine* 3 (2015).

Rosenthal, E. "New Treatment of Silicosis." *Colliery Guardian* (October 16, 1952): 461–464.

Rosner, David, and Gerald Markowitz. *Deadly Dust: Silicosis and the On-Going Struggle to Protect Workers' Health*. Ann Arbor: University of Michigan Press, 2006.

———. *Deadly Dust: Silicosis and the Politics of Occupational Disease*. Princeton, NJ: Princeton University Press, 1991.

———. "The Trials and Tribulations of Two Historians: Adjudicating Responsibility for Pollution and Personal Harm." *Medical History* 53, 2 (2009): 271–292.

Rovida, Carlo. "Un caso di silicosi del polmone, con analisi chimica" [One case of lung silico-sis, with chemical analysis]. *Annali di chimica applicata alla medicina* 53 (1871): 102–106.

Sayers, R. R. "Anthraco-Silicosis of Anthracite Miners." In ILO, *Supplement to Occupation and Health: Encyclopaedia of Hygiene, Pathology and Social Welfare* [2 vols., 1930–1934], 1938: 13–24.

Sayers, R. R., and Anthony Lanza. "History of Silicosis and Asbestosis." In Lanza (ed.), *Silicosis and Asbestosis*, 3–30. London: Oxford University Press, 1938.

Schaad, Nicole. *Chemische Stoffe, giftige Körper: Gesundheitsrisiken in der Basler Chemie* [Chemical substances, toxic body: Health hazards in the Basel chemical industry]. Zurich: Chronos, 2003.

Schenker, Marc B., Kent E. Pinkerton, Diane Mitchell, Val Vallyathan, Brenda Elvine-Kreis, and Francis H. Green. "Pneumoconiosis from Agricultural Dust Exposure among Young California Farmworkers." *Environmental Health Perspectives* 117, 6 (2009): 988–94.

Schlipköter, H. W., and A. Brockhaus. "The Effects of Polyvinylpyridine on Experimental Silicosis." *Deutsche medizinische Wochenschrift (1946)* 85, 21 (1960): 920–923.

Schwartz, Olivier. *Le monde privé des ouvriers: Hommes et femmes du Nord* [The private world of workers: Men and women from northern France]. Paris: Presses Universitaires de France, 1990.

Schweber, Libby. *Disciplining Statistics: Demography and Vital Statistics in France and England, 1830–1835.* Durham, NC: Duke University Press, 2006.

Seibert, Julia. "More Continuity than Change? New Forms of Unfree Labor in the Belgian Congo, 1908–1930." In Marcel van der Linden (ed.), *Humanitarian Intervention and Changing Labor Relations: The Long-Term Consequences of the Abolition of the Slave Trade,* 369–386. Leyden, the Netherlands: Brill, 2011.

Sellers, Christopher. *Hazards of the Job: From Industrial Disease to Environmental Health.* Chapel Hill: University of North Carolina Press, 1997.

"70,000 child workers in the coal mines of Jaintia Hills." *Morung Express,* 19 March 2010.

Sherson, D. "Silicosis in the Twenty First Century." *Occupational and Environmental Medicine* 59, 11 (2002): 721–722.

Shryock, Richard Harrison. *The Development of Modern Medicine.* New York and London: Hafner, 1969 [originally published 1936; reprint of 2nd ed., 1947].

"Silico-Anthracosis." *American Journal of Public Health* 23 (April 1933): 369–370.

"Silicosis Review." *Industrial Medicine* 4 (January 1935): 22.

Sorenson, J. R. J., I. R. Campbell, L. B. Tepper, and R. D. Lingg. "Aluminum in the Environment and Human Health." *Environmental Health Perspectives* 8 (1974): 3–95.

Soutar, C. A., J. F. Hurley, B. G. Miller, H. A. Cowie, and D. Buchanan. "Dust Concentrations and Respiratory Risks in Coalminers: Key Risk Estimates from the British Pneumoconiosis Field Research." *Occupational and Environmental Medicine* 61, 6 (2004): 477–481.

Starobinski, Jacques. "Sur la chlorose" [On chlorosis]. *Romantisme* 31, 11 (1981): 113–130.

Stassen, J.-J. *L'après-Marcinelle: Quarante ans d'Europe sociale dans le cadre du Traité de la CECA pour l'amélioration des conditions de travail des mineurs; Protection du travail dans les mines belges après la catastrophe de Marcinelle* [Post-Marcinelle: Forty years of social Europe under the ECSC treaty to improve working conditions for miners; Worker protection in Belgian mines after the Marcinelle catastrophe]. Liège, Belgium: CEFAL [European Consortium for Training and Upgrading Workers], 2006.

Stassen, J.[-J.], R. Stenuit, and H. Van Kerckhoven. *Code des mines, minières et carrières* [Code for mining, mines, and quarries]. Brussels: Éditions Techniques et Scientifiques, 1957.

Steedman, Carolyn. *Dust: The Archive and Cultural History.* Manchester, UK: Manchester University Press, 2001.

Steenland, Kyle, and David F. Goldsmith. "Silica Exposure and Autoimmune Diseases." *American Journal of Industrial Medicine* 28, 5 (1995): 603–608.

Stewart, Alice. "Pneumoconiosis of Coal-Miners: A Study of the Disease after Exposure to Dust Has Ceased." *British Journal of Industrial Medicine* 5, 3 (1948): 120–140.

Stonecipher, Linda J., and Gerald C. Hyner. "Health Practices before and after a Worksite Health Screening." *Journal of Occupational Medicine* 35 (1993): 297–305.

Stout, N., and C. Bell. "Effectiveness of Source Documents for Identifying Fatal Occupational Injuries: A Synthesis of Studies." *American Journal of Public Health* 81, 6 (1991): 725–728.

Sturdy, Steven Waite. "A Co-Ordinated Whole: The Life and Work of John Scott Haldane." PhD dissertation, University of Edinburgh (1987).

Suarthana E., A. S. Laney, E. Storey, J. M. Hale, and M. D. Attfield. "Coal Workers' Pneumoconiosis in the United States: Regional Differences 40 Years after Implementation of the 1969 Federal Coal Mine Health and Safety Act." *Occupational and Environmental Medicine* 68 (2011): 908–913.

Sumiya, Mikio. *Shokkô oyobi kôfu chôsa* [A survey on factory workers and miners]. Tokyo: Kôseikan, 1970.

Takahashi, K. "The Silica Carcinogenicity Issue in Japan." *Occupational and Environmental Medicine* 60, 11 (2003): 897–898.

Tardieu, Ambroise. "Étude hygiénique sur la profession de mouleur en cuivre" [Study on health conditions in copper molding]. *Annales d'hygiène publique et de médecine légale*, ser. 2, 2 (1854): 5–33, 308–347.

Teleky, Ludwig. *History of Factory and Mine Hygiene.* New York: Columbia University Press, 1948.

Thackrah, C. T. *The Effects of Arts, Trades, and Professions on Health and Longevity,* 2nd ed. London: Longman, 1832.

Thébaud-Mony, Annie. *La reconnaissance des maladies professionnelles en France: Acteurs et logiques sociales* [The recognition of occupational diseases in France: Actors and social dynamics]. Paris: La Documentation Française, 1991.

Thomann, Bernard. "L'hygiène nationale, la société civile et la reconnaissance de la silicose comme maladie professionnelle au Japon (1868–1960)" [National hygiene, civil society, and the recognition of silicosis as an occupational disease in Japan (1868–1960)]. *Revue d'histoire moderne et contemporaine* 56, 1 (2009): 142–176.

———. *La naissance de l'État social japonais: Biopolitique, travail et citoyenneté dans le Japon impérial (1868–1945)* [The birth of Japan's social state: Biopolitics, work, and citizenship in imperial Japan (1868–1945)]. Paris: Presses de Sciences Po, 2015.

Tibbetts, John. "Under Construction: Building a Safer Industry." *Environmental Health Perspectives* 110, 3 (2002): A134.

Tiwari, Rajnarayan R., Yashwant K. Sharma, and Habibullah N. Saiyed. "Tuberculosis among Workers Exposed to Free Silica Dust." *Indian Journal of Occupational and Environmental Medicine* 11, 2 (2007): 61–64.

Tofani, Loretta. "American Imports, Chinese Deaths." *Salt Lake Tribune,* 21 October 2007.

Topalov, Christian, ed. *Laboratoires du nouveau siècle: La nébuleuse réformatrice et ses réseaux en France, 1800–1914* [New-century laboratories: The reform nexus and its networks in France, 1800–1914)]. Paris: Éditions de l'EHESS [École des Hautes Études en Sciences Sociales], 1999.

US Department of Labor, Division of Labor Standards. *National Silicosis Conference: Summary of Reports.* Bulletin 13. Washington, DC: Government Printing Office, 1937.

Valiante, David J., Donald P. Schill, Kenneth D. Rosenman, and Edward Socie. "Highway Repair: A New Silicosis Threat." *American Journal of Public Health* 94, 5 (2004): 876–880.

Van Daele, Jasmien, ed. *ILO Histories: Essays on the International Labour Organization and Its Impact on the World during the Twentieth Century,* vol. 12. Bern and New York: Peter Lang, 2010.

Van Mechelen, V. "Critères médicaux de l'efficacité de la lutte contre les poussières" [Medical criteria to assess the effectiveness of the fight against dusts]. *Communication—Institut d'Hygiène des Mines* 102, 20 (1952): 1–9.

———. "Evolution des idées en matière de classification radiologique des pneumoconioses" [Evolving ideas about the radiological classification of pneumoconiosis]. *Cahiers de médecine du travail* 5, 2 (1967): 7–18.

———. "Les lacunes de nos connaissances en matière de silicose" [Our knowledge gaps about silicosis]. *Communication—Institut d'Hygiène des Mines* 33, 8 (1948): 8–10.

Van Oorschot, Wim. "Non-Take-Up of Social Security Benefits in Europe." *Journal of European Social Policy* 1, 1 (1991): 15–30.

van Sprundel, M. "Mijnwerkerspneumoconiose" [Mineworkers' pneumoconiosis]. *Instituut voor Mijnhygiene: Mededeling*, ser. 2, 7 (1986): 17.

Varaschin, Denis, and Ludovic Laloux, eds. *10 mars 1906: Courrières, aux risques de l'histoire* [10 March 1906: Courrières, at the risks of history] Vincennes, France: GRHEN [Groupe de Recherche en Histoire de l'Énergie], 2006.

Vergara, Angela. "The Recognition of Silicosis: Labor Unions and Physicians in the Chilean Copper Industry, 1930s–1960s." *Bulletin of the History of Medicine* 79, 4 (2005): 723–748.

Vernon, H. M. "Methods of Investigating and of Improving the Health of Industrial Workers." *Journal of the Royal Society for the Promotion of Health* 51 (1930): 211–216.

Viet, Vincent, and Michèle Ruffat. *Le choix de la prévention* [Choosing prevention]. Paris: Economica, 1999.

Vigliani, Enrico C., and Benvenuto Pernis. "Immunological Aspects of Silicosis." *Advances in Tuberculosis Research* 17 (1963): 230–280.

Villermé, L. R. *Tableau de l'état physique et moral des ouvriers employés dans les manufactures de coton, de laine et de soie* [Portrait of the physical and moral state of workers in cotton, wool, and silk factories], 2 vols. Paris: Louis Renouard, 1840.

Vincent, Julien. "La réforme sociale à l'heure du thé: La porcelaine anglaise, l'Empire britannique et la santé des ouvrières dans le Staffordshire (1864–1914)" [Social reform at tea time: English porcelain, the British empire, and the health of workers in Staffordshire (1864–1914)]. *Revue d'histoire moderne et contemporaine* 56, 1 (2009): 29–60.

———. "Ramazzini n'est pas le précurseur de la médecine du travail" [Ramazzini is not the forerunner of occupational medicine]. *Genèses* 89, 4 (2012): 88–111.

Vincent, Michel, and M. Lievre. "Sarcoïdose et empoussièrement pulmonaire, une hypothèse pathogénique qui prend du crédit" [Sarcoidosis and pulmonary dust exposure, a plausible pathogenic link]. *Revue des maladies respiratoires* 19, 1 (2002): 103–104.

Virchow, Rudolph. "The Pathology of Miners' Lung." *Edinburgh Medical Journal* 4 (1858–1859): 204–213.

Von Zenker, Friedrich Albert. "Ueber Staubinhalationskrankheiten der Lungen" [Dust inhalation and related lung diseases]. *Deutsches Archiv für klinische Medicin* 2 (1867): 116–172.

"Voto della Commissione nominate del V. Congresso degli Scienziati Italiani per riferire sul lavoro dei fanciulli negli opifici Italiani" [Vote of the commission appointed by the Fifth Congress of Italian Scientists to report on child labor in Italian factories], *Annali Universali di Statistica*, ser. 2, 1, 2 (1844): 301–328.

Walters, Vivienne, and Ted Haines. "Workers' Use and Knowledge of the 'Internal Responsibility System': Limits to Participation in Occupational Health and Safety." *Canadian Health Policy* 14 (1988): 411–423.

Wang, M. L., L. A. Beeckman-Wagner, A. L. Wolfe, G. Syamlal, and E. L. Petsonk. "Lung-Function Impairment among US Underground Coal Miners, 2005 to 2009: Geographic Patterns and Association with Coal Workers' Pneumoconiosis." *Journal of Occupational and Environmental Medicine* 55 (2013): 846–850.

Wang, M. L., Z. E. Wu, Q. G. Du, E. Petsonk, K. Peng, Y. D. Li, S. K. Li, G. Han, and M. Attfield. "A Prospective Cohort Study among New Chinese Coal Miners: The Early

Pattern of Lung Function Change." *Occupational and Environmental Medicine* 62 (2005): 800–805.

Ward, Leonard. "The Effect, as Shown by Statistics, of British Statutory Regulations Directed to the Improvement of the Hygienic Conditions of Industrial Occupations." *Journal of the Royal Statistical Society* 68, 3 (1905): 435–525.

Watt, A. "Personal Experiences of Miners' Phthisis on the Rand, 1903 to 1916." In ILO, *Silicosis: Records* (1930), 589–596.

Weale, Mr. "A Letter from Mr. Weale of the Royal Naval Hospital at Plymouth to Dr. Barham, on the Diseases of Miners and Sailors." *Twenty-Second Annual Report of the Royal Institution of Cornwall* (1840): 34–37.

Weeks, James L. "The Fox Guarding the Chicken Coop: Monitoring Exposure to Respirable Coal Mine Dust, 1969–2000." *American Journal of Public Health* 93, 8 (2003): 1236–1244.

———. "The Mine Safety and Health Administration's Criterion Threshold Value Policy Increases Miners' Risk of Pneumoconiosis." *American Journal of Industrial Medicine* 49 (2006): 492–498.

———. "Tampering with Dust Samples in Coal Mines (Again)." *American Journal of Industrial Medicine* 20, 2 (1991): 141–144.

Weindling, Paul, ed. *International Health Organisations and Movements, 1918–1939.* Cambridge: Cambridge University Press, 1995.

———. "Social Medicine at the League of Nations Health Organisation and the International Labor Office Compared." In Weindling (ed.), *International Health Organisations and Movements*, 134–153.

Weisz, George. *Chronic Disease in the Twentieth Century: A History.* Baltimore: Johns Hopkins University Press, 2014.

White, Jenny, and Lisa A. Bero. "Corporate Manipulation of Research: Strategies Are Similar across Five Industries." *Stanford Law & Policy Review* 21, 1 (2010): 105.

Willoughby, E. F. "Some Prevalent Fallacies in Vital Statistics." *Journal of the Royal Society for the Promotion of Health* 20 (1899): 107–123.

Wilson, Francis. *Labour in the South African Gold Mines.* Cambridge: Cambridge University Press, 2001.

Wilson, Richard A. *Human Rights, Culture, and Context: Anthropological Perspectives.* London: Pluto Press, 1997.

Wu, Zongzhi. "Les maladies professionnelles constituent un problème social majeur" [Occupational diseases are a major social problem]. *ChinAfrique* (May 2005), www.chinafrique.com.

Xu, X. Z., X. G. Cai, X. S. Men, P. Y. Yang, J. F. Yang. S. L. Jing, J. H. He, and W.Y. Si. "A Study of Siliceous Pneumoconiosis in a Desert Area of Sunan County, Gansu Province, China." *Biomedical and Environmental Sciences* 6 (1993): 21–22.

Yassi, Annalee. *Recent Developments in Worker's Compensation, Toronto.* Report prepared for the Ministry of Labour of Ontario, 1983.

Yingratanasuk, Tanongsak, Noah Seixas, Scott Barnhart, and Drew Brodkin. "Respiratory Health and Silica Exposure of Stone Carvers in Thailand." *International Journal of Occupational and Environmental Health* 8, 4 (2002): 301–308.

Yudelman, David. *The Emergence of Modern South Africa.* Cape Town: David Philip, 1984.

Zhao J. D., J. D. Liu, and G. Z. Li. "Long-Term Follow-Up Observations of the Therapeutic Effect of PVNO on Human Silicosis." *Zentralblatt für Bakteriologie, Mikrobiologie und Hygiene, Serie B: Umwelthygiene, Krankenhaushygiene, Arbeitshygiene, präventive Medizin* 178, 3 (1983): 259–262.

Editor

Paul-André Rosental is a professor of contemporary history at Sciences Po, Paris, and an associate researcher at the Institut National d'Études Démographiques (INED). He specializes in the history of demographic, social, and health-related policies, an area in which he directs the ESOPP (Études Sociales et Politiques des Populations [Social and Political Studies on Populations] research team. At Sciences Po's Center for European Studies and its Center for History, he directs the European Research Council Senior Advanced Grant project "From Silicosis to Silica Hazards," which combines the disciplines of history, medicine, and the social sciences. The author of 90 articles or book contributions, he has also edited or coedited a number of special issues of academic journals, including "From Silicosis to Silica Hazards: An Experiment in Medicine, History, and the Social Sciences" for the *American Journal of Industrial Medicine* (2015). In 2016 he published *Destins de l'Eugénisme* (Destinies of eugenics).

Authors

Alberto Baldasseroni is an occupational physician and epidemiologist with CeRIMP (Centro Regionale Infortuni e Malattie Professionali [Regional Center for the Study of Work Injuries and Occupational Diseases]) for the Tuscany region, based in Florence, and a professor in the School of Specialization in Public Health and Hygiene at the University of Florence. His research field is in occupational medicine: public health and epidemiology. He is the author or coauthor of more than 80 medical papers cited in PubMed and many other contributions in books, congress proceedings, and the like.

Francesco Carnevale is an occupational physician. His research field is in occupational medicine: public health, pulmonology, neurology, oncology, epidemiology, and the history of occupational health. He is the author or coauthor of over 300 medical papers in journals and books, including a 2012 English edition of Bernardino Ramazzini's *Opera medica & phisiologica* [Works: medical and physiological] and a 2015 book (with Alberto Baldasseroni), *Malati di lavoro: Artigiani e lavoratori, medicina e medici da Bernardino Ramazzini a Luigi Devoto (1700–1900)* [Sick from work: Artisans and workers, medicine, and physicians from Bernardino Ramazzini to Luigi Devoto (1700–1900)].

Éric Geerkens holds a PhD in history. His doctoral dissertation on *La rationalisation dans l'industrie belge de l'Entre-deux-guerres* [Scientific management in Belgian industry in the interwar period] was published in 2004. He is currently researching the history of workplace health. Since 2010, he has been teaching economic and social history at the University of Liège. He is the author of numerous publications, including peer-reviewed journal articles and book chapters.

Martin Lengwiler is a professor of modern history in the Department of History at the University of Basel. In 2006 he was a visiting professor at the École des Hautes Études en Sciences Sociales, Paris, and he has taught at the Universities of Heidelberg, Zurich, and Bern, as well as Humboldt-University, Berlin. He is also a founding member of the Science Policy Studies research group at the Social Science Research Institute, Berlin (Wissenschaftszentrum Berlin). His work focuses on the comparative history of European welfare states, the history of science and knowledge, and historiographical methods.

Gerald Markowitz is the Distinguished Professor of History at John Jay College of Criminal Justice and the Graduate Center, City University of New York. He holds a PhD in history from the University of Wisconsin. The recipient of numerous grants from private and federal agencies, including the National Science Foundation, he was awarded the Viseltear Prize for Outstanding Work in the History of the Public Health from the American Public Health Association, as well as awards from the American Industrial Hygiene Association. With David Rosner, he has authored and edited books and articles on public health, occupational safety and health, and environmental health, including *Deadly Dust: Silicosis and the Politics of Occupational Disease in Twentieth-Century America* (2002).

Jock McCulloch teaches in the School of Global Studies at RMIT University, Australia. He is the author of *Asbestos Blues* (2002), a study of mining in South Africa; *The Global Asbestos Industry and Its Fight for Survival* (2008, with Geoff Tweedale); and *South Africa's Gold Mines and the Politics of Silicosis* (2012).

Joseph Melling is a historian of work, management, and the environment. He has published on the history of insanity, the social history of housing, and occupational health, where he has coedited *Dangerous Trade: Histories of Industrial Hazard across a Globalizing World* (2011). His current interests are in the history of occupational and social stress and the history of physical culture (including nudism) in Europe since the 1880s. He has been involved in projects on mental health since 1945, as well as on stress in the modern workplace. He teaches at the University of Exeter, where he codirects the Centre for Medical History.

Julia Moses is Lecturer in Modern History at the University of Sheffield, where she leads the Risk, Policy, and Law research group, and Marie Curie Fellow in the Institute of Sociology at the University of Göttingen. She was previously a lecturer at the University of Oxford, and received her PhD at Cambridge. Her research concentrates on social welfare and its regulation, with a special focus on the role of the law in addressing "risks" and shaping the family in modern Europe. She has coedited (with Michael Lobban) *The Impact of Ideas on Legal Development* (2012), and her books, *The First Modern Risk: Workplace Accidents and the Origins of European Social States* and *Marriage, Law, and Modernity: Global Histories*, are forthcoming.

David Rosner is the Ronald H. Lauterstein Professor of Sociomedical Sciences History at Columbia University and codirector of the Center for the History of Public Health at Columbia's Mailman School of Public Health. He received his BA from the City College of New York, his MPH from the University of Massachusetts, and his PhD (in the history of science) from Harvard University. He was elected to the National Academy of Medicine of the National Academy of Sciences and has won numerous prizes, including the Viseltear Prize for Outstanding Work in the History of Public Health and the McGovern Prize. He and Gerald Markowitz were awarded the Upton Sinclair Memorial Lectureship for Outstanding Occupational Health, Safety, and Environmental Journalism by the American Industrial Hygiene Association.

Bernard Thomann, a historian, is a full professor at the National Institute of Oriental Languages and Civilizations, Paris, and a former fellow of the Maison Franco-Japonaise in Tokyo. He was a visiting fellow at the University of Tokyo from 2002 to 2005. He is currently researching the emergence of the

Japanese welfare state, the history of occupational health, and labor relations in the mining industry of Japan. He is the author of *Le salarié et l'entreprise dans le Japon contemporain: Formes, genèse et mutations d'une relation de dépendance (1868–1999)* [Employees and businesses in present-day Japan: Forms, origin, and changes in a dependent relationship (1868–1999)] (2008) and *La naissance de l'Etat social japonais: Biopolitique, travail et citoyenneté dans le Japon impérial (1868–1945)* [Birth of the Japanese social state: Biopolitics, work, and citizenship in imperial Japan (1868–1945)] (2015).

Index

Abraham, J. H., 43, 44
accidents, industrial, 116–117, 141; insurance programs for, 109, 112, 123, 124, 126; medicine and, 111; prevention organizations and, 109–110
ACGIH. *See* American Conference of Governmental Industrial Hygienists
aerosols, 41, 185
Algeria, stone carving in, 206
Amalgamated Miners Association (Australia), 113
American Association of Industrial Physicians and Surgeons, 19–20
American Bradden Copper Company, 159
American Conference of Governmental Industrial Hygienists, 223
Amoudru, Claude, 171n74, 188
anthraco-silicosis, 174, 175–176, 188
anthracosis, 27, 95, 176, 187
antibiotics, 22–23, 28n18, 174
anticontagionism, 38–39, 44, 46
Anti-Slavery International (UK), 214–215
Areva, 217–218
Arlidge, John Thomas, 36–37, 47, 49, 51–52, 54
asbestos, 2, 228–229
asbestos-related diseases, 6, 15, 26, 86, 95–96
Asia, silicosis's spread in, 208–209. *See also* individual nations
Asian Network for the Rights of Occupational and Environmental Victims, 217
Association of Italian Industrialists for the Prevention of Industrial Accidents, 109
Australia: compensation systems in, 86; gold mining in, 53; medical studies in, 118; mutual-aid societies in, 113; prevention in, 156, 180; silicosis policies in, 153
Austria, silicosis policies in, 151
Austria-Hungary, mining regulations in, 112

bacteriology, 21, 114
Barry, G. E., 69, 81
Beijing Workers' Autonomous Federation, 216
Belgium, 20, 30, 79, 109, 163; dust monitoring in, 199; epidemiological research in, 196, 197; exposure thresholds in, 194, 195, 199; occupational illness policy in, 121; prevention in, 178–179, 183, 184; silicosis policies in, 132–133; wet drilling in, 175
Benin, 158
Bergbau-Forschung GmbH Forschungs-institut des Steinkohlenberg-bauvereins (Germany), 192
Bergmannsheil (Germany), 110, 126, 192
Bergsucht [mountain disease], 31
black lung, 26, 39, 189
black phthisis, 49
bladder cancer, 111
blasting, end-of-shift, 175, 180
Brazil, 2, 207,
Britain. *See* United Kingdom
British Colonial Office, 81
British Medical Association, 45, 54
bronchitis, 56
brown lung, 26
Bureau of Mines (US), 194
byssinosis (brown lung disease), 26

Canada, 158; aluminum therapy in, 184; miners' wives in, 162–163; prevention in, 180; silicosis policies in, 154; workplace injuries in, 162–163, 171n71
Canadian McIntyre Porcupine Gold Mine Company, 184
carbon dust, 52–53
Cardiff-Douai standards, 192
Carozzi, Luigi, 75–79, 84–95, 123, 143, 153

prevention (*cont.*)
    investment in, 82; medical approaches to,
    184–186; necessity of, 200; occupational
    health policies and, 221; productivity and,
    181; resistance to, 181–184, 200; strategies
    for, 175; technical approaches to, 180–184;
    workforce selection and, 185
productivist ideology, 148, 140
Professional Mining Association (Germany),
    124–127
progressive massive fibrosis, 189
PRU. *See* Pneumoconiosis Research Unit
Prudential Life Insurance Company, 21
Prussia, 105, 109
Public Health Service (US), 118, 194
public opinion, 5, 10, 42, 44, 59
public-works sector, silicosis risk in,
    220–221
pulmonary cirrhosis, 61n16
pulmonary diseases. *See* lungs
pulmonary fibrosis, 53, 54, 57, 59, 90, 187,
    226
PVNO. *See* synthetic polymers

Queensland (Australia), 142, 164–165

radiography, 92, 115, 189–193
Rajchman, Ludwik, 76–77
Ramazzini, Bernardino, 4, 31, 158
Rand mining, 5, 6, 66–68, 70, 81, 87, 183
Reagan, Ronald, 219
Red Internacional Mujeres y Mineria, 214
research centers (Europe), 191–192
respiration, 31, 34, 40
risk: length of exposure to, 154; outsourcing
    of, 210
Rovida, Carlo Leopoldo, 39
Royal Society of Arts of London, 43
Rush, Benjamin, 32

Samuel, Herbert, 119
Samuel Committee (UK), 153
sandblasting, 2, 209, 216–217, 220
Sartre, Jean-Paul, 117, 171n75
Satire of Trades, 31
scientific management, 4, 16–17

Scotland, 49, 89, 159, 183, 199
self-help associations. *See* mutual-aid
    associations
Sheffield (Eng.), grinders in, health crises of,
    42–46
Sherpa Association, 217–218
siderosis, 39
silica (silica dust): ailments resulting from, 30,
    229; alternate effects of, 222; vs. asbestos,
    228–229; carcinogenicity of, 222–224; vs.
    coal dust, 54, 225; danger of, 27, 57, 91, 225;
    effect of, 141; exposure to, 1–2; industrial
    sectors working with, 85; international
    conferences on, 65; kidney disease and, 226;
    lung cancer and, 223, 232n72; lung diseases
    associated with, 222–223; measuring, 124;
    medical status of, 64–65; mixed with other
    dusts, 85, 224; researchers' focus on, 39–40,
    65; silicosis and, 225–226
silicosis, 20–23, 73, 156, 223
—controlling: 219; delaying onset of, 177;
    eradication program for, 2; exposure
    threshold for, 141, 144–145; medical exams
    for, 142–143; medical monitoring and, 152,
    177; medical prevention of, 184–186;
    prevention of, 67, 180 (*see also* prevention);
    radiological classification of, 153, 189–190;
    respiratory function measurements and, 40
—medical knowledge on, history of: 3–4,
    8–9, 15–16, 30, 32, 41, 57–59, 78, 82–83, 92,
    94, 113, 115, 140–141, 143, 150, 211;
    associated with South Africa, 67; consensus
    on, 84–85, 118; global medical forum on,
    79; identification of, 65; invisibility of, 3–4,
    27; as king of occupational diseases, 4, 8,
    14–15; medical debate on, 91–92, 222–226;
    misdiagnosis of, 22; pharmacological
    approach to, 184; uncertainties about, 115;
    visibility of, 140, 152
—medicolegal and insurance issues of:
    accident insurance programs and, 121;
    compensation for, 4–5, 6, 9, 20, 63n76,
    69–72, 81–82, 108, 122, 125, 129, 131–133,
    211; included in occupational disease
    tables, 176; legal developments and, 126;
    legislation on, 114, 143, 145, 146, 220;